Lecture Notes in Computer Science 1901

Edited by G. Goos, J. Hartmanis, and J. van Leeuwen

W0246061

Berlin
Heidelberg
New York
Barcelona
Hong Kong
London
Milan
Paris
Singapore
Tokyo

Opher Etzion   Peter Scheuermann (Eds.)

Cooperative Information Systems

7th International Conference, CoopIS 2000
Eilat, Israel, September 6-8, 2000
h Proceedings

Series Editors

Gerhard Goos, Karlsruhe University, Germany
Juris Hartmanis, Cornell University, NY, USA
Jan van Leeuwen, Utrecht University, The Netherlands

Volume Editors

Opher Etzion
IBM Research Laboratory
Matam 31905, Haifa, Israel
E-mail: opher@il.ibm.com

Peter Scheuermann
Northwestern University, Department of Electrical and Computer Engineering
2145 Sheridan Road, Evanston, IL 60208, USA
E-mail: peters@ece.nwu.edu

Cataloging-in-Publication Data applied for

Die Deutsche Bibliothek - CIP-Einheitsaufnahme

Cooperative information systems : 7th international conference ;
proceedings / CoopIS 2000 Eilat, Israel, September 6 - 8, 2000. Opher
Etzion ; Peter Scheuermann (ed.). - Berlin ; Heidelberg ; New York ;
Barcelona ; Hong Kong ; London ; Milan ; Paris ; Singapore ; Tokyo :
Springer, 2000
    (Lecture notes in computer science ; Vol. 1901)
    ISBN 3-540-41021-X

CR Subject Classification (1998): H.2.4, H.5, C.2.4, H.3, I.2.11

ISSN 0302-9743
ISBN 3-540-41021-X Springer-Verlag Berlin Heidelberg New York

Springer-Verlag Berlin Heidelberg New York
a member of BertelsmannSpringer Science+Business Media GmbH
© Springer-Verlag Berlin Heidelberg 2000
Printed in Germany

Typesetting: Camera-ready by author
Printed on acid-free paper   SPIN: 10722620   06/3142   5 4 3 2 1 0

Foreword

Cooperation among systems has gained substantial importance in recent years: electronic commerce virtual enterprises and the middleware paradigm are just some examples in this area. CoopIS is a multi-disciplinary conference, which deals with all aspects of cooperation. The relevant disciplines are: collaborative work, distributed databases, distributed computing, electronic commerce, human-computer interaction, multi-agent systems, information retrieval, and workflow systems. The CoopIS series provides a forum for well-known researchers who are drawn by the stature and the tradition of these conference series and has a leading role in shaping the future of the cooperative information systems area.

CoopIS 2000 is the seventh conference in the series and the fifth conference organized by the International Foundation on Cooperative Information Systems (IFCIS). It is sponsored by the IFCIS, the IBM Research Laboratory in Haifa and Compaq, Tandem labs Israel. It replaces the former international workshops on Interoperability in Multidatabase systems (IMS) and the conference series on Cooperative Information Systems (CoopIS & ICICIS).

In response to the call for papers 74 papers were submitted. Each of them was reviewed by at least three reviewers, and at the end of this process 24 papers were accepted for presentation at the conference. Six additional papers were selected for short presentations. In addition the conference includes two panels, two keynote speakers (Professor Calton Pu from Georgia Tech and Professor Sheizaf Rafaeli from Haifa University) and one tutorial. A special issue of the International Journal of Cooperative Information Systems will follow.

August 2000   Opher Etzion & Peter Scheuermann

General Chairs

Avigdor Gal
Rutgers University, USA
E-mail: avigal@rci.rutgers.edu

Michele Missikoff
IASI-CNR, Italy
E-mail: missikoff@iasi.rm.cnr.it

Program Chairs

Opher Etzion
IBM Research Laboratory in Haifa, Israel
E-mail: opher@il.ibm.com

Peter Scheuermann
Northwestern University, USA
E-mail: peters@ece.nwu.edu

Publicity and Proceedings Chairs

David Carmel
IBM Research Laboratory in Haifa, Israel
E-mail: carmel@il.ibm.com

David Botzer
IBM Research Laboratory in Haifa, Israel
E-mail: botzer@il.ibm.com

Organization Chairs

David Botzer
IBM Research Laboratory in Haifa, Israel
E-mail: botzer@il.ibm.com

Tova Berger
IBM Research Laboratory in Haifa, Israel
E-mail: tova@il.ibm.com

Program Committee Members

Yariv Aridor – Israel
Israel Ben-Shaul – Israel
Alex Borgida – USA
Mokrane Bouzeghoub – France
Andrei Broder – USA
Yuri Breitbart – USA
Tiziana Catarci – Italy
Christopher Clifton – USA
Umesh Dayal – USA
Stefan Decker – USA
Eric Dubois – Belgium
Asuman Dogac – Turkey
Ahmed Elmagarmid – USA
Ramez Elmasri – USA
Opher Etzion – Israel (co-chair)
Jiawei Han – Canada
David Hawking – Australia
Mike Huhns – USA
Stefan Jablonski – Germany
Anant Jhingran – USA
Yahiko Kambayashi – Japan
Dimitris Karagiannis – Austria
Kamal Karlapalem – Hong Kong
Rao Kotagiri – Australia
Ling Liu – USA
Stuart Madnick – USA

Robert Meersman – Belgium
Tova Milo – Israel
Renée J. Miller – Canada
Ami Motro – USA
John Mylopoulos – Canada
Erich Neuhold – Germany
Aris Ouksel – USA
Tamer Ozsu – Canada
George Papadopoulos – Cyrpus
Mike Papazoglou – The Netherlands
Evaggelia Pitoura – Greece
Yael Ravin – USA
Tore Risch – Sweden
Jeff Rosenschein – Israel
Ron Sacks Davis – Australia
Hans Schek – Switzerland
Peter Scheuermann – USA (co-chair)
Peretz Shoval – Israel
Oded Shmueli – Israel
Jacob Slonim – Canada
Arne Solvberg – Norway
Moshe Tennenholtz – Israel
Jeff Ullman – USA
Kyu-Young Whang – Korea
Jian Yang – Australia

External Reviewers

Klemens Bohm
Terje Brasethvik
Jaelson Castro
Anat Eyal
Paolo Giorgini
Necip Hamali
Timour Katchaouov
Manuel Kolp
Tsvika Kuflik
Aristidis Likas

Jianguo Lu
Jian Pei
Heiko Schuldt
Guttorm Sindre
Avi Telyas
Hakki Toroslu
Hallvard Traetteberg
Arif Tumer
Anthony K. H. Tung
Ozgur Ulusoy

Table of Contents

Information Services

Workflow Execution

CSCW and Organizational Aspects

Mobile Cooperation

Multi Agents Systems

Formalizing (and Reasoning About) the Specifications of Workflows

Goce Trajcevski[1] and Chitta Baral[2] and Jorge Lobo[3]

[1] Univ. of Illinois at Chicago, Dept. of EECS, gtrajcev@eecs.uic.edu
[2] Bell Labs, jlobo@research.bell-labs.com
[3] Arizona State Univ., Dept. of CSE, chitta@asu.edu

Abstract. We address the problem of *workflow requirements specifications* under realistic assumptions that it involves experts from different domains (different business policies), where not all the possible execution scenarios known beforehand. Using recent results on *reasoning about actions*, we formalize the notion of the specifications' correctness. To address this, we propose a high level language $\mathcal{A}_W$ as a basis of our prototype tool for process specification. We go "one step" before actual analysis and design, and offer a formalism which enables the experts to specify their knowledge in terms of the effects that the activities have on the workflow environment. Our methodology allows expressing not only the knowledge, but also the "ignorance" (the semantics allows unknown values to reflect a realistic situation of agents dealing with incomplete information) and the possibility of exceptional situations. We define an entailment relation which enables reasoning about the correctness of the specifications, in terms of achieving a desired goal, and testing about consequences of modifications in the workflow descriptions.

1 Introduction and Motivation

A *workflow* (WF) is a *process* which executes various cooperative and coordinated *activities* in order to achieve a desired *goal* [22]. Workflow Management Systems (WFMS) provide tools for modeling, executing and monitoring workflows [27, 40] and they need well – defined correctness/reliability criteria [1, 17, 44] and the ability to adapt to changes in a flexible manner. Recent works have addressed several of these issues [20, 25, 30, 32, 41, 50] and identified solutions of many problems of interest in WFMS. Among the other contributions, several formalisms have been proposed (e.g. OGWL (Opera Graphical Workflow Language) [30]; State and Activity Charts [50]; Concurrent Transaction Logic (CTR) [25]; Transaction Datalog (TD) [14]) which enable representation, reasoning and execution of workflows.

Since the beginning of eighties, the software engineering research has been pointing out the importance of *knowledge representation* being thoroughly captured during the requirements specifications stage, before moving on with analysis/design and implementation [13, 46, 47]. This is an important aspect in workflow/ process specification in many applications (e.g. Virtual Enterprises) [2, 24]. The specification stage involves experts from different domains, representatives

O. Etzion and P. Scheuermann (Eds.): CoopIS 2000, LNCS 1901, pp. 1–17, 2000.
© Springer-Verlag Berlin Heidelberg 2000

of different organizations and policies (as Whorf's hypothesis from psycholinguistics says: " ... *the language a person uses to describe his or her environment is a lens through which he or she views that environment ...*") [49]. Typically, not all the possible executional scenarios are known; participants need not know the details of how other partners are implementing certain (business) policies. Also, a participant may not be willing to fully reveal a decision – making process and (s)he should have the ability to choose to what extent a process will be a "black box" for the other partners (or to what extent it should be "opened"). When it comes to cooperation and synchronization, a particular domain expert typically states the "weakest preconditions" and the "strongest effects" expected.

Thus, during the early specification stage, the main problems are: has there been enough domain *knowledge* collected; can we *reason* about its *correctness* (which, at this stage is concerned with being able to achieve a desired *goal*); given the tendency of domain experts to specify mostly *plausible* scenarios, can we handle the occurrence of *exceptional* cases.

1.1   An Overview of Our Approach

In this work, we view workflows as a collection of cooperative agents and use recent results on reasoning about actions [4, 6, 29, 36] to formalize the process of their specification and test their correctness. Our approach, in a philosophical sense, resembles formalization of database updates [43] and transactions [15, 16].

Our main contributions are as follows. We present a very simple, high level language $\mathcal{A}_W$ and, based on it, a prototype tool, which facilitates the process specification (i.e. the domain where the workflow activities will execute). The tool enables dual (textual and visual) representation of workflow specification AND enables the user to toggle between the representations at any time. The domain experts are enabled to specify the constraints on valid states and valid transitions among them, and can specify not only their knowledge but also their "ignorance" (e.g. incomplete state specification) and the possibility of abnormal (exceptional) cases. The users can express behavioral and control aspects in terms of *reactive module* (again, both textual and visual representations are available and an user can flip between the two at any time). With all these flexibilities (– the language allows *unknown* values to reflect the situations of dealing with incomplete information (essential during dynamic modifications of a workflow/construction of *ad-hoc* workflows); – we give an *entailment* relation for querying the correctness of the specifications, and reasoning about consequences of modifications to its description ("what – if" scenarios)), $\mathcal{A}_W$ is still based on a strict logical foundation and has a formal semantics. Hence, we have a formal notion of a *correctness*. of a workflow description. The rest of the paper is structured as follows. Section 2 introduces the basis of our formalism, describes the basic aspects of the language $\mathcal{A}_W$ and our current prototype tool. In Section 3 we specify how we address the issues of cooperativity and exceptions and Section 4 presents the formalization of the notion of correctness. In Section 5 we summarize, compare with the relevant literature and propose the directions for the future work.

2   Basic Aspects of Formalizing the Workflow Specifications

Specification and reasoning about activities in our approach is done using a tool based on a high level language $\mathcal{A}_W$, developed in the spirit of the action description language $\mathcal{A}$ [26] (the description of the language is based on $\mathcal{A}_K$ in [11]; $\mathcal{L}_{active}$ in [7]; and $\mathcal{ADC}$ in [6]). Action theories have been successfully used in reasoning about robot control programs [37] and in the logical formalization of active databases [5, 7] (reasoning about parameterized actions, qualification and ramification constraints, concurrent execution of actions [29]). The later use makes it more appropriate than the traditional approach of program correctness [23] which has been designed for standard programming languages and lacks the flexibility of defining new operators/ activities. Recall that during the requirements specification of workflows, we do not want to generate "fully correct" but *sound* and *"mostly" complete* descriptions, similar to the incomplete specifications in [21]. This enables avoiding "full blown" theorem provers and using planners to generate modules. Levesque et al. [37] discuss the difference between the "action" approach and traditional approach of "program correctness".

For the implementation of our tool, we followed the principles of process languages design surveyed in [47](e.g.: – pictures help in improving intuition and communication/ cooperation; – they work best when they depict modest ammount of information; – the use of semantically deep formalism supports many desirable properties). There are 3 main classes: 1. *MainFrame.java* – the "brain" which creates the actions listeners that invoke appropriate methods to handle user input; 2. *WorkflowArea.java* which is responsible for the graphical representation of the workflow being specified (e.g. redrawing an obscured area, dragging the nodes of activities around so that they are arranged in a most appealing manner); 3. *Mediator.java* is responsible for generating an internal representation and using it to convert between textual and visual parts of the specification.

Our tool will cooperate and guide the users through specifications of each proposition of the language in both textual and visual representations, with a set of pulldown menus. Figure 1 illustrates the specification of a rule in a control module (defined below) of a particular workflow[4]. The detailed description of the functionality is specified in [35].

2.1   Activities' Domain Description

$\mathcal{A}_W$ has three disjoint nonempty sets of symbols, called *facts*, *events* and *activity names*. Facts are the data items which describe the environment of the workflow (i.e. a tuple in a relational database, or an attribute value of an object). They correspond to the notion of *fluents* in AI parlance, used by McCarthy [39] in the

---

[4] The current version of $\mathcal{A}_W$ based prototype tool is available via anonymous ftp at *www.eecs.uic.edu/ ~ gtrajcev/workflowtool*.

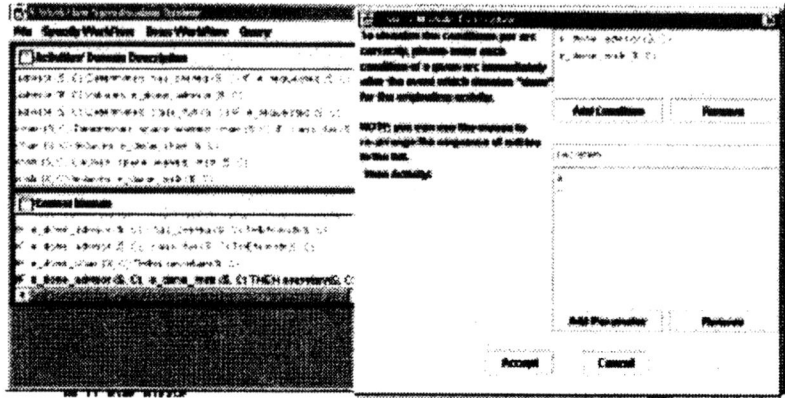

Fig. 1. Specification of a workflow

context of reasoning about actions. A *literal* is a fact or event, possibly preceded by ¬.

An *activity description* in the language $\mathcal{A}_W$ consists of a collection of three kinds of "propositions":

a **causes** f if $p_1, \ldots, p_n, e_1, \ldots, e_m$ (an "ef-proposition")

a **determines** f if $p_1, \ldots, p_n, e_1, \ldots, e_m$ (a "k-proposition")

a **induces** e if $p_1, \ldots, p_n, e_1, \ldots, e_m$ (an "event definition")

• An "ef-proposition" describes the effect of an activity on the truth value of a fact. Here, a is an activity; each of $f, p_1, \ldots, p_n$ ($n \geq 0$) and $e_1, \ldots, e_m$ ($m \geq 0$) is a literal.

Note that the *facts* can have **unk** values (i.e. are evaluated wrt 3-valued logic), but the events cannot (negation of an event indicates that it is not a part of the environment). Intuitively, the literals p_i, e_j are *preconditions* on the effects of the activity a, meaning, if a is executed when the preconditions are true then f becomes true after the execution of a. Observe that an action may have different effects on the environment, depending on the state in which it is executed (one can specify "simultaneous" effects too) similar to Vortex [32].

Example 1. Observe an E–commerce scenario where, upon login, a customer should be presented with a "welcome" promotional message. If its an old customer, the content of the message should be based on several criteria like: – credit status; – history of purchases reflecting his/her preferences; – new "hot" products which may be of interest for the particular customer. On the other hand, a new customer should "view" a more broad welcoming menu which shows general categories and enables him to specify particular interest(s).

The example (simplified from [33]) reveals a subtle issue. When specifying the workflow, all that the business partners need to know is that there is a template activity, say *welcoming_message*, which requires certain input/output parameters. It should further be decided, upon negotiations among the partners involved, which details (if any) of *how* that activity is implemented should be given.

To represent input/output parameters of the activities, we use variables. Hence, strictly speaking, the syntax of an "ef-proposition" looks like:

$a(\overline{X_{a_1}}, \ldots, \overline{X_{a_n}})$ **causes** $f(\overline{X_f})$ **if** $p_1(\overline{X_1}), \ldots, p_n(\overline{X_n}), e_1(\overline{Y_1}), \ldots, e_m(\overline{Y_m})$

If some variable in $(\overline{X_f})$ or negated literal in the preconditions, does not appear in the positive literal in the precondition (*unsafe* negation), our tool will automatically warn the user of the possibility of unsafe evaluation and the need for the variable to be instantiated at the invocation time of the activity.

• An "event definition" is a proposition which describes the occurrence of an *entity of interest* during the course of execution of a workflow. Events are useful when enforcing *order constraints* [25] on the execution of the workflow, as we'll explain shortly. Also, they are essential for inter–process communication [31]. Heterogeneous workflow tools may be integrated/synchronized by a common event notification mechanism (instead of using common API and/or fully shared database). Events are also used to denote which is the current state of the workflow. In our implementation of $\mathcal{A}_W$ [35], upon specifying an "ef–proposition", the tool automatically generates an "event definition" signaling the end of the particular activity. We distinguish among two types of events: (i) internal events, given by the definitions, because at specification time we know which action could induce them; (ii) external events – generated by other workflow agents, which notify the main workflow about the occurrence of "something of interest" which is not controlled by the main agent.

• A "k-proposition" stipulates that if a is executed in a state in which its preconditions are true, then in the resulting state the truth value of f becomes known. However, the value can not be predicted and it will be known only at run time. The activities in "k-proposition"s are what we have referred to as *sensing* activities (we also call them *knowledge producing activities*), and they have been studied formally in the context of planning problems [12, 28]. However, as we will discuss shortly, we need to slightly modify the "k-propositions" if they are to be used in workflow specification.

Example 2. Observe a simple workflow which automates a course registration process of a graduate student. Some of the activities description are:

$advisor(S, C)$ **determines** $has\_prereq(S, C)$ **if** $e\_requested(S, C)$
$advisor(S, C)$ **determines** $class\_full(S, C)$ **if** $e\_requested(S, C)$

which illustrate that it is the advisor's responsibility to check if the student is eligible to register.

Once everything is completed, the secretary should grant the registration password of a particular course to the student:

$secretary(S, C)$ **causes** $passwd(S, C)$ **if** $has\_prereq(S, C), \neg class\_full(S, C)$

Of course, the effect of the activity "secretary" may be different, depending on the status of the environment in which it is executed. For example, if the student does not have the prerequisites and the course instructor did not agree to waive them, then the secretary will deny the registration password to the student:

$secretary(S,C)$ **causes** $\neg passwd(S,C)$ **if**
$\neg has\_prereq(S,C), \neg prereq\_waived(S,C)$

In the example[5] above, although the activity *advisor* is a cooperative one, the registration workflow has no influence/impact on *how* the advisor workflow agent operates. Moreover, the main registration workflow agent is someone that is "harrasing" the advisor by asking him/her to execute an activity on its behalf (especially when the advisor has a grant-proposal deadline). Similar to activity *welcoming_message* in the context of Example 1 where the business partner decides to which extent it will be unfolded or kept as a black box, as far as $\mathcal{A}_W$ is concerned, an activity like the *advisor(S,C)* in Example 2 may be a template, or a workflow itself.

2.2   Control Modules

The set of activities' description specifies the effects of executing a particular action in a particular state. But we need to allow the users of our tool to specify their knowledge about *how* activities execution is coordinated in order to achieve a desired goal. Recall that in the specification stage the complete information about the environment may not be available and not all the possible execution scenarios are known. To define the *execution* of workflow agents, we rely on a *control module* of reactive rules. Such control modules, similar to production rule systems, have been used for real-time robot control [10, 42].

A control module is a collection of rules of the form:
if $e_1,\ldots,e_n,f_1,\ldots,f_k,$ **unk** $f_{k+1},\ldots,$ **unk** f_m **then** a
where:
- each e_i is an event literal (possibly negated)
- each $f_i(1 \le i \le k)$ is a (positive or negated) fact
- each **unk** f_j specifies a particular fact whose truth value is *unknown* at a given state.
- a is the action to be executed in a state in which the conjunction on the left-hand side (LHS) of the rule is true.

The set of rules reflects the user's knowledge about the *data* and *control flow* (i.e. how to sequence the activities, what are pre-conditions on their execution; the input/output parameters). The module can be in several possible states: *active/running* in which it executes actions of the RHS of some rule which LHS conditions are satisfied in the given state of the environment; *HALT* which is reached upon a "successful termination"; *SUSPEND*, which is a state that the module has entered because it has to "wait" (e.g. termination of some cooperative activity). However, this state of the control module illustrates the "knowledge" of the user about the particular state of the workflow environment; *failure* state of the control module illustrates the case where the workflow environment does not match any condition in the LHS of any rule in the module

---

[5] The complete specification of the registration workflow is given in [9].

(which, in cooperative terms could mean a "deadlock"). The difference between *failure* and *SUSPEND* is that the former illustrates a possibility which can not be "predicted" at specification stage. The "state" of the control module is a part of the overall state of the workflow and it can be captured using the set of facts and events. Formally, for a given workflow specification (domain description of each activity and the control module), the state is a triplet $s = [\Sigma, \mathcal{E}, \mathcal{R}]$ where: $\Sigma = \langle T, F \rangle$ where T denotes the set of facts which are known to be *true* and F denotes the set of facts which are known to be *false* (the rest of the facts are assumed to be *unknown*); $\mathcal{E} = \mathcal{E}_i \cup \mathcal{E}_e$ denotes the set of events (internal and external) which are known to be true in a particular state; and $\mathcal{R}$ denotes the set of the *enabled* rules from the control module (i.e. the set of ground instances of rules whose LHS evaluates to *True* for the given Σ and $\mathcal{E}$). The semantics is given by defining a (partial) transition function Ψ_w which specifies how the state changes by executing rules from the control module (see [9] for a complete specification of the semantics of $\mathcal{A}_W$).

For example, a particular instance of the module "wakes – up" (is triggered) when an external event is generated. In the context of Example 2 this happens when a particular student requests a registration (e.g. the event $e\_requested(john, eecs361)$ becomes true in the workflow state). We introduce the **unk** connector because agents are constantly dealing with incomplete information that they complete by making requests to other workflow agents (i.e. remote procedure calls or consults to the external world). The "unknown" value may very well be implemented with having a *null* value for an attribute in a database. However, it is unlikely that the domain/ business expert is familiar with the meaning of *null* values (or any implementation details). This implies reasoning in 3-valued logic. In the context of the Example 1, if a new customer applies for a credit line with the on-line shopping enterprise, the goal of the workflow is to determine the eligibility for credit and the credit line. However, evaluated under 3-valued logic, the formula: $grant\_credit(Customer, Limit) \vee \neg grant\_credit(Customer, Limit)$ need not be a tautology, which makes the goal of the workflow a non – simple one. The set of propositions in the activities' domain description and the set of rules in the control module provide enough flexibilities for specifying workflows (as prescribed by [22]: *sequencing* ; *AND/OR–splits and joins; iteration nesting*).

Figure 2 illustrates a case of AND – join in context of Example 2 (if a section is full, and both the department head and the particular course instructor decide if the space should be waived, the two "activities" can be executed concurrently).

Ramifications A description using "ef-propositions" and "k-propositions" can only describe the direct effects of an activity in a given state. However, executions of actions may have indirect effects in a particular state (e.g. a database update may cause an integrity constraint violation). Ramification effects are usually derived from the set of facts and events, and they can be used to specify which are the valid states of the workflow evolution (as well as the valid transitions among those states). Thus, we introduce the following ramification propositions in $\mathcal{A}_W$:

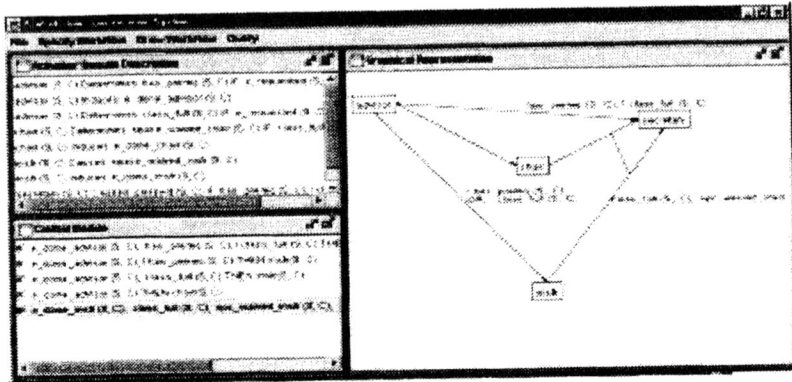

Fig. 2. An example of a registration workflow

- $p_1, \ldots, p_n, e_1, \ldots e_m$ suffice for f – with the intuitive meaning that in any state in which $p_1, \ldots, p_n, e_1, \ldots e_m$ are true, we can infer that f is also true. Observe that f can be either a fact or an event. Although we do not address the issue of composite events in this work, a ramification proposition can be readily used to specify a conjunction of events.

3   Cooperation of Activities and Exceptions

Assume that a new customer enters the virtual enterprise of Example 1. In order to determine if (s)he should be granted a credit (and the limit value), it is very likely that the workflow will make a "cooperative" request to another workflow agent – credit history agency. All that the main workflow agent *knows* is that the request for the service of credit history check has been sent. It cannot know beforehand when the request will be actually served. However, this should not prevent the main workflow agent of the enterprise from guiding the user through the list of products and their prices/availability. Periodically, the main workflow may re-send the request to the credit agency workflow, until it gets a response. In case the request has not been served after some predefined time period, the workflow may decide to inform the new user that the decision about granting him/her a credit line will be determined later. The situation is more extreme in the Example 2. Here, the registration workflow cannot continue its execution until the response from the *advisor* agent has been received and the truth value of *has_prereq(S,C)* is determined.

However, in general there may be several other processes running concurrently and it is not practical to suspend the entire execution in a given state, waiting for a response from a cooperative agent. Let us reiterate the flip-side of the coin: although the activity *advisor(S,C)* is a cooperative for the main workflow, for the advisor workflow agent the request to act on behalf of registration workflow is an "interference". It is likely that the advisor has his own policy on how to respond to external requests, not known to the registration workflow agent.

This is why we assume the existence of two types of events, internal and external. Namely, when the main workflow asks the advisor to determine *has_prereq(S,C)* it generates its *internal* event so that it is "aware" that the request for service has been made. Within the world of the advisor workflow this generates an *external* event notifying him of a particular service being requested. Once the advisor finds out if the student has the prerequisites, it may send the value back to the registration workflow. Upon that, he records that he had completed the request (internal event). The notification to the registration workflow that its request has been served is an external event (the truth value of *has_prereq(S,C)* is known). The work in [31] uses *exported event list* and *imported event queue*[6].

To formalize the discussion above, we modify the "k-proposition" in the activity descriptions as follows. The cooperative activity like the *advisor(S,C)* in the registration workflow description consists of two parts[7]:

$advisor(S,C)^{\rightarrow}$ **induces** $e\_advisor\_asked(S,C)$ **if** $\neg e\_advisor\_responded(S,C)$

$advisor(S,C)_{\leftarrow}$ **determines** $has\_prereq(S,C)$ **if** $e\_advisor\_responded(S,C)$

In the particular setting of the registration example, we may want to add the following rule to the control module:

if $e\_advisor\_asked(S,C), \neg e\_advisor\_responded(S,C)$ **then** $SUSPEND(S,C)$

to specify that the main workflow agent should wait for the response from the advisor. Since, in general, there may be several other activities that could be executed in a given state, even though we may have a $SUSPEND$ rule in the control module, the workflow instance itself need not enter that particular state. We have the following definition:

Definition 1. Let A $= [a_1, a_2, \ldots a_n]$ be a sequence of activities executed by a workfow agent. We call the sequence legal iff for every $a_j = action_{\leftarrow}(X)$ there exists at least one $a_i = action^{\rightarrow}(X)$ such that $i < j$.

Observe that each a_k will have ground values for the variables, corresponding to a particular workflow instance. Also note that Definition 1 does not preclude a sequence of actions in which several occurrences of a particular instance $action^{\rightarrow}(m, n, \ldots, r)$ will not have a matching $action_{\leftarrow}(m, n, \ldots, r)$. In the setting of Example 1 this corresponds to the case where the main enterprise workflow agent has repeated the request for a credit history check but, for whatever reasons, it has not obtained an answer from the cooperative agent yet. Clearly, this is not the desired executional scenario and it may lead to an *exception*, formalized below.

---

[6] The authors also discuss different event revocation policies for exceptional cases.

[7] This, of course, would be appropriately reflected in the specification of the rules in the control module

3.1   Defeasibility and Exceptions

The workflow research community has only recently tackled the problem of exceptions [18, 19, 30] and identified several types of failures (c.f. [18]): 1. basic (hardware/network/DBMS); 2. application failures (WMFS invokes an application which returns an error code or does not return any value). For the most part, these types of failures are handled by relying on the recovery mechanisms of the underlying DBMS (e.g. *Exotica* project offers tools for specification of compensating tasks, which are subsequently translated into *FDL* – FlowMark Definition Language).

Since we are concerned in formalizing and testing the correctness of workflow specification, we are interested in *expected* and *unexpected* categories of failures [19]. Expected exceptions correspond to the executions which are not desirable but may happen (hopefully, very rarely). This approach is similar to the standard exception handling in programming languages like Smalltalk and C++.

Let us reiterate that in a real situation the domain experts may not be aware of all the possible executional scenarios during the specification. This may yield some cases of unexpected exceptions, for which the main workflow agent may not know how to react. In the context of Example 2, the agent *advisor* is considered a cooperative one, but it may not respond to the messages from the main (registration) workflow agent. This is an exceptional situation for which the main workflow may not know how to react (i.e. it assumed at specification time that any advisor will always respond to a request from a workflow instance). Once a workflow instance encounters an unexpected situation, there are several steps that need to be taken: 1. modify the schema (workflow definition) so that it recognizes and reacts to the exceptional case in the future; 2. modify the schema with rules to "repair" the current failure instances. 3. modify the schema so that the workflow instances "beyond repair" are aborted (possibly re–started). These steps correspond to managing a workflow definition with a so–called progressive case policy. Clearly, steps 2. and 3. will not be needed after the "infected" workflow instances are managed. The modifications done in step one, however, will become propositions which remain in the schema for the future–expected exceptions. The constructs of $\mathcal{A_W}$ that we introduced so far are sufficient to specify the repair policies in steps 2. and 3.

Hence, we must allow for some activities (i.e. the consequences of their executions) and some ramifications to be *defeasible*, in a sense that their effects to not apply in a particular state s because that state is considered to be exceptional. To handle this exceptional behavior, we extend $\mathcal{A_W}$ by introducing exceptional causality and ramification with the following propositions:

$p_1, \ldots, p_n, e_1, \ldots, e_m$ **exceptionally_suffice_for** f

a **exceptionally_causes** f **if** $p_1, \ldots, p_n, e_1, \ldots, e_m$

a **exceptionally_induces** e **if** $p_1, \ldots, p_n, e_1, \ldots, e_m$

a **exceptionally_determines** f **if** $p_1, \ldots, p_n, e_1, \ldots, e_m$

In the exceptional situations, the effects of the activities are determined by the exceptional propositions and the effects of the defeasible propositions are ignored. To illustrate the concept, in the registration example we could add:

$advisor(S, C) \leftarrow$ **exceptionally_causes** $advisor\_no\_available(S, C)$
if $e\_advisor\_timeout$

in case a student request for the advisor's response has reached a deadline marked by an event and the workflow is still waiting for the effects of the activity $advisor(S, C)$. In this situation the exceptional effect is assumed. Now we can have *corrective* actions that will execute in an environment in which $advisor\_no\_available(S, C)$ is true. Moreover, the set of exceptional ramification propositions will induce new facts/ events that can create a new state for the workflow (say, by "cleaning" some events and facts from the state before the exception was detected). Although it is not obvious from the preceding discussion, there is a noteworthy observation regarding the flexibility of the extended $\mathcal{A}_\mathcal{W}$. Namely when iterating, say, over a collection of elements, if one element is exceptional we need not terminate the entire iteration. The repair policy (exceptional ramification propositions) may specify a state in which that particular cycle of the iteration is ignored, but yet the conditions for iterating over the rest of the collection are still valid (i.e. why throwing the entire bucket of apples if we can remove the rotten one). The main benefit of extending $\mathcal{A}_\mathcal{W}$ with exceptional propositions is that we allow very early, in the specification stage, to separate the failure semantics and exception handling from the control logic. The formal treatment of the defeasible and exceptional propositions is given in [6], based on the language $\mathcal{ADC}$.

4   Checking the Correctness of the Workflow Specifications

We allow two types of testing of the workflow specifications. The first type corresponds to "off-line" deliberation on the data and control flow. Here we assume that each of the experts involved in the specifications has provided (what (s)he believes is) the sufficient information about the effects of the activities. In other words, we assume a "current" version of the domain description D as a set of ef-propositions, k-propositions and event-definitions.

Definition 2. Given a domain description D and a legal sequence of activities A $= [a_1, a_2, \ldots, a_n]$, a sequence_query is an expression of the form φ **after** A **at** s, where where φ is a formula (evaluated in 3-valued logic) and s is a state.

Given a set of states S and a domain description (action theory) D, let $S' = Closure(S, D)$ denote the minimal set of states (with respect to the $\subseteq$ ordering) such that: (i) $S \subseteq S'$; (ii) $(\forall s \in S)$ if s' is reachable from s by executing legal sequence of actions described in D, then $s' \in S'$; and (iii) $(\forall s' \in S')(\exists s \in S)$ such that s' is reachable from s by executing legal sequence of actions described in D.

The formula φ in Definition 2 will denote a *goal* that the workflow should achieve. We say that a domain description D entails a sequence_query $q \equiv \varphi$ **after** $[a_1, a_2, \ldots, a_n]$ **at** s, $(D \models q)$ if q is true in all the *models* of D (c.f. [9]).

Definition 3. A domain description D is sufficient with respect to a goal G iff there exists a state s and for every $s' \in Closure(s,D)$ there exists a legal sequence of actions $A = [a_1, a_2, \ldots, a_n]$ such that $D \models G$ **after** A **at** s'.

Definition 3 describes the means which the domain experts can use to test if they have specified enough of the domain description. Moreover, by assigning a cost value to the actions, it can be used as a tool to check the cost of executing a particular sequence of actions which achieves the desired (business) goal.

If the experts involved in the workflow specification are confident, there may be no need for any off-line deliberation: they may complete the workflow specification at a single "negotiation", both the domain description D and the control module M. In any case, once the complete workflow description is available, we have the other type of query for testing its correctness:

Definition 4. Given an activity description D and a control module M, a workflow_query is an expression of the form φ **after** M **at** s where φ is a formula (evaluated w.r.t. the 3-valued logic) and s a state.

Workflow_queries enquire about the consequences of executing a control module M, for a given activities (domain) description D. Definition 4, as opposed to Definition 2, implicitly requires that the legal sequence of actions consists only of the actions specified as a RHS of some rule in the control module. In order to have a definition similar to Definition 3 above, we need to slightly modify the notion of a closure. Given a set of states S, a control module M and a domain description (action theory) D, let $S' = Closure(S,M,D)$ denote the minimal set of states (with respect to subset ordering) such that: (i) $S \subseteq S'$; (ii) $(\forall s \in S)$ if s' is reachable from s by executing legal sequence of actions from M described in D, then $s' \in S'$; and (iii) $(\forall s' \in S')(\exists s \in S)$ such that s' is reachable form s by executing legal sequence of actions from M described in D.

Definition 5. A workflow specification is said to be correct with respect to a control module M, a set of states S, a set of activities description D, and a goal G if, $S = Closure(S, M, D)$ and for all states $s \in S$, $D \models G$ **after** M **at** s.

as a tool to formally state the correctness of the workflow control module (and verify it for a given goal).

There is a special subclass of workflows for which we can do even more during the specification stage. The class of *sequential* workflows consists of all the workflows in which the set of rules in their control modules have the property that all the rules whose LHS are satisfied at a given state, have the same RHS. Informally, sequential workflows rule out the AND-joins (OR-rules do not result in concurrent execution of activities). For the class of sequential workflows we can directly apply the results in [12] to actually *generate* the control module from a given domain description and a given goal[8]. (in [12] control modules are referred as *plans*).

---

[8] The conditions of soundness and completeness for sequential workflows are given in [8].

5   Concluding Remarks, Related Literature and Future Work

In this work we have extended previous results in formalizing reactive control using action theories [12] and applied it to cooperative workflow agents. The main advantage of the language $\mathcal{A_W}$ is that it allows an expert to express his/her domain knowledge in terms of the effects that an activity or task may have on the environment, without any specific knowledge about *how* the activity is implemented. Also note that the semantics of $\mathcal{A_W}$ incorporates the events as a part of the state unlike, for example, process algebra – based approaches where transitions are modeled explicitly and the states in between consecutive transtions are implicit (c.f. [48]). This is an important aspect during the specification stage, where experts from different domains are involved. We allow the users to specify the control logic AND reason if the specifications that they have provided (so far) are sufficient to achieve a desired goal. More importantly, given the description of the effects of the activities, we can help the users "generate" enough control-logic information to achieve their goal. We have implemented a prototype tool which enables both dual (textual and graphical) representations of the workflow specifications.

There are several formalisms for workflow representation. Graphic – based ones like OGWL (Opera Graphical Workflow Language) [30] (which is subsequently converted to internal textual representation) similar to IBM's FDL [38] and State and Activity Charts [50] (which uses ECA rules for describing transitions among states), which is close to the UML standard[9]. The works [25, 24] use CTR (Concurrent Transaction Logic) to design and reason about workflows (in presence of a rich set of constraints) and [14] presents TD ('Transaction Datalog) as a concurrent programming language and uses it to determine computational complexity of workflows. All these formalisms, in a sense, do not strictly formalize the specification stage per se. It is somehow assumed that through intellectual negotiations, the representation indeed corresponds to what the users wanted to specify. On the other hand, we go one step behind in the workflow design, and propose a methodology to formalize the specification phase. $\mathcal{A_W}$ for example, offers more flexibility than CTR or TD, in a sense that none of the two languages allows expressing multiple effects of a same action, or takes a clear account for exceptions.

The closest approach to ours is CONGOLOG [36], where correctness of a concurrent agent language is formulated. Our language is simpler that CONGOLOG – we do not have non-deterministic activities, but we consider exogenous/cooperative activities, which are not considered in CONGOLOG and are essential to model workflows. The problem of planning with incomplete information has also been addressed in the Description Logic [28], however it is too specialized formalism to be used in workflow specification. A formal approach for the workflow computation is given in [45], but the problem of requirements

---

[9] Both OPERA and Mentor projects have addressed other very important problems [3, 41].

specification stage is not treated as a separate aspect, which is the core of our approach.

Another formal approach to modeling and analysis of workflows is based on Petri Nets [48]. The author presents a detailed description of the dimensions/ aspects of the Worflow Management Systems and how they can be mapped into a Petri Net – based specification (actually, there is a formal definition of a *WF–net*) and presents construction of all the routing constructs of interest, like AND/ OR spits and joins, iteration, etc. A benefitial aspect of this approach is that Petri Nets (and their higher – level versions: colored, timed . . .) are very well studied and have formal foundation for investigating various properties of interest to process – based systems (e.g. liveness, boundedness) and there are many Petri Nets tools available. Note that in our formalism, we are much more "liberal" for the specification stage (not necessarily complete) and we also have a tool which can toggle between visual and textual representation. We do not require that the user is familiar with a specialized formalism and we allow incorporating the exceptional scenarios. Let us point that the comparison between logic programs and high – level Petri nets presented in [34] (recall that the specifications in $\mathcal{A_W}$ can be translated to logic program).

Some recent works, addressing the issue of exceptions are [31] (Opera) and [18, 19] defining the Chimera–Exc language (in FAR system). However, the main difference in our work is that we tackle the exceptions handling in the context of specification stage, so that a domain expert can express its knowledge about exceptional situations and their handling according to a given (business) policy.

The programming paradigm Vortex [32, 33] provides a choice-based execution of "attribute centered" workflows. The authors provide a form of incremental decision-making in collecting the values of specific attribute. We view our work as something that can be used as a pre–processor of Vortex based design of workflows.

Observe that one of the salient features of $\mathcal{A_W}$ is its modularity as a spec- ification formalism. New activities descriptions and control module rules can be added independent of the rest of the domain description. There are few im- mediate extensions of our work. We would like to formalize the treatment of composite events (contexts and consumption policies) and we are planning to investigate the possibility of translating between $\mathcal{A_W}$ based specification and other workflow representation formalisms. Also, we are looking into making the visual part of our tool close/ compatible with the existing visual modeling tools, like UML. Currently, we are incorporating the unexpected exception handling and full correctness analysis in the prototype implementation, and we are devel- oping a collaborative version of it.

Acknowldgements: The authors would like to thank Mr. Maxim Kondratyev for implementing part of our formalism in the prototype specification tool. We are grateful to the anonymous referees for their valuable comments and sugges- tions.

References

1. G. Alonso, D. Agrawal, A. El Abadi, and C. Mohan. Functionalities and limitations of current workflow management systems. *IEEE Experts – Special Issue on Cooperative Information Systems*, 12(5), 1997.
2. G. Alonso, U. Fiedler, C. Hagen, A. Lazcano, H. Schuldt, and N. Weiler. Wise: Business to business e-commerce. In *Research Issues on Data Engineering (RIDE)*, 1999.
3. G. Alonso, C. Hagen, and A. Lazcano. Processes in electronic commerce. In *ICDCS Workshop on Electronic Commerce in Web-Based Applications*, 1999.
4. C. Baral, M. Gelfond, and A. Provetti. Representing Actions: Laws, Observations and Hypothesis. *Journal of Logic Programming*, 1996.
5. C. Baral and J. Lobo. Formal characterization of active databases. In *International Workshop on Logic in Databases (LID'96)*, 1996.
6. C. Baral and J. Lobo. Defeasible specifications in action theories. In *Intl. Joint Conference on AI*, 1997.
7. C. Baral, J. Lobo, and G. Trajcevski. Formal characterization of active databases: Part ii. In *5th Intl. Conf. on Deducive and Object – Oriented Databases (DOOD'97)*, 1997.
8. C. Baral, J. Lobo, and G. Trajcevski. Formalizing workflows as collection of condition – action ruls. Technical report, UIC – EECS – 1998 – 2, Univ. of Illinois at Chicago, 1998.
9. C. Baral, J. Lobo, and G. Trajcevski. Formalizing (and reasoning about) the specification of workflows. Technical Report UIC–EECS–00–3, University of Illinois at Chicago, Dept. of EECS, 2000.
10. C. Baral and T. Son. Relating theories of actions and reactive robot control. In *AAAI 96 Workshop on Reasoning about actions, planning and robot control: bridging the gap*, 1996.
11. C. Baral and T. Son. Approximate reasoning about actions in presence of sensing and incomplete information. Technical report, Dept of Computer Science, University of Texas at El Paso, 1997.
12. C. Baral and T. Son. Relating theories of action and reactive control. In *Linkoping Electronic Articles in computer and Information Science*, volume 3. 1998.
13. S. Bergamaschi and C. Sartori. On taxonomic reasoning in conceptual design. *ACM Transactions on Database Systems*, 3(17), 1992.
14. A. Bonner. Workflow, transactions and datalog. In *Principles of Database Systems (PODS)*, 1999.
15. A. Bonner and M. Kifer. Transaction logic programming (or a logic of declarative and procedural knowledge). Technical report, Univ. of Toronto, 1995.
16. A. Bonner and M. Kifer. Concurrency and communication in transaction logic. In *Joint Intl. Conference and Symposium on Logic Programming*, September 1996.
17. U.M. Borgholf, P. Bottoni, P. Mussio, and R. Parechi. Reflective agents for adaptive workflows. In *2nd Intl. Conf. on Practical Applications of Intelligent Agents and Multi – Agent Technology (PAAM'97)*, April 1997.
18. F. Casati. *Models, Semantics and Formal Methods for the Design of Workflows and their Exceptions*. PhD thesis, Politecnico di Milano, 1999.
19. F. Casati and G. Pozzi. Modeling exceptional behavior in commercial workflow management systems. In *4th Intl. Conf. on Cooperative Information Systems (CoopIS)*, 1999.

20. F. Cassati, S. Ceri, B. Pernici, and G. Pozzi. Deriving active rules for workflow enactment. In *7th Intl. Conf. on Database and Expert Systems Application*, 1996.
21. A. Cichocki and M. Rusinkiewicz. Migrating workflows. In *NATO-ASI, Advances in Workflow Management Systems and Interoperability*. 1997.
22. The Workflow Management Coalition. Terminology and glossary. Technical Report WFMC-TC-1011, The Workflow Management Coalition, June 1996.
23. P. Cousot. Methods and logics for proving programs. In *Handbook of theoretical computer science*, volume B, pages 841–994. MIT Press, 1990.
24. H. Davulcu, M. Kifer, R.L. Pokorny, C. Ramakrishnan, and S. Dawson. Modeling and analysis of interactions in virtual enterprises. In *Research Issues on Data Engineering (RIDE)*, 1999.
25. H. Davulcu, M. Kifer, C.R. Ramakrishnan, and I.V Ramakrishnan. Logic based modeling and analysis of workflows. In *ACM Principles of Database Systems*, 1998.
26. M. Gelfond and V. Lifschitz. Representing action and change by logic programs. *Journal of Logic Programming*, 17:301–321, 1993.
27. D. Georgakopoulos, M. Hornick, and A. Sheth. An overview of workflow management: From process modeling to workflow automation infrastructure. *Distributed and Parallel Databases*, 3:119–153, 1995.
28. G. De Giacomo, L. Iocchi, D. Nardi, and R. Rosati. Descriptoin logic-based framework for planning with sensing action. In *Description Logic*, 1997.
29. E. Giunchiglia and V. Lifschitz. An action language based on causal logic. In *AAAI - 98*, 1997.
30. C. Hagen and G. Alonso. Flexible exception handling in the opera process support system. In *18th Intl. Conf. on Distributed Computing Systems (ICDCS 98)*, April 1998.
31. C. Hagen and G. Alonso. Beyond the black box: Event-base inter-process communication in pss. In *19 International Conferrence on Distributed Computing Systems (ICDCS)*, 1999.
32. R. Hull, F. Llirbat, E. Simon, J. Su, G. Dong, B. Kumar, and G. Zhou. Declarative workflows that support easy modifications and dynamic browsing. In *Intl. Joint Conference on Work Activities Coordination and Collaboration (WACC)*, 1999.
33. R. Hull, F. Llirbat, J. Su, G. Dong, B. Kumar, and G. Zhou. Efficient support for decision flows in e–commerce applications. In *2nd Intl. Conf. on Telecommunications and Electronic Commerce (ICTEC)*, 1999.
34. J. Jeffrey, J. Lobo, and T. Murata. A high – level petri net for goal – directed semantics of horn clause logic. *IEEE Transactions on Knowledge and Data Engineering*, 8(2), 1996.
35. M. Kondratyev. Dual representation of workflow specifications. Master's Project Report, March 2000. University of Illinois at Chicago.
36. Y. Lesperance, H. Levesque, F. Lin, D. Marcu, R. Reiter, and R. Scherl. Foundations of a logical approach to agent programming. In *Intelligent Agents - II*. 1995.
37. H. Levesque, R. Reiter, Y. Lesperance, F. Lin, and R. Scherl. Golog: A logic programming language for dynamic domains. *Journal of Logic Programming*, May 1997.
38. F. Leymann and W. Altenhuber. Managing business processes as an information resource. *IBM Systems Journal*, 2(32), 1994.

39. J. McCarthy and P. Hayes. Some philosophical problems from the standpoint of artificial intelligence. In *Machine Intelligence*, volume 4, pages 463–501. Edinburgh University Press, 1969.

40. C. Mohan. Tutorial: State of the art in workflow management system research and products, March 1996.

41. P. Muth, J. Weissenfels, M. Gillman, and G. Weikum. Integrating light-weight wfms with existing business environments. In *International Conferrence on Data Engineering (ICDE)*, 1999.

42. N. Nilsson. Teleo-reactive programs for agent control. *Journal of AI research*, pages 139–158, 1994.

43. R. Reiter. On specifying database updates. *Journal of Logic Programming*, 19,20:1–39, 1994.

44. A. Sheth, D. Georgakopoulos, S.M.M. Joosten, M. Rusinkiewics, W. Scacchi, J. Wileden, and A. Wolf. Report from the nsf workshop on workflow and process automation in information systems. *ACM SIGSOFT - Software Engineering Notes*, 22(1), 1997.

45. M.P. Singh. Formal semantics for workflow computations. Technical report, TR – 96 – 08, North Carolina State University, 1996.

46. I. Sommerville. *Software Engineering*. Addison – Wesley, 1992.

47. S. M. Sutton, P. L. Tarr, and L. J. Osterweil. An analysis of process languages. Technical Report 95 – 78, Dept. of Computer Science, University of Massachusetts, Amherst, 1995.

48. W.M.P van der Aalst. The application of petri nets to workflow management. *The Journal of Circuits, Systems and Computers*, 8(1), 1998.

49. B. Whorf. *Language, thought and reality*. MIT Press, 1956.

50. D. Wodtke and G. Weikum. A formal foundation for distributed workflow execution based on state charts. In *6th Intl. Conf. on Database Theory (ICDT 97)*, 1997.

Advanced Workflow Patterns

W.M.P. van der Aalst[1★] and A.P. Barros[2] and A.H.M. ter Hofstede[3] and B. Kiepuszewski[4★★]

[1] Eindhoven University of Technology, Faculty of Technology and Management, Department of Information and Technology, P.O. Box 513, NL-5600 MB, Eindhoven, The Netherlands. w.m.p.v.d.aalst@tm.tue.nl
[2] Distributed Systems Technology Centre, The University of Queensland, Brisbane Qld 4072, Australia, abarros@dstc.edu.au
[3] Cooperative Information Systems Research Centre, Queensland University of Technology, P.O. Box 2434, Brisbane Qld 4001, Australia, arthur@icis.qut.edu.au
[4] Mincom Limited, P.O. Box 1397, Brisbane Qld 4001, Australia, bartek@mincom.com

Abstract. Conventional workflow functionality like task sequencing, split parallelism, join synchronization and iteration have proven effective for business process automation and have widespread support in current workflow products. However, newer requirements for workflows are encountered in practice, opening grave uncertainties about the extensions for current languages. Different concepts, although outwardly appearing to be more or less the same, are based on different paradigms, have fundamentally different semantics and different levels of applicability - more specialized for modeling or more generalized for workflow engine posit. By way of developmental insight of *new* requirements, we define workflow patterns which are described imperatively but independently of current workflow languages. These patterns provide the basis for an in-depth comparison of 12 workflow management systems. As such, the work reported in this paper can be seen as the academic response to evaluations made by prestigious consulting companies. Typically, these evaluations hardly consider the workflow modeling language and routing capabilities and focus more on the purely technical and commercial aspects.

1 Introduction

Background

Workflow technology continues to be subjected to on-going development in its traditional application areas of business process modeling and business process

---

★ Part of this work was done at CTRG (University of Colorado, USA) during a sabbatical leave.
★★ This research was partially supported by an ARC SPIRT grant "Component System Architecture for an Open Distributed Enterprise Management System with Configurable Workflow Support" between QUT and Mincom.

O. Etzion and P. Scheuermann (Eds.): CoopIS 2000, LNCS 1901, pp. 18–29, 2000.

coordination, and now in emergent areas of component frameworks and inter-workflow, business-to-business interaction. Addressing this broad and rather ambitious reach, a large number of workflow products, mainly workflow management systems (WFMS), are commercially available, which see a large variety of languages and concepts based on different paradigms (see e.g. [1, 4–6, 9, 10, 12–14, 16, 17]).

As current provisions are compared and as newer concepts and languages are embarked upon, it is striking how little, other than standards glossaries, is available for central reference. One of the reasons attributed to the lack of consensus of what constitutes a workflow specification is the organizational level of definition imparted by workflows. The absence of a universal organizational "theory", it is contended, explains and ultimately justifies the major differences - opening up a "horses for courses" diversity for different business domains. What is more, the comparison of different workflow products winds up being more of a dissemination of products and less of a critique - "bigger picture" differences of workflow specifications are highlighted, as are technology, typically platform dependent, issues.

Workflow specifications can be understood, in a broad sense, from a number of different perspectives (see [10]). The *control-flow* perspective (or process) perspective describes activities and their execution ordering through different constructors, which permit flow of execution control, e.g., sequence, splits, parallelism and join synchronization. Activities in elementary form are atomic units of work, and in compound form modularize an execution order of a set of activities. The *data perspective* layers business and processing data on the control perspective. Business documents and other objects which flow between activities, and local variables of the workflow, qualify in effect pre- and post-conditions of activity execution. The *resource perspective* provides an organizational structure anchor to the workflow in the form of human and device roles responsible for executing activities. The *operational* perspective describes the elementary actions executed by activities, where the actions map into underlying applications. Typically, (references to) business and workflow data are passed into and out of applications through activity-to-application interfaces, allowing manipulation of the data within applications.

Clearly, the control flow perspective provides an essential insight into a workflow specification's effectiveness. The data flow perspective rests on it, while the organizational and operational perspectives are ancillary. If workflow specifications are to be extended to meet newer processing requirements, control flow constructors require a fundamental insight and analysis. Currently, most workflow languages support the basic constructs of sequence, iteration, splits (AND and OR) and joins (AND and OR) - see [13]. However, the interpretation of even these basic constructs is not uniform and it is often unclear how more complex requirements could be supported. Indeed, vendors are afforded the opportunity to recommend implementation level "hacks" such as database triggers and application event handling. The result is that neither workflow specifications or clean insight into newer requirements is advanced.

Problem

Even without formal qualification, the distinctive features of different workflow languages allude to fundamentally different semantics. Some languages allow multiple instances of the same activity type at the same time in the same workflow context while others do not. Some languages structure loops with one entry point and one exit point, while in others loops are allowed to have arbitrary entry and exit points. Some languages require explicit termination activities for workflows and their compound activities while in others termination is implicit. Such differences point to different insights of *suitability* and different levels of *expressive power*.

The challenge, which we undertake in this paper, is to understand how complex requirements can be addressed in the current state of the art. These requirements, in our experiences, recur quite frequently in the analysis phases of workflow projects, and present grave uncertainties when looking at current products. Given the fundamental differences indicated above, it is tempting to build extensions to one language, and therefore one semantic context. Such a strategy is rigorous and its results would provide a detailed and unambiguous view into what the extensions entail. Our strategy is more practical. We wish to draw a more *broader* insight into the implementation consequences for the big and potentially big players. With the increasing maturity of workflow technology, workflow language extensions, we feel, should be levered across the board, rather than slip into "yet another technique" proposals.

Approach

We indicate new requirements for workflow languages through workflow *patterns*. As described in [15], a pattern "is the abstraction from concrete form which keeps recurring in specific non-arbitrary contexts". Gamma et al. [8] first catalogued systematically some 23 design patterns which describe the smallest recurring interactions in object-oriented systems. The design patterns, as such, provided independence from the implementation technology and at the same time independence from the essential requirements of the domain that they were attempting to address (see also e.g. [7]).

For our purpose, patterns address business requirements in an imperative workflow style expression, but are removed from specific workflow languages. Thus they do not claim to be the only way of addressing the business requirements. Nor are they "alienated" from the workflow approach, thus allowing a potential mapping to be positioned closely to different languages and implementation solutions. Along the lines of [8], patterns are described through: conditions that should hold for the pattern to be applicable; examples of business situations; problems, typically semantic problems, of realization in current languages; and implementation solutions.

The rest of the paper describes only four workflow patterns. These patterns are just a small sample of the many patterns we have identified. In [3] we report 26 patterns. It will be assumed throughout that the reader is familiar with the basic functionality of current workflows: sequence, splits (OR and AND), joins (OR and AND) and iteration. The goal of this paper is not to provide a comprehensive overview of workflow functionality: It only shows the flavor of the research that has been conducted. For a more complete overview we refer to [3].

2   Advanced Synchronization Patterns

In most workflow engines two basic forms of synchronization are supported, AND-join and OR-join. Although the actual semantics of these constructs differ from system to system, it can be safely assumed that the intention of the AND-join is to synchronize two (or more) concurrent threads, whereas the intention of the OR-join is to merge two threads into one with the (implicit) assumption that only one thread will be active during run-time. Many different business scenarios require more advanced synchronization patterns. An example of such an advanced synchronization pattern is the so-called Synchronizing Merge.

Pattern 1 (Synchronizing Merge)
Description A point in the workflow process where multiple paths converge into one single thread. If more than one path is taken, synchronization of the active threads needs to take place. If only one path is taken, the alternative branches should reconverge without synchronization.
Synonyms Synchronizing join
Examples
   - After executing the activity *evaluate_damage* the activity *contact_fire_department* or the activity *contact_insurance_company* is executed. However, it is also possible that both need to be executed. After either or both of these activities have been completed, the activity *submit report* needs to be performed (exactly once).
Problem The main difficulty with this pattern is to decide when to synchronize and when to merge. Synchronizing alternative flows leads to potential deadlocks and merging parallel flows may lead to unwanted, multiple execution of the activity that follows the standard OR-join construct.
Solutions
   - The two workflow engines known to the authors that provide a straight-forward construct for the realization of this pattern are MQSeries/Workflow and InConcert. As noted earlier, if a synchronising merge follows an OR-split and more than one outgoing transition of that OR-split can be triggered, it is not until runtime that we can tell whether or not synchronization should take place. MQSeries/Workflow works around that problem by passing a False token for each transition that evaluates to False and a True token for each transition that evaluates to True. The merge will wait until it receives tokens from each incoming transition. InConcert does not use a False token concept. Instead it passes a token through every transition in a graph. This token may or may not enable the execution of an activity depending on the entry condition. This way every activity having more than one incoming

transition can expect that it will receive a token from each one of them, thus deadlock cannot occur. The careful reader may note that these evaluation strategies require that the workflow process does not contain cycles.

- In all other workflow engines the implementation of the synchronizing merge is not straightforward. The common design pattern is to avoid the explicit use of the OR-split that may trigger more than one outgoing transition and implement it as a combination of AND-splits and OR-splits that guarantee to trigger only one of the outgoing transitions (we will call such splits XOR-splits for the remaining of this paper). This way we can easily synchronize corresponding branches by using AND-join and OR-join constructs.

□

The synchronizing merge is just an example of an advanced synchronization pattern. In [3] we have identified additional ones such as the Multi-merge, the Discriminator, and the N-out-of-M Join.

3 Structural Patterns

Different workflow management systems impose different restrictions on their workflow models. These restrictions (e.g., arbitrary loops are not allowed, only one final node should be present, etc.) are not always natural from a modeling point of view and tend to restrict the specification freedom of the business analyst. As a result, business analysts either have to conform to the restrictions of the workflow language from the start, or they model their problems freely and transform the resulting specifications afterwards. A real issue here is that of suitability. In many cases the resulting workflows may be unnecessarily complex which impacts end-users who may wish to monitor the progress of their workflows.

An example of a typical structural requirement imposed by some of the workflow products is that the workflow model is to contain only one ending node, or in case of many ending nodes, the workflow model will terminate when the first one is reached. Again, most business models do not follow this pattern - it is more natural to think of a business process as terminated once there is nothing else to be done.

Pattern 2 (Implicit Termination)
Description A given subprocess should be terminated when there is nothing else to be done. In other words, there are no active activities in the workflow and no other activity can be made active (and at the same time the workflow is not in deadlock).
Examples
- This semantics is typically assumed for every workflow model at the analysis stage.
Problem Most workflow engines terminate the process when an explicit *Final* node is reached. Any current activities that happen to be running by that time

will be aborted.
Solutions

- Some workflow engines (Staffware, MQSeries/Workflow, InConcert) would terminate the (sub)process when there is nothing else to be done.

- The typical solution to this problem is to transform the model to an equivalent model that has only one terminating node. The complexity of that task depends very much on the actual model. Sometimes it is easy and fairly straightforward, typically by using a combination of different join constructs and activity repetition. There are cases when it is not possible to do so. Clearly one of the cases when it is impossible is a model that involves multiple instances (see section 4). The required semantics is impossible to achieve without resorting to external triggers.

□

Another pattern described in [3] is the so-called Arbitrary Cycle (cf. [11]). Virtually every workflow engine has constructs that support the modeling of loops. Some of the workflow engines provide support only for what we will refer to as *structured cycles*. Structured cycles can have only one entry point to the loop and one exit point from the loop and they cannot be interleaved. They can be compared to WHILE loops in programming languages while arbitrary cycles are more like GOTO statements. This analogy should not deceive the reader though into thinking that arbitrary cycles are not desirable as there are two important differences here with "classical" programming languages: 1) the presence of parallelism which in some cases makes it impossible to remove certain forms of arbitrariness and 2) the fact that the removal of arbitrary cycles may lead to workflows that are much harder to interpret (and as opposed to programs, workflow specifications also have to be understood at runtime by their users).

4   Patterns involving multiple instances of an activity

Many workflow management systems have problems with the phenomenon that we will refer to as *multiple instances*. From a theoretical point of view the concept is relatively simple and corresponds to more than one token in a given place in a Petri-net representation of the workflow graph. From a practical point of view it means that one activity on a workflow graph can have more than one running, active instance at the same time. As we will see, it is a very valid and frequent requirement. The fundamental problem with the implementation of this pattern is that due to design constraints and lack of anticipation for this requirement most of the workflow engines do not allow for more than one instance of the same activity to be active at the same time. As an example we discuss one pattern dealing with multiple instances.

Pattern 3 (Multiple Instances Requiring Synchronization)
Description For one case an activity is enabled multiple times. The number of instances may not be known at design time. After completing all instances of

that activity another activity has to be started.

Examples

- When booking a trip, the activity *book_flight* is executed multiple times if the trip involves multiple flights. Once all bookings are made, the invoice is to be sent to the client.

- The requisition of a 100 computers results in a certain number of deliveries. Once all deliveries are processed, the requisition has to be closed.

Problem Most workflow engines do not allow multiple instances. Languages that do allow multiple instances (e.g. Forté and Verve) do not provide any construct that would allow for synchronization of these instances. Languages that support the asynchronous subprocess invocation (e.g. Visual WorkFlo through the *Release* construct) do not provide any means for for the synchronization of spawned off subprocesses.

Solutions

- If the number of instances (or maximum number of instances) is known at design time, then it is easy to synchronize the multiple instances implemented through activity repetition by using basic synchronization.

- If the language supports multiple instances *and* decomposition that does not terminate unless all activities are finished, then multiple instances can be synchronized by placing the workflow sub-flow containing the loop generating the multiple instances inside the decomposition block. The activity to be done once all instances are completed can then follow that block.

- MQSeries/Workflow's *Bundle* construct can be used when the number of instances is known at some point during runtime to synchronize all created instances.

- In most workflow languages none of these solutions can be easily implemented. The typical way to tackle this problem is to use external triggers. Once each instance of an activity is completed, the event should be sent. There should be another activity in the main process waiting for events. This activity will only complete after all events from each instance are received.

□

Pattern 3 is just an example of a pattern dealing with multiple instances. In [3] we have identified additional ones. Figure 1 illustrates some design patterns for dealing with multiple instances. Workflow (a) can be implemented in languages supporting multiple concurrent instances of an activity as well as implicit termination (see Pattern 2). An activity B will be invoked here many times, activity C is used to determine if more instances of B are needed. Once all instances of B are completed, the subprocess will complete and activity E can be processed. Implicit termination of the subprocess is used as the synchronizing mechanism for the multiple instances of activity B. Workflow (b) can be implemented in languages that do not support multiple concurrent instances. Activity B is invoked asynchronously, typically through an API. There is no easy way to synchronize

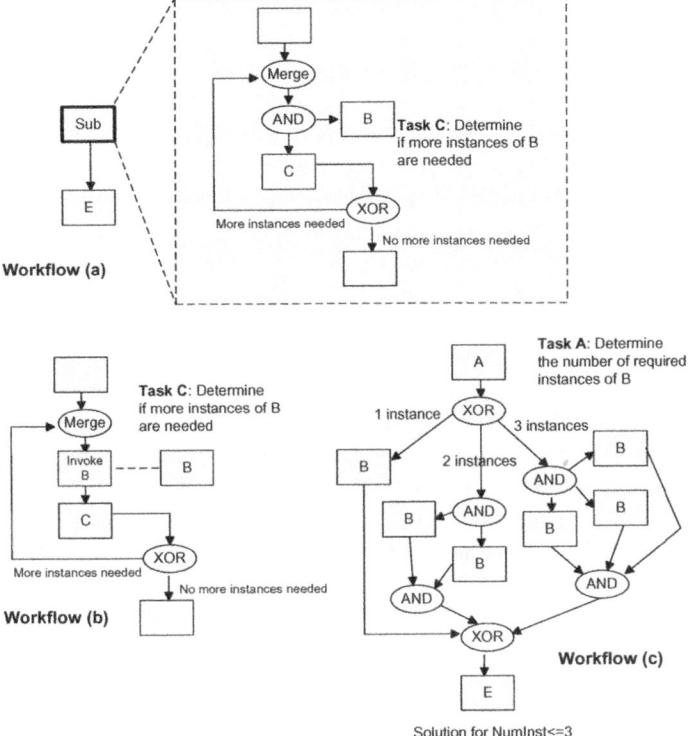

Fig. 1. Design patterns for multiple instances

all instances of activities B. Finally workflow (c) demonstrates a simple implementation when it is known during design time that there will be no more than three instances of B.

5   State-based Patterns

In real workflows, most workflow instances are in a state awaiting processing rather than being processed. Most computer scientists, however, seem to have a frame of mind, typically derived from programming, where the notion of state is interpreted in a narrower fashion and is essentially reduced to the concept of data. As this section will illustrate, there are real differences between work processes and computing and there are business scenarios where an explicit notion of state is required. As the notation we have deployed so far is not suitable for capturing states explicitly, we adopt the variant of Petri-nets as described in [2] when illustrating the patterns in this section. Petri-nets provide *a* possible solution to modeling states explicitly (an example of a commercial workflow management system based on Petri-nets is COSA).

Moments of choice, such as e.g. supported by constructs as XOR-splits/OR-splits, in workflow management systems are typically of an *explicit* nature, i.e., they are based on data or they are captured through decision activities. This means that the choice is made a-priori, i.e., before the actual execution of the selected branch starts an internal choice is made. Sometimes this notion is not appropriate. Consider Figure 2 adopted from [2]. In this figure two workflows are depicted. In both workflows, the execution of activity A is followed by the execution of B or C. In workflow (a) the moment of choice is as late as possible. After the execution of activity A there is a "race" between activities B and C. If the external message required for activity C (this explains the envelope notation) arrives before someone starts executing activity B (the arrow above activity B indicates it requires human intervention), then C is executed, otherwise B. In workflow (b) the choice for either B or C is fixed after the execution of activity A. If activity B is selected, then the arrival of an external message has no impact. If activity C is selected, then activity B cannot be used to bypass activity C. Hence, it is important to realize that in workflow (a), both activities B and C were, at some stage, simultaneously scheduled. Once an actual choice for one of them was made, the other was disabled. In workflow (b), activities B and C were at no stage scheduled together.

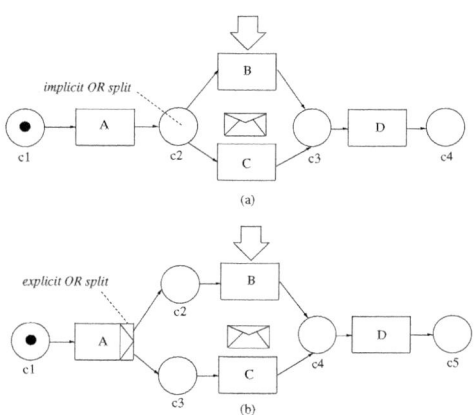

Fig. 2. Illustrating the difference between implicit (a) and explicit (b) XOR-splits

Many workflow management systems abstract from states between subsequent activities, and hence have difficulties modeling implicit choices.

Pattern 4 (Deferred Choice)
Description A point in the workflow process where one of several branches is chosen. In contrast to the XOR-split, the choice is not made explicitly (e.g., based on data or a decision) but several alternatives are offered to the environment. However, in contrast to the AND-split, only one of the alternatives is executed. This means that once the environment activates one of the branches the other

alternative branches are withdrawn. It is important to note that the choice is delayed until the processing in one of the alternative branches is actually started, i.e., the moment of choice is as late as possible.

Synonyms External choice, Implicit choice.

Examples

- After receiving the products there are two ways to transport the products to the department. The selection is based on the availability of the corresponding resources. Therefore, the choice is deferred until a resource is available.

- See the choice between B and C in Figure 2. Activity A may represent the sending of a form to a customer. Activity C corresponds to the processing of the form once it is returned. Activity B corresponds to situation where the form is not received in time and some alternative action is taken.

Problem Many workflow management systems support the XOR-split but do not support the implicit XOR-split. Since both types of choices are desired (see example), the absence of the implicit OR-split is a real problem.

Solutions

- Assume that the workflow language being used supports AND-splits and the cancellation of activities. The implicit XOR-split can be realized by enabling all alternatives via an AND-split. Once the processing of one of the alternatives is started, all other alternatives are cancelled. Consider the implicit choice between B and C in Figure 2(a). After A both B and C are enabled. Once B is selected/executed, activity C is cancelled. Once C is selected/executed, activity B is cancelled. Note that the solution does not always work because B and C can be selected/executed concurrently.

- Another solution to the problem is to replace the implicit XOR-split by an explicit XOR-split, i.e., an additional activity is added. All triggers activating the alternative branches are redirected to the added activity. Assuming that the activity can distinguish between triggers, it can activate the proper branch. Consider the example shown in Figure 2. By introducing a new activity E after A and redirecting triggers from B and C to A, the implicit XOR-split can be replaced by an explicit XOR-split based on the origin of the first trigger. Note that this solution moves part of the routing to the application or task level.

□

In [3] we have identified several patterns related to the Deferred Choice. An example of such a pattern is the so-called Milestone. In this pattern one branch of a parallel process is offered a time window by another branch to executed certain parts of the process. Other related patterns are Cancel Activity, Cancel Case, and Interleaved Parallel Routing. These patterns have in common that an explicit notion of states is required and that they are supported by only a few workflow management systems.

It is interesting to think about the reason why many workflow products have problems dealing with state-based patterns. The systems that abstract from states are typically based on messaging, i.e., if an activity completes, it notifies or triggers other activities. This means that activities are *enabled* by the receipt of one or more messages. State-based patterns have in common that an activity can become *disabled* (temporarily). However, since states are implicit and there are no means to disable activities (i.e., negative messages), these systems have problems dealing with the constructs mentioned. Note that the synchronous nature of patterns such as the deferred choice (i.e., Pattern 4) further complicates the use of asynchronous communication mechanisms such as message passing using "negative messages" (e.g., messages to cancel activities).

6   Epilogue

The four workflow patterns described in this paper correspond to routing constructs encountered when modeling and analyzing workflows. These patterns illustrate the more complete set of 26 workflow patterns reported [3]. Several patterns are difficult, if not impossible, to realize using many of the workflow management systems available today. As indicated in the introduction, the routing functionality is hardly taken into account when comparing/evaluating workflow management systems. The system is checked for the presence of sequential, parallel, conditional, and iterative routing without considering the ability to handle the more subtle workflow patterns described in this paper. The evaluation reports provided by prestigious consulting companies such as the "Big Six" (Andersen Worldwide, Ernst & Young, Deloitte & Touche, Coopers & Lybrand, KPMG, and Price Waterhouse) typically focus on purely technical issues (Which database management systems are supported?), the profile of the software supplier (Will the vendor be taken over in the near future?), and the marketing strategy (Does the product specifically target the telecommunications industry?). As a result, many enterprises select a workflow management system that does not fit their needs.

We have used a comprehensive set of workflow patterns to compare the functionality of 12 workflow management systems (COSA, Visual Workflow, Forté Conductor, Meteor, Mobile, MQSeries/Workflow, Staffware, Verve Workflow, I-Flow, InConcert, Changengine, and SAP R/3 Workflow), cf. [3]. From the comparison it is clear that no tools support all the selected patterns. In fact, many of these tools only support a fraction of these patterns and the best of them only support about 50%. Specifically the limited support for state-based patterns and advanced synchronization patterns (e.g., multiple instances, merge, N-out-of-M) is worth noting. Typically, when confronted with questions as to how certain complex patterns need to be implemented in their product, workflow vendors respond that the analyst may need to resort to the application level, the use of external events or database triggers. This however defeats the purpose of using workflow engines in the first place. Therefore, it is worthwhile to use the set of patterns given in [3] as a check list when selecting a workflow product.

Disclaimer. We, the authors and the associated institutions, assume no legal liability or responsibility for the accuracy and completeness of any product-specific information contained in this paper. However, we made all possible efforts to make sure that the results presented are, to the best of our knowledge, up-to-date and correct.

References

1. W.M.P. van der Aalst. Chapter 10: Three Good reasons for Using a Petri-net-based Workflow Management System. In T. Wakayama et al., editor, *Information and Process Integration in Enterprises: Rethinking documents*, The Kluwer International Series in Engineering and Computer Science, pages 161–182. Kluwer Academic Publishers, Norwell, 1998.
2. W.M.P. van der Aalst. The Application of Petri Nets to Workflow Management. *The Journal of Circuits, Systems and Computers*, 8(1):21–66, 1998.
3. W.M.P. van der Aalst, A.P. Barros, A.H.M. ter Hofstede, and B. Kiepuszewski. Workflow Patterns. Unpublished (46 pages), 2000.
4. W.M.P. van der Aalst and A.H.M. ter Hofstede. Verification of Workflow Task Structures: A Petri-net-based Approach. *Information Systems*, 25(1):43–69, 2000.
5. A. Doğaç, L. Kalinichenko, M. Tamer Özsu, and A. Sheth, editors. *Workflow Management Systems and Interoperability*, volume 164 of *NATO ASI Series F: Computer and Systems Sciences*. Springer-Verlag, Berlin, 1998.
6. C.A. Ellis and G.J. Nutt. Modelling and Enactment of Workflow Systems. In M. Ajmone Marsan, editor, *Application and Theory of Petri Nets 1993*, volume 691 of *Lecture Notes in Computer Science*, pages 1–16. Springer-Verlag, Berlin, 1993.
7. M. Fowler. *Analysis Patterns: Reusable Object Models*. Addison-Wesley, Reading, Massachusetts, 1997.
8. E. Gamma, R. Helm, R. Johnson, and J. Vlissides. *Design Patterns: Elements of Reusable Object-Oriented Software*. Addison-Wesley, Reading, Massachusetts, 1995.
9. D. Georgakopoulos, M. Hornick, and A. Sheth. An Overview of Workflow Management: From Process Modeling to Workflow Automation Infrastructure. *Distributed and Parallel Databases*, 3:119–153, 1995.
10. S. Jablonski and C. Bussler. *Workflow Management: Modeling Concepts, Architecture, and Implementation*. International Thomson Computer Press, 1996.
11. B. Kiepuszewski, A.H.M. ter Hofstede, and C. Bussler. On Structured Workflow Modelling. In B. Wangler and L. Bergman, editors, *12th International Conference, CAiSE 2000*, volume 1789 of *Lecture Notes in Computer Science*, pages 431–445, Stockholm, Sweden, June 2000. Springer-Verlag, Berlin.
12. T.M. Koulopoulos. *The Workflow Imperative*. Van Nostrand Reinhold, New York, 1995.
13. P. Lawrence, editor. *Workflow Handbook 1997, Workflow Management Coalition*. John Wiley and Sons, New York, 1997.
14. F. Leymann and D. Roller. *Production Workflow: Concepts and Techniques*. Prentice-Hall PTR, Upper Saddle River, New Jersey, USA, 1999.
15. D. Riehle and H. Züllighoven. Understanding and Using Patterns in Software Development. *Theory and Practice of Object Systems*, 2(1):3–13, 1996.
16. T. Schäl. *Workflow Management for Process Organisations*, volume 1096 of *Lecture Notes in Computer Science*. Springer-Verlag, Berlin, 1996.
17. WFMC. Workflow Management Coalition Terminology and Glossary (WFMC-TC-1011). Technical report, Workflow Management Coalition, Brussels, 1996.

Extending UML with Workflow Modeling Capabilities

Guido Wirtz[1], Mathias Weske[2], and Holger Giese[1]

[1] Institute for Computer Science, Westfälische Wilhelms-Universität
Einsteinstrasse 62, 48149 Münster, GERMANY
{guidow,gieseh}@cs.uni-muenster.de
[2] Department of Information Systems, Westfälische Wilhelms-Universität
Steinfurter Strasse 109, 48149 Münster, GERMANY
weske@helios.uni-muenster.de

Abstract. Nowadays application systems are modeled in object-oriented design languages like the Unified Modeling Language (UML). Although workflow management has to deal with such environments, typically propriatory modeling languages are used. We try to remedy the use of seperate languages by proposing an extension of the UML to allow workflow modeling, thereby providing a seamless integration of workflow functionality in object-oriented application systems.

1 Introduction

Workflow management is an important technology for modeling and controlling the execution of business processes in commercial applications [4, 9]. While the construction of complex software systems nowadays uses object-oriented analysis and design [1], workflow modeling is often performed separately, using different methods, techniques, and tools. This situation is especially unfortunate because automating workflows means implementing the needed processes in the environment at hand where the gap between application object modeling and workflow modeling may lead to inadequate workflow support for object-oriented applications, both with respect to maintainability of the software and the reuse of workflow schemas. Although organizations tend to be complex but strictly structured, the process-oriented view found in most workflow approaches declines to use this fact as a means of structuring models which is close to the application domain and hence is highly useful, especially for managing overall complexity and scalability of workflow specifications. This makes a workflow modeling methodology which is compatible to the used software engineering techniques even more desirable. To overcome this unsatisfying situation, this paper proposes such an integrated approach. As stated similarly in [12], one of the basic assumptions of this work is that the problems arising in workflow modeling are similar to those occurring with the analysis, design and implementation of complex sequential and distributed software systems. Hence a compatible methodology for both worlds is feasible. Our work is based on object-oriented notation. For modeling static aspects, we use the UML [11]. Additionally, so-called Object Coordination

O. Etzion and P. Scheuermann (Eds.): CoopIS 2000, LNCS 1901, pp. 30–41, 2000.

Nets (OCoNs) [5], a visual formalism for describing system dynamics are integrated into the UML context. This leads to a set of notations which are suitable to specify not only application objects, but also workflows.

2   Background and Rationale

Depending on the workflow language and on the workflow management system employed, several dimensions are covered in workflow schemas; these dimensions are also known as workflow aspects [7]: the *functional* aspect specifies what has to be done within a workflow. The *operational* aspect determines how it is done, i.e., which techniques and tools are used to perform the workflow. The *behavioral* aspect defines when and under which conditions a workflow is executed. The *informational* aspect specifies the data objects which are being manipulated during workflow executions and the flow of data between workflow activities. The *organizational* aspect describes the roles and personnel which are involved in workflow executions. There are two conflicting goals regarding these aspects, namely *independence* and *consistency*. At the first glance, the *independence* of different aspects of a workflow schema has at lot of benefits. It makes sure that changes w.r.t. one particular aspect do not involve the others. However, in real-world workflow applications, aspects are normally not that independent from each other, for instance due to interrelationships between the operational aspect (external applications) and the informational aspect (data used by them). Moreover, complete independence of aspects may not be desirable. Whereas the different aspects of workflow applications are helpful to concentrate on specific views separately when modeling workflows, afterwards questions of *overall consistency* of the specification become important: which parts of an organization are involved in a specific workflow, what are the roles of the organizational units, are they capable of or really the best guess for performing their specific subtask or is, for example, the flow of data consistent with the security policy of an organizational structure. Thus, the organizational aspect may give important hints how to specify the functional and behavioural aspects or even place restrictions on the operational aspect in a given context, e.g., if a task is performed in a specific part of an organisation, a specific external application has to be used which differs from those of other divisions due to a non-uniform software (version) environment. On the other hand, during the restructuring of a complex workflow environment, modeling the functional and behavioural aspects of the most important workflow schemas first, provides the detailed specification for *use cases* [11] needed to discuss the overall organizational design. Workflow languages typically allow the specification of workflow schemas in a manner which puts its focus on the fact that the aspects are defined independently. The approach described in this paper employs object-oriented methods to deliver to some extent a combination of both goals: focussing on the aspect currently at hand in the well-defined context of a structured specification of all relevant aspects.

The use of object-oriented methods implies two additional benefits in the workflow context. Traditionally, workflow schemas are described using specific and often propriatory languages. These workflow languages often use formalisms based on directed graphs [16] or Petri Nets [13] in a manner which does not fit very well into the technical environment of modern information system infrastructures. Often, these systems are (and definitely will be in the future) developed using object-oriented methods. For the modeling of such systems, object-oriented design languages and recently the quasi-standard of the Unified Modeling Language [11] are widely used. The usage of these notations when specifying workflow applications helps to close the gap between both worlds and eases the incorporation or adaption of off-the-shelf software as well as the implementation of software. Describing, e.g., the informational aspect of a workflow in the same language as the data interfaces of the applications permits the re-use of the data format descriptions or at least provides a clear basis for the adaption of formats. If no legacy code is available, the description of a specific task of a workflow schema using UML diagrams provides an ideal starting point for implementing the needed piece of software with state-of-the-art methods. The second benefit comes for free and is due to the capabilities of OO methods for managing complexity. Workflow systems are as complex as application software systems and their development can make use of OOA and OOD to deal with the complexity. Here, using structure modeling to capture the organizational aspect [7] of a workflow system like, e.g., geographically distributed branches of an organization with distinguished roles and permissions to perform (parts of) the work to be done, can provide a basis for keeping an eye on the consistency w.r.t. all other aspects from the very beginning. If all aspects of a workflow application are specified in an integrated design language, independence of aspects gets a new chance by explicitly specifying dependencies and assumed independence may even be checked in the model. More important, a different dimension of independence is introduced which is of much more use: the means of structuring the design of a workflow system using OO methodology into subsystems with interfaces and specifying dependencies between subsystems explicitly deals much better with managing overall complexity and change management for workflow applications in-the-large than the abovementioned independence of aspects which is provided to some extent by different diagrams when specifying workflow in-the-small.

In order to be close to the standard for OO applications, workflow specifications should also be described with the diagrams provided by the UML wherever suitable. Although the UML subsumes a variety of techniques to model different aspects of software systems, there remain some problems. First, there are simply too many kinds of diagrams to be used in a specific application. Overlapping aspects of behaviour may be described by annotating class diagrams in so-called collaboration diagrams, sequence diagrams, activity diagrams or statechart diagrams. Second, there is no clear semantics for most of these diagrams regarding the internal correspondence to other diagrams used in the same model. This is a serious flaw in the UML because the really essential aspects of system dynamics which are important especially for the functional and behavioural aspects of a workflow system are not that well-covered. Using such notations would make the intended notation of consistency hard to implement (for a detailed discussion see [5]). In the context of workflow modeling, a pragmatic approach helps to overcome the problems with the UML. In order to introduce as few new notation as possible, only those notations of the UML which are used to describe static structures like systems, subsystems, classes, associations and so on are utilized. So-called Object Coordination Nets (OCoNs) [17] provide a high-level Petri-Net [2] formalism for specifying system dynamics. To avoid the problems with consistency, OCoNs are seamlessly integrated into the UML and have a formal semantics. In contrast to most high-level net approaches working with complex textual and formal annotations which are hard to use for the non-expert in formal methods, the net dialect puts its focus on the visual expressiveness. Principal different aspects of a workflow system are expressed in different diagrams whereas related aspects are described in the same diagram but represented by distinguishable graphical entities.

3   The Object Coordination Net Approach

We assume the reader to be familiar with place-transition nets [2] and the basic concepts of object orientation. Transitions in our context are interpreted to be *actions* which occur through calls to services provided by objects. For places which are called *pools*, we distinguish between two principle entities: simple data and control flow using untyped tokens and objects typed according to the type system obtained by the informational aspects of workflows are stored in so-called *event pools* (circles). More permanent objects which are in the object-oriented view the carrier of activity or provider of services are interpreted as *resources* the system uses to perform its work. Places which hold resources are represented by *resource pools* (hexagons).

In order to support a method for workflow modeling as described in the previous section, structuring a system into encapsulated subsystems and a well-defined and expressive formalism to describe interfaces and interface-based interaction are crucial. The OCoN approach introduced in [17] fulfills these requirements by putting its focus on a system design which is ruled by the *contract principle* [10]. Organisational aspects are used to obtain a coarse-grained structure of the context in which workflows are to be modeled. Using UML structure diagrams this results in a set of (nested) subsystems providing services specified in contracts to the outside and possibly using services from other subsystems via their contracts to implement the provided functionality (see Fig. 5). A single contract is a traditional signature specifying the names and required parameters of all provided services which is extended by a state-machine-like *protocol net* (PN) to specify externally visible behaviour if not all services are always available. This kind of specification enhances the benefits of interfaces in case of services which obtain nonuniform service availability as it is often found in systems acting according to complex organizational rules. The example shown in Fig. 1 specifies a simple contract to deal with an object of type Media like, e.g., a book or CD using the services getout and putback. The PN adds important usage information to the signature. Only if the required entity is in state [Free], is the service getout available. Moreover, the contract requires that a getout which brings the object to state [InUse] has to be followed definitely by a putback. Hence, the contract specifies restrictions for its users. Finally, a hint that the object may not be available for some (finite) time due to internal regulations of the implementation is specified by introducing a third state [Check] and an anonymous step (shaded transition). However, the protocol guarantees that eventually the object will be in state [Free] again. Using states as pre- and post-conditions for service availability supports the abstract description of the behavioural workflow aspect.

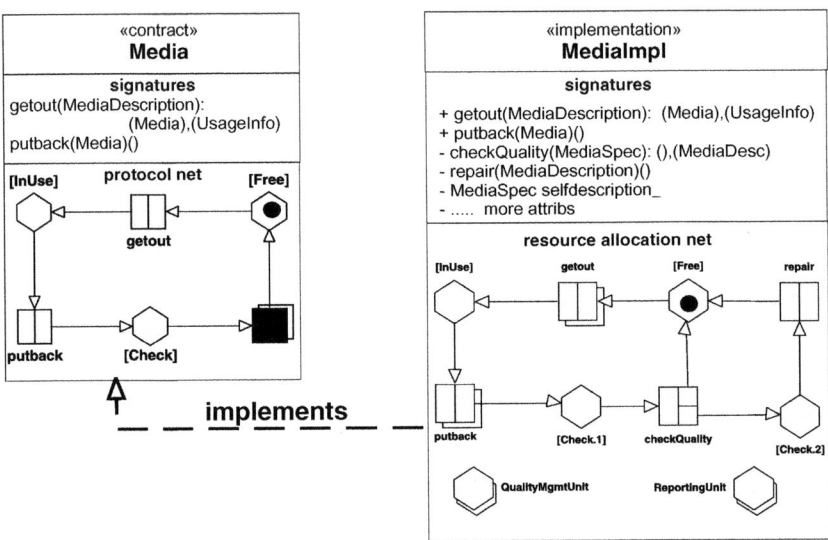

Fig. 1. Media contract and its implementation MediaImpl

For decoupling subsystems properly, we distinguish clearly between the external information provided by a contract and its internal implementation. Moreover, we rigorously permit the usage of services by means of provided contracts only. The internals of a subsystem itself may have a complex structure as well as complicated rules of handling control and data. This leads in practice to a hierarchical design of such systems. Besides the internal subsystem structure, there are two aspects of special importance inside a single system: the internal details of the *implementation* of the provided services and the overall *management of resources* to accomplish that goal. The concepts needed to model these aspects include two additional variants of Petri-nets, namely *service nets* (SN) for describing the detailed workflow when performing a single service and *resource allocation nets* (RAN) for the resource management.

The interaction mechanism of the nets is visualized in Fig. 2: calling a provided service as described in the corresponding PN activates the RAN of the instance which provides the call with the needed resources and delegates it to the requested service (SN). If the service uses external services from other contracts, parts of the work are delegated to instances of the used type. For the Media example, the implementation MediaImpl in Fig. 1 (right) defines the local attributes needed for the implementation, publishes the services to implement getout and putback, but uses additional private services, e.g., checkQuality to control incoming Media whether they are ok to be used again or not. Moreover, the RAN implements the protocol provided by the PN. It states that two external resources imported from other subsystems (shaded hexagons), namely QualityMgmtUnit and ReportingUnit, are needed for the implementation of the contract. The initial state of a new instance of MediaImpl is defined to be [Free] by putting a token in the corresponding resource place. Compared to Media, the possible states of MediaImpl are refined. Where [Free] and [InUse] are used to represent the corresponding states of the PN, [Check] is partitioned into [Check.1] and [Check.2]. This reflects the fact that the work which has to be done inside the implementation is splitted into two parts checkQuality and repair in the case of incoming objects which are in bad shape. However, the only thing w.r.t. these details which is of any interest for the contract, is the existence of internal work which prevents Media in state [InUse] from becoming [Free] immediately after a putback. MediaImpl fulfills the protocol because either checkQuality decides that everything is ok and the object is put back in state [Free] or the object is put into state [Check.2] and has to undergo a repair after which it is put back in state [Free], too. Because this part of the behaviour depends on the object at hand, the RAN uses a transition checkQuality with two possible alternative outcomes.

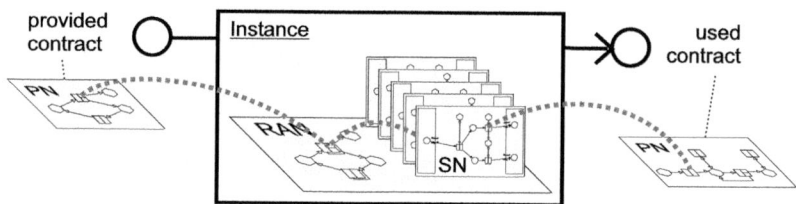

Fig. 2. OCoN architecture and usage of Net types

The usage of shaded transitions indicates that the net (PN or RAN) at hand does not have complete control over the operation or how it is called. As well as the implementation details are out of control of the anonymous transition in the PN, are the number and time of calls to getout and putback from the outside not under control of the implementation.

The detailed subworkflows implementing a service are specified in a *service net* (SN). It adopts the object-oriented view of method invocation by supporting an intuitive call semantics which is well-known from procedural programming languages and remote procedure calls. Fig. 3 visualizes the concept: a transition is interpreted to represent a call to a method-like service. As a precondition for firing, a *carrier of activity* (here obj1 of type Resource1), i.e., the object which processes the call, is required as well as the parameters (here an object of type InType) and a simple Event. Moreover, the carrier has to be not only of type

Resource1 but especially a resource in state [State1]. If the call to fun fires, it consumes all preconditions in the first step, performs some durable activity inside the service fun and produces all postconditions afterwards in a second step. The effect is an object of type ResultType in place resu and a state change for the carrier which is afterwards in state [State2].

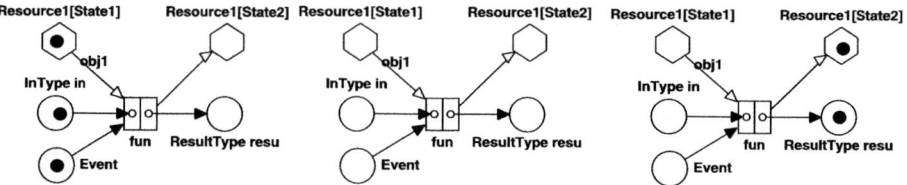

Fig. 3. Steps during execution of resu = obj1.fun(in)

The hierarchical design of the service nets allows for calls to other services during firing inside a transition. Due to the synchronous nature of call and return, this works across hierarchies and can also be used as a wrapper call to services implemented by legacy code. The concept is explained by means of the internal MediaImpl service checkQuality (see Fig. 4). In order to support hierarchical abstraction but keep the essentials also on the abstract call level, calling transitions visualize the signature of the service they call (see Fig. 4, left). The transition here requires a single data parameter and produces an alternative output to abstract from an internal decision.

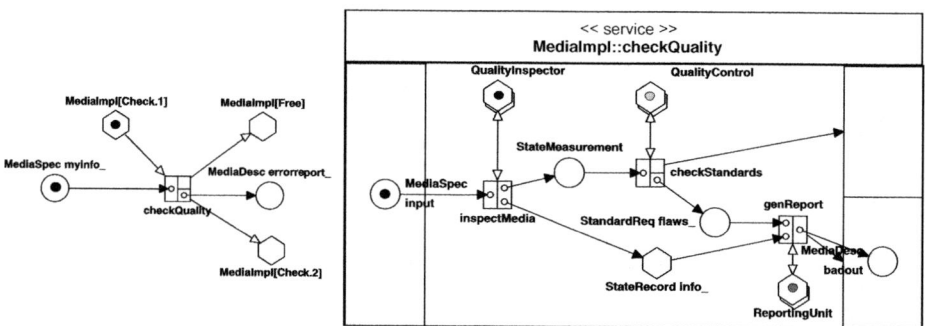

Fig. 4. Call semantics of OCoNs

In conformance with the RAN in Fig. 1, the operation can only be carried out by instances of the resource MediaImpl in state [Check.1]. Because this is specified in the RAN, it is not explicitly stated in the textual signature. The signature requires an additional parameter of type MediaSpec which is represented by the precondition pool myInfo in the calling net. The result MediaDesc which is expected only in one of the possible decision outcomes is handled in a similar manner. Because both preconditions are fulfilled, the action is enabled to fire. The unfolded version of the calling transition (see Fig. 4, right) uses two bars to represent the input and output parameters. The figure shows the initial situation after consuming the preconditions. Additional resources are present from the

QualityMgmtUnit and the ReportingUnit (cf. the RAN in Fig. 1) in order to carry out the delegated work. The object is inspected, a status record is generated and the QualityControl decides whether the object is ok (event to upper output alternative) or a kind of error report has to be produced. Depending on the decision taken, the final state of the object will be [Free] or [Check.2].

4   Usage of OCoNs for Workflow Modeling

A media store renting books, CDs, videos etc. and its surroundings are used for the case study. These include normally the interaction with customers as well as companies producing, advertising and selling new media via external business partners like a transport agency and, of course, a banking service. Omitting cash flow and explicit user modeling, in the simplest scenario there are three principle business partners which are represented by different subsystems in the structural model (see Fig. 5, left).

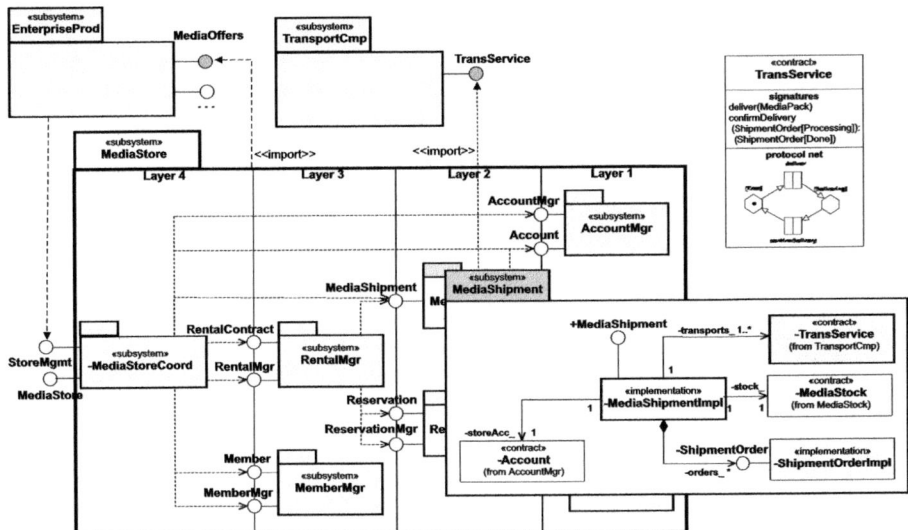

Fig. 5. The MediaStore and its context

The subsystems are interconnected by providing and importing contracts from each other. The MediaStore provides two different contracts. One is used for management issues, e.g., ordering new media, filling the stock etc. via the EnterpriseProd company whereas customers are served by the MediaStore contract. Both contracts are implemented within the subsystem itself using an internal subsystem MediaStoreCoord which coordinates and delegates all work which has to be done to the different subsystems for member management, media renting with reservation handling and so on. The subsystem imports two external contracts, namely the MediaOffers for ordering new media and the TransService from the TransportCmp subsystem for the shipment of rented media. Besides the dependencies which are made explicit via the usage of local or imported contracts,

been designed in a manner which provides contracts implemented by subsystems
for the different kinds of functionality. Using these resources when specifying
a workflow schema introduces information about the operational aspect and
combines it with behavioural aspects. Additionally, the schema now deals with a
more complex situation: some of the wanted media may be not available because
they are in use by other customers and the member may require to be notified
when they become available. Because this is a special kind of service, it is not a
good idea to implement that in the RentalMgr. Instead, it is done in parallel by an
additional subsystem, namely the ReservationMgr, implementing a fair reservation
policy.

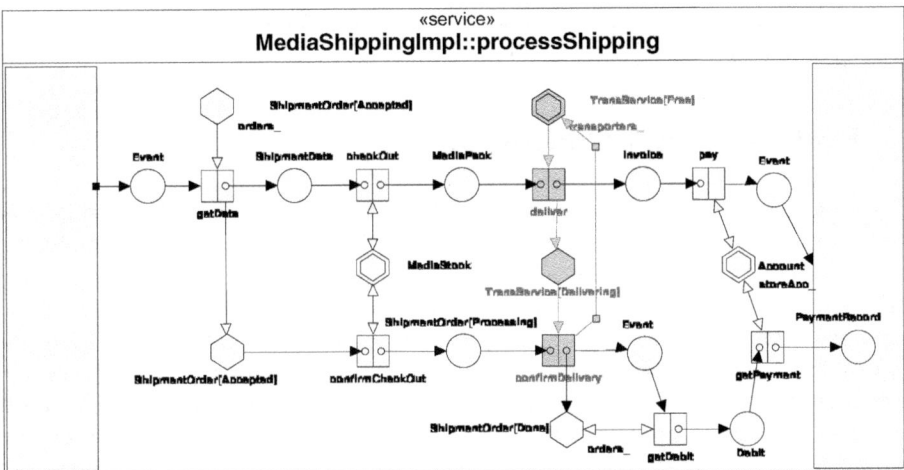

Fig. 7. Service ProcessShipping uses external contract TransService

In order to keep the example manageable, we only go into some of the details of the shipment of rented media. The MediaShipment subsystem in Fig. 5
(right) offers this functionality by means of a simple contract using the same
name. Although the subsystem needs an external subworkflow, this is handled
much like using the local resources by importing the contract TransService which
is from a completely different subsystem in contrast to, e.g., the contracts Account or MediaStock which are in the same subsystem as MediaShipment itself. The
details of shipment orders and how they are handled are implemented locally in
the ShipmentOrderImpl. The partial workflow using all these entities is encapsulated within the service processShipping which performs the real work. Because
all details of the subsystem are hidden, the contract may well be re-used in a
completely different context. The service itself is specified using the service net
shown in Fig. 7. Only confirmed ShipmentOrders in state [Accepted] are processed,
the MediaStock is used to check out the ordered media which are delivered using
the TransService. Besides the real delivering, the state of this job (represented
by a ShipmentOrder) is observed in parallel in the subsystem. The contract Account is used to pay for the transport as well as to compute the shipping costs.
These are represented by a PaymentRecord (which is assumed to be specified as

a class in the informational aspect) and built the final output of this service. The only thing of specific interest here is how the external subworkflow from the contract TransService is used for handling the transport of media itself (see highlighted area in Fig. 7). The contract is used as a shared resource, because other systems may also use this contract. However, for performing the action, only a [Free] resource can be used, and it has to be used exclusively, i.e. not in parallel with other usages. This is because the action changes the state of the resource to [Delivering] until the confirmDelivery has been executed, too. Afterwards, the resource state is changed again into [Free]. All this is easily done in complete conformance with the contract TransService because its protocol net (see Fig. 5, right) is visually embedded into the using service net which makes the consistent usage of subworkflows even from different system parts an easy manageable task.

5   Evaluation and Conclusions

UML diagrams are widely accepted nowadays and their use for the workflow aspects they are suited for eases the communication among all people involved in workflow modeling, implementation, and monitoring. Moreover, the gap in languages and notations between workflow and application development is closed to some extent. The presented example should illustrate that the Petri-Net formalism used permits the gradual change from informal descriptions to correct nets including typing as a means of integrating workflow aspects consistently. In the long term, there are strategic benefits w.r.t. the availability of important management information: having specified a complex workflow system in the proposed way, almost all important information about the organizational structure, responsibilities, dependencies between subsystems and workflow schemas as well as the resource usage and requirements present in the system are available in a structured set of documents in a nearly formal language. Hence, there is a proper basis for the overall analysis, consistency checking, and optimization of structures and processes. Moreover, possible effects of changes can be found in explicit specifications which provides information crucial for local change management as well as more advanced situations like, e.g., finding (subsystem) candidates for outsourcing.

Although there are many approaches dealing with a diversity of graphical descriptions, the usage of Petri-Net variants in workflow management is widespread, e.g. FUNSOFT Nets [3], HOON [6] and especially the work of van der Aalst, e.g., [13] and colleagues. However, most of the work and even recent approaches dealing with interorganizational workflows (e.g., [14]) put their focus on the process aspect and fail to utilize structure to overcome scalability and encapsulation problems. The approach described in [15] tries to combine all aspects, but its puristic use of mechanisms based solely on nets and their interaction makes the resulting models too complex for real-life applications. Moreover, the underlying so-called *reference nets* [8] use the metaphor of nets flowing through nets which seems to be too complicated for a non-expert in high-level Petri-Nets. In the Mentor project [18], state-charts and activity-charts are used to model workflows. The main focus of that project is distributed workflow execution control based on persistent message queues. Whereas these description techniques are close to some of the UML notations, workflow modeling is not embedded in an object-oriented design in that project.

The method sketched in this paper has been used for two years now by students in classes modeling distributed software systems but recently also to describe workflow systems. At the moment, case studies of business processes and workflows in companies are performed in order to evaluate the approach in real-life business settings.

References

1. Grady Booch. *Object-Oriented Analysis and Design with Applications*. Addison-Wesley, Menlo Park CA, 1993. (Second Edition).
2. W. Brauer, W. Reisig, and G. Rozenberg [eds]. *Petri Nets: Central Models (part I)/Applications (part II)*, volume 254/255 of *LNCS*. Springer Verlag, Berlin, 1987.
3. W. Deiters and V. Gruhn. The FUNSOFT Net Approach to Software Process Management. *Int. Journal on SWE and Knowledge Engineering*, 2(4), 1994.
4. D. Georgakopoulos, M. Hornick, and A. Sheth. An Overview of Workflow Management. *Distributed and Parallel Databases*, 3:119–153, 1995.
5. Holger Giese, Jörg Graf, and Guido Wirtz. Closing the Gap Between Object-Oriented Modeling of Structure and Behavior. In Robert France and Bernhard Rumpe, editors, *UML'99*, volume 1723 of *LNCS*, pages 534–549, October 1999.
6. Y. Han and H. Weber. Adaptive Workflow and Software Architecture Thereof. *Journal of Integrated Design and Process Science*, 2(2):1–21, 1998.
7. S. Jablonski and C. Bussler. *Workflow Management: Modeling Concepts, Architecture and Implementation*. Int. Thomson Computer Press, 1996.
8. O. Kummer and F. Wieberg. Renew homepage. Dept. of CS, University of Hamburg, Germany,URL: http://www.renew.de, 1999.
9. F. Leymann and D. Roller. *Production Workflow: Concepts and Techniques*. Prentice Hall, New Jersey, 2000.
10. Bertrand Meyer. *Object-Oriented Software Construction*. Prentice Hall, 1997. 2nd.
11. Object Management Group. *OMG UML 1.3*, June 1999. OMG doc ad/99-06-08.
12. S.K. Shrivastava. Workflow Management Systems. *IEEE Concurrency*, 7(3), 1999.
13. W.M.P. van der Aalst. The Application of Petri Nets to Workflow Management. *Journal of Circuits, Systems and Computers*, 8(1):21–66, 1998.
14. W.M.P. van der Aalst. Interorganizational Workflows: An Approach based on MSCs & Petri Nets. *System Analysis–Modelling–Simulation*, 34(3):335–367, 1999.
15. W.M.P. van der Aalst, D. Moldt, R. Valk, and F. Wienberg. Enacting Interorganizational Workflows Using Nets in Nets. In *Proc. of the 1999 Workflow Management Conference*, pages 117–136. University of Muenster, Muenster, Germany, 1999.
16. M. Weske and G. Vossen. *Workflow Languages*, pages 359–379. International Handbooks on Information Systems. Springer, Berlin, 1998.
17. Guido Wirtz, Jörg Graf, and Holger Giese. Ruling the Behavior of Distributed Software Components. In H. R. Arabnia, editor, *PDPTA*, July 1997.
18. D. Wodtke, J. Weissenfels, G. Weikum, and K. Dittrich. The Mentor Project: Steps towards Enterprise-Wide Workflow Management. In *Proceedings of the 12th International Conference on Data Engineering*, pages 556–565. IEEE CS, 1996.

ConSearch: Using Hypertext Contexts as Web Search Boundaries

Zhanzi Qiu, Matthias Hemmje, Erich J. Neuhold

GMD-IPSI, Darmstadt, Germany
{qiu, hemmje, neuhold}@darmstadt.gmd.de

Abstract. This paper describes a schema for searching on the Web by making use of hypertext contexts that can be represented with new Web standards as search boundaries and argues that this would help to provide users more accurate results in their searches concerning specific topics or subject domains. It also proposes several issues to be addressed in making the schema applicable and presents a prototype system that addresses these issues and supports hypertext context-based search.

1 Introduction

The ability to browse is generally regarded as one of the most important reasons for using hypertext, while searching facilities should also be supported in modern hypertext environments [9]. The World Wide Web is such a hypertext environment. Because of its huge scale and arbitrary structure, it creates many challenges for the development of its searching capabilities.

In the current Web, most links are not typed, and there is no link-based composition mechanism. Thus the Web lacks explicit structural meta information [18], and the search engines on it are typically keyword-based. With such engines, people usually get a large amount of pages that they can not process, or even more, many of the pages are totally irrelevant to their information needs, especially when they search for information on specific topics.

To improve the ability of expressing structures and semantics on the Web, several new standards, mainly XML (Extensible Markup Language) [21] and RDF (Resource Description Framework) [15], are developed or under development. These standards open new opportunities to improve the information access on the Web. However, it is an open question how to make use of the structural and semantic information that can be represented with the standards efficiently for search purposes. This paper describes a part of our effort to answer this question.

In this work, we focus on making use of hypertext contexts, one of the main high-level hypermedia structures that can be represented with the new Web standards for searching on the Web. We view a hypertext context as a mechanism to specify the scope of the information space to be examined in a search and argue that this would help to improve the search response time and the quality of the results of searches concerning a specific topic or subject domain.

The rest of the paper is organized as follows. Section 2 describes the concept of hypertext contexts and gives simple examples. Section 3 answers the question how hypertext contexts can be represented with new Web standards. Section 4 proposes a

O. Etzion and P. Scheuermann (Eds.): CoopIS 2000, LNCS 1901, pp. 42–53, 2000.

schema for searching on the Web by making use of hypertext contexts and discusses issues to be addressed to make the schema applicable. Section 5 presents a prototype system that supports hypertext context-based search. Section 6 mentions related work. Finally, Section 7 summarizes this work and outlines our future activities.

2 Hypertext Contexts

2.1 Concepts

A *hypertext context* is a generic high-level hypermedia structure that groups together a set of nodes and links into a logical whole. The idea of *hypertext contexts* was first introduced by Schwartz and Delisle [16]. *Contexts* partition the data within a hypertext graph. A hypertext graph contains one or more *contexts*; each *context* has one *parent context* and zero or more *child contexts* [3].

Precisely, if C is a *hypertext context*, then its contents must define a pair (N, L), where N is a set of nodes in a hypertext graph and L is a set of links whose end nodes belong to N. We say that C contains a node M if M is in N and that C contains a link l if l is in L. M is a *node component* of C, while l is a *link component* of C.

If C1, C2 are two *hypertext contexts*, we say that C1 contains C2 only when all nodes and links in C2 are contained in C1. That is, if C1 defines a pair (N1, L1), C2 defines a pair (N2, L2), and C2 $\subseteq$ C1, then N2$\subseteq$ N1 and L2$\subseteq$ L1. Contrary, if N2$\subseteq$ N1 and L2$\subseteq$ L1, then C2 $\subseteq$ C1. We say C1 is the *parent context* of C2, and C2 is one of the *child contexts* of C1.

Usually, a *hypertext context* is said to be a container for a group of nodes, while the links between the nodes are thought to be included implicitly in the context. We adopt this meaning of hypertext contexts later in this paper. That is to say that unless clearly specified, the *components* of a *hypertext context* refer to the nodes contained in it.

In practice, *hypertext contexts* can be used to support configuration, private workspaces, and version history trees [16]. They can be used as a mechanism to describe different context views of the same hyperdocuments, tuned to different applications or classes of users of the documents [4]. In this sense, a (group of) hyperdocument(s) may contain any number of *hypertext contexts*. Such *hypertext contexts* can exist statically in hypertext document collections or can be created dynamically by hypertext based information systems.

2.2 Examples

Typical examples of hypertext contexts that exist statically in hypertext document collections are various maps, paths, guided tours and focused node lists related to a particular topic or subject domain. These hypertext contexts are usually encoded in concrete nodes, maybe one context in one node, or several contexts in one node. Many such nodes (pages) exist on the current Web but can not be recognized automatically. So are the hypertext contexts described in them.

For instance, the page "DELITE publications" (http://www.darmstadt.gmd.de/delite/Publications/) contains a complete list of all publications from the division DELITE of GMD-IPSI (http://ipsi.gmd.de/), and each item in the list points to a DELITE publication. What the list describes is actually a hypertext context that is composed of all nodes (pages) about DELITE publications.

Moreover, it can be said that the items listed under each year constitute a child context of the above large one.

As for the hypertext contexts that are created dynamically by hypertext based information systems, the most typical examples are various search results, which are attained by computation against certain query criteria. Like static hypertext contexts, they can not be recognized automatically on the current Web. In addition to these typical examples, dynamic hypertext contexts can apparently be attained from Boolean operations performed to hypertext contexts existing in systems.

3   Standard Representation of Hypertext Contexts

Link any other information, hypertext contexts, no matter static or dynamic, can be shared and reused in a large information space like the Web only when they are represented in a standard format. Fortunately, the new Web standards, XML and RDF, have made this possible. With them information providers can describe the hypertext contexts in their Web resources explicitly and browser and search systems can recognize the contexts automatically.

3.1   Representing Hypertext Contexts with XML Extended Links

In the XML model, the linking mechanisms supported are specified in the XML Linking Language (XLink) [20]. A hypertext context that contains Web resources as its components can be described with a linking element for an `extended link`. Each component of the hypertext context is given in a `locator` element, which is a child element of the linking element.

For instance, the following encoding (an out-of-line extended link) describes a hypertext context *mycontext* that is composed of 3 nodes:

```
<mycontext xml:link="extended" inline="false">
   <locator href="doc1" role="description">
   <locator href="doc2" role="commentary">
   <locator href="doc3" role="reference">
</mycontext>
```

A `locator` may indicate a resource, which itself contains an extended link, i.e., also describes a hypertext context. In this way, the *parent-child* relationship between hypertext contexts can be represented.

Especially, hypertext contexts and their parent-child relationship may be described with `extended link group` elements (a special kind of `extended links`) and `extended link document` elements (a special kind of `locator` elements). The `Steps` attribute of the `extended link group` elements can be given a numeric value that serves as a hint from the author to any system as to how many levels hypertext contexts exist.

That is, an `extended link group` element may be used to store a list of links to other resources that together constitute an interlinked group. Each such resource is identified by means of an `extended link document` element and may itself contain an `extended link`. In this case, the `group` element describes a hypertext context that is the parent of the hypertext contexts described in the resources indicated by the `document` elements.

To give an example, suppose the above descriptions about *mycontext* are stored in *mycontext.xml*, a possible parent context of *mycontext* can be described as follows:

```
<group xml:link="group" steps=2>
<document xml:link="document" href="mycontext.xml" role="recommend"/>
<document xml:link="document" href="..." role="..."/>
...
</group>
```

These descriptions are contained in a document other than *mycontexts.xml*.

3.2   Representing Hypertext Contexts with RDF Containers

In the RDF model, a hypertext context can be represented in a `container`. Each component (node) of the context is referred to with a `resource`. (In RDF, the term *resource* is in most cases a metaphor of *node*).

RDF defines three types of container objects: `bag`, `sequence`, and `alternative`. The first two are used to declare the multiple values of a property, and the third is to declare alternatives for the (single) value of a property. For representing hypertext contexts, the first two types of `containers` fit better. Besides, the difference between them, i.e., one declares unordered lists and another declares ordered lists, does not make much sense, as the sequence of components in a hypertext context is not cared.

For example, a hypertext context that consists of resources about people working in the project *delite-online* can be described as follows:

```
<rdf:RDF><rdf:Description
about="http://www.darmstadt.gmd.de/delite/projects/delite-
online.html">
   <s:people><rdf:Bag>
       <rdf:li resource="http://www.darmstadt.gmd.de/~qiu/">
       <rdf:li resource="http://www.darmstadt.gmd.de/~lhuang/">
       <rdf:li resource="http://www.darmstadt.gmd.de/~moelle/">
    </rdf:Bag></s:people>
 </rdf:Description></rdf:RDF>
```

Such RDF descriptions can exist in a separate RDF document, or be contained in the head of an HTML document.

It is clear that by embedding a RDF `container` in another RDF `container`, the parent-child relationship between hypertext contexts can be represented.

4   Using Hypertext Contexts as Web Search Boundaries

With the possibility to represent hypertext contexts in a standard way, it is time for us to consider how to make use of the information contained in these objects for various purposes. We believe that a few new search methods may be developed for Web users.

A very straightforward consideration is to use hypertext contexts as a mechanism to specify the information space to be examined in a search activity. This is because a hypertext context effectively cuts a boundary between its containing nodes and links from other nodes and links that are out of it (as shown in Figure 1). This mechanism should prove to be useful for improving the results of searches concerning specific topics or subject domains. On the current Web, this kind of search activity is

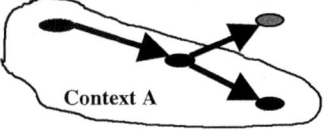

Figure 1. A simple hypertext context

usually frustrating. With the typically keyword-based search engines, users usually get a large amount of pages that they can not easily process, while on the other hand many of the pages are totally irrelevant to their information needs.

4.1   Primary Experiments

To explore our idea of using hypertext contexts as Web search boundaries, we have developed a prototype system called delite-WebGlimpse and performed some experiments with it [14]. This system allows users to define hypertext contexts themselves when they browse and search on the Web and then submit searches within the context boundaries. For instance, if one wants to find out which people in GMD IPSI are doing research related to "data mining", one can define a hypertext context that contains all the personal homepages of GMD IPSI staff as its components. One then submits query "data mining" and asks the system to search only in the context. In this case, one gets only 3 hits and the precision of this result is 100%. Comparatively, if the search is done in the whole GMD IPSI Web site (start from http://ipsi.gmd.de/), the user will get 375 hits (at the time we performed the experiments) and has to filter the pages himself. Apparently this situation will be much more serious when the search is done in the whole Web with global search engines.

Our experiments have demonstrated that using hypertext contexts as Web search boundaries is really useful. A large amount of non-relevant pages can be filtered out before any further search activities or pattern matching processes take place, and the search results are thus more specific and more relevant to users' information needs.

4.2   Issues for Supporting the Use of Hypertext Contexts as Web Search Boundaries

In practice, to enable the use of hypertext contexts as Web search boundaries, there are a few issues to be addressed.

The first issue is to represent hypertext contexts in a standard way and make it sharable and reusable throughout the Web. This issue has been discussed in Section 3 above in this paper and can be seen as the prerequisite for addressing other issues. With this prerequisite, a Web search system that intends to support the use of hypertext contexts as search boundaries should be able to

- extract from the Web sufficient hypertext context information and index the information efficiently so that the hypertext contexts themselves can be queried with the information later,
- efficiently organize the hypertext context information after indexing internally so that the hypertext contexts can be retrieved at a speed acceptable by users,
- provide a user-friendly interface to enable users to search for hypertext contexts and specify hypertext contexts as search boundaries in a comfortable way, and
- implement the searches within the boundaries of specified hypertext contexts with acceptable performance and provide sound search results.

In the following, we will present how our prototype system, ConSearch, addresses these issues.

5   ConSearch - A Prototype System

ConSearch is the prototype system we design to test our idea of using hypertext contexts that can be represented with new Web standards as Web search boundaries. In the following we first give a high-level discussion of its architecture and then introduce several technologies in its implementation. Finally, some evaluation issues about it are discussed.

5.1   Architecture Overview

The overall picture of ConSearch is shown in Figure 2. It includes four basic engines representing different aspects.

The **info agent** is responsible for gathering hypertext context information from the Web and storing the information in databases. It contains a **URI server**, an **extractor**, a **storage server**, and an **indexer**. The URI server sends lists of URIs to be fetched to the extractor. The extractor fetches the data resources (including HTML, XML and RDF documents), extracts hypertext context information from the resources, represents the information with a specific ConSearch internal format, and sends the documents of the internal format to the storage server. The storage server stores the document of the internal format into a repository, from which the indexer reads the documents, parses them and performs indexing functions. The indexing results are sent to the database for hypertext contexts.

The **query engine** receives queries, lets users search for hypertext contexts, specify hypertext contexts as search boundaries, transfers the queries to the retrieval engine, and presents search results derived by the retrieval engine to users. The engine will be implemented as Web browser clients with a form-based user interface.

The **retrieval engine** is responsible for using information in the database to derive hypertext contexts specified, implementing searches within the hypertext contexts, and sending search results to the query engine. This engine is the part in which the system cooperates with other search systems, as described in Section 5.5 later.

The **database manager** is a backbone of the entire system. It receives data from the info agent and provides data to the retrieval engine. In ConSearch, the database manager is an object relational Informix Universal Server DBMS.

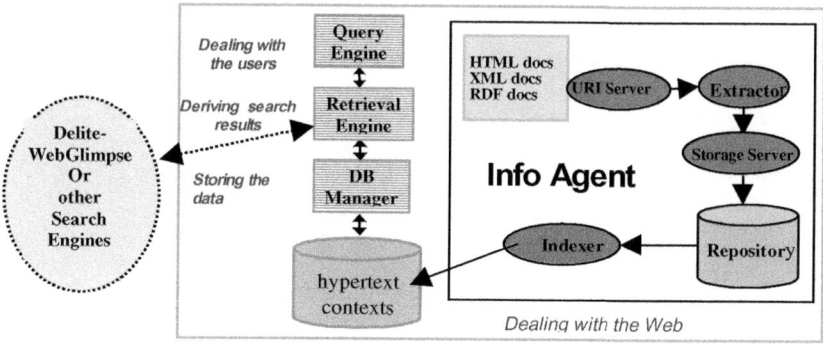

Figure 2. Architecture Overview

5.2   Hypertext Context Information Gathering and Indexing

Corresponding to how XML and RDF represent hypertext contexts, ConSearch gathers and indexes the following information (referred to as hypertext context information in this paper) for each hypertext context:

1. the URI of the Web resource that the context talks about (called aboutURI later),
2. the URI of the Web resource that describes the context (called sourceURI later), and,
3. descriptive keywords, which can be extracted from RDF property types, sourceURI, aboutURI, roles of external links, names of the link elements that contain the context, and special descriptive information about the context with regards to certain Web resources.

All this information is gathered with the JEDI (Java Extraction and Dissemination of Information) [6] tool, which is used in ConSearch as the extractor. The tool consists of a wrapper that can collect information by navigating through multiple documents and by explicating their implicit logical structure, and a mediator that maps the collected information to an integrated view.

Since a Web search system like ConSearch is fed by heterogeneous textual information sources, the translation of the incoming texts to an internal format is inevitable. The internal ConSearch format is provided in form of an XML DTD and aims to cover the demand of describing the hypertext context information exhaustively. Figure 3 shows an example of a hypertext context encoded in the ConSearch internal format. The hypertext context is assigned a name. All the descriptive keywords extracted are listed in the content of the *description* element. Besides, its sourceURI, aboutURI, components are all contained in this document.

Such documents are compressed and stored into a repository by the storage server. The indexer reads the repository, uncompresses the documents, parses them and performs keyword-indexing functions to the content of the element *description*. The indexing results and all URIs related to the hypertext contexts are sent to the database, which owns the schema as described in the following section.

```
<context name="DelitePub1999">
  <source>http://www.darmstadt.gmd.de/delite/publication/1999.rdf</source>
  <about>http://www.darmstadt.gmd.de/delite/publication/index.html</about>
  <description>delite, publication, 1999</description>
  <components>
    <component>
      http://www.darmstadt.gmd.de/delite/publication/1999/pub1.html
    </component>
    <component>
      http://www.darmstadt.gmd.de/delite/publication/1999/pub2.html
    </component>
    ...
  </components>
</context>
```

Figure 3. A hypertext context produced by JEDI

5.3   Internal Organization of Hypertext Context Information

In ConSearch, hypertext context information after indexing is stored in an Informix Universal Server database. Every hypertext context has an associated ID number (called contextID) which is assigned whenever a new hypertext context is parsed out of a Web resource. To represent the components of hypertext contexts and the aboutURIs and sourceURIs of hypertext contexts in a non-redundant way, every Web resource also has an ID number (called docID later) whenever a new URI is parsed out. Similarly, every keyword used to describe hypertext contexts is assigned an ID number (called wordID later) in order not to waste space.

Based on the above basic point of view, the database of hypertext contexts is built with the schema as shown in Figure 4. The *URI Table* contains URIs that are parsed and the primary serial numbers assigned to the URIs. The *Word Table* contains keywords that are used to describe the hypertext contexts and their primary serial numbers. The *Context Table* contains the primary serial number of hypertext contexts and IDs for aboutURIs and sourceURIs of the contexts. The *Context Component Table* lists the components of hypertext contexts. The *Context Parent Table* represents the parent-children relations between hypertext contexts. Finally, *The Context-Word Table* builds relationships between hypertext contexts and the keywords used to describe them.

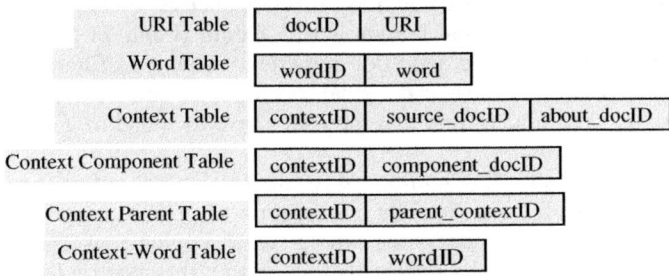

Figure 4. Database for hypertext contexts

With this internal organization of hypertext context information, ConSearch is able to support the specification of hypertext contexts as search boundaries, not only single hypertext contexts, but the combination of hypertext contexts as well. Furthermore, searching for hypertext contexts themselves by inputting keywords and/or the aboutURIs and sourceURIs is also possible.

5.4   User Interface for Querying and Specifying Hypertext Contexts

ConSearch provides a form-based interface to enable users to query hypertext contexts and specify hypertext contexts. As shown in Figure 5, users can query hypertext contexts by specifying sourceURIs, aboutURIs, and keywords. After users confirm the specification, the system will display all the candidate contexts (in some case, maybe not only one context is found) by showing their sourceURIs, aboutURIs, and all their descriptive keywords (as shown in Figure 6). Then users can adjust their queries or go to take a look at the components of the candidate contexts (as shown in Figure 7) and/or make their choice of the contexts to be used as the search boundaries for their queries. As Figure 6 shows, users can also ask the system to do Boolean combination of the hypertext contexts found and use the resulting hypertext context as search boundaries.

5.5   Implementing Searches within Hypertext Contexts

To implement searches within the boundaries of specified hypertext contexts, ConSearch is designed to be able to cooperate with other keyword-based search systems, which are either global or local. For instance, the current version of ConSearch is integrated with our delite-WebGlimpse [14], which uses Glimpse [7] as its search engine.

In this integration, ConSearch is responsible to provide the URLs of the component pages of the specified hypertext contexts to delite-WebGlimpse and delite-WebGlimpse maps these URLs to the file names of the pages it collects[1] and save the file names in a context file. This context file is then compressed and sent to Glimpse, which supports very flexible functions to limit the search to only parts of the files in a collection[2].   In this way, searching within the boundaries of specified hypertext contexts is implemented.

When integrated with global search systems, such as InfoSeek [10] and AltaVista [1], ConSearch works as a meta search engine.   It sends queries to one or more other systems according to users' selection (as shown in Figure 6 and 7) to get results, combining the results and using the specified hypertext context as filters. With this process, it provides users more specific final results that are relevant to their information needs and saves much time that the users have to spend to get the results in current normal ways.

In case search engines restrict the number of results to e.g. 200 out of the possible thousands, ConSearch asks for a more tight cooperation with those engines. That is, ConSearch should be allowed to access the whole search engine ranking list or the large part of the list. In this way, the results that are within the specified context but are in the tail of the search engine ranking will not be missed.

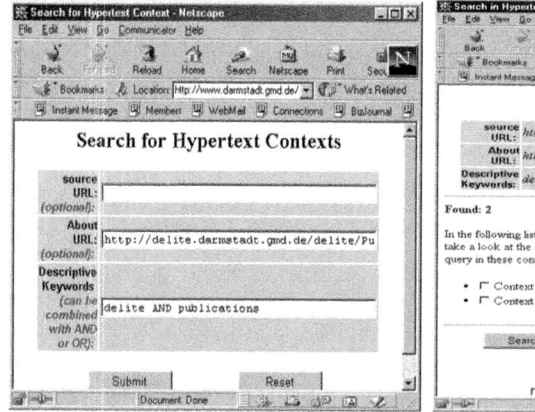

Figure 5. Search for hypertext contexts

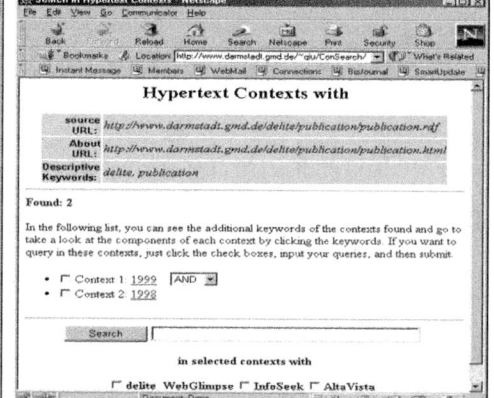

Figure 6. Show found hypertext contexts and enable search in selected hypertext contexts

---

[1] delite-WebGlimpse collects all remote pages locally with a mapping mechanism from urls to file names.

[2] Glimpse provides several options to enable users to filter files in search. One option is –f, which reads a list of file names from a given file and uses only those files in search.

5.6   Evaluation Issues

The most important measure of a search engine is the quality of its search results. It is quite certain that by supporting the use of hypertext contexts as Web search boundaries, ConSearch provides users with more accurate search results. Our experiments with delite-WebGlimpse [14] have proved this. As described in 4.1, if one asks the system to search within a hypertext context containing the personal homepages of GMD-IPSI (http://ipsi.darmstadt.gmd.de/) staff (at present 81) for one's query "data mining", one will get only 3 hits (as shown in Figure 8). And the precision of the result is 100%. Similarly, for the query "information retrieval", one will get 5 hits with also the precision 100%. In this way, the special information needs of searching for GMD-IPSI members who have research interests in the fields of "data mining" and "information retrieval" are satisfied. Comparatively, if the searches are done on the whole GMD-IPSI site, for such queries, one will get several hundreds of hits and has to filter the hits themselves.

Aside from search quality, a thorough evaluation about a system which intends to support hypertext context-based search should cover its storage requirements, its performance in extracting and indexing the information, its quality and performance in searching hypertext contexts, and its performance in implementing searches within specified hypertext contexts. Until now, we have not done such a thorough evaluation for ConSearch. However, there is some significance that ConSearch can scale well to the size of the Web as the Web grows, as it chooses a scalable DBMS and stores all hypertext context information gathered and indexed in databases.

As the new Web standards become more adopted and more hypertext contexts represented with the standards will be provided on the Web, a thorough evaluation about the method and the system presented in this paper will be done.

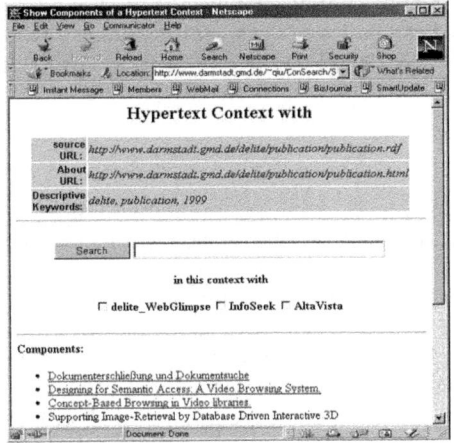

Figure 7. Show components of a hypertext context and enable search in the context

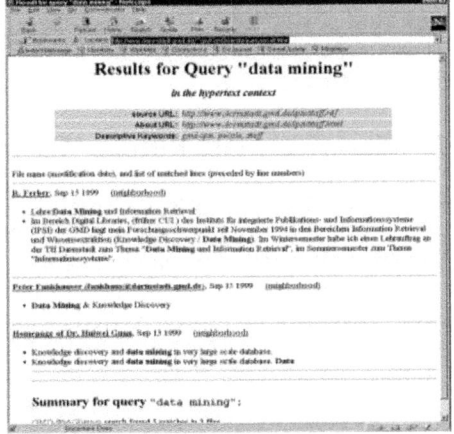

Figure 8. Result for query "data mining" in the context "GMD-IPSI staff"

6   Related Work

The idea of drawing a boundary for the information space to be examined in search activities has been reflected in some popular search systems which provide category search, fielded search, "search within results", "find similar pages", and so on, such as Yahoo [22], InfoSeek [10] and Lycos [12]. It can also be seen in search agents that traverse the Web looking for specific information in real time [17] or allow users to set up their own local searches [13]. In comparison, the schema we present in this paper for searching in the Web space by using hypertext contexts is more general and covers the schemas proposed by other systems. Furthermore, it meets the development of the Web in its ability of expressing structures and semantics.

There is a trend of making use of additional structural information to improve Web searching. Structural information has so far been used for enhancing relevance judgements, ranking Web pages or other purposes. Among the work in this area the achievements of Google [8; 2] and Clever [5; 11] are most attractive. Both systems use weighted link popularity as a primary criteria in their ranking mechanism. As far as we know, none of these systems have taken into account the Web's new abilities in expressing structural and semantic information in their search algorithms yet.

Delite-WebGlimpse [14] is our starting effort to explore our idea of using hypertext contexts as Web search boundaries. It aims at the current Web (with no explicitly represented hypertext contexts) and provides facilities to help users to define hypertext contexts themselves and enable them to search in those hypertext contexts. The results we get from the experiments done with it are the first proof for the value of our idea.

XML [21] and RDF [15] are ongoing effort of W3C [19] to improve Web's ability in expressing structure and semantics. Accompanying W3C's effort, a number of XML and RDF software tools have been developed or under development. A list of such tools can be found under http://www.w3.org/XML/ and http://www.w3.org/RDF/. Most of them are parsers, generators, editors and browsers. They can be integrated into more complicated systems that intend to handle XML and RDF resources.

7   Summary and Future Work

This paper describes a part of our effort to answer the open question how to make use of the structural and semantic information that can be represented with new Web standards efficiently for search purposes.

The general schema presented in this paper of using hypertext contexts as Web search boundaries has been proved to a large degree by our work and some work from other people. It may further prove to be useful by being integrated into large search engines and allowing users to get more accurate results, as the new standards become more widely adopted and a large number of hypertext contexts are provided with the standard formats.

The prototype developed for implementing the schema is currently still primitive. More facilities to help users to specify a hypertext context for a given query should be provided. Further thorough evaluation will be done to determine to what degree hypertext contexts work in their role as search boundaries, and how Web search engines will index data efficiently if hypertext contexts are to be supported. It will be also a concern of this work how to enable information providers to produce hypertext contexts easier and efficiently.

In addition to using hypertext contexts as Web search boundaries, we intend to develop more search methods that make use of this kind of information. Furthermore, the value of other kinds of high-level hypermedia structures that can be represented with new Web standards for search purposes will also be explored in our future work.

References

1. AltaVista: http://www.altavista.com/
2. Brin, S. and Page, L., "The anatomy of a large-scale hypertextual Web-search engine," *Proc. 7th International World Wide Web Conference*, 1998.
3. Campbell, B., Goodman, J. M., "HAM: A general purpose hypertext abstract machine," *Communications of the ACM*, 31(7), July 1988, pp. 856-861.
4. Casanova, M. A., Tucherman, L., "The nested context model for hyperdocuments," *Proc. of Hypertext'91*, pp. 193-201.
5. Clever: http://www.almaden.ibm.com/cs/k53/clever.html
6. Huck, G., Fankhauser, P., Aberer, K., Neuhold, E., "Jedi: Extracting and synthesizing information from the Web," *Proc. 3rd IFCIS International Conference on Cooperative Information Systems (CoopIS'98)*, New York City, August 1998, pp. 32-43.
7. Glimpse: http://glimpse.cs.arizona.edu/
8. Google: http://google.stanford.edu/
9. Halasz, F.G., "Reflections on Notecards : seven issues for the next generation of hypermedia systems," *Communication of the ACM*, 31(7), pp.836-852, 1988.
10. InfoSeek: http://www2.infoseek.com/
11. Kleinberg, J., "Authoritative sources in a hyperlinked environment," *Proc. ACM-SIAM Symposium on Discrete Algorithms*, 1998. Also appears as IBM Research Report RJ 10076(91892), May 1997.
12. Lycos: http://a2z.lycos.com/
13. Miller, R., Bharat, K., "SPHINX: A framework for creating personal, site-specific Web crawlers," *Proc. 7th International World Wide Web Conference*, Brisbane Australia, April 1998.
14. Qiu, Z., Hemmje, M., Neuhold, E., "Towards Supporting User-Defined Hypertext Contexts in Web Searching", Proceedings of IEEE ADL'2000 , May 22-24, 2000, National Institutes of Health, Bethesda, MD, USA.
15. RDF: http://www.w3.org/TR/REC-rdf-syntax/
16. Schwartz, M., Delisle, N., "Contexts – A partitioning concept for hypertext," *ACM Transactions on Office Information Systems*, 5(2), April 1987, pp. 168-186.
17. Sumner, R. G., Yang, K, and Dempsey, B. J., "An interactive WWW search engine for user-defined collections," *Digital Libraries 98*, Pittsburgh PA, USA.
18. Trigg, R. H., "Hypermedia as integration: Recollections, reflections and exhortations," Keynote Address in *Hypertext'96 Conference*. Xerox Palo Alto Research Center.
19. W3C: http://www.w3.org/
20. XLink: http://www.w3.org/TR/xlink/
21. XML: http://www.w3.org/XML
22. Yahoo: http://www.yahoo.com/

Combining the Power of Searching and Querying*

Sara Cohen[1], Yaron Kanza[1], Yakov Kogan[1], Werner Nutt[2], Yehoshua Sagiv[1], and Alexander Serebrenik[3]

[1] Computer Science Dept., The Hebrew University, Jerusalem, Israel
{sarina,yarok,yakov,sagiv}@cs.huji.ac.il
[2] Department of Computing and Electrical Engineering
Heriot-Watt University, Edinburgh, Scotland
nutt@cee.hw.ac.uk
[3] Computer Science Dept., K. U. Leuven, Heverlee, Belgium
Alexander.Serebrenik@cs.kuleuven.ac.be

Abstract. EquiX is a search language for XML that combines the power of querying with the simplicity of searching. Requirements for search languages are discussed and it is shown that EquiX meets the necessary criteria. Both a graphical abstract syntax and a formal concrete syntax are presented for EquiX queries. In addition, the semantics is defined. It is shown that EquiX has an evaluation algorithm that is polynomial under combined complexity.
EquiX combines pattern matching, quantification and logical expressions to query both the data and meta-data of XML documents. The result of a query in EquiX is a set of XML documents. A DTD describing the result documents is derived automatically from the query.

1 Introduction

The widespread use of the World-Wide Web has given rise to a plethora of simple query processors, commonly called search engines. Search engines query a database of semi-structured data, namely HTML pages. It is difficult to query the meta-data content in such pages using a search engine. Only the data can easily be queried. For example, one can use a search engine to find pages containing the word "villain". However, it is difficult to obtain only pages in which "villain" appears as a character in a Wild West movie. More and more XML pages are finding their way onto the Web. Thus, it is becoming increasingly important to be able to query both the data and the meta-data content of Web pages. We propose a language for querying (or searching) the Web that fills this void.

Search engines can be viewed as simple query processors. The query language of most search engines is rather restricted. Both traditional database query languages, such as SQL, and newly proposed languages, such as XQL [7], XML-QL [4] and Xmas [6], are much richer than search-engine query languages. However, the limited expressiveness of search engines appears to be an advantage

---

* This research was supported by grant 9481-1-98 of the Israeli Ministry of Science.

O. Etzion and P. Scheuermann (Eds.): CoopIS 2000, LNCS 1901, pp. 54–65, 2000.

in the context of the Web. Many Internet users would find it hard to formulate SQL queries. In comparison, experience has proven that even novice Internet users can easily ask queries using a search engine. It is likely that this is true because of the inherent simplicity of the search-engine query languages.

Consequently, an apparent disadvantage of search-engine languages is really an advantage when it comes to querying the Web. We believe that the Web gives rise to a new concept in query languages, namely *search languages*. A search language is a language that can be used to search for data. We differentiate between the terms *search* and *query*. Roughly speaking, a search is an imprecise process in which the user guesses the content of the document that she requires. Many times the schema is (partially) unknown when a search is performed. It is virtually impossible to perform many types of searches in traditional database languages, such as SQL. For example, without knowing the schema of a database, it is impossible to find all tuples in all tables that contain the word "Jones". In fact, even if the schema is known, it is quite difficult to formulate such a query. Querying is a precise process in which the user specifies exactly the information she is seeking and where it is located in relation to the schema. In this paper we define a language that has both searching and querying capabilities. We call a language that allows both searching and querying a *search language*.

We call a query written in a search language a *search query* and the query result a *search result*. Similarly, we call a query processor for a search language a *search processor*. From analyzing popular search engines, one can define a set of criteria that should guide the designing of a search language and processor:

1. **Format of Results:** A search result of a search query should be a set of documents or sections of documents that satisfy the query. When searching, the user is interested in *finding* information. Thus, restructuring of documents to compute results is not necessary.
2. **Pattern Matching, Quantification and Logical Expressions:** Search engines allow pattern matching, quantification (using "+" and "-" symbols, etc.) and logical expressions (using AND, OR and NOT, etc.). Currently, these can be performed on the data only. We propose to extend these capabilities to be performed on meta-data. Pattern matching on the meta-data allows a user to formulate a search query without knowing the exact structure of the document. Allowing quantification and logical expressions on both data and meta-data enriches the query language and makes it more powerful.
3. **Iterative Searching Ability:** The result of a search query may contain hundreds, if not thousands, of documents. Thus, it is important to allow requerying of previous results. This enables users to search for the desired information iteratively, until such information is found.
4. **Polynomial Time:** The database over which search queries are computed is large and is constantly growing. Hence, it is desirable for a search query to be computable in polynomial time under combined complexity (i.e., when both the query and the database are part of the input).

When designing a search language, there is an additional requirement that is more difficult to define scientifically. A search language should be *easy to use*.

5. **Simplicity:** One should be able to formulate queries easily and the queries, once formulated, should be intuitively understandable.

The definition of requirements for a search language is interesting in itself. In this paper we present a specific language, namely EquiX, that fulfills the requirements 1 through 4. From our experience, we have found EquiX search queries to be intuitively understandable. Thus, we believe that EquiX satisfies the additional language requirement of simplicity. EquiX is rather unique in that it combines both polynomial query evaluation (under combined complexity) with several powerful querying abilities. In EquiX, both quantification and negation can be used. In an extension to EquiX we allow aggregation and a limited class of regular expressions ([3]). Both searching and querying can be performed using the EquiX language. EquiX also simplifies the querying process by automatically generating the format of the result and a corresponding DTD.

This paper extends previous work [2]. An extended version of this paper can be found in [3]. In Section 2 we present a data model for XML documents. Both the concrete and abstract syntax for EquiX queries are described in Section 3. In Section 4 we define the semantics of EquiX, and in Section 5 the evaluation of EquiX queries is discussed. Section 6 concludes.

2   Data Model

We define a data model for querying XML documents [1]. At first, we assume that each XML document has a given DTD. In [3] this assumption is relaxed. The term *element* will be used to refer to a particular occurrence of an element in a document. The term *element name* will refer to a name of an element and thus, may appear many times in a document. Similarly we use *attribute* to refer to a particular occurrence of an attribute and *attribute name* to refer to its name. At times, we will blur the distinction between these terms when the meaning is clear from the context.

We introduce some necessary notation. A *directed tree* over a set of nodes N is a pair $T = (N, E)$ where $E \subseteq N \times N$ and E defines a tree-structure. We say that the edge (n, n') is *incident from* n and *incident to* n'. Note that in a tree, there is at most one edge incident to any given node. We assume throughout this paper that all trees are finite. A directed tree is *rooted* if there is a designated node $r \in N$, such that every node in N is reachable from r in T. We call r the *root* of T. We denote a rooted directed tree as a triple $T = (N, E, r)$.

An XML document contains both data (i.e., atomic values) and meta-data (i.e., elements and attributes). The relationships between data and meta-data, (and between meta-data and meta-data) are reflected by use of nesting. We will represent a document by a directed tree with a labeling function. The data and meta-data in a document correspond to nodes in the tree with appropriate labels. Nodes corresponding to meta-data are *complex nodes* while nodes corresponding to data are *atomic nodes*. The relationships in a document are represented by edges in the tree. In this fashion, a document is represented by its parse tree.

Note that using ID and IDREF attributes one can represent additional relationships between values. When considering these relationships, a document may no longer be represented by a tree. In the sequel we will utilize ID and IDREF attributes to answer search queries.

In general, a parsed XML document need not be a rooted tree. However, we can assume, without loss of generality, that all XML documents are rooted trees. An XML document that gives rise to a rooted tree is said to be *rooted* and the element that corresponds to the root of the tree is called the *root element*.

We now give a formal definition of an XML document. We assume that there is an infinite set A of atoms and infinite set $\mathcal{L}$ of labels.

Definition 1 (XML Document). *An* XML document *is a pair* (T, l) *s.t.*

- $T = (N, E, r)$ *is a rooted directed tree*[1];
- $l : N \to \mathcal{L} \cup A$ *is a labeling function that associates each complex node with a value in $\mathcal{L}$ and each atomic node with a value in A.*

We assume that each DTD has a designated element name, called the *root element name* of the DTD. Consider a DTD d with a root element name e. We say that a document $X = (T, l)$ with root r *strictly conforms to d* if

1. the document X conforms to d (in the usual way [1]) and
2. the function l assigns the label e to the root r (i.e., $l(r) = e$).

The following DTD with root element name movieInfo describes information about movies.

```
<!ELEMENT movieInfo    (movie+,actor+)>
<!ELEMENT movie        (descr,title,character+)>
<!ELEMENT actor        (name)>
<!ATTLIST actor
           id          ID        #REQUIRED>
<!ELEMENT descr        (#PCDATA)>
<!ELEMENT title        (#PCDATA)>
<!ELEMENT name         (#PCDATA)>
<!ELEMENT character    EMPTY>
<!ATTLIST character
           role        CDATA     #REQUIRED
           star        IDREF     #REQUIRED>
```

In Figure 1 an XML document containing movie information is depicted. This document strictly conforms to the DTD presented above. Note that the nodes in Figure 1 are numbered. The numbering is for convenient reference and is not part of the data model.

A *catalog* is a pair $C = (d, S)$ where d is a DTD and S is a set of XML documents, each of which strictly conforms to d. A *database* is a set of catalogs.

---

[1] Note that an XML document is a sequence of characters. Thus, to properly model the ordering of elements in a document, an ordering function on the children of a node should be introduced. For simplicity of exposition we omit this in the paper.

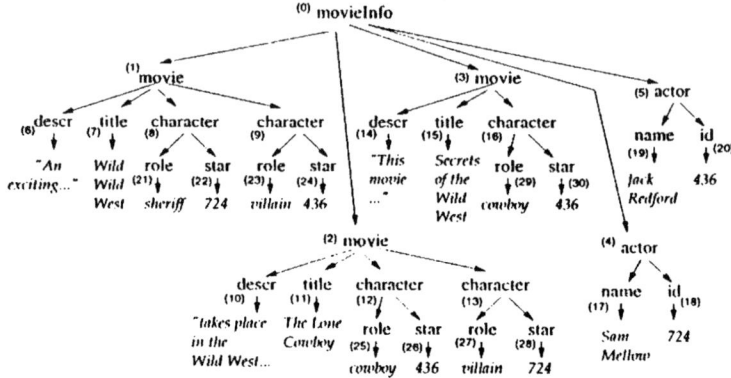

Fig. 1. An XML document describing information about movies.

Note the similarity of this definition to the relational model where a database is a set of tuples conforming to given relation schemes. This data model is natural and useful. Our assumption that each XML document conforms to a given DTD implies that the documents are of a partially known structure. We can display this knowledge to the user. Thus, it is not necessary to first query the database for its structure before searching for the desired information.

3   Search Query Syntax

In this section we present both a concrete and an abstract syntax for EquiX search queries. A search query written in the concrete syntax is a *concrete query* and a search query written in the abstract syntax is an *abstract query*.

3.1   Concrete Query Syntax

The concrete syntax is described informally as part of the graphical user interface currently implemented for EquiX. Intuitively, a query is an "example" of the documents that should appear in the output. By formulating an EquiX query the user can specify documents that she would like to find. She can specify constraints on the data that should appear in the documents. We call such constraints *content constraints*. She can also specify constraints on the meta-data, or structure, of the documents. We call such constraints *structural constraints*. In addition, the user can specify *quantification constraints* which constrain the data and meta-data that should appear in the resulting documents by determining how the content and structural constraints should be applied to a document.

The user formulates her query interactively. The user chooses a catalog (d, S). Only documents in S will be searched (queried). At first a *minimal query* is displayed. In a minimal query, only the root element name of d is displayed. A minimal query looks similar to an empty form for querying using a search engine (see Figure 2). The user can then add content constraints by filling in the form, or add structural constraints by expanding elements that are displayed. When an element is expanded, its attributes and subelements, as defined in d, are displayed. The user can add content constraints to the elements and attributes. The user can also specify the quantification that should be applied to each element and attribute, i.e., quantification constraints. This can be one of *exists*, *not exists*, *for all*, and *not for all* (written in a user friendly fashion). In addition, the user can choose which elements in the query should appear in the output.

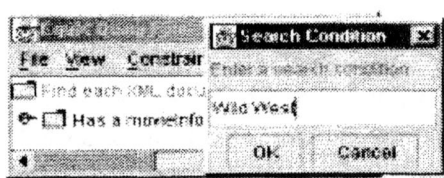

Fig. 2. Minimal query that finds documents containing the phrase "Wild West".

In Figure 3 an expanded concrete query is depicted. This query was formulated from the DTD presented in Section 2. It retrieves the title and description of Wild West movies in which Redford does not star as a villain. Intuitively, answering this query is a two part process. First, *search* for Wild West movies. The phrase "Wild West" may appear anywhere below the movie element. This is similar to a search in a search engine. Second, *query* the movies to find those in which Redford does not play as a villain. This condition is rather exact. It specifies where the phrases should appear and it contains a quantification constraint. Thus, conceptually, this is similar to a traditional database query.

3.2   Abstract Query Syntax

We present our abstract syntax. A boolean function that associates each sequence of alpha-numeric symbols with a truth value among $\{\bot, \top\}$ is a *string matching function*. We assume that there is an infinite set C of string matching functions, that C is closed under complement and that the function $\top$ is a member of C.

Definition 2 (Abstract Query). *An abstract query is a rooted directed tree T augmented by four functions and an output set, denoted (T, l, c, o, q, O) where*

- $l : N \to \mathcal{L}$ *is a labeling function that associates each node with a label;*
- $c : N \to C$ *is a content function that associates each node with a string matching function;*
- $o : N \to \{\wedge, \vee\}$ *is an operator function that associates each node with a logical operator;*

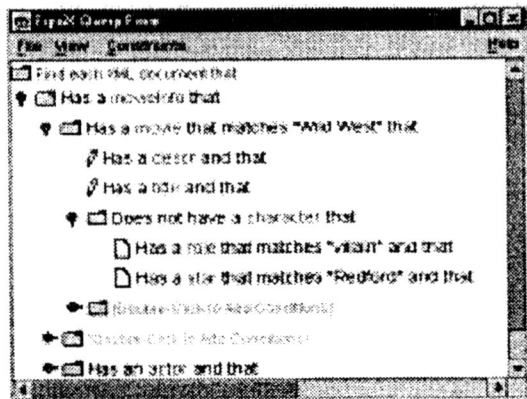

Fig. 3. Query for the titles and descriptions of movies in which Redford isn't a villain.

- $q : E \rightarrow \{\exists, \forall\}$ is a quantification function *that associates each edge with a quantifier;*
- $O \subseteq N$ is a set of projected nodes, *nodes that should appear in the result.*

Consider a node n. If $o(n) = \wedge$, we will say that n is an *and-node*. Otherwise we will say that n is an *or-node*. Similarly, consider an edge e. If $q(e) = \exists$, we will say that e is an *existential-edge*. Otherwise, e is a *universal-edge*.

We give an intuitive explanation of the meaning of an abstract query. The formal semantics is presented in Section 4. When evaluating a query, we will attempt to *match* nodes in a document to nodes in the query. In order for a document node n_X to match a query node n_Q, the function $c(n_Q)$ should hold on the data below n_X. In addition, if n_Q is an and-node (or-node), we require that each (at least one) child of n_Q be matched to a child of n_X. If n_X is matched to n_Q then a child n'_X of n_X can be matched to a child n'_Q of n_Q, only if the edge (n_Q, n'_Q) can be *satisfied* w.r.t. n_X. Roughly speaking, in order for an universal-edge (existential-edge) to be satisfied w.r.t. n_X, all children (at least one child) of n_X that have the same label as n'_Q must be matched to n'_Q.

Note that in a concrete query the user can use the quantifiers $\{\exists, \forall, \neg\exists, \neg\forall\}$ and all nodes are implicitly and-nodes. In an abstract query only the quantifiers $\{\exists, \forall\}$ may be used and the nodes may be either and-nodes or or-nodes. When creating a user interface for our language we found that the concrete query language was generally more intuitive for the user. We present the abstract query language to simplify the discussion of the semantics and query evaluation. Note that the two languages are equivalent in their expressive power. Translating one to the other is straightforward and is not presented due to space limitations.

The concrete query in Figure 3 can be represented by the abstract query in Figure 4. The string matching functions are specified in italics next to the nodes.

Black nodes are output nodes. In the sequel, unless otherwise specified, the term *query* will refer to an abstract query.

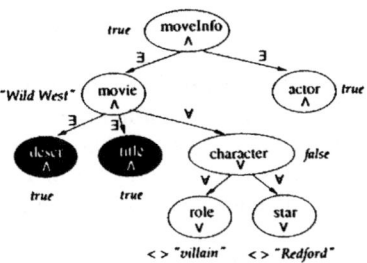

Fig. 4. Abstract query for the concrete query in Figure 3. Output nodes are black.

Recall the search language requirements we presented in Section 1. We postulated that in a search language, it should not be necessary for the user to specify format of the result (Criterion 1). In EquiX, by defining the set O, the user only specifies what information should she wants the result to include, and does not explicitly detail the format in which it should appear. We suggested that it is important for there to be pattern matching, quantification, and logical expressions for constraining data and meta-data (Criterion 2). For data, these can all be specified using the content function c. For meta-data, the pattern to which the structure should be matched is specified by T and l, the quantification is specified by q, and logical operators can be specified using o. The result of an EquiX query is a set of XML documents. In [3] we show how a DTD for the result documents can be computed. Thus, requerying of results is possible in EquiX (Criterion 3). In Section 5 we show that EquiX queries can be evaluated in polynomial time, and thus, EquiX meets Criterion 4.

4 Search Query Semantics

When describing the semantics of a query in a relational database language, such as SQL or Datalog, the term *matching* can be used. The result of evaluating a query are all the tuples that match the schemas mentioned in the query and satisfy the constraints. We describe the semantics of an EquiX query similarly.

We first define when a node in a document matches a node in a query. Consider a document X, and a query Q. Suppose that the labeling function of X is l_X and the labeling function of Q is l_Q. We say that a node n_X in X *matches* a node n_Q in Q if $l_X(n_X) = l_Q(n_Q)$. We denote the parent of a node n by $p(n)$. We now define a matching of a document to a query.

Definition 3 (Matching). *Let $X = (T_X, l_X)$ be an XML document, with nodes N_X and root r_X, Let $Q = (T_Q, l_Q, c, o, q, O)$ be a query tree with nodes N_Q and root r_Q. A matching of X to Q is a function $\mu : N_Q \to 2^{N_X}$, such that*

1. **Roots Match:** $\mu(r_Q) = \{r_X\}$;
2. **Node Matching:** *if* $n_X \in \mu(n_Q)$, n_X *matches* n_Q;
3. **Connectivity:** *if* $n_X \in \mu(n_Q)$ *and* $n_X \neq r_X$, *then* $p(n_X) \in \mu(p(n_Q))$.

Note that Condition 1 requires that the root of the document is matched to the root of the query, Condition 2 insures that matching nodes have the same label, and Condition 3 requires matchings to have a tree-like structure.

We define when a matching of a document to a query is satisfying. We first present some auxiliary definitions. Consider an XML document $X = (T_X, l_X)$, where $T_X = (N_X, E_X, r_X)$. Consider a node n_X in T_X. We differentiate between the *textual content* (i.e., data) contained below the node n_X, and the structural content (i.e., meta-data). When defining the textual content of a node, we take ID and IDREF values into consideration. We say that n'_X is a *child* of n_X if $(n_X, n'_X) \in E_X$. We say that n'_X is an *indirect child* of n_X if n_X is an attribute of type IDREF with the same value as an attribute of type ID of n'_X. We denote the textual content of a node n_X as $t(n_X)$, defined

- If n_X is an atomic node, then $t(n_X) = l_X(n_X)$;
- Otherwise, $t(n_X)$ is a concatenation[2] of the content of its children and indirect children.

We demonstrate the textual content of a node with an example. Recall the XML document depicted in Figure 1. The textual content of Node 9, is "villain 436 Jack Redford". Note that the $t(24)$ includes the value "Jack Redford" since Node 5 is an indirect child of Node 24.

We discuss when a quantification constraint is satisfied. Consider a document X, a query Q and a matching μ of X to Q. Let n_X be a node in X and let $e = (n_Q, n'_Q)$ be an edge in Q. We say n_X *satisfies e with respect to* μ if

- e is an existential-edge and there is a child n'_X of n_X such that n'_X matches n'_Q and $n'_X \in \mu(n'_Q)$.
- e is a universal-edge and for all children n'_X of n_X, if n'_X matches n'_Q, then $n'_X \in \mu(n'_Q)$.

We define a satisfying matching of a document to a query.

Definition 4 (Satisfying Matching). *Let $X = (T_X, l_X)$ be an XML document, and let $Q = (T_Q, l_Q, c, o, q, O)$ be a query tree. Let μ be a matching of X to Q. We say that μ is a satisfying mapping of X to Q if for all nodes n_Q in Q and for all nodes $n_X \in \mu(n_Q)$ the following conditions hold*

1. if n_Q is a leaf then $c(n_Q)(t(n_X)) = \top$, i.e., n_X satisfies the string matching condition of n_Q;

---

[2] Note that an XML document may be cyclic as a result of ID and IDREF attributes. We take a finite concatenation by taking each child into account only once. In addition, the order in which the concatenation is taken and the ability to differentiate between data that originated in different nodes may affect the satisfiability of a string matching function. This is a technical problem that is taken into consideration in the implementation. We will not elaborate on this point any further.

2. *otherwise (n_Q is not a leaf):*
   (a) *if n_Q is an or-node then n_X satisfies either $c(n_Q)$ or at least one edge incident from n_Q with respect to μ;*
   (b) *if n_Q is an and-node then n'_X satisfies both $c(n_Q)$ and all edges that are incident from n_Q with respect to μ.*

Condition 1 implies that the leaves satisfy the content constraints in Q. Conditions 2a and 2b imply that X satisfies the quantification constraints in Q. The structural constraints are satisfied by the existence of a matching.

Example 1. Recall the query in Figure 4 and the document in Figure 1. Note that there is no satisfying matching that matches Node 1 to the movie node in the query because the universal quantification on the edge connecting movie and character cannot be satisfied. One satisfying matching of the document to the query is: $\mu(\text{movieInfo}) = \{0\}$, $\mu(\text{movie}) = \{2\}$, $\mu(\text{descr}) = \{10\}$, $\mu(\text{title}) = \{11\}$, $\mu(\text{character}) = \{12, 13\}$, $\mu(\text{role}) = \{25, 27\}$, $\mu(\text{star}) = \{26, 28\}$, $\mu(\text{actor}) = \{4\}$.

We presented several matchings of a document to a query. Let μ and μ' be matchings of a document X to a query Q. We define the *union* of μ and μ' in the obvious way. Formally, given a query node n_Q, then $(\mu \cup \mu')(n_Q) := \mu(n_Q) \cup \mu'(n_Q)$. There may be an exponential number of matchings of a given document to a given query. Note, however, that the following holds.

Proposition 1 (Union of Matchings). *Let X be an XML document and let Q be a query. Let $\mathcal{M}$ be the set of all matchings of X to Q. Then the union of all the matchings in $\mathcal{M}$ is a matching. Formally, $(\bigcup_{\mu \in \mathcal{M}} \mu) \in \mathcal{M}$.*

We say that a document X *satisfies* a query Q if there exists a satisfying matching μ of X to Q. We now specify the output of evaluating a query on a single XML document. The result of a query is the set of documents derived by evaluating the query on each document in the queried catalog.

Intuitively, the result of evaluating a query on a document is a subtree of the document (as required in Criterion 1). The subtree contains nodes of three types. Document nodes corresponding to *output* query nodes appear in the resulting subtree. In addition, we include *ancestors* and *descendents* of these nodes. The ancestors insure that the result has a tree-like structure and that it is a projection of the original document. Recall that the textual content of the document is contained in the atomic nodes of the document tree. Hence, the result must include the descendents to insure that the the textual content is returned.

For a given document, query processing can be viewed as the process of singling out the nodes of the document tree that will be part of the output. Consider a document $X = (T_X, l_X)$ with $T_X = (N_X, E_X, r_X)$ and a query Q with projected nodes O. Let $\mathcal{M}$ be the set of satisfying matchings of X to Q. The output of evaluating the query Q on the document X is the the document defined by projecting N_X on the set $N_R := N_{\text{out}} \cup N_{\text{anc}} \cup N_{\text{desc}}$ defined as

- $N_{\text{out}} := \{n_X \in N_X \mid (\exists n_O \in O)(\exists \mu \in \mathcal{M}) \, n_X \in \mu(n_O)\}$;
- $N_{\text{anc}} := \{n_X \in N_X \mid (\exists n'_X \in N_{\text{out}}) \, n_X \text{ is an ancestor of } n'_X\}$;

– $N_{\text{desc}} := \{n_X \in N_X \mid (\exists n'_X \in N_{\text{out}})\ n_X$ is an descendent of $n'_X\}$.

Note that nodes in N_{out} are document nodes that correspond to projected nodes in Q. The ancestors (descendents) of the nodes in N_{out} are in N_{anc} (N_{desc}). We call N_R the *output set* of X with respect to Q.

The result of applying the query in Figure 4 to the document in Figure 1 is depicted in Figure 5. Note that the values of "descr" and "title" are grouped by "movie". This follows naturally from the structure of the original document.

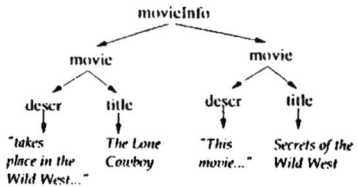

Fig. 5. Result of applying the query in Figure 4 to the document in Figure 1.

5   Query Evaluation

A query is defined by choosing a catalog and exploring its DTD. Consider a query Q generated from a DTD d in the catalog (d, S). Evaluating Q on the database results in the set of documents created by evaluating Q on each document in S.

There may be an exponential number of matchings of a query to a document. Concrete queries contain both quantification and negation. Thus, it would seem that computing the output of a query on a document should be computationally expensive. Roughly speaking, however, query evaluation in this case is analogous to evaluating a two variable first-order query. Therefore, using dynamic programming we can in fact derive an algorithm that runs in polynomial time, even when the query is considered part of the input (i.e., combined complexity). Thus, EquiX has polynomial evaluation time (Criterion 4).

Consider a query Q with nodes N_Q and a document X with nodes N_X. Let $|D|$ be the size of the data in document X, i.e., the size of X when ignoring X's meta-data. Let $C(m)$ be an upper-bound on the runtime of computing a string-matching constraint on a string of size m. The theorem below gives the complexity of query evaluation. Its proof can be found in [3].

Theorem 1 (Polynomial Complexity). *The result of evaluating the query Q on the document X can be computed in time $O(|N_X| \cdot |N_Q| \cdot (|N_Q| \cdot |N_X| + C(|D|)))$.*

Query evaluation generates a set of documents. A query is formulated by exploring a DTD. Thus, in order to allow *iterative querying* or *requerying of results*, a DTD for the resulting documents must be defined. In [3] we present a polynomial procedure that computes a DTD for the resulting documents of a given query. This DTD is linear in the size of the DTD from which the query was originated. The compactness of the result DTD makes the requerying process simpler, since requerying entails exploring the result DTD. Thus, EquiX fulfills the search language requirement of ability to perform requerying (Criterion 3).

6 Conclusion

Several XML query languages have been proposed recently, such as XQL [7], XML-QL [4] and Lorel [5]. They are powerful in their querying ability. However, they do not fulfill some of our search language requirements. In these languages the format of the result must be specified, in contradiction to Criterion 1. Furthermore, XML-QL and XQL are limited in their ability to express quantification constraints (Criterion 2). Most importantly, none of these languages guarantee polynomial evaluation under combined complexity (Criterion 4).

EquiX fulfills all the requirements presented in Section 1. It also has a user-friendly concrete syntax. In our language, complex queries with negation, quantification and logical expressions can be expressed. We have also extended EquiX to allow aggregation and limited regular expressions [3]. As future work, we plan to extend the ability of querying ontologies [3] and to allow use of more complex regular expressions. We also plan to refine EquiX with the ability to deal with incomplete information and to add a metric for ranking the results that considers both the data and the meta-data.

References

1. T. Bray, J. Paoli, and C. M. Sperberg-McQueen. Extensible markup language (XML) 1.0, 1998. Available at http://www.w3.org/XML.
2. S. Cohen, Y. Kanza, Y. Kogan, W. Nutt, Y. Sagiv, and A. Serebrenik. EquiX—Easy querying in XML databases. In *Proc. 2nd International Workshop on the Web and Databases*, Philadelphia, (Pennsylvania, USA), June 1999.
3. S. Cohen, Y. Kanza, Y. Kogan, W. Nutt, Y. Sagiv, and A. Serebrenik. Equix—A search and query language for XML. Technical Report 2000-28, Departement Computer Science, Hebrew University, Jerusalem, Israel, 2000. Available at http://www.cs.huji.ac.il/leibniz/research/2000.html.
4. A. Deutsch, M. Fernandez, D. Florescu, A. Levy, and D. Suciu. XML-QL: A query language for XML, 1998. Available at http://www.w3.org/TR/NOTE-xml-ql.
5. R. Goldman, J. McHugh, and J. Widom. From semistructured data to XML: Migrating the Lore data model and query language. In *Proc. 2nd International Workshop on the Web and Databases*, Philadelphia, (Pennsylvania, USA), June 1999.
6. B. Ludäscher, Y. Papakonstantinou, and P. Velikhov. A framework for navigation-driven lazy mediators. In *Proc. 2nd International Workshop on the Web and Databases*, Philadelphia, (Pennsylvania, USA), June 1999.
7. J. Robie, J. Lapp, and D. Schach. XML query language (XQL), 1998. Available at http://www.w3.org/TandS/QL/QL98/pp/xql.html.

Cooperative Indexing, Classification, and Evaluation in BoW

Dror G. Feitelson

School of Computer Science and Engineering,
The Hebrew University, 91904 Jerusalem, Israel,
feit@cs.huji.ac.il,
WWW home page: http://www.cs.huji.ac.il/~feit

Abstract. BoW is an on-line bibliographic Dynamic Ranked Information-space (DyRI). It provides the infrastructure for users to add bibliographical information, classify it, index it, and evaluate it. Thus users cooperate by contributing and sharing their experience in order to advance the most problematic aspects of information retrieval: finding the *most relevant* and *high quality* information for their needs.

1 Introduction

The basic problem in information retrieval today is filtering the massive amounts of information that are available in order to find high-quality relevant information. The quest for high quality means that the available information must be evaluated and ranked in some way. The quest for relevance means that the information must also be classified and indexed according to pertinent concepts.

Current information retrieval systems often leave much of this filtering to the users. They focus on an effort to be comprehensive, producing a superset of the desired information. The user then shifts through this information, discarding most of it, and selecting those items that seem to best answer the needs. But the effort expanded in this selection process — in which *a human user with understanding of the domain checks the system's classification and performs an evaluation* — is lost. The system does not keep track of which data items were selected in the end, and does not have the means to match them with a refined version of the user's original query.

The BoW project is an attempt to investigate the possibility of tapping the work done by users to improve the system. The scope chosen is a bibliographic repository for a limited domain (BoW stands for "Bibliography on the Web", and our prototype contains approximately 3000 entries from the domain of parallel systems). Within this scope, users are provided with facilities to contribute to the classification and indexing of entries, and the same facilities are used for the incremental construction of queries. In addition, the system keeps track of users' searches and their results, and uses this information to reorganize the way data is presented to subsequent users. Thus valuable user experience contributes to improving the system's service, rather than being lost.

O. Etzion and P. Scheuermann (Eds.): CoopIS 2000, LNCS 1901, pp. 66–77, 2000.
© Springer-Verlag Berlin Heidelberg 2000

2   Dynamic Ranked Information Spaces

2.1   The Vision

Consider a situation where you are a university professor specializing in parallel systems, and one of your students comes to you with an idea for a new network topology. You recall that you have seen something like this in the past, but you do not remember the name given to this topology or who did the work. An altavista search using the term "network topology" produces 12,338 hits, and those you check either describe specific installations or are dangling links pointing to nothing. Your only recourse is to try and call up some colleagues who might have a better memory.

Now consider what might have happened if the parallel processing community maintained a dynamic ranked information space with technical publications in this field. You would enter at the root node, and traverse the path "architecture" → "interconnection networks" → "topologies" to arrive at a page listing hundreds of proposed topologies, grouped according to their attributes. For each one you will be able to get a concise description, the text of research articles describing the topology and its uses, commentary on these articles, links to descriptions of systems that actually use this topology, and an indication of how many other researchers are also interested in it. If you find that any of this information is stale or misleading, you will be able to either leave a comment about it, or alert an editor that a link should be removed. Thus your experience will immediately contribute to the maintenance of the site, as the experiences of others have contributed before you.

This example is not unique to parallel systems or even to searching in the scientific literature. For example, a similar situation can occur with an architect looking for data on designing public libraries in a dynamic ranked information space dedicated to that topic. The basis is the existence of a tightly knit community of users that contribute to the maintenance and updating of the repository by submitting information, commentary, and suggestions for structural changes. As a result, the repository changes dynamically with time (rather than just accumulating more and more items), and contains feedback and evaluations in addition to the original raw data items. In addition, using the repository shortens the publication time of new information to zero, and makes it available in multiple cross sections. It is a large scale extension of the concept of peer review, coupled with an indexing service.

The project follows the "field of dreams" approach, which is actually the basis for the growth of the Internet [5]: we just *provide the technology* for creating the information space, and *leave it to the users to supply the content*[1]. The resulting system is called a "**Dynamic Ranked Information-space**", or DyRI for short.

---

[1] However, initially it is necessary to prime the information spaces with enough content to make them sufficiently attractive so that potential users overcome the "new technology" barrier.

2.2   The Design

While the concepts explored here apply to any information repository, we use a bibliographic repository for concreteness. This also simplifies the prototype by limiting it to rather structured data.

User Types   Users of DyRIs are classified into three types: users, contributors, and editors.

Users are those who use the information space to search for information. The main search method is by traversing a concept index that classifies the available information according to content. This allows for refining the search as one proceeds, rather than requiring one to have a clear notion of the required information at the outset.

While general users do not add information to the information space, they do register feedback relating to existing data. One form of feedback is simply by traversing the concept index: the system keeps counts of visits to each page, and uses this information to identify the more popular ones to future users. In addition, users may register positive or negative feedback to each page, to note their level of satisfaction. Again, the system displays this information as part of the indication of a page's popularity.

Contributors are users who not only search for data, but also contribute data. In principle any user may become a contributor; the only requirement is to identify oneself to the system. Such identification is required both in order to attribute contributions such as annotations to their authors, and in order to identify the arguing parties in case of disputes. In extreme cases of misuse, it may be necessary to limit certain users.

Contribution can take any of three forms:

- Adding a new entry to the repository.
- Adding an annotation to an existing entry, providing additional insight into its importance or content.
- Adding a link between related pages or entries.

Links create the fabric of the concept index, allowing it to be traversed incrementally, at the same time narrowing the scope of the search. Whenever a new entry is added to the repository, it should be linked to appropriate pages in the concept index. Contributors who discover additional meaningful links later may also add them.

In addition, contributors can make minor modifications to existing data, e.g. in order to correct errors. Contributors can also *suggest* major modifications, such as deleting entries or links. However, acting upon such suggestions is left to *editors*, after proper solicitation of a rebuttal from the original contributor. Thus the editor's main task is to resolve conflicts and maintain the quality of the repository, based on input from the contributors.

The Concept Index Most search engines are unsatisfactory because users are required to have a good notion of what they are looking for before they start. The most common approach is to describe the query using keywords and logical operations; for example, the query (scheduling & (parallel | distributed)) is read as "find documents including the word 'scheduling' and either of 'parallel' or 'distributed' ". The intent is probably to find references regarding scheduling in parallel or distributed systems. However, the issue of whether we mean job scheduling by the operating system, task scheduling by the runtime system, or task scheduling by the compiler is left open. A good search engine will find all three types (and maybe more) and leave it to the user to shift through them. Adding keywords can reduce this burden, but runs the risk of false negatives, where items of interest are rejected because they do not contain all the specified

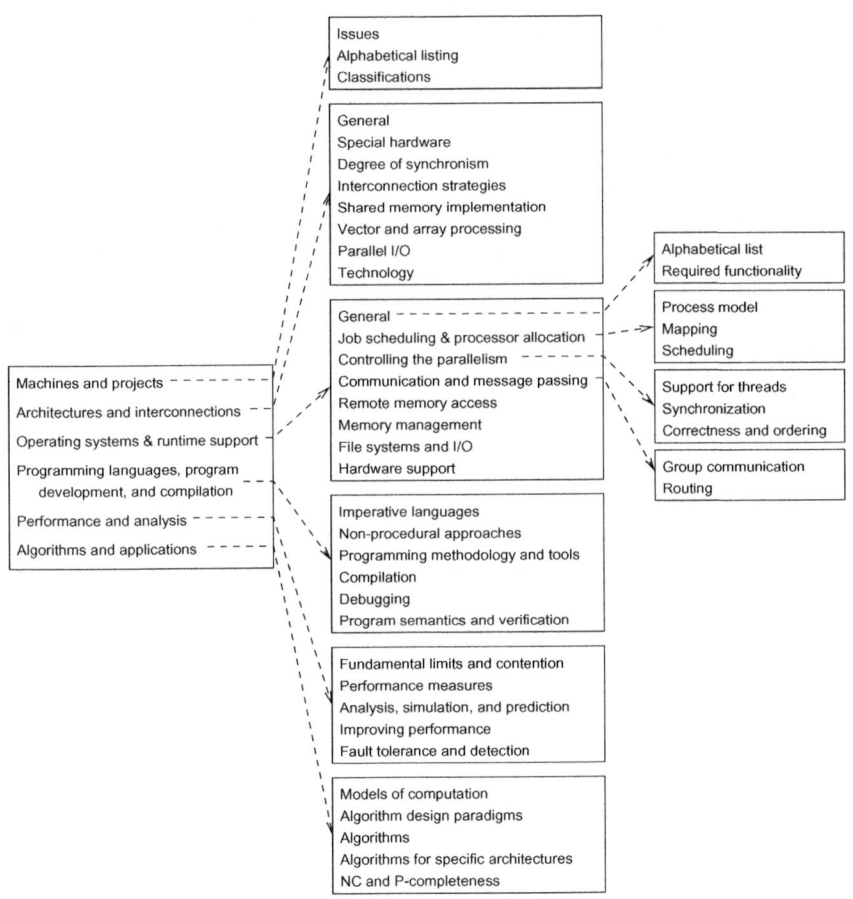

Fig. 1. *Example of the top levels of a concept index for an information space on parallel systems.*

keywords (and without any typos 8-).

In contrast, the concept index allows users to formulate their search incrementally on-line, and does not depend on matching keywords. Essentially it can be viewed as a menu-driven search. The top level of the index (the root) contains links to several broad topics. Following such a link leads to a page representing the chosen topic (a *concept page*), and including a list of subtopics and/or bibliographic entries. The index is navigated using a hypertext interface such as a Web browser, by going from one concept page to another. The leaves contain only bibliographic entries that pertain to a narrow and focused topic.

An example of the top levels of a concept index for the domain of parallel systems is shown in Fig. 1. Using such a structure, a user looking for information on the scheduling of parallel jobs will follow the "operating systems and runtime support" link from the top level, and then the "Job scheduling & processor allocation" link. A user looking for information about on-line task scheduling would diverge at the second level, and choose the "controlling the parallelism" link. A user looking for information about task scheduling by the compiler would start with the "programming languages, program development, and compilation" link at the top level, and then choose "compilation".

As noted above, the structure of the concept index is of utmost importance. For any specialized domain, it seems advisable to create a special index based on a thorough understanding of the domain. This should be done with an eye for what users might look for. The topics need not be (and probably should not be) completely disjoint: the index structure can easily be a DAG rather than a tree. Thus any subtopic that is relevant to two or more larger topics (e.g. if it represents their intersection) is simply linked to all of them, and can be found by several distinct routes in the index. For example, it would be convenient if information on "virtual memory" was accessible both via "architectures" → "shared memory implementation" and "operating systems" → "memory management".

An important question is the "right" size for pages, and the resulting depth of the index [2]. The tradeoff is between scrolling and loading. Using small pages that do not require scrolling leads to a deeper index, and therefore requires more pages to be loaded from the server. If we want to reduce the average number of pages loaded in order to reduce the accumulated waiting time, we need to use larger pages. A possible way out is to use a relatively low branching factor, but show *two levels* of the index in each page. The pages are then bigger, but their internal structure makes them easier to use.

User Feedback An important part of the interface is the support for registration and display of user feedback. The feedback feature is embedded naturally into the concept index, so as to be usable and useful without any training. Registering feedback about links in the concept index is done as a byproduct of traversing these links. One simple form of feedback is popularity: the system keeps count of the number of times that each link is traversed, and displays this *at the head of the link* (rather than displaying a count of visits in the page itself). Note that if a page has more than one link pointing at it, the counts for

Fig. 2. *Composite "back" button used to obtain feedback.*

these links will be different, as they well should be, because they represent the perceived relevance of the page *in different contexts.*

The problem with mere counts is that they represent the *initial perception* of users, but not their *final satisfaction with their choice.* To capture user satisfaction, pages have composite "back" buttons embedded in them (Fig. 2). By selecting the happy or sad face, the user can distinguish between a "happy back after finding what I wanted" and a "frustrated back after failing". Clicking elsewhere just performs the back function, without registering any feedback.

The problem with the composite back buttons is that we do not want to burden the user with them. Therefore *inferential* feedback is used as well. One form of inferential feedback is that positive feedback is applied to the whole path from the root to the page on which the happy face is pressed, thus saving the need to go all the way back to register satisfaction. Negative feedback, on the other hand, is applied only to the last link, allowing for backtracking and trying of other links. Another form of inferential feedback is that using the "export" facility is deemed to represent positive feedback, based on the assumption that the user is exporting data because he likes what he found.

Once the system has the feedback information, it should display it in a useful manner. The suggested approach is to decorate each link with a small icon that presents the information graphically. Specifically, a set of marks can be used, with green check-marks denoting positive feedback and red X's denoting negative feedback. The number of marks indicates the degree of positiveness or negativeness, while their size reflects the total number of visits. Such a display allows users to focus immediately on "big check-mark" links, which are those that many other users have found useful.

The specific formula used combines the ratio of good to bad feedback with a logarithmic scale, so as to allow for a large dynamic range. The formula for the number of check-marks n is

$$n = \lg\left(\frac{g-b}{b+1} + 0.7\right) + 1$$

where g and b are the numbers of good and bad feedbacks, respectively. For X's, exchange g and b. This leads to numbers as indicated in Fig. 3.

An additional use of feedback is the internal organization of the concept pages. It is envisioned that at lower levels of the index concept pages will be divided into topics, each listing a set of relevant bibliographic entries. The order of entries in such a set should be

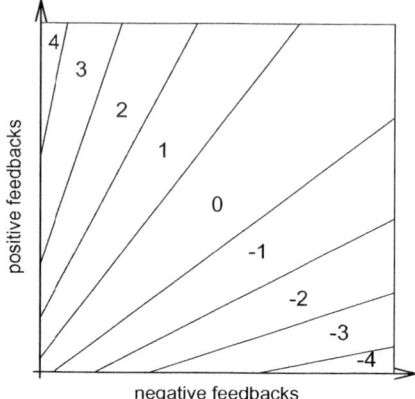

Fig. 3. *dependence of feedback visualization on actual number of positive and negative feedbacks.*

1. New documents that were only recently added to the repository. Such documents are kept on top for a few months or until they get some feedback from users.
2. Documents that have received positive feedback.
3. Documents about which users are ambivalent, or no feedback is available, possibly for lack of popularity.
4. Documents that have received negative feedback. These documents are candidates for removal.

3   Comparison with Other Approaches

The issue of finding relevant information according to one's needs is obviously of paramount importance. It has therefore motivated considerable research and development activity, and the creation of a large industry that indexes and provides access to on-line information. There are three main approaches: using links, using keywords, and using experts.

3.1   Finding Information Using Links

The Science Citation Index is based on the notion that related papers in the scientific literature are "linked" by their bibliographical citations: either they cite each other, or they share many citations. Thus if you have a starting point for your search, namely some scientific paper on this topic, you can use both *its* citations and citations *to it* to find additional related papers. Citations in a paper are easy to find: they appear in the paper itself. The Science Citation Index provides the other direction: for any given paper, it lists other papers that cite it.

This idea has been extended in two ways using the WWW. One is to make references into hyperlinks, and collect on-line documents that reference each other. An example is the NEC Research Index (http://csindex.com), which is based on an automatic tool that crawls the Web looking for scientific papers, analyzes them, and creates a citation index from them [4]. A related example is the hypertext bibliography project (http://theory.lcs.mit.edu/~dmjones/hbp). This project contains information about all papers published in a host of journals and conferences, mainly related to Theoretical Computer Science, and maintains two-way links among these papers according to their citations.

The other extension is to apply these ideas directly to the structure of the WWW itself. The thrust of the work in this direction is based on Kleinberg's classification of Web sites into hubs and authorities, based on the the links emanating from them and pointing to them [3].

3.2 Finding Information Using Keywords

Indexing services are another well-known search facility. They don't require you to have a starting point — only a good notion of what you are looking for. They survey the scientific literature as it is published, and collect papers by topic. Thus they provide a much needed mapping from topics to journal pages, much as an index at the end of a book provides a mapping from topics to the pages of the book.

The enormous quantity of information that is available, and its exponential growth rate, has lead to much interest in automatic indexing [7]. Direct improvements to simple indexing include the ability to derive related words, and knowledge about synonyms based on a thesaurus [1, 8]. Using these facilities, it is possible to find useful information even in cases where a direct match to the user's query does not exist.

A more sophisticated approach is based on learning from examples using boosting algorithms [6]. These algorithms combine multiple inaccurate heuristic classifications (e.g. based on keywords) into a more accurate final classification (e.g. a prediction of the topic being addressed in the document). The methodology involves iterative learning using pre-classified examples. Each example attaches a set of labels to a document. The system learns to attach such labels automatically, by iteratively refining its notion of how combinations of inaccurate classifications lead to final classifications. This in turn is based on giving higher weights to those examples that are hardest to classify.

3.3 Indexing by Experts

While machine learning can help achieve good classifications based on keywords, some believe that ultimately there is no alternative to human understanding. Indeed, most Internet portals now include large indexes (usually called Internet Directories) maintained by their staff in addition to the traditional keyword search facility (Table 1). These indexes classify the whole Internet according to a hierarchical structure, and provide lists of generally useful web pages for each

Table 1. *The sizes of major Internet directories at end of 1999, according to Search Engine Watch (*http://www.searchenginewatch.com*).*

directory	editors	categories	links
Yahoo!	100+	?	1200000+
LookSmart	200	60000	1000000
Open Directory	15400	153000	950000
Snap	30–50	64000	600000

topic. The Yahoo! index is especially interesting, as it is a DAG rather than a tree, with explicit indication that some pages are shared by several branches (http://www.yahoo.com). The Open Directory (whose slogan is "HUMANS do it better") also has a very useful structure: The home page displays two levels of the directory, with links to pages on the main topics, and below each one, links to more focused subtopics. About.com (http://www.about.com) is a network of sites maintained by experts in various fields, which makes a point of parading the human experts rather than the technology.

3.4   Problems and Comparison

There are various problems with the abovementioned approaches. One is that many of them *lack interpretation*. This means that papers are associated according to superficial attributes (citations or keywords), not according to an understanding of what the papers are actually about and how they relate to each other. There is no real editorial work on classification and organization. Moreover, users cannot augment these mechanisms with private annotations that do contain interpretation.

Another is that they are often *source oriented*. This relates to the choice of papers that are covered: certain journals are selected, and all the papers that appear in them are included, starting from a certain year. Granted, an effort is made to select as many journals as possible, and to focus on the best journals, but economic and business considerations may sometimes prevail over technical ones. Moreover, even good journals sometimes contain not-so-good papers, and some good papers are published in obscure journals. Results that are only published in conferences or technical reports are excluded outright. So are old papers that were published before the indexing commenced.

A third problem is that of *coverage and quality*. This problem is especially common in keyword-based search, where hits that do indeed contain the requested keywords have widely different levels of importance and usefulness. In the extreme case we have false positives, which contain the desired keywords but are totally irrelevant. An example is a search for "gang scheduling"[2] which retrieved a web page that included the sentence "The RV6 forum got off to a

---

[2] A scheduling technique used on parallel computers whereby a job's processes are scheduled simultaneously on distinct processors.

rocky start due to a scheduling misunderstanding with the Van's gang". A related problem is false negatives, that is relevant and useful documents that use synonyms or related terms are therefore not found.

The problem with human experts is that they are expensive, so there is a necessary tradeoff between the number of experts and the size of the fields that they have to cover. As a result, the human classifiers cannot in general have cutting edge knowledge about all their fields.

The BoW project is based on the idea that indexing by paid experts is futile. Instead, indexing and ranking must be done by the users of the information, thus tapping their enormous combined pool of knowledge and experience. Of special importance is the support of ranking and evaluation of documents, which does not exist in other projects. It is this ranking which counteracts the exponential growth of information, and ensures that high-quality information becomes more visible. The thrust of our work is to create the infrastructure and technology to enable such a mode of cooperation.

4   The BoW Prototype

The BoW project has been ongoing for a couple of years, and two generations have been completed. An example screen dump of a page from the concept index of a parallel systems information space is shown in Fig. 4. The prototype supports insertion of new bibliographic entries, addition of annotations, creation of links from concept pages to entries, among entries, and to external web pages (thus supporting the publication of full text rather than only references), user feedback and display, and exporting of bibliographical entries. It has a concept index of 142 pages, in which 8201 links to entries are grouped according to 3167 topics. In all, there are 3046 entries, for an average of 2.7 links per entry. This is all based on an automatic conversion of a bibliographic database kept in LaTeX/BibTeX format since 1988. It can be accessed on-line at URL http://www.bow.cs.huji.ac.il.

The implementation is based on using perl mode in an Apache Web server. The concept index is mirrored in a directory hierarchy, and concept pages are generated on-line as required by reading the appropriate directory. Thus all updates and changes appear automatically once the underlying directory structure is modified.

Several problems arise from the fact that the http protocol is stateless, and provides only limited support for continuous sessions (using cookies). Currently this causes problems with collecting a list of entries that should be exported upon demand; when user registration is implemented, we will also need to keep track of the user. The initial solution was to send the whole export list back and forth in each transaction. The second version improved on this by keeping the list in a memory segment shared by all the httpd processes in the server, and only sending a session ID in each transaction.

Features that are now being implemented as part of the third generation include

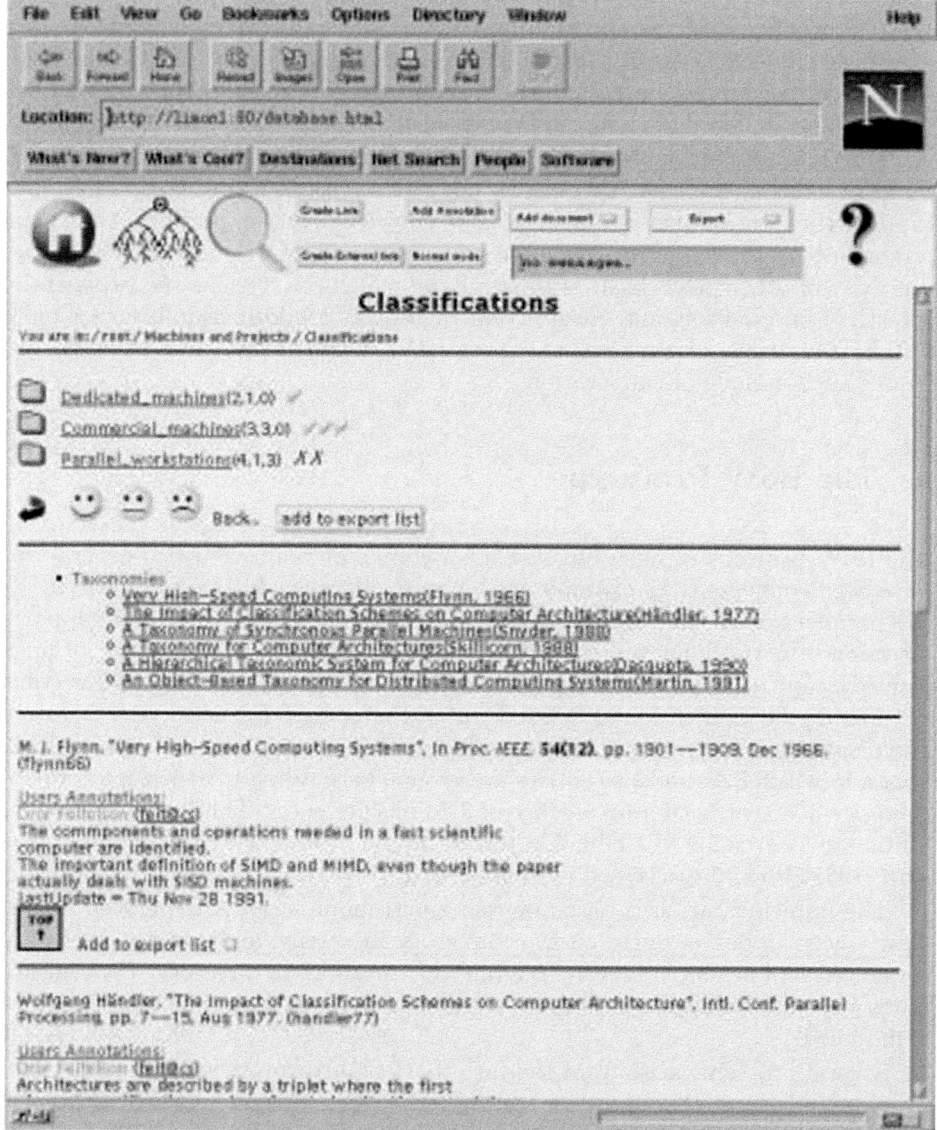

Fig. 4. Example of concept page from the prototype information space on parallel systems. It includes links to sub-topics with an indication of user feedback, a listing of entries that belong in this page, and then the entries themselves, including bibliographic information and annotations.

- Mechanization of the citation format to enable better identification of duplicate entries. In particular, journal and proceedings titles should come from a menu.
- Control over the structure of the concept index with an XML-based format.
- Provision of an automated listing of suggested concept pages, where a newly inserted entry may be indexed. This is generated based on similarity between the new entry and entries that are already indexed and linked to these pages.

5   Conclusions

The main idea behind DyRIs is that *users* can and should cooperate to improve the quality and usefulness of an information space. We designed and implemented one way of doing so, which is based on minimal active participation by users: they are invited to (but not forced to) add annotations and links to concept pages, and can provide feedback by using back-with-feedback buttons. This was a basic design decision, based on the fear that more extensive features such as feedback forms will go unused. We hope that the annoyance for users with our minimal design will be small enough that they will actually use these features. We intend to make the prototype information space on parallel systems publicly available once version 3 is ready, in order to test it in a real world setting.

Acknowledgements

This research was supported in part by the Ministry of Science. The first versions of the prototype were implemented by David Er-El and Roy Peleg.

References

1. H. Chen, J. Martinez, A. Kirchhoff, T. D. Ng, and B. R. Schatz, *"Alleviating search uncertainty through concept association: automatic indexing, co-occurrence analysis, and parallel computing"*. J. Am. Soc. Inf. Sci. **49(3)**, pp. 206–216, 1998.
2. S. H. Kim and C. M. Eastman, *"An experiment on node size in a hypermedia system"*. J. Am. Soc. Inf. Sci. **50(6)**, pp. 530–536, 1999.
3. J. M. Kleinberg, *"Authoritative sources in a hyperlinked environment"*. In 9th ACM-SIAM Symp. Discrete Alg., pp. 668–677, Jan 1998.
4. S. Lawrence, C. L. Giles, and K. Bollacker, *"Digital libraries and autonomous citation indexing"*. Computer **32(6)**, pp. 67–71, Jun 1999.
5. R. W. Lucky, *"New communications services — what does society want?"*. Proc. IEEE **85(10)**, pp. 1536–1543, Oct 1997.
6. R. E. Schapire and Y. E. Singer, *"BoosTexter: a boosting-based system for text categorization"*. Machine Learning **39(2/3)**, pp. 135–168, May 2000.
7. B. R. Schatz, *"Information retrieval in digirtal libraries: bringing search to the net"*. Science **275(5298)**, pp. 327–334, Jan 17 1997.
8. L. W. Wright, H. K. Grosetta Nardini, A. R. Aronson, and T. C. Rindflesch, *"Hierarchical concept indexing of full-text documents in the unified medical language system information sources map"*. J. Am. Soc. Inf. Sci. **50(6)**, pp. 514–523, 1999.

Complex View Selection for Data Warehouse Self-Maintainability

Dimitri Theodoratos

Department of Electrical and Computer Engineering
Computer Science Division
National Technical University of Athens
Zographou 157 73, Athens, Greece
dth@dblab.ece.ntua.gr

Abstract. A Data warehouse (DW) integrates data from multiple distributed heterogeneous data sources. A DW can be seen as a set of materialized views defined over the source relations. The materialized views are eventually updated upon changes of the source relations. For different reasons (e.g. reduction to the view maintenance cost, unavailability of the sources etc) it is desirable to make the DW self-maintainable. This means that the materialized views can be maintained, for every source relation change, without accessing the sources.

In this paper we deal with the problem of selecting auxiliary views to materialize in the DW such that the original materialized views and the auxiliary views taken together are self-maintainable. A distinguishing feature of our approach is that we consider that a data source can store multiple source relations referenced by the materialized views. Further, the data sources are of cooperative type, that is, they can compute and transmit to the DW the changes for (complex) views defined over their own relations. We first formally model the problem by using an AND/OR dag structure for multiple views that allows the representation of common subexpression sharing. We then provide a method for computing auxiliary views that fit in the space available for materialization and minimize the cost of computing the changes to be applied to the materialized views during the maintenance process.

1   Introduction

Data Warehouses (DWs) integrate, in advance, selected information from one or many, usually remote, autonomous data sources into a single database. A DW can be abstractly seen as a set of materialized views defined over the relations stored in the data sources. User queries are processed using these views. When the source relations change, the data at the DW are eventually updated. Current DWs often accumulate enormous quantities of data. The size of the stored data affects both the querying and the maintenance process. Reducing the view maintenance cost is one of the most significant challenges when implementing a DW.

The materialized views are usually maintained incrementally. In an incremental strategy, only the changes that must be applied to the view are computed

O. Etzion and P. Scheuermann (Eds.): CoopIS 2000, LNCS 1901, pp. 78–89, 2000.

using the changes of the source relations [12, 2, 3, 9]. The expressions used to compute the changes to be applied to a view involve the changes of the source relations, and are called *maintenance expressions*. In general, the maintenance expressions involve also source relations. Therefore, their evaluation requires *contacting the (remote) data sources*. Further, concurrent changes of the source relations can result in "anomalies" if traditional algorithms are applied. *Additional queries* need to be issued against the source relations to compensate for the effect of these concurrent changes [18].

When the source relation changes affect more than one materialized view, multiple maintenance expressions need to be evaluated. The techniques of multiquery optimization can be used to detect "common subexpressions" between maintenance expressions in order to derive an efficient global evaluation plan. The maintenance expressions can be evaluated more efficiently if they can be partially rewritten over views already materialized at the DW. Materialized views that are added to the DW exclusively for reducing the view maintenance cost (and not for contributing to the evaluation of user queries) are called *auxiliary views* [11, 15].

The data sources can be of different types ranging from *cooperative sources* to *legacy* systems [17]. A cooperative source can use the view definition to filter out source relation changes that are irrelevant [2] to the view materialization, and to project out useless attributes from the changes.

Self-maintainable views. A materialized view is *self-maintainable* if it can be maintained, for any instance of the source relations over which it is defined, and for all source relation changes, using only these changes, the view definition, and the view materialization [5, 6].

By adding auxiliary views to a set of materialized views, we can make the whole view set self-maintainable. There are different reasons for making a view set self-maintainable: (a) The source relations need not be contacted in turn for evaluating maintenance expressions during view updating. (b) "Anomalies" due to concurrent changes are eliminated and the view maintenance process is simplified. (c) The materialized views can be maintained efficiently even if the sources are not able to answer queries (e.g. legacy systems), or if they are temporarily unavailable (e.g. in mobile systems).

If the auxiliary views are appropriately selected, they may fit in the space available at the DW for this purpose and, at the same time, satisfy the desired goal of making the whole view set self-maintainable, while reducing the cost of computing the changes of the materialized views.

The problem. In this paper we deal with the issue of making a set of materialized views self-maintainable by adding auxiliary views. All the previous approaches consider that a data source either it transmits to the DW the changes of each relation or at most it filters the changes of each relation by appropriately selecting some tuples and projecting out some attribute values. However, changes of different relations in the same source are not combined together. Here we follow a different approach. We assume that:

(a) Each data source can hold multiple relations, and

(b) Data sources are of cooperative type. They can be aware of some DW views defined over their relations. These views are called source views. The data sources are able to compute, store, and transmit to the DW the changes of the source views.

In view of the previous assumptions, we address the following problem: given a set of views materialized at the DW, define source views and decide which of them to additionally materialize as auxiliary views in the DW such that:

(a) The materialized view set (that is the initial views and the auxiliary ones) is self-maintainable.

(b) The materialized auxiliary views fit in the space available in the DW for this end.

(c) The cost of computing the changes of all the materialized views from the changes of the source views is minimal.

Contribution and outline. The main contributions of the paper are the following:

- We present a generic model of a self-maintainable DW over distributed data sources. In contrast to previous approaches, we consider that the data sources can store multiple relations and can compute and transmit to the DW the changes of complex views defined over their own relations.
- We formalize this model using an AND/OR dag structure for multiple views that represents multiple ways of evaluating the views and "common subexpression" sharing. Using AND/OR dags, we show how source view changes can be propagated to multiple materialized views that are affected by these changes without accessing the data sources.
- In this context we address the problem of making a set of materialized views self-maintainable by determining source views and by additionally materializing some of them at the DW as auxiliary views. The materialization of the auxiliary views is subjected to a space constraint while the selection of source views has to minimize the cost of propagating source view changes.
- We present a method for detecting source views that can be left virtual without affecting the self-maintainability of the DW, thereby resulting in important space savings.
- Finally, using this method, we design an algorithm that provides an optimal solution to the problem.

The rest of the paper is organized as follows. The next section reviews related work. In Section 3 we present the DW model. Section 4 introduces multiexpression AND/OR dags and their derivatives, and describes source view change propagation at the DW. In Section 5 we present the method that detects source views that can be left virtual. The algorithm that computes the optimal solution is outlined in Section 6. Section 7 contains concluding remarks.

2   Related Work

Self-maintainability here is meant at "compile-time", that is, the instance of the source relation changes is not known when deciding about self-maintainability.

Self-maintainable views with respect to a type of source relation changes (insertion, deletion, or modification) are first introduced in [5], where conditions for an SPJ view to be self-maintainable are provided for different types of changes.

In [10] the problem of deriving a minimal set of auxiliary views that make a given SPJ view self-maintainable, with respect to insertions, deletions and modifications to the source relations, is addressed. Given a generalized project-select-join view, [1] provides an algorithm for identifying a minimal set of auxiliary views that makes the original view self-maintainable. [8] addresses the problem of making a view self-maintainable when additional relational operators, under set semantics are involved. All three approaches [10, 1, 8] concern a single view and make use of key and referential integrity constraints in order to derive the auxiliary views. In contrast to these approaches, we consider multiple views and we derive auxiliary views which, taken together with the original views, are self-maintainable, minimize the overall cost of incrementally computing the changes of the materialized views and fit in the space available for materialization. In this process, we are not constraint by the availability of integrity constraints.

In [17, 6] self-maintainability for multiple views is achieved by pushing down selections and projections to the source relations and by storing the resulting auxiliary view at the DW. [7] elaborates this approach in the context of multiple SPJ views. In contrast to these approaches, we consider a generic class of views, and we exploit the fact that multiple source relations can be stored at the same data source. Therefore, we are able to derive complex auxiliary views that combine multiple source relations from the same source and involve different binary and unary operators.

3   Data Warehouse model

The basic architecture of our DW model [14] comprises a central component (the DW) and components for the remote data sources.

The DW component. The DW contains a set of materialized views. Some views may be defined over other views, thus forming hierarchies. Views may also share common subexpressions.

User queries use these materialized views, either exclusively or partially, in order to get evaluated. This is done through complete or partial rewritings of the queries (initially defined over the source relations) over the materialized views.

In each DW there is a set of views, called *source views*, that satisfies the following properties:
(a) Each source view is defined over source relations from the same data source.
(b) All the materialized views in the DW can be completely rewritten over the source views.
Note that source views need not necessarily be materialized. There might also be virtual.

Initially, the DW contains some materialized views. These views are used mainly for answering queries. We call these views here *primary views*. Some source views may be primary views (and thus are materialized). The rest of the source views are added to the DW for ensuring self-maintainability. These source views are called here *auxiliary views*, and they can be materialized or virtual.

The data sources. Each data source is autonomous and contains one or more relations referenced by the DW views. A data source is aware of all the source views that are defined over its own relations. The data sources compute incrementally the changes to be applied to the source views that are defined over their own relations. The source view changes are then transmitted to the DW.

Different maintenance timing policies, immediate or deferred, are possible. In an immediate policy, the changes of the source views are computed and propagated from the sources to the DW triggered by the transaction that updates the source relations. In a deferred policy, the propagation of the changes is delayed.

Change propagation at the DW. The source view changes are incrementally propagated to the materialized views that are affected by these changes, in the order they arrive at the DW. During this propagation, common subexpressions between the views are taken into account. Moreover, other materialized views that are not affected by these changes (in particular other source views, auxiliary or not) are exploited.

Our goal in this paper is to select source views that minimize the cost of computing the changes of the views materialized at the DW. If all these views are materialized, the DW is self-maintainable. However, we will show that in some cases, some or all of these views can be left virtual without compromising self-maintainability.

4   Multiexpression dags and change propagation at the DW

In this section, we introduce the notion of multiexpression AND/OR dags and their derivatives, and we show how we can propagate changes at the DW using change propagation dags.

4.1   Multiview dags

The views we consider here are algebraic expressions that have the SQL bag (multiset) semantics. Besides the traditional operators [3], the algebra includes also generalized projection operator [4, 9] to account for grouping/aggregation operations.

We use multiexpression AND/OR dags to compactly represent alternative evaluations of an algebraic expression and common subexpression sharing between different expresssions [11], extended with marked nodes to account for views materialized at the DW [13, 16].

Definition 1. Given a set of expressions **E** defined over a set of views (and/or relations) **U**, a *multiexpression AND/OR dag* $\mathcal{G}$ *for* **E** *over* **U** is a bipartite dag. The nodes of $\mathcal{G}$ are partitioned in AND nodes and OR nodes. An AND node is called *operation node* and is labeled by an operator while an OR node is called *view node* and is labeled by the expression (view) it computes. In the following we may identify nodes with their labels. An operation node has one or two outgoing edges to view nodes and one incoming edge from a view node. A view node has one or more outgoing edges (if any) to operation nodes and one or more incoming edges (if any) from an operation node. $\mathcal{G}$ is not necessarily a rooted dag (that is it does not necessarily have a single root). All the expressions in **E** appear in $\mathcal{G}$. All the root nodes of $\mathcal{G}$ are view nodes labeled by expressions in **E** (but not all the expressions in **E** label necessarily root nodes). The sink nodes in $\mathcal{G}$ are labeled by views in **U**. View nodes in a multiexpression AND/OR dag *can be marked*. Marked nodes represent materialized views.   □

A multiexpression dag is a special case of a multiexpression AND/OR dag that provides a single way for evaluating multiple expressions (AND dag). Let **V** be the set of views materialized in the DW, defined over a set of source relations **R**. These views are called *primary views.*

Definition 2. Consider the set **V** of primary views over a set of source relations **R**. A *multiview (AND/OR) dag* for **V** over **R** is a multiexpression (AND/OR) dag for **V** over **R** such that the views in **V** are the only marked nodes.   □

Example 1. Consider the source relation schemes $R_1(E, F)$, $S_1(A, B)$, $S_2(B, C)$, $S_3(C, D)$, $T_1(A, G)$, $T_2(G, H)$, and $T_3(H, D)$. Suppose that the corresponding relations are partitioned in three data sources. R_1 is stored in the first, S_1, S_2 and S_3 in the second, and T_1, T_2 and T_3 in the third. Let primary views V_1, V_2 and V_3 be defined over these relations. Figure 1 shows a multiview AND/OR

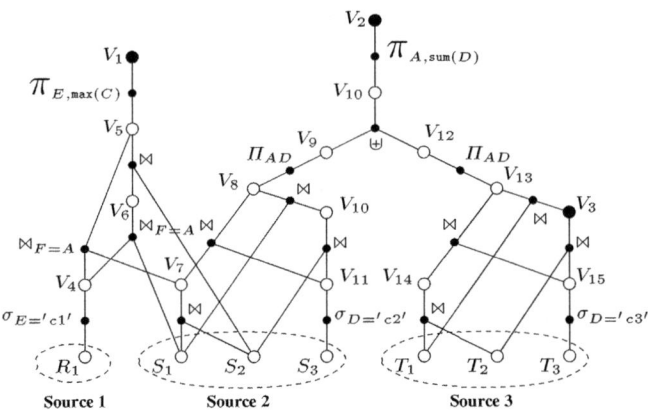

Fig. 1. A multiview AND/OR dag for $\{V_1, V_2, V_3\}$

dag $\mathcal{G}$ for $\{V_1, V_2, V_3\}$. Small circles represent operation nodes, while bigger ones represent view nodes. Black filled circles represent marked view nodes. Different ways of evaluating views V_1, V_2, and V_3 are represented by $\mathcal{G}$. Two of them are

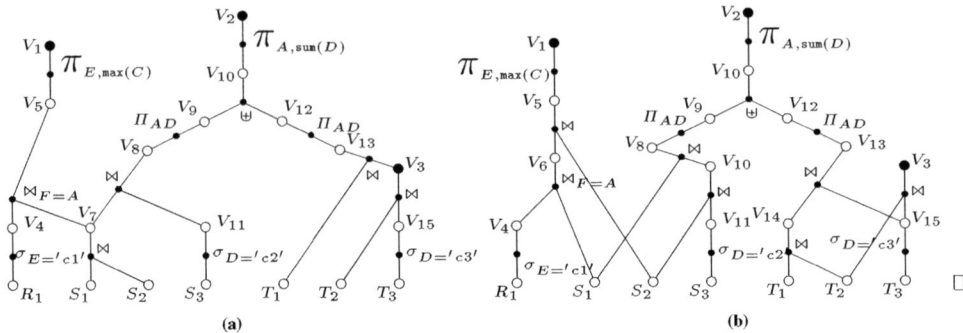

Fig. 2. Multiview dags for $\{V_1, V_2, V_3\}$

shown in Figure 2. Each of these two multiview dags depicts a way of evaluating the views V_1, V_2, and V_3.   □

4.2   Change propagation at the Data Warehouse

In order to discuss change propagation at the DW we use the notions of source view set and change propagation dag for a source view.

Definition 3. Let $\mathcal{G}$ be a multiview dag for a set of primary views $\mathbf{V}$ over a set of source relations $\mathbf{R}$. Assume that the relations in $\mathbf{R}$ are partitioned between different data sources. A *source view set* $\mathbf{V}_S$ in $\mathcal{G}$ is a set of views in $\mathcal{G}$ such that:
(a) every view in $\mathbf{V}_S$ is defined over relations from the same data source,
(b) for every marked node V in $\mathcal{G}$, V is in $\mathbf{V}_S$, or every path from V to a sink node includes a view node in $\mathbf{V}_S$, and
(c) every path from a marked node V to a view node U in $\mathbf{V}_S$ does not include a view node in $\mathbf{V}_S$ other than U, unless, U is a marked node, or there is a path from another marked node to U that does not include V.   □

Given $\mathbf{V}_S$, its elements are called *source views*. Some primary views may be source views as well, that is, $\mathbf{V}$ and $\mathbf{V}_S$ are not necessarily disjoint. The views in $\mathbf{V}_S - \mathbf{V}$ are called *auxiliary views*.

Clearly, there may be many different source view sets in a multiview dag. Also, a set of views can be a source view set in different multiview dags. A trivial source view set in any multiview dag is the set of source relations.

Example 2. Figure 2(a) shows a multiview dag. The view sets $\{V_4, V_7, V_{11}, T_1, V_3\}$ and $\{V_4, V_7, V_9, V_{12}, V_3\}$ are source view sets in this multiview dag. The view set $\{V_4, S_1, S_2, V_{10}, V_{14}, T_2, V_{15}\}$ is a source view set in the multiview dag of Figure 2(b).   □

Definition 4. Consider a multiview dag $\mathcal{G}$, a source view set $\mathbf{V}_S$ in $\mathcal{G}$, and a source view V in $\mathbf{V}_S$. Let $\mathbf{V}'$ be the set of views V' in $\mathbf{V}$ such that there is a path in $\mathcal{G}$ from V' to V that does not include a source view node in $\mathbf{V}_S$ other than V. A *change propagation dag for V in $\mathcal{G}$* is a multiexpression dag $\mathcal{G}_V$ for $\mathbf{V}'$ over $\mathbf{V} \cup \mathbf{V}_S$ such that: (a) $\mathcal{G}_V$ is a subdag of $\mathcal{G}$, (b) V is a sink node in $\mathcal{G}_V$, (c) the source views in $\mathbf{V}_S$ that appear in $\mathcal{G}_V$ are sink nodes, and (d) the marked view nodes that appear in $\mathcal{G}_V$ are sink nodes or ancestor nodes of V.   □

Example 3. Consider the multiview dag of Figure 3(a) and the source view set $\{V_4, V_7, V_{11}, T_1, V_3\}$. Figure 3 shows a change propagation dag for V_7. In the same multiview dag, consider the source view set $\{V_4, V_7, V_9, V_{12}, V_3\}$. Figure

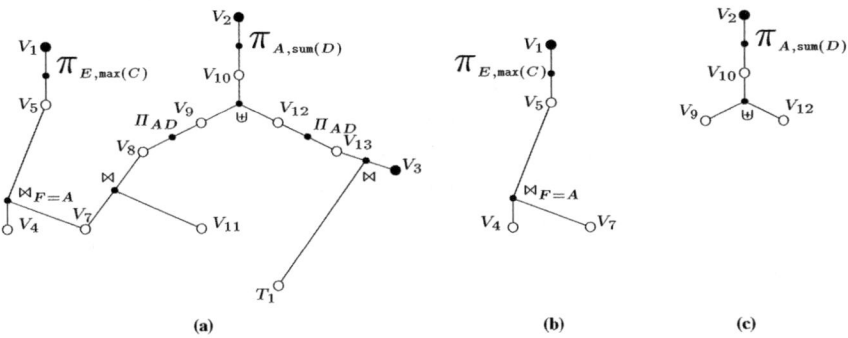

(a)   (b)   (c)

Fig. 3. Change propagation dags (a) for V_7, (b) for V_7 (and V_4), (c) for V_9 (and V_{12}).

3(b) shows a change propagation dag for V_7. This is also a change propagation dag for V_4. Figure 3(c) shows a change propagation dag for V_9 (and for V_{12}). □

Change propagation dags can be used to propagate source view changes to the primary views. We consider deletions and insertions of multisets of tuples. Thus, the changes of a view or relation V are represented by a multiset of tuples, ∇V, to be deleted from, and a multiset of tuples, ΔV, to be insert into V. Modifications are modeled by deletions followed by insertions. In order to avoid wasteful insertions and deletions, as well as wasteful data transmissions, we assume that ∇V and ΔV are defined to be strongly minimal [3]: $\nabla V \doteq V = \emptyset$ and $\nabla V \min \Delta V = \emptyset$.

The propagation of the changes of the source views to the primary views that are affected by these changes can be performed separately for each affected primary view. Using change propagation dags in this process allows the exploitation of common subexpressions between the views, and the use of other materialized views (primary or auxiliary) that are not affected by these changes. Changes are propagated bottom-up along a change propagation dag $\mathcal{G}_V$ for a source view V, starting with view V. The changes of V are computed by the corresponding data source. Clearly, the view nodes that are affected by the changes of V in $\mathcal{G}_V$ are the ancestor nodes of V. The changes of an affected view node in $\mathcal{G}_V$ are computed using the changes of its child view node(s). The maintenance expressions provided in [3] for the typical algebraic operators and in [9] for the generalized projection operator allow this computation.

It is not difficult to see that if we additionally materialize in the DW all the auxiliary views of a source view set, the resulting DW is self-maintainable.

5   Determining virtual views in a source view set

Consider a set of source views $\mathbf{V}_S$ in a multiview dag $\mathcal{G}$ for a set of primary views $\mathbf{V}$. In this section we show that in some cases self-maintainability is preserved, even if some or all of the auxiliary views are virtual. For a given source view set $\mathbf{V}_S$, this characterization of the auxiliary views depends on the multiview dag $\mathcal{G}$. Our goal is to derive a materialized/virtual function $mv(G)$ on $\mathbf{V}_S$ − $\mathbf{V}$ that determines which auxiliary views have to be materialized and which auxiliary views can be left virtual. The method is based on the approach of [13] for detecting redundant views in a DW.

The expressions that compute the changes of a view node using the changes of its child view node(s) in a change propagation dag do not necessarily involve this view node and its child view node(s). Our method uses information derived by these expressions and proceeds by a top-down scan of a change propagation dag. This way, it can be deduced whether the materialization of an auxiliary view node U is needed for the computation of the changes of an ancestor view node of U in the change propagation dag. If it is not needed by any ancestor view node in any of the change propagation dags for the source views of $\mathbf{V}_S$ in $\mathcal{G}$, the auxiliary view U can be left virtual. Thus $mv(\mathcal{G})(U) = 0$. Otherwise, U must be materialized and $mv(\mathcal{G})(U) = 1$. We outline the method by an example.

Example 4. Figure 2(a) shows a multiview dag $\mathcal{G}$ for the set of primary views $\mathbf{V} = \{V_1, V_2, V_3\}$. The set $\mathbf{V}_S = \{V_4, V_7, V_9, V_{12}, V_3\}$ is a source view set in $\mathcal{G}$. The set of auxiliary views is $\mathbf{V}_S - \mathbf{V} = \{V_4, V_7, V_9, V_{12}\}$.

Consider the change propagation dag for V_9 in $\mathcal{G}$ (Figure 3(c)). View node V_{10} is not needed for the computation of the changes of view node V_2. This can be derived from the expression that computes the changes of a view defined by a generalized projection operation, involving the aggregate function *sum*, on another view [9]. The changes of V_{10} are computed using only the changes of V_9: $\nabla V_{10} = \nabla V_9$ and $\Delta V_{10} = \Delta V_9$. Therefore, the auxiliary views V_9 and V_{12} are not needed in the change propagation dag for V_9 in $\mathcal{G}$. By symmetry, V_9 and V_{12} are not needed in the change propagation dag for V_{12} in $\mathcal{G}$ (which is again the change propagation dag shown in Figure 3(c)). The other change propagation dags for the source views of $\mathbf{V}_S$ in $\mathcal{G}$ do not involve V_9 or V_{12}. We deduce that the auxiliary views V_9 and V_{12} can be left virtual with respect to $\mathcal{G}$, that is $mv(\mathcal{G})(V_9) = mv(\mathcal{G})(V_{12}) = 0$. □

6   Selecting an optimal source view set

In this section we show how an optimal source view set can be computed. To do so we first introduce the notion of an export view set. We then outline an algorithm that computes the optimal source view set.

6.1   Export view sets

Export view sets are defined as follows:

Definition 5. Consider a multiview dag $\mathcal{G}$ for a set of primary views **V** over a set of source relations **R**. Assume that the relations in **R** are partitioned between different data sources. The *export view set* $\mathbf{V}_E$ in $\mathcal{G}$ is a set that contains the following views: (a) the primary views in $\mathcal{G}$ that are defined over relations from the same data source, and (b) every view in $\mathcal{G}$, defined over relations from the same data source, that has a parent view node defined over relations from more than one data source.   □

Example 5. Figures 2(a) and (b) show two multiview dags. The view sets $\{V_4, V_7, V_9, V_{12}, V_3\}$ and $\{V_4, S_1, S_2, V_9, V_{12}, V_3\}$ are the export view sets in these multiview dags respectively.   □

Intuitively, the export views in a multiview dag represent the most "complex" views that can be "exported" from each data source to construct the primary views in the DW. It can be shown that an export view set is a source view set. A procedure that computes all the export views sets in a multiview AND/OR dag is provided in [14].

6.2   An algorithm for selecting an optimal source view set

We outline now an algorithm [14] that computes an optimal solution to the problem. This algorithm operates on the multiquery AND/OR dag $\mathcal{G}$ and returns as output a solution, that is, a source view set $\mathbf{V}_S$ in a multiquery dag $\mathcal{G}$, the set of change propagation dags in $\mathcal{G}$, and the materialized/virtual function $mv(\mathcal{G})$ on $\mathbf{V}_S - \mathbf{V}$. The algorithm systematically generates, considers and examines different source view sets in $\mathcal{G}$. Source view sets that have to be considered are kept in the set $OPEN$. Those that have already been examined are kept in the set $CLOSED$. The triple $SOLUTION$ keeps the best solution found that far, while the variable MS keeps the corresponding change propagation cost.

When a source view set $\mathbf{V}_S$ under examination contains views that are not source relations or primary views, new source view sets can be generated from it as follows: for every view V in $\mathbf{V}_S$ that is not a source relation or a primary view, and for every child operation node O of V in $\mathcal{G}$, V is replaced in $\mathbf{V}_S$ by its child view node(s) in $\mathcal{G}$.

The following remark is central in the design of the algorithm. Let $\mathbf{V}_S$ and $\mathbf{V}'_S$ be two source view sets in a multiview dag $\mathcal{G}$ such that $\mathbf{V}'_S$ is generated from $\mathbf{V}_S$. This implies that every view node in $\mathbf{V}'_S$ is a descendant of or coincides with a view node in $\mathbf{V}_S$. Thus, every change propagation dag in $\mathcal{G}$ for a view in $\mathbf{V}_S$ is a subdag of a change propagation dag in $\mathcal{G}$ for a view in $\mathbf{V}'_S$. Consequently, the change propagation cost of $\mathbf{V}'_S$ in $\mathcal{G}$ is greater than that of $\mathbf{V}_S$ in $\mathcal{G}$. The same holds in every multiview dag in which $\mathbf{V}_S$ and $\mathbf{V}'_S$ are source view sets and $\mathbf{V}'_S$ can be generated from $\mathbf{V}_S$. Exploiting this remark in the algorithm, new source view sets are not generated from a source view set $\mathbf{V}_S$ under examination if the change propagation cost associated with the best solution found that far is less than or equal to that of $\mathbf{V}_S$. Note however that a source view set $\mathbf{V'}_S$ that has not been generated by $\mathbf{V}_S$ may be examined during the execution of the algorithm since it may be generated by another source view set.

Initially the algorithm generates the set of export view sets in $\mathcal{G}$, and keeps them in the set $OPEN$ for consideration. The algorithm repeatedly considers source view sets from the set $OPEN$. When a source view set is considered, it is removed from the set $OPEN$ and is compared with the source views sets in the set $CLOSED$. The algorithm examines a source view set under consideration only if it is not found in $CLOSED$. Thus, the reexamination of the same source view set is avoided. When a source view set $\mathbf{V}_S$ is examined, its change propagation cost, $mcost(\mathbf{V}_S)$, is compared with the change propagation cost, MS, associated with the best solution found that far. It is further examined only if $mcost(\mathbf{V}_S) < MS$. Examination continues by computing the materialized/virtual function $mv(\mathcal{G})$ for all the multiview dags $\mathcal{G}$ in which $\mathbf{V}_S$ is a source view set. From these multiview dags those that determine a materialized/virtual function on $\mathbf{V}_S - \mathbf{V}$ satisfying the space constraint on the auxiliary views of $\mathbf{V}_S$ are selected. The minimal change propagation cost M of $\mathbf{V}_S$ in a multiview dag $\mathcal{G}$ that can be obtained by considering only the last multiview dags is compared with MS. If $M < MS$, $SOLUTION$ and MS are updated using $\mathbf{V}_S$, $\mathcal{G}$, and M. Otherwise, new source view sets are generated from $\mathbf{V}_S$, if possible, and are added to the set $OPEN$. The algorithm stops when no source view sets are left in the set $OPEN$ for consideration. If no source view set is found that satisfies the space constraint in a multiview dag, an empty solution is returned.

An important feature of the previous algorithm is that it computes the optimal solution without necessarily examining all possible source view sets in the multiview AND/OR dag $\mathcal{G}$. If there are no space constraints, the algorithm computes the optimal solution by generating only the export view sets in $\mathcal{G}$.

7   Conclusion

Reducing the cost of incrementally maintaining materialized views is an important challenge when implementing a DW. One way to satisfy this goal is to make the DW self-maintainable by additionally materializing auxiliary views. Previous approaches to this issue, in the absence of additional information, materialize auxiliary views that are select-project views on the source relations, and restrict the role of the data sources in filtering the changes of each source relation. Changes of different source relations are not combined together.

Here we consider that the data sources are of cooperative type, and can hold multiple relations. Under this assumption we present a generic model for a self-maintainable DW over these sources. Using an AND/OR dag structure for representing multiple views, we formalize the problem of making the DW self-maintainable by materializing complex auxiliary views. These auxiliary views are defined over relations from the same data source and can involve multiple unary and binary operators. We provide an algorithm that selects such a set of views, while satisfying a constraint on the space available for materialization and minimizing the cost of propagating the changes to the materialized views. We show that in certain cases self-maintainability is not compromised if some auxiliary views are left virtual. This can result in important space savings and is due to the fact that the auxiliary views can be complex, involving multiple relations.

An extension of the present work involves addressing the problem of making a DW self-maintainable by selecting complex views in the presence of integrity constraints.

References

1. M. O. Akinde, O. G. Jensen, and M. H. Böhlen. Minimizing Detail Data in Data Warehouses. In *Proc. of EDBT*, pages 293–307, 1998.
2. J. A. Blakeley, N. Coburn, and P. A. Larson. Updating derived relations: detecting irrelevant and autonomously computable updates. *ACM TODS*, 14(3), 1989.
3. T. Griffin and L. Libkin. Incremental Maintenance of Views with Duplicates. In *Proc. ACM SIGMOD*, pages 328–339, 1995.
4. A. Gupta, V. Harinarayan, and D. Quass. Aggregate-Query Processing in Data Warehousing Environments. In *Proc. of VLDB*, pages 358–369, 1995.
5. A. Gupta, H. Jagadish, and I. S. Mumick. Data Integration using Self-Maintainable Views. In *Proc. of EDBT*, pages 140–144, 1996.
6. R. Hull and G. Zhou. A Framework for Supporting Data Integration Using the Materialized and Virtual Approaches. In *ACM SIGMOD*, pages 481–492, 1996.
7. W. Liang, H. Li, H. Wang, and M. E. Orlowska. Making Multiple Views Self-Maintainable in a Data Warehouse. *DKE*, 30(2):121–134, 1999.
8. M. Mohania and Y. Kambayashi. Making Aggregate Views Self-Maintainable. *Data and Knowledge Engineering*, 32(1):87–109, 2000.
9. D. Quass. Maintenance Expressions for Views with Aggregation. In *Workshop on Materialized Views: Techniques and Applications*, pages 110–118, 1996.
10. D. Quass, A. Gupta, I. S. Mumick, and J. Widom. Making Views Self Maintainable for Data Warehousing. In *Proc. of PDIS*, pages 158–169, 1996.
11. K. A. Ross, D. Srivastava, and S. Sudarshan. Materialized View Maintenance and Integrity Constraint Checking: Trading Space for Time. In *Proc. of the ACM SIGMOD Intl. Conf. on Management of Data*, pages 447–458, 1996.
12. O. Shmueli and A. Itai. Maintenance of Views. In *Proc. of the ACM SIGMOD Intl. Conf. on Management of Data*, pages 240–255, 1984.
13. D. Theodoratos. Detecting Redundancy in Data Warehouse Evolution. In *Proc. of the 18th Intl. Conf. on Conceptual Modeling*, pages 340–353, 1999.
14. D. Theodoratos. Complex View Selection for DW Self-Maintainability. *Technical Report, Knowledge and Data Base Systems Laboratory, Electrical and Computer Engineering Dept., National Technical University of Athens*, Apr. 2000.
15. D. Theodoratos and T. Sellis. Designing Data Warehouses. *Data and Knowledge Engineering*, 31(3):279–301, Oct. 1999.
16. D. Theodoratos and T. Sellis. Incremental Design of a Data Warehouse. To appear in *Journal of Intelligent Information Systems*, 2000.
17. G. Zhou, R. Hull, and R. King. Generating Data Integration Mediators that Use Materialization. *Journal of Intelligent Information Systems*, 6(2):199–221, 1996.
18. Y. Zhuge, H. Garcia-Molina, J. Hammer, and J. Widom. View Maintenance in a Warehousing Environment. In *Proc. of ACM SIGMOD*, pages 316–327, 1995.

Integrating Snapshot Isolation Into Transactional Federations

Ralf Schenkel and Gerhard Weikum
University of the Saarland
P.O.-Box 15 11 50
D-66041 Saarbrücken
Fax +49 681 302 4014
email {schenkel,weikum}@cs.uni-sb.de

Abstract. This paper reconsiders the problem of transactional federations, more specifically the concurrency control issue, with particular consideration of component systems that provide only snapshot isolation, which is the default setting in Oracle and widely used in practice. The paper derives criteria and practical protocols for guaranteeing global serializability at the federation level. The paper generalizes the well-known ticket method and develops novel federation-level graph testing methods to incorporate sub-serializability component systems like Oracle. These contributions are embedded in a practical project that built a CORBA-based federated database architecture suitable for modern Internet- or Intranet-based applications such as electronic commerce. This prototype system, which includes a federated transaction manager coined Trafic (Transactional Federation of Information Systems Based on CORBA), has been fully implemented with support for Oracle and O₂ as component systems and using Orbix as federation middleware. The paper presents performance measurements that demonstrate the viability of the developed concurrency control methods.

1 Introduction

1.1 Objectives of a Transactional Federation

With the ever-increasing demand for information integration both within and across enterprises, on one hand, and the proliferation of gateway and other middleware technologies such as ODBC, DCOM, JEB, or CORBA, on the other hand, there is renewed interest in providing seamless access to multiple, independently developed and largely autonomously operated databases [Ston98,HSC99,MK+99]. Such a setting is known as a database federation or heterogeneous multidatabase system. More specifically, the approach of building an additional integration software layer on top of the underlying component systems is referred to as a *federated database system* [SL90,ÖV98]. Among the challenges posed by such a system architecture is the problem of enforcing the consistency of the data across the boundaries of the individual component systems. Transactions that access and modify data in more than one component system are referred to as *federated* or *global transactions* [BGS92]; for example, an electronic commerce application could require a transaction to update data in a merchant's database as well as the databases of a credit card company and a service broker that pointed the customer to the merchant and requests a provisioning fee for each sale. Providing the usual ACID properties for such federated transactions is inherently harder than in a homogeneous, centrally administered distributed database system, one reason being that the underlying component systems of a federation may employ different protocols for their local transaction management.

Problems of ensuring the global serializability and atomicity of federated transactions have been intensively studied in the past. The proposed solutions range from imposing additional constraints on the transaction protocols of the component systems to building an additional transaction manager in the federated software layer [Weihl89, BGRS91,BS92,Raz92,GRS94]. However, none of the proposed approaches can by any means be considered as the universally "best" strategy for federated concurrency control. Rather the choice of the most appropriate strategy depends on the transaction protocols of the component systems, the operational characteristics of the applications, and other factors. Therefore a federated transaction manager should support a suite of different strategies and allow the application builder (or administrator staff) to select

O. Etzion and P. Scheuermann (Eds.): CoopIS 2000, LNCS 1901, pp. 90–101, 2000.
© Springer-Verlag Berlin Heidelberg 2000

the most suitable protocols for the federation. In addition, it should be extensible to incorporate new transaction management strategies, specifically tailored to the needs of the application at hand. Furthermore, the federation must be able to cope with different isolation levels [BBGM+95] in the underlying component systems, for example, the "snapshot isolation" provided by Oracle [Orac99]. Such options for relaxed (local) serializability are widely popular in practice. They have only recently attracted also the research community with emphasis on formal properties [ALO00,ABJ97,BLL00, FLO+99,SW+99], but have still been more or less disregarded in the literature on federated transaction management.

1.2   Problems With Component Systems Providing Snapshot Isolation

This paper specifically addresses the problem of federated concurrency control for transactional federations based on component systems some of which provide only snapshot isolation. Note that Oracle falls into that category; although it can provide also full serializability using table locking, snapshot isolation is the best setting that can be achieved without extra coding in the application programs and widely used in practice. Further note that already running global transactions against multiple, autonomous Oracle instances all of which use the same snapshot-isolation protocol poses severe correctness problems as the resulting global execution cannot even be guaranteed to be globally snapshot-isolated. When different Oracle instances employ different isolation levels or the federation includes also database systems that provide full serializability, it becomes even more unclear how to guarantee global data consistency. As for global transaction atomicity and durability, on the other hand, a transactional federation can rely on the logging and recovery capabilities of the underlying component systems in conjunction with a standardized distributed commit protocol like XA or its CORBA counterpart OTS, as supported by virtually all commercial database systems. Therefore, this paper focuses on the concurrency control dimension of transactional federations.

For (local) transactions run under the *snapshot isolation* level, or *SI* for short, all operations read the most recent versions as of the time when the transaction began, thus ensuring a consistent view of the data through the transaction. A particularly beneficial special case is that all read-only transactions are perfectly isolated in the sense of the multiversion serializability theory [BHG87]. For read-write transactions, on the other hand, the sketched protocol cannot ensure (multiversion) serializability. In addition, Oracle performs the following check upon acquiring a write lock: if the data object to be locked has been written by another, already committed transaction that ran concurrently to the considered one (i.e., committed after the considered transaction began), then the current transaction is aborted and rolled back. This check aims to provide an additional level of sanity. Nonetheless, the protocol cannot ensure full (multiversion) serializability, with the following schedule as a counterexample (operation subscripts are transaction identifiers, x_i denotes the version of x generated by transaction t_i, and t_0 is a fictitious initializing transaction):

$$r_1(x_0)\ r_1(y_0) \qquad r_2(x_0)\ r_2(y_0) \qquad\qquad w_1(x_1)\ c_1 \qquad\qquad w_2(y_2)\ c_2$$

The example may lead to inconsistent data, for example, violating a constraint such as $x + y < 100$ although both transactions alone would enforce the constraint. Given that such anomalies appear to be infrequent in practice, the protocol is widely used in Oracle applications. However, although application architects accept the risk of inconsistencies, they are not happy with his state of affairs, especially as applications become more complex, span organizational boundaries, and become even more mission-critical for business success.

1.3   Contribution and Outline of the Paper

The paper's contributions are threefold:

- We develop a formal model that allows us to reason about local versus global snapshot isolation and serializability in the context of federated transactions.
- Based on this model, we develop novel algorithms for federated concurrency control to ensure global serializability. Our algorithms leverage prior proposals, specifically the ticket method [GRS94] and federation-level graph testing with edges derived from SQL-

statement predicates [BGS92,SSW95], and generalize them for the newly considered setting with component systems that provide only local snapshot isolation (e.g., Oracle). In particular, we introduce a novel type of *online Snapshot-Isolation Multiversion-Serializability Graph (OSI-MVSG)* that allows us to enforce global serializability on top of component systems that merely provide snapshot isolation.

- We have implemented a full-fledged prototype of a transactional federation supporting Oracle and O_2 as component systems and using Orbix as middleware technology. We present performance measurements in a real system environment (as opposed to mere simulations) that demonstrate the viability of the developed methods and compare their performance properties.

The rest of the paper is organized as follows. In Section 2, we introduce the basic model and notations, and we develop the theoretical underpinnings for coping with snapshot isolation in concurrent transaction executions. Section 3 reconsiders established protocols for global serializability in the case that some systems provide only snapshot isolation, and develops a practically viable protocol to guarantee global serializability in this case. Section 4 presents the architecture of the fully operational prototype implementation. In Section 5, we discuss performance measurements of the presented algorithms. We conclude the paper with an outlook on future work.

2   Formal Underpinnings and Basic Techniques

2.1   Notation

A *transaction* t_i is a sequence, i.e., total order $<$, of read and write actions on data objects from one or more databases, along with a set of begin and commit actions, one for each database accessed by t_i, such that all begin actions precede all read and write actions in the order $<$ and all commit actions follow all other actions w.r.t. $<$. For all transactions, we further restrict the sequence of read and write accesses to allow a write on object x only if there the transaction includes also a read on x that precedes the write in the action order $<$.

A *global transaction (GT)* is a transaction that accesses objects from at least two different databases. In contrast, a *local transaction (LT)* accesses only a single database. The projection of a global transaction t_i onto a database DB_k is the set of actions of t_i that refer to objects from DB_k, along with their corresponding order $<$. This projection will be referred to as a *global subtransaction (GST)* and denoted by $t_i^{(k)}$. For the scope of this paper, we assume that all LTs are known to the federation layer. This can be accomplished by simple request/reply re-routing without any modification of the code of LT applications.

A *schedule* of transactions $T=\{t_1, ...\}$ is a sequence, i.e., total order $<$, of the union of the actions of all transactions in T such that the action ordering within transactions is preserved. A *multiversion schedule* of transactions $T=\{t_1, ...\}$ is a schedule with an additional *version function* that maps each read action $r_i(x)$ in the schedule to a write action $w_j(x)$ that precedes the read in the order $<$. The read action is then also written as $r_i(x_j)$ with x_j denoting the version created by the write of t_j. A *monoversion schedule* of transactions $T=\{t_1, ...\}$ is a multiversion schedule whose version function maps each read action $r_i(x)$ to the most recent write action $w_j(x)$ that precedes it (i.e., $w_j(x) < r_i(x)$ and there is no other write action on x in between).

The usual correctness criterion for multiversion concurrency control is that a given multiversion schedule should be view-equivalent to a serial monoversion schedule, with view-equivalence being defined by the reads-from relation among the actions of a schedule [BHG87]. A means of testing this is the *multiversion serialization graph* (MVSG) for a schedule, which is acyclic if and only if the schedule is multiversion serializable.

A multiversion schedule of transactions $T=\{t_1, ...\}$ satisfies the criterion of *snapshot isolation (SI)* if the following two conditions hold:

(SI-V)   *SI version function*: The version function maps each read action $r_i(x)$ to the most recent committed write action $w_j(x)$ as of the time of the begin of t_i,

(SI-W)   *disjoint writesets*: The writesets of two concurrent transactions are disjoint.

MVSR and SI are incompatible in that neither of the two classes contains the other. In [SW+99], we developed a graph characterization for schedules in SI, the so-called SI-MVSG, that extends the MVSG from multiversion serializability theory.

2.2   Characterization of Serializability on Top of Snapshot Isolation

In our context of transactional federations we are faced with the problem of having to guarantee serializability on top of an existing mechanism that we know to guarantee snapshot isolation. This problem is of practical interest already for a single component system like Oracle if the application demands full serializability. Oracle's recommendation to this end is to have the application programs explicitly lock, e.g., through the SQL "Select ... For Update ..." command, all relevant data in a transaction including read-only data. Another approach, inspired by earlier work on graph-based techniques for multidatabase transactions [BGS92], that we are going to exploit in our protocols is to maintain an online version of the SI-MVSG on top of the component system(s) and test it for cycles. Note that the earlier work was restricted to conventional conflict graphs aiming at conflict-serializability, whereas we consider a multiversion serialization graph. We introduce our novel concept here for the centralized (i.e., single-component) case, and will later leverage the result for the distributed (i.e., multi-component) case.

Definition: (OSI-MVSG)
The Online Snapshot Isolation Multiversion Serialization Graph *(OSI-MVSG)* for a given execution s satisfying (SI-V) is a directed graph with transactions as nodes and edges built by the following rules, as operations are submitted:

(i)   When a transaction begins, it is added to the graph.

(ii)   When a transaction t_i issues operation $r_i(x)$, then for all transactions t_j in the graph that issued an operation $w_j(x)$ before,
   a)   an edge $t_i \rightarrow t_j$ is added to the graph if t_j and t_i are concurrent,
   b)   an edge $t_j \rightarrow t_i$ is added to the graph if t_j was committed before t_i began,
   and each of the edges is labeled with x.

(iii)   When a transaction t_i issues operation $w_i(x)$, then for all transactions t_j in the graph that issued an operation $r_j(x)$ before, an edge $t_j \rightarrow t_i$ labeled with x is added to the graph. Additionally, if there is a transaction t_j in the graph concurrent to t_i that issued $w_j(x)$ before, an edge $t_j \rightarrow t_i$ labeled with x is added to the graph.

(iv)   A transaction is removed from the graph as soon as it is committed, all the transactions running concurrently with it are committed, and it is a source in the graph.   ∎

Note that although the OSI-MVSG is very similar to a standard conflict graph, it differs from a conflict graph in a subtle but important way by the edges created according to rule (ii) a) which capture the (SI-V) property of snapshot isolation. The practical relevance of the OSI-MVSG construction stems from the following theorem.

Theorem 1 (correctness of OSI-MVSG cycle testing):
A concurrency control algorithm based on OSI-MVSG allows only executions that are
(i)   serializable if it rejects an operation when the added edges lead to a cycle in the graph,
(ii)   snapshot isolated if it rejects an operation on object x when the added edges lead to a cycle that consists only of edges labeled with x.   ∎

The OSI-MVSG can be implemented on top of one or more component systems. The resulting global OSI-MVSG is a nicely versatile data structure as it can be used for 1) testing if an execution is serializable (i.e., no cycle exists) and 2) testing if an execution is snapshot isolated (i.e., no cycle exists where all predicates on the edges are conflicting with each other), whichever is considered the appropriate correctness criterion for the transactional federation.

As we cannot directly observe the underlying read and write accesses to the stored data, we need to build an approximation of the reads-from relationship or the conflict relations of the various component systems based on the operations that global transactions submit. In our implementation, we have adopted the approach of [SSW95] for analyzing potential conflicts between the predicates of SQL commands. We monitor the actions of global subtransactions and derive predicates that characterize the objects accessed by those subtransactions. Read operations are usually caused by SQL select statements, so we can use the search predicate of that statement to characterize all objects returned by that statement. For example, if a subtransaction submits the query "select p from parts where p.color=green or (p.price>100 and p.weight>7)", the predicates "color=green" and "price=100 and weight<7" characterize exactly those subsets of the complete relation "parts" that the subtransaction reads. When the query involves a join, the join predicates are decomposed into separate predicates on each of the joined tables thus disregarding the join predicate itself but keeping all filter predicates on each of the tables; these filter predicates are themselves converted into disjunctive normal form for efficient bookkeeping and conflict testing. Using the same technique, we can analogously derive predicates for SQL updates, inserts and deletes. Based on those predicates, we then say that a subtransaction t_j *potentially reads from* another committed subtransaction t_i, if the subsets that t_i updated and those that t_j read are overlapping, i.e., the conjunction of the predicates is satisfiable. This may actually add nonexisting reads-from or conflict relations, because we can only approximate the set of objects being accessed. However, this approximation is conservative in capturing all real reads-from relationships, so that we can guarantee the correctness of an algorithm that is based on the approximated reads-from or conflict relation.

3   Guaranteeing Global Serializability

Although SI is a popular option in practice, many mission-critical applications cannot afford the (whatever small) risk of data becoming inconsistent and therefore require full serializability. Then global SI as a correctness criterion, albeit "almost correct" with regard to the applications' needs, will not be good enough.

As an example consider the following federated version of the introduction's example for a non-serializable but SI schedule:

$$DB_1 \qquad r_1^{(1)}(x) \qquad\qquad r_2^{(1)}(x) \qquad\qquad w_1^{(1)}(x) \qquad\qquad c_1\ c_2$$
$$DB_2: \qquad\qquad r_1^{(2)}(y) \qquad\qquad r_2^{(2)}(y) \qquad\qquad w_2^{(2)}(y)\ c_1\ c_2$$

In this scenario, a global consistency constraint that relates the values of objects x and y could not be guaranteed. For example, a condition such as $x + y < 100$ could be violated although each individual transaction would preserve the constraint if it were executed alone. The problem could be rectified, of course, by requesting the application programmers to take additional measures such as manually acquiring stronger locks in the underlying component systems or extending the programs by an application-level notification or other synchronization mechanism. However, this would seriously impede application development productivity, and make applications more complex and thus more software-failure-prone. Federated systems should become no more difficult to use than today's centralized systems, neither at the application nor the system-administration level.

3.1   Extending the Ticket Technique

The ticket technique was introduced by Georgakopoulos et al [GRS94] as an elegant and flexible way to derive local serialization orders and, based on that, guarantee global serializability, for local SR schedulers. It requires that each global subtransaction reads the current value of a dedicated counter-type object, the so-called ticket, and writes back an increased value at some point during its execution. The ordering of the ticket values read by two global subtransaction reflects the local serialization order of the two subtransactions. Incompatible serialization orders are detected by the means of a *ticket graph* that is maintained at the federation level and whose edges reflect the local serialization orders. The global schedule is serializable if and only if the ticket graph does not contain a cycle.

This technique is easy and efficient to implement. For component systems with special properties (e.g., allowing only rigorous local schedules) further optimizations are possible, so that the ticket technique has the particularly nice property of incurring only as much overhead as necessary for each component system. This makes the ticket method a very elegant and versatile algorithm for federated concurrency control.

The ticket method has two potential problems, however. First, the ticket object may be a potential bottleneck in a component database. Second and much more severely, having to write the ticket turns read-only transactions into read-write transactions.

When the ticket technique is applied on top of local SI schedulers, it is evident that every global subtransaction in a component database writes at least one common object, namely the ticket. Because SI enforces disjoint writesets of concurrent transactions, all but one of several concurrent subtransactions will be aborted by the local scheduler. The resulting local schedule is therefore trivially serializable, because it is in fact already serial, and the ordering of the ticket values of two global subtransactions reflects their local serial(ization) order. Nevertheless, sequentializing all global subtransactions in SI component systems is a dramatic loss of performance and would usually be considered as an overly high price for global consistency.

The results we have presented up to now may lead to the impression that the ticket technique is unusable for SI component systems. In [SW+99] we developed an extension of the ticket technique that can overcome its disadvantages for many typical applications; we only give a short overview here. In fact, many real-life application environments are dominated by read-only transactions, but exhibit infrequent read-write transactions as well. Each global subtransaction and local transaction has to be marked "read-only" or "read-write" at its beginning; an unmarked transaction is supposed to be read-write by default. A global transaction is read-only if all its subtransactions are read-only; otherwise it is a global read-write transaction.

Our extended ticket method requires that all global read-write transactions are executed serially. That is, the federated transaction manager has to ensure that at most one global read-write transaction is active at a time. Each read-write subtransaction of a global transaction takes a ticket as in the standard ticket, its read-only subtransactions are treated as those of a global read-only transaction. Note that tickets are still necessary for global read-write transactions to correctly handle the potential interference with local transactions. Although the sequentialization of global read-write transactions appears very restrictive, it is no more restrictive than in the original ticket method if SI component systems are part of the federation.

In our extension of the ticket versions, read-only subtransactions, on the other hand, need only read the ticket. This avoids making them read-write and being forced sequential. A feasible solution is to assign to a read-only subtransaction a ticket value that is strictly in between the value that was actually read from the ticket object and the next higher possible value that a read-write subtransaction may write into the ticket object. This approach can be implemented very easily. The fact that this may result in multiple read-only subtransactions with the same ticket value is acceptable in our protocol.

3.2   Multilevel Transactions

Multilevel transactions have been pursued for transactional federations in the earlier work of [DSW94,SSW95] as a means for reducing the duration for which locks are held in the underlying component systems (or, more generally, the scope of the local concurrency control measures if a non-locking protocol is used). To this end, each high-level operation that is passed to a component system is handled as if it were a separate, purely local and fairly short, transaction. This ensures the atomicity and isolation of individual high-level operations. On top of this, the federation layer needs to keep additional, long-duration higher-level locks or take equivalent steps such as cycle testing on a graph in order to guarantee that the entire, multi-operation transactions appear atomic and semantically serializable to the clients. The high-level operations at the federation layer could be semantically rich methods on appropriately defined object types such as deposit or withdraw operations on bank account objects, or they could correspond to the SQL commands that typically constitute the interface of a component system. In the latter case, which has been studied in detail in [SSW95], the federation layer needs to extract appropriate predicates from the SQL commands as the basis for its own additional predicate locking. An inevitable consequence of committing each high-level operation as a separate transaction as early as possible is that undoing an entire client transaction, e.g., on behalf of a client-requested rollback, entails issueing compensating actions for the already committed transactions of the underlying component systems.

In the context of component systems that merely support SI, multilevel transactions do not necessarily guarantee semantic serializability. The reason is that the individual high-level operations from different client transactions are not fully isolated. So the pathological (i.e., consistency-violating) scenario shown at the beginning of Section 3 could arise between two individual high-level operations (on behalf of two different client transactions), and this effect would not be known to the federation layer. However, if such critical cases can be identified by the application architect, the federation layer could acquire appropriately strong semantic locks so as to prevent such concurrent scenarios in the underlying component systems. So whenever local SI is potentially insufficient, the federation layer would simply block the second high-level operations from being issued to the component system until the ongoing operation is completed. Obviously this approach requires a deep understanding of the application's semantics and consistency requirements. Thus we do not consider the multilevel-transaction protocol as the method of choice for transactional federations with local SI schedulers, but include it in the spectrum of supported methods for specific application cases. For the experiments reported in Section 5, we have designed our benchmark application and the form of high-level locks kept at the federation layer such that semantic serializability for entire client transactions is guaranteed even with local SI schedulers.

3.3   Global Cycle Testing Based on the Online SI-MVSG

The online SI-MVSG, or OSI-MVSG for short, introduced in Section 2 is a means for ensuring serializability on top of an SI scheduler. As explained in Section 2, we simply need to test the OSI-MVSG for cycles and reject operations that would lead to a cycle by aborting the corresponding transaction. In a transactional federation, the additional problems arise that the OSI-MVSG needs to be built across all underlying component systems and needs to include also component systems that do provide local serializability, not just the ones that provide local SI. It turns out, however, that both problems are relatively easy to solve:

- The global OSI-MVSG to be maintained at the federation layer is simply the union of the OSI-MVSGs that we would maintain on top of each component system separately. We need to ensure, however, that nodes are not removed too early from this union graph: for the generalization to federations, the rule is that a transaction can be removed from the graph only if all transactions that have run concurrently with it in *anyone* of the underlying databases are committed, and the transaction to be deleted is a source in the global graph.

- As for the incorporation of component systems that guarantee full local conflict-serializability, the construction of edges in the OSI-MVSG requires an additional mechanism for observing conflict orders rather than the version-based reads-from relationship. In our implementation, we require such component systems to use tickets (possibly the implicit tickets given by the commit order if the component system has the rigorousness property). The OSI-MVSG adds edges for subtransactions on these component systems such that the edges correspond to the observed ticket orders between subtransactions.

Putting these considerations together yields the following result: a global concurrency control algorithm based on cycle testing on a global OSI-MVSG for transactional federations with component systems that guarantee either local snapshot isolation or local conflict-serializability allows only executions that are globally serializable if it rejects an operation when the added edges lead to a cycle in the graph. As discussed already in Section 2, the construction of the graph's edges requires observing reads and writes at the component system's interfaces. In our setting, this entails extracting simple predicates from the SQL operations that are issued to the various component systems. Section 2 already discussed how this can be accomplished.

3.4   Comparison and Combination of Protocols

None of the three presented families of protocols dominates the others; rather each of them has specific advantages in certain situations but also drawbacks with regard to certain aspects. In principle, the most powerful approach in terms of possible concurrency is the *multilevel trans-action protocol*, as the locks in the underlying component systems are held only for the duration of an operation and the federation layer can exploit the semantics of high-level operations to a large extent. However, its drawback is that it requires significant additional care for setting up the appropriate style of operations and corresponding locks, the compensating actions to be logged, etc. Even if the approach is restricted to standard SQL operations, for which all these aspects can be set up generically (as opposed to application-specific methods such as withdraw-als and deposits), one still needs to specify the high-level conflicts between these operations such that local SI can be tolerated for the isolation of operations, which may be application-specific. In addition, the management of high-level locks at the federation layer and the logging of compensating actions may incur significant overhead. The *family of ticket methods*, on the other hand, is clearly the best in terms of low overhead at the federation layer. In particular, its overhead "scales" with the correctness degrees of the underlying component systems: for systems with locally rigorous schedules, no explicit tickets are needed, for systems with the formal property of avoiding cascading aborts no edges need to be kept in the global ticket-order graph. However, tickets may well incur substantial performance degradation. Finally, the *cycle testing protocol* on the global online SI-MVSG is positioned in between the other two approaches with regard to both potential concurrency, which we would expect to be higher than with tickets, and overhead as well as application-specific setup complexity, which should be lower than with multilevel transactions.

The three protocol families are complementary not only in that differently configured federa-tions may choose different protocols, but also in that different protocols may be combined within the same federation, either on a per transaction or per component system basis. So a single transaction that accesses multiple component systems may use different protocols on different component systems depending on the properties of these systems.

4   Prototype Implementation

The practical viability of our theoretical results is demonstrated by a federated transaction man-ager, coined TRAFIC, that we have built as part of the VHDBS system [HWW98], a compre-hensive prototype system for federated databases that has been developed by the Fraunhofer Institute for Software and Systems Engineering and the Research Lab of the German Telekom AG. The VHDBS architecture is based on the wrapper-mediator paradigm [Wied92]. System-specific adapters wrap the existing component systems and translate data definitions and queries between the federated level and the native languages of the underlying database systems. Cur-rently, there are adapters to integrate Oracle 8i and O_2 Release 5. The VHDBS federation server acts as a mediator on the federated level, integrating metadata and decomposing federated que-ries and transactions into the corresponding subqueries and subtransactions. The common data model at the federation level is a subset of the ODMG object model, the query language is essentially ODMG's OQL, extended by operations to modify object attributes. The databases in a federation remain locally accessible, in addition to the integrated access through the federation layer.

Transactions are supported in VHDBS by the federated transaction manager *Trafic* [SW99]. Whenever a client embeds a data-access operation in the context of a transaction, VHDBS passes them through Trafic. There, appropriate steps are taken to guarantee global atomicity and global serializability. Trafic consists of several modules, which are specified in CORBA's IDL interface definition language. All modules can be integrated into a single CORBA server, or each module can be instantiated as a separate CORBA server with all servers distributed over a number of hosts.

Trafic generally provides a clear separation between transaction management *mechanisms* and *strategies*. Mechanisms such as lock management, graph cycle testing, or logging provide generic functionality; strategies make use of those mechanisms to guarantee a globally correct execution. Trafic supports a suite of different strategies; currently, there are implementations of all the strategies presented in Section 3.

To guarantee the atomicity of distributed transactions, Trafic makes use of Iona's OrbixOTS, an implementation of OMG's Object Transaction Service OTS. OTS essentially provides a two-phase commit protocol with CORBA-style interfaces and allows integrating existing resource managers via the standardized XA interface. Trafic uses OTS in the following way. When a client requests to start a new transaction using Trafic's transaction factory, Trafic begins a corresponding OTS transaction. All subsequent data-access operations are then passed through Trafic. Whenever a database is accessed for the first time in the context of the transaction, the local OTS agent automatically registers it with the transaction. Finally, upon the transaction's commit, OTS coordinates the subtransactions in the involved component systems, applying the standard two-phase commit protocol. Thus, our prototype architecture requires that all component systems provide an XA interface; this is the case for the currently supported systems Oracle and O_2.

All the logging that is necessary for the two-phase commit protocol is done by the underlying component system and OTS (for the coordinator log). Additionally, Trafic provides its own LogManager to support compensating actions for the multilevel transaction management strategy presented in Section 3.2. With this strategy, a client transaction is broken down into a sequence of independently committed OTS transactions. The standard case for all other strategies presented in this paper, however, is that each client transaction constitutes a single OTS transaction, and this guarantees global atomicity by OTS and the underlying component systems alone.

5   Experimental Evaluation

5.1   Benchmark Setup

The experimental evaluation of the presented suite of protocols has been carried out on the full-fledged implementation within the VHDBS federated database system on top of Oracle 8i databases. To this end, we designed an oversimplified stock brokerage scenario with three databases and very few data so that data contention would be the main performance bottleneck in multi-user access. So the experiments were designed as extreme stress tests rather than trying to capture all aspects of a real application.

We consider two stock brokers and a bank. Each stock broker manages 100 customers, and each one of them operates an Oracle 8i database with the following schema (identical for both of them):

- A first relation Stocks(StockID, Price) contains the available stocks, identified by the primary key StockID, and the current price for each stock. This relation contains 100 tuples.
- The second relation StockList(CustomerID, StockID, Amount) holds information about the stocks owned by the customers. Each customer owns ten randomly selected, different stocks.

In addition to these two stock brokers, the bank operates another Oracle 8i database with the following schema:

- A relation Portfolio(CustomerID, StockID, Amount) holds information about the stocks owned by the customers. It is essentially the union of the stock brokers' StockList relations.

On top of these three databases, we ran two classes of transactions: The *Investment* transaction models one customer buying several shares of one stock, by reading the current stock price in the one of the two stock broker's database and updating the customer's entry in the broker's and the bank's databases. The *Value* transaction computes the total value of all shares that a customer owns by querying both stock brokers' databases for the stocks that the customer owns and their current prices. These two transaction types are sketched in Figure 1.

```
Investment(cid,sid,amount):
determine stock broker database SB from sid;
select price from SB.Stocks where StockID=sid;   number:=amount/price;
if (customer already owns shares of this stock)
{ update SB.StockList set Amount=Amount+number; }
else { insert into SB.StockList values(cid,sid,number); }
if (customer already owns items of this stock)
{ update Bank.Portfolios set Amount=Amount+number; }
else { insert into Bank.Portfolios valules(cid,sid,number); }

Value(cid):
totalvalue:=0;
for StockID,Amount in (select StockID,Amount from SB1.StockList where CustomerID=cid)
{ select Price from SB1.Stocks where stockid=StockID;   totalvalue+=Amount*Price; }
for StockID,Amount in (select StockID,Amount from SB2.StockList where CustomerID=cid)
{ select Price from SB2.Stocks where stockid=StockID;   totalvalue+=Amount*Price; }
```

Figure 1 – Pseudocode of the Two Benchmark Transactions

All the benchmarks were run with Trafic's modules implemented as separate CORBA servers, distributed over five Sun Sparcstations in such a way that the CPU load was balanced across the machines, to the best possible extent. As for the underlying database servers, the Oracle instances were run on a Sun Ultra Enterprise 4000 with eight processors and two PCs running Windows NT. As it turned out during the measurements, all these machines were far from being performance bottlenecks.

5.2   Performance Measurements

This section presents results from the performance measurements for the following four experiments:

- a multi-user combination of Value and Investment transactions with input parameters chosen according to a 90-10 skewed distribution, with the read-write Investment transactions as the dominating load,
- the same multi-user combination of Value and Investment transactions, but with the read-only Value transactions as the dominating load,
- a multi-user load of a conflict-free variation of Investment transactions such that no two concurrent transactions accessed any common stocks or customers, as a means for assessing the pure bookkeeping overhead of the various techniques,
- a multi-user load of read-only Value transactions, to assess the bookkeeping overhead for the important special case of read-only transactions.

All experiments measured transaction throughput for a particular number of clients each of which spawns a new transaction upon the completion of the last transaction issued by the same client. So we used a fixed multiprogramming level (MPL) in a single run, and then varied this MPL to produce a complete performance chart. For the read-write dominated mixed workload experiments, the MPL of the Value transactions was constantly five, and only the MPL of the Investment transactions was varied. For the read-only dominated mixed workload experiments, the MPL of the Investment transactions was constantly five. Note that in all experiments the absolute throughput figures are fairly low for several reasons: VHDBS is merely a prototype system that incurs substantial overhead (e.g., copying fine-grained Orbix objects across machines), the experiments were run on rather low-end hardware, and our experimental setup really was an extreme stress test in terms of data contention.

In the following, we use *ETT* for the extended ticket technique presented in Section 3.1, *OTT* for the traditional (optimistic) ticket technique, *MLTM* for the multilevel transaction strategy presented in Section 3.2, and *MVSG* for the Online SI-MVSG strategy presented in Section 3.3. To assess the overhead of the various strategies, we also measured a strawman strategy *NONE* that completely ignores global concurrency control (and thus cannot guarantee any global correctness criterion at all), but simply drives the two-phase commit protocol at commit time.

Figure 2 shows the throughput results for the read-write dominated (left chart) and the read-only dominated (right chart) settings. Throughput of Value transactions turned out to be roughly the same for all strategies, so it was omitted from the charts. As for the Investment transactions in the read-write dominated setting, we see that the OSI-MVSG technique outperforms all other techniques until a certain MPL, after that, MLTM allows the highest throughput of Investment transactions. The ticket method performs poorly for read-write transactions because of the additional contention for ticket objects. In the read-only dominated setting, the OSI-MVSG strategy again shows the best throughput for Investment transactions. MLTM's throughput rapidly drops with increasing MPL of Value transactions, because an increasing amount of lock conflicts with the long-running Value transactions causes long blockings of Invest transactions.

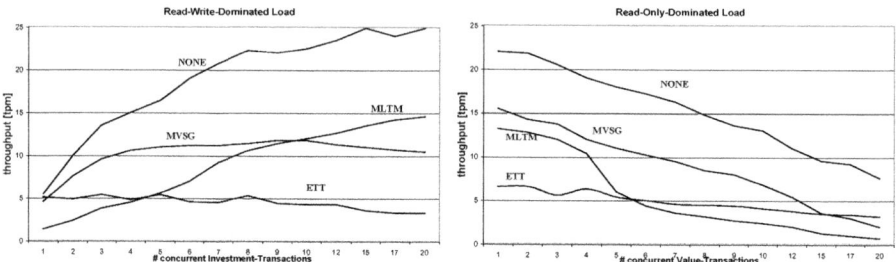

Figure 2 – Benchmark results for read-write dominated load

To study the overhead of the strategies for read-only transactions, we also measured the throughput of Value transactions alone for varying MPL. Here, the extended ticket technique developed in this paper performs equally well as the MVSG technique, whereas the original ticket technique again suffers from the bottleneck of the ticket objects. MLTM shows a relatively low throughput because of the additional cost of committing subtransactions (note that a single transaction comprised 60 subtransactions on average). Similar measurements with the conflict-free variant of Investment Transactions convey the overhead of the various strategies for read-write transactions. Again, MVSG shows the clearly best performance. The additional logging of MLTM accounts for its lower performance.

We conclude this section with a summary of our experimental findings:

- The Online SI-MVSG has proven to be the method of choice for mixed environments with both read-write and read-only transactions. It even outperforms the strategies for global SI, even though providing globally serializable executions.
- The extended ticket technique has the best performance for read-only transactions, but has major performance disadvantages with read-write transactions.
- Multilevel transactions exhibit decent overall performance, without any extraordinary results, however, which is partly caused by the fact that our benchmark did not include any operations with special semantics such as withdrawals or deposits that could have been exploited for higher concurrency.

6   Conclusion

In this paper we have re-opened the subject of transactional federations with particular focus on the previously neglected issue of component systems that support "only" snapshot isolation (SI) rather than full serializability (SR). We have presented a suite of techniques for ensuring global serializability on top of heterogeneous federations with a mix of both SI- and SR-oriented components. Our techniques leverage prior work, most notably, the ticket method and the technique of deriving reads-from and conflict relations from observing SQL-statement predicates at the federation layer. In addition, we have presented a generalization of the ticket technique and a novel technique based on cycle testing in a federation-level online multiversion-serialization graph. All techniques have been implemented in a full-fledged federated database system, and we have presented stress-test performance measurements on this real-system platform to demonstrate the viability and performance advantages of the novel techniques.

Federated database systems were considered impractical for much of the last decade, but the proliferation of gateway and other middleware technology and especially the pressing application demand for integrated access to multiple data sources have recently led to a revival of the federation concept [Ston98,MK+99,HSC99]. This paper has addressed a significant part of the transactional aspects of federations, and we believe that the incorporation of snapshot isolation is of particular practical interest given its wide use for operational (Oracle) databases. Our future work will mostly aim to make our framework, protocols, and also prototype implementation more comprehensive in that we also want to support other forms of relaxed isolation levels such as the ANSI SQL "read committed" level and especially combinations of different isolation levels on a per component-systems or transaction-class basis.

References

[ALO00] A. Adya, B. Liskov, P. O'Neil: *Generalized Isolation Level Definitions.* ICDE, San Diego, 2000.

[ABJ97] V. Atluri, E. Bertino, S. Jajodia: *A Theoretical Formulation for Degrees of Isolation in Databases*, Information and Software Technology 39(1), Elsevier Science, 1997.

[BBGM+95] H. Berenson, P. Bernstein, J. Gray, J. Melton, E. O'Neil, P. O'Neil: *A Critique of ANSI SQL Isolation Levels.* SIGMOD, San Jose, 1995.

[BLL00] A.J. Bernstein, P.M. Lewis, S. Lu: *Semantic Conditions for Correctness at Different Isolation Levels.* ICDE, San Diego, 2000.

[BGRS91] Y. Breitbart, D. Georgakopoulos, M. Rusinkiewciz, A. Silberschatz: *On Rigorous Transaction Scheduling.* IEEE Transactions on Software Engineering 17(9), 1991.

[BGS92] Y. Breitbart, H. Garcia-Molina, A. Silberschatz: *Overview of Multidatabase Transaction Management.* VLDB Journal 1(2), 1992.

[BHG87] P.A. Bernstein, V. Hadzilacos, N. Goodman: *Concurrency Control and Recovery in Database Systems.* Addison Wesley Press, 1987.

[BS92] Y. Breitbart,A. Silberschatz: *Strong Recoverability in Multidatabase Systems*, RIDE, Tempe, 1992.

[DSW94] A. Deacon, H.-J. Schek, G. Weikum: *Semantics-based Multilevel Transaction Management in Federated Systems.* ICDE, Houston, 1994.

[FLO+99] A. Fekete, D. Liarokapis, E. O'Neil, P. O'Neil, D. Shasha: *Making Snapshot Isolation Data Item Serializable*, Manuscript, 1999.

[GRS94] D. Georgakopoulos, M. Rusinkiewicz, A.P. Sheth: *Using Tickets to Enforce the Serializability of Multidatabase Transactions.* IEEE Transactions on Knowledge and Data Engineering 6(1), February 1994.

[HSC99] J.M. Hellerstein, M. Stonebraker, R. Caccia: *Independent, Open Enterprise Data Integration*, IEEE Data Engineering Bulletin 22(1), 1999.

[HWW98] B. Holtkamp, N. Weißenberg, X. Wu: *VHDBS: A Federated Database System for Electronic Commerce*, EURO-MED NET, 1998.

[MK+99] N. M. Mattos, J. Kleewein, M. T. Roth, K. Zeidenstein: *From Object-Relational to Federated Databases.* Invited Paper, in: A. P. Buchmann (Ed.): *German Database Conference (BTW)*, 1999.

[ÖV98] M.T. Özsu, P. Valduriez: *Principles of Distributed Database Systems.* 2nd Edition, Prentice Hall, 1998.

[Orac99] Oracle Corporation: *Oracle8i Concepts: Chapter 27, Data Concurrency and Consistency*, 1999.

[Raz92] Y. Raz: *The Principle of Commit Ordering or Guaranteeing Serializability in a Heterogeneous Environment of Multiple Autonomous Resource Managers Using Atomic Commitment.* VLDB, Vancouver, 1992

[SL90] A.P. Sheth, J.A. Larson: *Federated Database Systems for Managing Distributed, Heterogeneous, and Autonomous Databases.* ACM Computing Surveys 22(2), 1990.

[SSW95] W. Schaad, H.-J. Schek, G. Weikum: *Implementation and Performance of Multi-level Transaction Management in a Multidatabase Environment.* RIDE, Taipeh, 1995.

[Ston98] M. Stonebraker: *Are We Working On The Right Problems? (Panel).* SIGMOD, Seattle, 1998.

[SW99] R. Schenkel, G. Weikum: *Experiences With Building a Federated Transaction Manager Based on CORBA OTS*, in: Proceedings of the 2nd International Workshop on Engineering Federated Information Systems, Kühlungsborn, 1999.

[SW+99] R. Schenkel, G. Weikum, N. Weißenberg, X. Wu: *Federated Transaction Management With Snapshot Isolation*, in: Proceedings of the 8th International Workshop on Foundations of Models and Language for Data and Objects – Transactions and Database Dynamics, Schloß Dagstuhl, Germany, 1999.

[Weihl89] W.E. Weihl: *Local Atomicity Properties: Modular Concurrency Control for Abstract Data Types.* ACM Transactions on Programming Languages and Systems 11(2), 1989.

[Wied92] G. Wiederhold: *Mediators in the Architecture of Future Information Systems.* IEEE Computer 25(3), 1992.

An Evaluation of the Java-Based Approaches to Web Database Access*

Stavros Papastavrou[1], Panos Chrysanthis[1], George Samaras[2], Evaggelia Pitoura[3]

[1] Dept. of Computer Science, University of Pittsburgh
{stavrosp, panos}@cs.pitt.edu
[2] Dept. of Computer Science, University of Cyprus
cssamara@cs.ucy.ac.cy
[3] Dept. of Computer Science, University of Ioannina
pitoura@cs.uoi.gr

Abstract. Given the undeniable popularity of the Web, providing efficient and secure access to remote databases using a Web browser is crucial for the emerging cooperative information systems and applications. In this paper, we evaluate all currently available Java-based approaches that support persistent connections between Web clients and database servers. These approaches include Java applets, Java Sockets, Servlets, Remote Method Invocation, CORBA, and mobile agents technology. Our comparison is along the dimensions of *performance* and *programmability*.

1 Introduction

Providing efficient and secure access to remote databases using a Web browser is crucial for the emerging cooperative information systems, such as Virtual Enterprises. A number of methods for Web database connectivity and integration have been proposed such as CGI scripts, active pages, databases speaking http, external viewers or plug-ins, and HyperWave [6]. These methods enhance the Web server capabilities with dynamic functionality for interactive and cooperative applications to create database connections, execute queries and transactions, and generate dynamic Web pages. However, there is an increasing interest in those that are Java-based due to the inherent advantages of Java, namely, platform independence support, highly secure program execution, and small size of compiled code, combined with a simple database connectivity interface (JDBC API) that facilitates application access to relational databases over the Web at different URLs [8].

Several Java-based methods are currently available that can be used for the development of Web cooperative information systems but in the best of our knowledge, there is no quantitative comparison of them in a database context. Existing studies either primarily focused on the various server side scripting mechanisms to support database connectivity (e.g., [5, 9]), or evaluated the Java client/server communication

---

* This work was partially supported by NSF IRI-9502091 and IIS-9812532, and AFOSR F49620-98-1-043 awards.

O. Etzion and P. Scheuermann (Eds.): CoopIS 2000, LNCS 1901, pp. 102› 113, 2000.

paradigm without any database connectivity or lengthy computations (e.g., [11]). This experimental paper contributes a comparison of the six Java-based approaches, specifically, Java applets using JDBC (Applet JDBC), Java Sockets [13], Java Servlets [4], Remote Method Invocation (RMI) [3], CORBA [10], and Java Mobile Agents (JMA) [2]. We focus on these methods because of their support for *persistent* database connections, which are essential for cooperative environments with long, and repeated data retrievals and updates.

For our evaluation, we used each approach to implement a Web client accessing and querying a remote database. Each approach differs in the way the client establishes connection with remote database servers with the help of a middleware and the implementation of the middleware. Depending on the way the client establishes connection with the middleware, the approaches can be classified as (1) *non-RPC* ones, that do not provide for remote method invocation mechanisms, (2) *RPC* ones with clear remote method invocation semantics, and (3) *RPC-like* ones involving mobile agent technology.

We compared the behavior of the different approaches along the following two dimensions: (1) *performance* expressed in terms of response time under different loads, and (2) *programmability* expressed in terms of the number of system calls at the client and the server site. The two salient results of our study are: (1) Best performance is not always achievable with high programmability and low resource requirements, and (2) the mobile agent technology needs to improve its programmability while giving particular emphasis in its infrastructure.

In the next section, we first discuss our experimental testbed and then elaborate on the implementation details of the six approaches under evaluation. In Section 3, we discuss our performance evaluation results whereas in Section 4, we compare the different approaches from programmability point of view.

2   The Experimental Testbed

We use each Java method to implement a Web client querying a remote database. Our testbed is structured along a three-tier *client/middleware/database* model. Two design principles were adopted in the selection of the various components during the development of the testbed. First, our Web clients should be lean for allowing fast downloads, and therefore increasing support for wireless clients. Second, no a-priori configuration of the Web client should be necessary to run the experiments in order to maintain portability, and therefore, support arbitrary clients. Thus, our Web client is a Java applet stored on a Web server. When the Java applet is downloaded and initialized at a client computer, queries can be issued through the applet's GUI to be executed on the remote database server (Figure 1). Our remote database server, a 3-table Microsoft Access, is on the same machine with the Web server.

The role of the middleware is to accept client requests, execute them on the database server, and return the results back to the client. Due to security restrictions of Java applets, part of the middleware has to execute on the Web server machine.

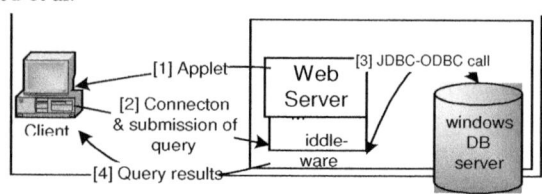

Figure 1: Basic configuration

Downloadable applets are not allowed to access any system resources or communicate with any site other that their originating web server. In our experiments, because the database server co-resides with the Web server, the entire middleware in all cases executes on the same machine. To enhance performance, if possible, the middleware connects to the database when it is activated and before any query is submitted.

Given that an Access database can only be accessed using ODBC, the middleware of all approaches except Applet JDBC, use a JDBC-ODBC bridge (type 1) driver to connect to the database. A type 1 JDBC driver cannot be used in the Applet JDBC approach in which the client applet downloads the JDBC driver, because a type 1 driver is not designed to be downloadable by Java applets. Instead we use a type 3 JDBC driver, which is the most flexible from all four types of JDBC drivers [14] with Java applets: it can be fully downloaded at run time, requiring no code pre-installation. Further, it supports multiple-vendor databases by translating clients' queries into an intermediate language that is converted into a vendor-specific protocol by a middle-tier gateway, including JDBC calls into ODBC ones.

In the rest of this section, we elaborate on the implementation of each approach. *Initialization phase* is the procedure for establishing database connectivity, and *execution phase* is the procedure for querying the database after the database connection is established.

2.1 Non-RPC Approaches: Java Socket and Java Servlet

Both the *Java Socket* and *Java Servlet* approaches use sockets to connect a client and the middleware program. In the Java Socket approach, sockets are created by the clients, whereas in the Servlet approach, are created by the run-time environment.

2.1.1 The Java socket approach. In this first approach, the middleware is a stand-alone Java application server running on the Web server machine. A client collaborates with the application server by establishing an explicit socket connection.

The applet submits the query through the socket connection to the application server, which decodes the incoming stream of data, and executes the query on the database server. The result table is then passed to the client applet again by the means of data streams.

The cost of the first query in this approach is
1. Initialization phase:
    A. The time for the client to open a socket connection with the application server.

2. Execution phase:
    A. The time for the client to pass to the application server the data stream containing the SQL statement.
    B. The time for the application server to execute the query, obtain the results and return them to the client.
All subsequent queries require only the execution phase.

2.1.2 Java Servlets Approach. In this approach, the middleware program is a Java servlet, which is a Java program that runs as a child process within the context of a Web server program. In our case, the *application servlet* was loaded during the Web Server start-up time. Client's queries are routed by the Web server to the application servlet, which submits them to the database server for processing. The results are returned to the client again through the Web server. All queries involve both an initialization and an execution phase. Thus, the cost of any query in this approach is

1. Initialization phase:
    A. The time for the client to establish a URL connection with the Web server.
2. Execution phase:
    A. The time for the applet to invoke the application servlet passing the query as a parameter (stating explicitly the servlet name and type of operation).
    B. The time for the servlet to execute the query, obtain and return the result table to the client.

2.2 RPC approaches: Java RMI, CORBA, and Applet JDBC

The RPC approaches can be classified based on whether or not the client directly maintains the database connection. In the RMI and CORBA approaches, the connection is maintained by the middleware whereas in the Applet JDBC approach, by the web client.

2.2.1 The RMI approach. Java RMI is a Java application interface for implementing remote procedure calls between distributed Java objects. In RMI, the middleware consists of two objects: the *application server* which handles the queries; and the *installer object*, which is used to start up the application server, and register it under a unique service name with the Java virtual machine running on the Web server.

To establish a database connection, a client calls the RMI bind method to obtain a reference to the application server. Using this reference, the client can submit a query by calling a method on the application server passing the query as a parameter. The application server executes the query at the database server, and returns the result table to the client as the return value of the method called.

The cost of the first query is

1. Initialization phase:
    A. The time for the applet to obtain a reference to the remote application server (bind to it) using a URL and a service name.
2. Execution phase:

A. The time for the client to invoke a method on the application server passing the SQL statement as a parameter.

B. The time for the application server to execute the SQL statement, obtain and return the results.

The time required for a subsequent query is the execution phase.

2.2.2 The CORBA approach. CORBA, the Common Object Gateway Request Broker Architecture, is an emerging distributed object standard that defines client/server relationships between objects in a common interface language. In order for a CORBA client object to utilize a CORBA server object, an implementation of CORBA's basic functionality, called the Object Request Broker (ORB), has to be loaded at both the client and the server sites. In our testbed, we use Visigenic's Visibroker for Java [15], which is also included in Netscape Navigator and hence, the client does not download the ORB classes from the Web server which would have been the alternative. For security purposes, CORBA allows an applet to bind to and communicate with a remote CORBA server object only through a firewall called the IIOP (Internet Inter-ORB Protocol) Gatekeeper, installed at the Web server machine from which the applet is downloaded.

Except from the IIOP Gatekeeper, the middleware in the CORBA approach is similar to the one in the RMI approach. There is an application server object and an installer object. The installer object in this case is also used to load the ORB, and register the application server with a unique service name with the ORB. The steps required for the first query are shown in Figure 2.

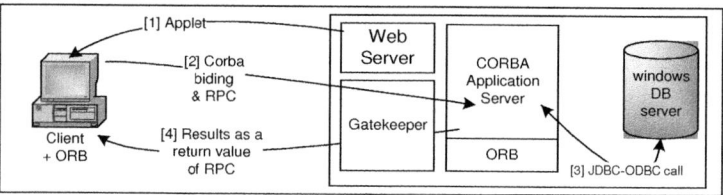

Figure 2: CORBA approach

The cost of the first query is
1. Initialization phase:
   A. The time for the client to load and initialize core ORB classes.
   B. The time for the client to bind to the application server using *only* the service name of the application server.
2. Execution phase:
   A. The time for the client to invoke a method on the application server passing the SQL statement as a parameter.
   B. The time for the application server to execute the SQL, obtain and return the results to the client as the return value of the method called.

Execution phase is only required for any subsequent query.

2.2.3 The Applet JDBC approach: Applets that use directly the JDBC API. In this approach, the client applet downloads a type 3 JDBC driver and uses directly the JDBC API to connect to the database. The Gateway of the type 3 driver plays the role of the middleware. After the client downloads the JDBC driver, it establishes database connectivity issuing JDBC calls on the Gateway, which maps them to ODBC calls on the database server. Queries are submitted in the same way using JDBC calls.

The cost for the first query is

1. Initialization phase:
    A. The time for JDBC driver to be downloaded from the Web server and initiated by the applet.
    B. The time for the applet to establish database connection via the gateway.
2. Execution phase:
    A. The time for the applet to issue an SQL statement to the database and obtain the results.

All subsequent queries require only the execution phase.

2.3 RPC-like approach: Java Mobile Agents (JMA).

Finally, in this subsection, we describe the approach of using mobile agents to achieve Web database connectivity, and specifically, the best of the three variants proposed in [12]. Mobile agents are processes capable of pausing their execution on one machine, dispatching themselves on another machine and resuming their execution on the new machine. The idea in the JMA approach is to use one or more mobile agents to implement the middleware and carry out the requests of the client.

For our experiments, we used *Aglets* [7], for two reasons: (a) availability of code, and (b) support for hosting mobile agents within applets without significant overhead based on our prior experience with their use. Aglets can be fired from within a special applet, called the *FijiApplet* that provides an aglet execution environment similar to the general stand-alone aglet runtime environment called the *Tahiti Server*.

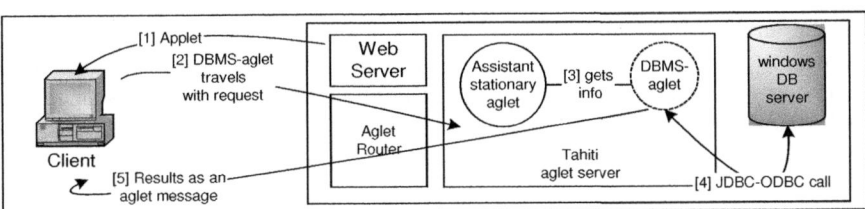

Figure 3: Mobile agents approach configuration (message variation)

In the JMA approach, the middleware consists of three components: The *DBMS-aglet*, the *(Stationary) Assistant-aglet* and the *Aglet Router*. The DBMS-aglet can connect to a database and submit queries. Each database server is associated with an Assistant-aglet identified by a unique aglet ID and a URL. An Assistant-aglet provides the information necessary for a DBMS-agent to load the appropriate JDBC driver and connect to the database server. An *Aglet Router* is required to route aglets and messages, dispatched from a FijiApplet to any destination, and vice versa, because of the Java security restrictions.

When the user enters the first query (Figure 3), the client applet (an extension of the FijiApplet) creates a DBMS-aglet with a specific URL-based itinerary (travel plan) and the specified query. The DBMS-aglet travels through the aglet router to the database server. Upon its arrival, the DBMS-aglet communicates with the Assistant-aglet to retrieve information on the database and drivers, loads the JDBC-ODBC driver, connects to the database server and executes the client's request. After returning the query result in a message to the client, the DBMS-aglet remains connected to the database server, waiting for a message with new requests from the client. This message passing is implemented implicitly as an RPC invocation from the client applet on the dispatched mobile agent. The cost of the initial query is

1. Initialization phase:
    A. The time for the client to create the DBMS-aglet
    B. The time for the client to initialize the DBMS-aglet (SQL statement, itinerary, etc.)
    C. The time for the DBMS-aglet to travel to the remote database server
    D. The time for the DBMS-aglet to negotiate with the assistant aglet
    E. The time for the DBMS-aglet to establish connection with the database
2. Execution phase:
    A. The time for the DBMS-aglet to query the database and send the results to the client using a message.

All subsequent requests require only one message from the client to DBMS-aglet, which includes the new SQL statement, plus the execution phase.

4 Performance Evaluation

We contacted two sets of experiments to evaluate the ability of each approach to support (1) *small interactions* that typically involve a small size of query results (128 bytes), and (2) *heavy cooperation* that involves a wide range of query results.

Given our interest to support both mobile clients and clients over a wide-area network with relatively slow communication links (limited bandwidth), we contacted our experiments on a wireless 1.2Mbps LAN of Pentium PCs. We used Netscape Navigator v4.6 as the Web client's Java-enabled browser. For each approach, a sufficient number of runs were performed to obtain statistically significant results.

4.1 Small Interactions

We measured the response time (a) of the first query and (b) of subsequent queries (Graph 1). Short-duration interactions consist of a single query as opposed to long-duration ones. The execution of the first query differs from the subsequent ones because it incurs the overhead of establishing the connection between the client and the remote database.

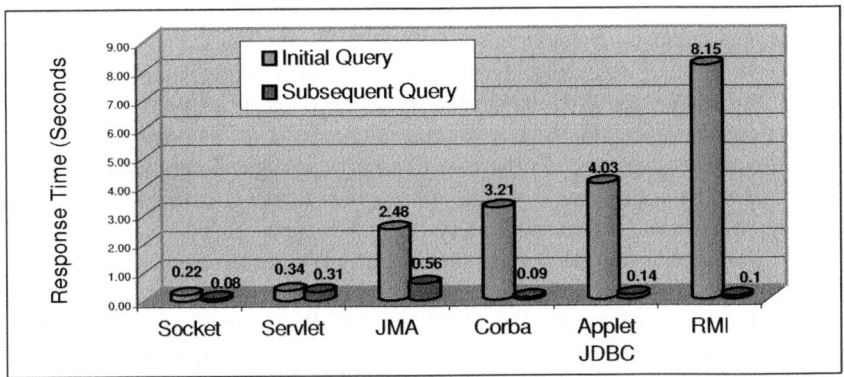

Graph 1. Performance of all approaches for 128 bytes result size

For the first query (short-duration interactions), the non-RPC approaches have by far the lowest response time. This can be explained by the fact that their initialization phase does not engage any special package loading by the client. Compared to the Socket approach, the Servlet approach performs slightly worse because (a) the communication between the client and the servlet is marshaled by the Web server, and (b) by executing as a Web server thread, the servlet receives less CPU time than the socket application server. Thus, servlets respond slower to requests and take more time to assemble the query results.

From the other approaches, the JMA approach offers the best performance for a single query. Significant part of its cost (around 2 sec) is due to the process of dispatching the DBMS-aglet from the client applet to the aglet router on the Web server and from there to the database server. In the case of the CORBA approach, the first query is slightly more expensive than the one in the JMA approach because of the overhead of initializing the necessary ORB classes and the binding to the application server. This overhead is quite significant (around 2.20 sec). Following the CORBA approach is the Java JDBC approach in which the response time of the first query is increased by a considerable amount of time by the downloading of the JDBC driver.

To our surprise, the RMI approach performs by far the worst for the first query. We expected the RMI approach to exhibit better performance because, as opposed to the other RPC approaches, it does not involve the loading of any specific package. The only way to explain this is to attribute the increased response time to the interpreted method of RMI calls when binding the client applet to the application server. CORBA compilers create hard-coded encoding/decoding routines for marshaling of objects used as RPC parameters, whereas RMI uses object serialization in an introspective manner. This means that (a) RMI encodes additional class information for each object passed as a RPC parameter, and (b) marshaling is done in an interpreted fashion. Consequently, RMI remote calls are more demanding in terms of CPU time and size of code transmitted, a fact that we observed in all our experiments.

For subsequent queries (long-duration interactions), the performance of the CORBA and RMI approaches dramatically improves, and becomes close to the best performance exhibited by the Socket approach. The reason is that the client applet is already bound to the application server and only a remote procedure call is required to query the database. For a similar reason, the JDBC applet approach also exhibits a significant performance improvement for subsequent queries.

Having the DBMS-aglet already connected to the remote database and ready to process a new query, the JMA approach also improves its response time for subsequent queries. However, this response time is the worst of all other approaches. We attribute this to two reasons: (1) the two required messages to implement subsequent queries have to be routed through the aglet router, and (2) a mobile agent is not a stand-alone process and it does not receive full CPU time.

Finally, the Servlet approach improves slightly its performance although the steps for executing any query are the same. This improvement is due to the fact that any subsequent connection between the client and the Web server require less time because the URL of the Web server has already been resolved in the initial query.

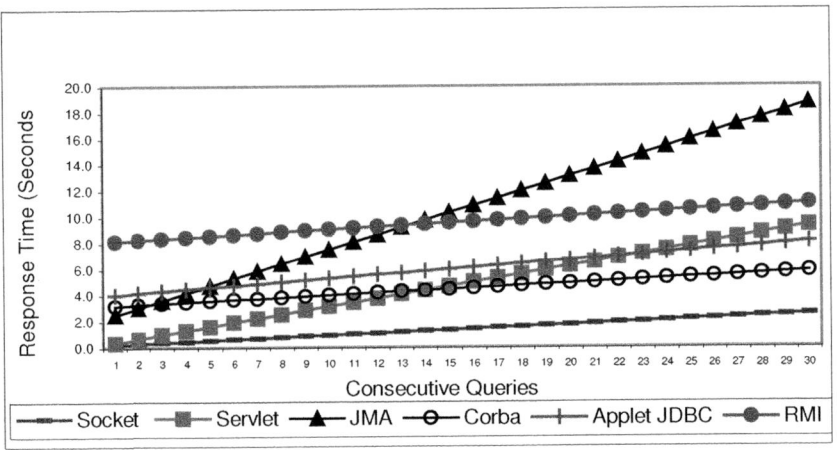

Graph 2: Average performance for up to 30 consecutive queries (128 bytes of result size)

In order to better illustrate the *overall performance* of each approach, we plotted in Graph 2 the average time required by each approach for a number of consecutive queries. It is clear that the socket approach is the most efficient for both short- and long –duration interactions. This is not a surprise since all other approaches are built on top of sockets. Both the Servlet and the JMA approaches scale very badly. The CORBA, JDBC applet, and RMI approaches appear to scale well, however, the RMI approach appears less attractive due to its worst performance for initial queries.

4.2 Heavy Cooperation

In order to evaluate heavy cooperation we adjusted the size of the query result from 5 kilobytes (95 tuples) to 64 kilobytes (1000 tuples) by changing the complexity of the SQL statement issued through the client applet.Query result size directly affects the

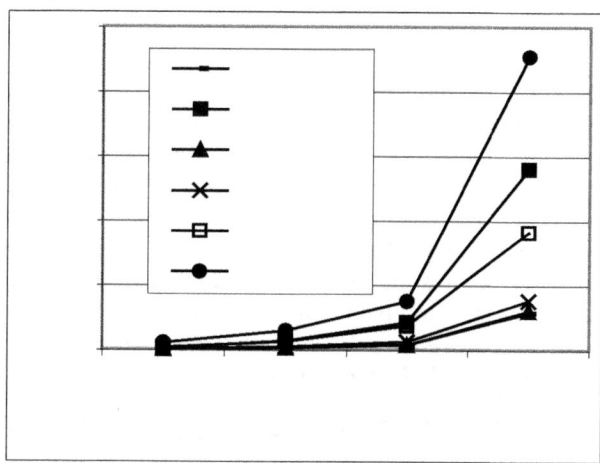

response time in two ways: (1) in the amount of time spent for the query to execute, and (2) in the transport time for the results to reach the client. For these experiments, we also measured response times of first and subsequent queries. In both cases, each approach exhibited the similar sensitivity, which is shown in Graphs 2.

The first observation is that the average response times of Java JDBC applet and JMA approaches increase exponentially with query result sizes larger than 20KB. The JDBC applet approach performs by far the worst for increased result size. This can be explained by the fact that in JDBC rows from a query result are retrieved one at a time. Specifically, to retrieve one row from the query result, the client must call a method on a Java ResultSet object, which is mapped on the remote database server through the Gateway. Consequently, for a large size of query result, a large number of those remote calls have to take place. In that case, large query results not only increase dramatically the response time but they also increase the Internet traffic.

The bad scaling of the JMA approach can be explained in the same way as the bad performance of the Servlet approach. Both mobile agents and servlets do not execute as stand-alone processes, and therefore, they do not receive full CPU time and heavily depend on the supporting execution environment. The other RPC approaches exhibit acceptable performances (close to linear for sizes above 20KB) with the CORBA approach being slightly better. As indicated above, the implementation of RPC calls in CORBA is much faster compared to the RMI's one.

5. Programmability Comparison

In this section, we compare the different approaches in terms of development effort. Our goal is to understand if there is any correlation or trade-off between performance and programming complexity. To quantify the development effort, we use the number of required system calls. The number of systems calls used in each approach is, in some sense, analogous to the number of code lines implementing each approach. Table 1 shows the total number of system calls required for each approach.

A first observation is that the development effort of the client is related to the level of abstraction of communication between the client and the middleware, in general, and the naming scheme used to identify the database services to establish communication, in particular. Not surprisingly, the RPC approaches involve less complex APIs, more transparent client/server communication and hence exhibit high programmability. All non-RPC approaches, including the JMA approach (the RPC-like one), require more development effort and hence have low programmability.

A second observation is that despite the fact that the JMA approach supports RPC-like communication, it exhibits the *lowest* programmability as indicated by the largest number of system calls required. Most of these system calls are used to construct, maintain and execute the URL-based itinerary.

		Socket	Servlet	CORBA	RMI	Applet JDBC	JMA
System Calls							
Total Number		29	25	25	12	6	29
Establish Connection	At the Client	7	11	2	1	3	11
	At the Middleware	11	3	8	6	0	11
Submit Query and Get Results	At the Client	3	3	1	1	3	2
	At the Middleware	8	8	4	4	0	5
Client Execution Code		6K	6K	23K	9K	50K	27K
Programmability		Low	Low	High	High	High	Low

Table 1: Programmability of the approaches

Finally, the level of programmability does not correspond to the size of the client executable code. Interestingly, the Non-RPC approaches, namely, Java Socket and Servlet, support the smallest client size (6K). On the other hand, the Applet JDBC has the largest client size of 50K: the Java applet is 6K and the JDBC driver is 46K. The JMA approach is the second most resource demanding approach after Applet JDBC with 27K: Java applet 10K, FijiApplet 10K and DBMS-Aglet 7K.

6 Conclusions and Future Work

In this experimental paper, we have implemented, evaluated, and compared all currently available Java-based approaches that support persistent Web database connectivity. Our comparison proceeded along the lines of the performance of query processing and of the programmability of each approach.

The results of our comparison showed that the CORBA approach offers high programmability and hence, is easy to develop, while its performance is comparable to the best performing approach that employs sockets. Therefore, the CORBA approach offers the best promise for the development of large Web applications, in particular, cooperative interactions involving multiple queries of varying result sizes. For small interactions, typically involving a single query, and environments with resource-starved clients, the socket and servlet approaches should be considered. These approaches yield a Web client with the smallest footprint, just 6 Kbytes. Clearly, the best performance is not always achievable with high programmability and low resource requirements.

The recent advancements of the Web technology and mobile computing led to a renewed interest on mobile agents technology. Given this renewed interest, our study provided an insight to potential scalability problems with the currently available mobile agent implementations. The JMA approach cannot support interactions that require movement or exchange of large amounts of data such as a large number of consecutive queries with increased size of query result. Hence, it is necessary to develop more efficient mobile agent infrastructures, if the full potential of mobile agents is to be explored. As part of our future work, we investigate the possibility of merging mobile agents and the CORBA technology in order to facilitate a scalable and efficient JMA-based Web database connectivity.

References

1. Anuff E. *Java Sourcebook*. Whiley Publishing, 1996.
2. Chess D., B. Grosof, C. Harrison, D. Levine, C. Parris, and G. Tsudik. Itinerant Agents for Mobile Computing. *IEEE Personal Communications*, Vol. 2, No. 5, Oct. 1992.
3. Downing T. B. *Java RMI: Remote Method Invocation*. IDG Books Worldwide, 1998.
4. Goodwill J. *Developing Java Servlets*. Sams Publishing, 1999.
5. Helmayer G., G. Kappel, and S. Reich. Connecting Databases on the Web: A Taxonomy of Gateways. *Proc. of the 8th DEXA Int'l Conference and Workshops,* Sept. 1997.
6. Maurer H. *Hyperwave: The Next Generation Web Solution*, Addison-Wesley, 1996.
7. IBM Japan Research Group. *Aglets Workbench*, <http:/www.trl.ibm.co.jp/aglets>
8. Jepson B. *Java Database Programming*. Wiley Computer Publishing, 1997.
9. Lambrinidis A., and N. Rousopoulos. Generating dynamic content at database-backed web server: cgi-bin vs mod_perl. *Sigmod Record*, Mar. 2000.
10. Object Management Group. The Common Object Request Broker: Architecture and specification. Feb. 1998.
11. Orfali R., and D. Harkley. *Client Server Programming with Java and CORBA*. Whiley Publishing, 1998.
12. Papastavrou S., G. Samaras, and E. Pitoura. Mobile Agents for WWW Distributed Database Access. *Proc. of the 14th IEEE Int'l Conf. on Data Engineering*, Mar. 1999.
13. Sun Microsystems Inc. Java Sockets Documentation, <http://java.sun.com/docs>
14. Sun Microsystems Inc., JDBC drivers, <http://java.sun.com/products/jdbc/drivers.html>
15. Visibroker for Java V.2.0. Borland, <http://www.inprise.com/visibroker>

A Framework for ASP-Marketplaces

Gerrit Tamm

Oliver Günther

gtamm@wiwi.hu-berlin.de
Institute of Information Systems
Humboldt University
Spandauer Strasse 1
D-10178 Berlin, Germany

guenther@wiwi.hu-berlin.de
Institute of Information Systems
Humboldt University
Spandauer Strssße 1
D-10178 Berlin, Germany

Abstract.

For organizations that plan to use *online software applications* via Internet one of the most important questions is, " How do you choose the right ASP for the companies corporate needs?". ASP marketplaces offer a plurality of pricing models and different levels of service. From whole system and whole service to single applications and methods, every digital product and service can be provided through an ASP marketplace. There is a need for ASP marketplaces, which gives the user a transparent insight into the ASP market. In this paper we define Application Service Providing in the context of Outsourcing. Then we analyze relevant software classes for ASP marketplaces. Finally we will set criteria to compare different levels of service of ASP marketplace. This paper gives an overview of key characteristics ASP marketplace provider must take into account by preparing the business process in order to successfully deliver application services.

Introduction

An Application Service Provider (ASP) is any organization or third-party that provisions software applications over the Internet, typically for a fee. ASPs host and manage the applications from their facilities or from co-location center(s), and coordinate the ongoing support, maintenance and upgrades of the applications [5]. The cost of using software online may be reduced dramatically, because the customer does not need to purchase dedicated hardware, or worry about in-house expertise for installation and maintenance. The classical market structures will be expanded by new relations between the market actors. ASP marketplaces will take on a central role in this new business area [3].
But before this kind of ASP marketplaces will become commonplace, several critical questions remain open to research [4]. It is not a technical but rather an economical problem ASP Marketplaces have to face. Software producers need to renew and extend their product line and pricing scheme for online business [2]. New business concepts, which allow the customization and personalization of software components in a product line (Versioning) and a personalized desktop configuration will determine either the success or the doom of software marketplace [15].

Types of Application Services

Outsourcing is increasingly accepted in business today. Organizations are concentrating on core competence, and use outside specialists to perform all non-essential functions [10]. The spectrum of application services now available as a managed service ranges from simple static website hosting, passing through hosted email and messaging, right up to high-end enterprise resource planning (ERP) applications. This new wave of outsourced application services is typically priced on a per-user, per-month subscription basis. Outsourcing allows concentrating

O. Etzion and P. Scheuermann (Eds.): CoopIS 2000, LNCS 1901, pp. 114, 119, 2000.
© Springer-Verlag Berlin Heidelberg 2000

on delivering strategic business value. For smaller enterprises, the issue is a lack of knowledge and resources to deploy and operate the new technologies they need to retain their competitiveness [6].

Application hosting

Internet service providers (ISPs) are specialised in providing servers and support for their customers to host web sites. Web sites get more and more sophisticated, from static content into interactive functions such as electronic commerce and customer self-service. Caused by this evolution ISPs find themselves hosting applications on their web server farms and they embrace the opportunity to offer the applications as managed services to their customers [14]. This ASP service is often described as application outsourcing. Providing access to the software as an application service allows customers to deploy it with less implementation effort and a much smaller upfront investment of money and resources.

Online Workspaces and Desktops

ASP marketplaces extend the application-hosting model to interactive desktops and workspaces. They offer application services online rental, either as a bundle or as individual choices from an online application catalogue [13]. Examples include email and collaborative applications, file and document storage, web and e-commerce administration software, simple desktop productivity tools, and others tailored to meet more specialist needs. ASPs and software producers must spend time preparing software for delivery. The ASP Marketplace carrier tailors an application to the customer's requirements, purchases the necessary software and hardware, and the customer receive the application as a managed service [14].

ASP Marketplaces

ASP Marketplaces offers an infrastructure for managing the deployment and use of distributed application services on the web and manages and delivers application capabilities to multiple entities [8]. ASP marketplaces enable software vendors to describe and to check in any kind of software application: complex ERP software, standard software, games and free software methods. For customers an ASP marketplaces is a decision support system for software applications and helps to select software components suitable to match individual requirements.
By using ASP Marketplaces (figure 1), organizations can keep their existing infrastructure, while deploying the newest applications across the enterprise.

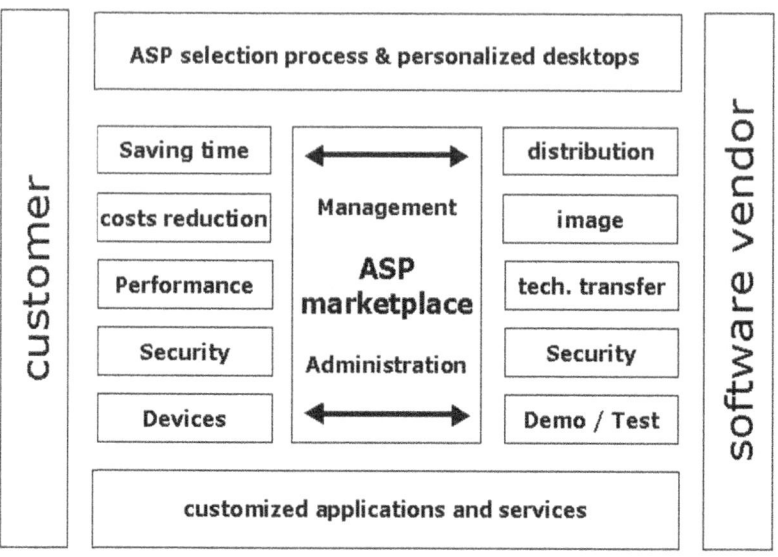

Fig. 1.: ASP Marketplace

Actors and their roles in ASP Marketplaces

Now we turn to the presentation of the actors and the roles they take on in an ASP marketplace (Figure 2).

Software producers develop, maintenance and host the applications.

Application Service Providers (ASPs) own the application or a special software license to offer the software product online.

Channel Partners publish and offer data and access to databases [4].

Network Service Providers offer and maintenance the computational services and provide network access to the applications.

ASP marketplaces offer a business logic that grants authorized users secure access to application server sites. They act as an intermediary between the buyer and the seller, which makes them responsible for the trade function of the online software marketplace [10]. Consequently they can be considered as the kernel of the new software market structure. The infrastructure provides functions to establish secure connections, to interoperate applications, and to manage services remotely. It also offers the business logic such as profiling, customization and pricing models. Moreover it offers new product strategies such as versioning and disaggregation of software suites [1].

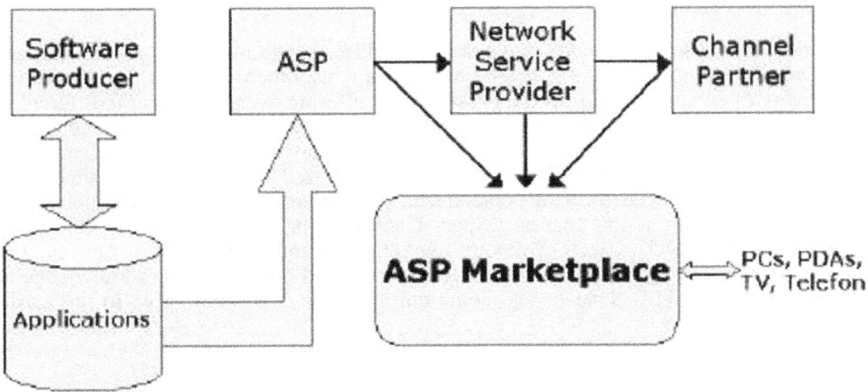

Fig. 2. Actors and their roles of an ASP Marketplace

Business models for ASP Marketplaces

The choice of a business model represents one of the most important decisions for ASPs, as it involves the basic questions of how and how much profit should be generated.

ASP Applications - Product strategies

Especially in the domain of software, consumers tend to have very specific and absolute preferences, leading to a great variety of software component combinations demanded. This generates an undeniable need for product differentiation in order to satisfy customers' needs [14].

Electronic-commerce applications
Vertical and horizontal electronic commerce marketplaces arise worldwide within incredible speed. For an ASP marketplace it is important to know and to offer suitable rules for special branches [9]. Product information has to be described in a common language like XML. ASP marketplaces offer the electronic purchasing application on a per-transaction, per-user, and per-month basis. Using the ASP marketplace model, setup costs and developing costs disappear, resulting in the fact that enterprises can begin to earn a return on investment (ROI) from day one.

Messaging and collaboration
Online massaging services like Hotmail and GMX are widely spread and very common. Messaging should have been one of the first applications to be offered by an ASP marketplace. In large organizations, messaging and collaboration applications are highly infrastructure intensive and vitally mission critical [13]. Messaging and collaboration are obvious complementary applications to electronic commerce and CRM. The ability to offer integrated solutions will be a core benefit of ASP Marketplaces, one of the evaluation criteria that potential customers of ASPs should take into account, ought to be the range of applications available [6].

ASP pricing strategies

ASP marketplaces can offer a wide range of pricing differentiation following individual criteria so that customers needs will be taken into account as much as possible [9]. The main characteristic of personal pricing is the possibility of offering every customer a different price. The price each customer has to pay may depend on the quality and quantity of consumption. Customers could be distinguished according to the type of enterprise (academic, small, corporate, government), the size of the organization, required databases, access time, duration time, and so on. A special form of personalized pricing are auctions [7]. Auctions are very common and popular in the Internet. Special software packages and promotion products auctions are very useful as well. Software marketplaces and ASPs should offer auctions to customers in addition to personalized pricing. Personalized pricing requires knowledge about individual customers [12]. One to one communication plays a central role in this customer information source.

ASP Selection Process

Migration to an ASP Marketplace puts any organization in a position of complete dependence on a third party. This is not unusual in business. Enterprises depend on banks to process financial transactions for them.

Service level agreements

Service Level Agreements are the most critical part of today's networked world. To prove the value of the outsourced applications, ASPs will need to provide assurances of performance and availability to their customers [13]. Service level agreements between network carriers and their customers are common and the concepts of SLAs can be applied to ASP Marketplace services as well.

Technology infrastructure and performance of the channel partner
The provider's technology infrastructure underpins the reliability and performance of any ASP solution, and should be expected to surpass the customer's own in-house setup [13]. The channel partner, who hosts the data center, should incorporate technology to maximize performance, with load-balancing across servers, high-bandwidth links to external networks and high-specification server platforms [6].

Data safeguarding and security
The ASP Marketplace data center should be able to show state of the art data protection capabilities, with Raid storage or similar, frequent backup, a disaster recovery plan and high standards of physical security. There should also be a clear procedure for the client to recover data from the provider at the termination of the relationship or contract.

Conclusion

The improvement of the Internet technologies and the increase of ASPs have given new confidence to ASP Marketplaces as a tactical and a strategic option for organizations .ASP marketplaces are gaining momentum but their impact on software vendors is still unclear [3]. The ASP model also reduces support costs, eliminates piracy, and creates an opportunity to sell customized, personalized and complementary software and services [11].

Early adopting ASP Marketplaces are helping to establish best practice standards for this young industry and demonstrating the benefits in proven customer implementations. Now the next generation of development of ASP Marketplaces starts, giving customers the ability to select customized personalized applications and pay for them on a usage base. ASP Marketplaces who can provide a secure proven infrastructure for integrating multiple applications and services have the most favorable terms to lead the ASP market. ASP marketplaces will be pioneering new economies of scale in the provision of computing to tomorrow's enterprises and organizations.

References

[1]   Bakos, Y. and Brynjolfsson, E., "Bundling and Competition on the Internet: Aggregation Strategies for Information Goods," Working Paper (1999)
[2]   Bakos, Y. and Brynjolfsson, E., "Bundling Information Goods: Pricing, Profits and Efficiency,", Management Science, 1999
[3]   Business Software Alliance, *Building an Information Economy*, Software Industry Positions U.S. for New Digital Era, 1999
[4]   Jacobsen, H.-A., Günther, O., Riessen, G., Component leasing on the World Wide Web, Proc. 1st ACM Conf. Electronic Commerce, ACM Press, 1999.
[5]   Kenneth S. Corts., *On the competitive effects of price-matching policies,* International Journal of Industrial Organization, 1997.
[6]   Klemenhagen, B., Application Service Providers (ASP) - Spotlight Report, Cherry Tree & Co., October 1999
[7]   Nevo, A., and Wolfram, C., Prices and coupons for breakfast cereals, Technical report, UC Berkeley, 1999. http://emlab.Berkeley.EDU/users/nevo/.
[8]   Tamm, G., Günther, O., On-demand application integration - Business Concepts and strategies for the ASP market, 4th Workshop FDBS-99, November 1999
[9]   Tamm, G., Günther, O., Business Models for ASP Marketplaces, ECIS 2000
[10] Tamm, G., Günther, O., Electronic Commerce Business Concepts for Server Based Computing, ITS 2000
[11] U.S. Government Working Group on Electronic Commerce, Annual Report (1st), November 1998
[12] Varian, Hal R., A model of sales, American Economic Review, 70:-659, 1980.
[13] Wainewrigt, P., Interlaint: ASP fusion for the enterprise, ASP News Review, September 1999
[14] Wainewrigt, P., Futurelink: Building the Information Utility, ASP News Review, May 1999
[15] Zwass, V., Structure and macro-level impacts of electronic commerce: From technological infrastructure to electronic marketplaces, Foundation of Information Systems, e-Commerce Paper, 1998.

Exploring the Semantic Structure of Technical Document Collections: A Cooperative Systems Approach[*]

Andreas Becks[1], Stefan Sklorz[1], and Matthias Jarke[1,2]

[1] Lehrstuhl für Informatik V, RWTH Aachen, Ahornstraße 55, 52056 Aachen, Germany
Phone: ++49 (241) 80-21516 – Fax: ++49 (241) 8888-321
{becks, sklorz, jarke}@informatik.rwth-aachen.de
[2] GMD-FIT, Schloss Birlinghoven, 53754 Sankt Augustin, Germany

Abstract. Identifying and analyzing the knowledge available in document form is a key element of corporate knowledge management. In engineering-intensive organizations, it involves tasks such as standard generation and evaluation, comparison of related cases and experience reuse in their treatment. In this paper, we present the design, implementation, and some application experiences with a modular approach that allows a variety of techniques from semantic document analysis to interoperate with a tailorable map-centered visualization of the structure of technical document collections.

1   Introduction

In knowledge management the identification and analysis of knowledge available in an enterprise is a key issue. Often it is not the lack of knowledge sources in a company that is a problem, but the flood of unstructured information hidden in document collections. Consider engineering-intensive organizations like the chemical industries. Here, management documents, requirement definitions, technical guidelines or manuals of chemical plants contain important information about the company's goals or issues regarding configuration and maintenance of machines. An important element in the mosaic of knowledge identification is to obtain a structured overview of such texts.

Whereas information retrieval systems aim at enabling a query-driven search in document collections, typical analysis tasks in knowledge management are characterized by a merely explorative and cooperative procedure: For example, in a system analysis effort consultants may want to find out what kind of documented knowledge is stored or what business processes are reflected in the produced documents. Fruitful exploration requires easily and intuitively accessible structure. Visualizing the often complex relationships between documents or classes of documents can serve as a common basis for discussion and cooperative exploration of documented knowledge.

---

[*] An extended version of this paper is available as technical report 2000-4, Dept. of Computer Science, RWTH Aachen, Germany (via anonymous FTP: ftp.informatik.rwth-aachen.de)

O. Etzion and P. Scheuermann (Eds.): CoopIS 2000, LNCS 1901, pp. 120–125, 2000.
© Springer-Verlag Berlin Heidelberg 2000

So-called document maps present the overall similarity structure of a corpus of texts. Documents are often represented as points in a 2D or 3D map display. The concept of 'document similarity' is reflected in the display by a notion of distance: The more similar documents or document groups are, the closer they appear in the map.

In our work we study the use of document maps in the context of knowledge management and specialized document collections. The process of knowledge elicitation is usually a collaborative effort which involves experts from different areas within the application domain, e.g. engineers, technical writers, etc.. In this paper we sketch a document map technique which powerfully visualizes the topological structure of a collection of texts and enables groups of experts to cooperatively discuss and analyze the company's documented knowledge assets. To provide a reliable basis for similarity computation we propose a modular framework for generating document maps and discuss experiences collected in different case studies.

Related Work

There are two groups of document map approaches to be found in literature. One group calculates a document space for visualization by using certain variations of Multidimensional Scaling (MDS) or related techniques. Coarsely spoken, based on a proximity measure between texts (adopted from information retrieval) for each document a point in a 2D or 3D metric space is calculated so that the distances between the points approximate the similarity of the corresponding documents. This space can be visualized directly, e.g. using a scatter plot: BEAD [3] presents similarity relationships between documents by 3-dimensional "particle" clouds. Using a similar visualization approach, STARLIGHT [11] aims to visualize the content of multimedia databases. Closely related to these approaches is GALAXIES [15] which yields a simple 2D scatter plot. VXINSIGHT [5] visualizes the document distribution density by means of a mountain terrain metaphor. These approaches are focused on the display of similarity between *individual* documents. The scaling techniques used try to optimize the distances between documents with respect to the given proximity measure. However, directly using a 2D or 3D space results in a relatively high information loss and can only very coarsely represent the original documents' similarity.

The second group uses self-organizing feature maps (SOM, [7]) as a basis for clustering and visualization. This simple neural network model tries to preserve the cluster structure rather than absolute metric distances between single objects. In [10, 4] topic navigation maps are presented for text categorization. These maps show the associative structure of document categories. WebSOM [8] uses a SOM as a browsing interface for collections of newsgroup articles. These SOM-based approaches more powerfully display the density or topical structure of a document space. In contrast to the MDS-related methods they perform an aggregation of information instead of presenting relationships of individual documents towards each other. However, when it comes to condensing and relating single texts and groups of documents against each other the presentation of individual items w.r.t. their overall topological structure – i.e. the cluster structure of the document space – is important: Which documents are grouped, and how do the respective groups relate to each other? Users may accept some local stretching of distance relationships but need a faithful cluster visualization.

To provide a reliable basis for visualization it is crucial to be able to choose an adequate indexing and comparison model for the document collection if available. Most approaches use a fixed term vector representation. In contrast, the design of our document map approach allows the flexible integration of different document comparison techniques, ranging from symbolic to term vector based text representations, combined with the powerful structure-preserving mapping of SOMs.

2   A Modular Approach for Generating Document Maps

The analysis of documents regarding their semantic similarity is the key concept for generating a document map. In our application domain we are interested in gaining a reliable overview of a specialized document collection. In information retrieval research and related fields many different models for document comparison have been developed: simple statistical information retrieval methods like the well-known vector space model [12], knowledge-based indexing and comparing methods for specialized text types, e.g. medical abstracts [2], or domain specific retrieval engines from case based reasoning [9]. Whether a specific method provides sufficient results depends on the linguistic style and the degree of knowledge which is necessary to assess the similarity of documents. As a consequence, the document indexing scheme should not be coupled with the visualization method actually used (as it is the case with the SOM approaches sketched in the last section).

In our framework the internal document representation method is not used for any calculation step except document comparison. The only interface we expect is a matrix of distance values for each pair of texts. Consequently, this module is exchangeable and can be chosen with respect to the characteristics of the corpus. By default our prototype uses the vector space model for indexing and similarity computation.

Given a similarity value for all pairs of documents we then compute a semantic document space which reflects the documents' similarity in its topology. For this we use techniques from multidimensional scaling. More precisely, we map objects (representing the documents) into m-space (where m is user-defined) so that the relative error of the distances in m-space regarding the 'true' distances of the objects (stress) is minimized. Therefore, similarity values s have to be transformed into distance values d. In cases where the similarity values fall into a predefined range [0, s_{max}] a linear conversion can be chosen, e.g. $d =_{def} s_{max} - s$. Some retrieval functions calculate similarity values where no maximal value is defined. In these cases a nonlinear inversion transformation, e.g. $d =_{def} b^{-s}$ for some fixed $b > 1$ can be applied. MDS does not require the distances between objects to respect the triangular inequality. In our implementation we use a geometrical scaling method introduced in [6] which performs the mapping in linear time with still satisfactory results if the distance measure used satisfies the properties of a metric.

The actual mapping and visualization step uses a self-organizing feature map [7]: This neural network model consists of one layer of active units which are disposed in a two dimensional grid structure. Each unit has m weighted connections to the input layer. During the unsupervised learning process the input vectors are sequentially presented to the network. In each learning step a single unit is determined where the weight vector is most similar to the input pattern. This so-called *cluster center* and units in a certain surrounding are then shifted towards the input vector. After the learning process the relative positions of different cluster centers towards each other in the grid show the similarity between corresponding input vectors. To visualize the information encoded in the neural network we use a powerful visualization technique, originally developed for data mining [13, 14]. This method reflects the density of the document space which is encoded in the weight vectors of the trained SOM.

3   The System DocMINER

Based on our method we have developed the interactive document map system DocMINER (<u>Doc</u>ument <u>M</u>aps for <u>I</u>nformation <u>E</u>licitation and <u>R</u>etrieval) in order to study the improvement of cooperative management of documented knowledge. This visual interface offers a common view and serves as the basis for analysis and discussion of the knowledge contained in a collection of technical documents.

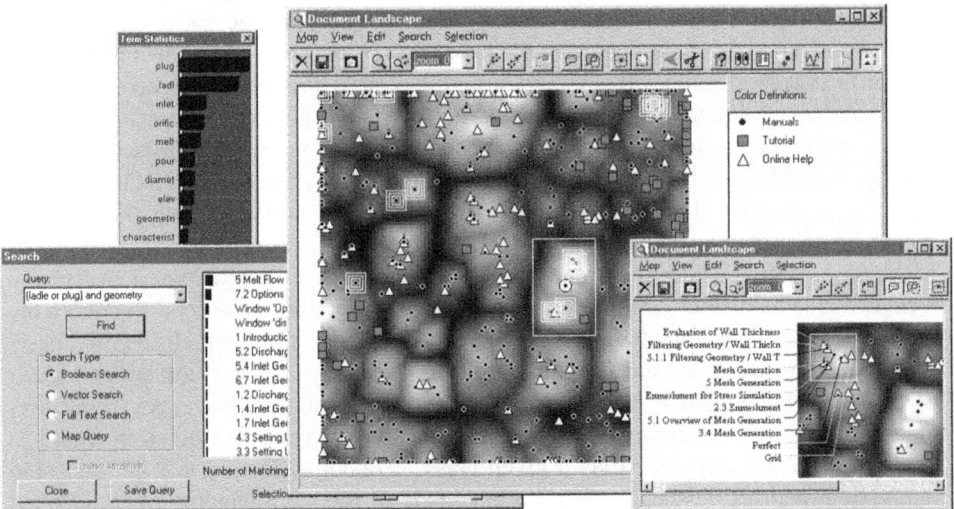

Figure 1: Interaction with a document map, the cooperative workspace

The figure shows a map of 679 documents which are represented as points in the display. Similar documents are grouped as neighbored points and are located in common bright shaded areas. Dark borders separate groups of related documents: The darker the color, the more dissimilar are the groups. To explore and analyze the collection users can zoom into marked areas, ask for significant key words of a field, view the titles of documents within a group, or open documents by point-and-click.

Our interaction paradigm allows a close coupling of query-driven and explorative search: In addition to browsing through the map analysts can use a query interface to highlight relevant documents w.r.t. an explicitly formulated information need. Given a query result, the map also helps to examine the context of matching texts.

Many analysis tasks involve the question of how predefined classes of documents correspond to each other. Therefore, individual documents can be color-coded so that the distribution of given classes within the 'information landscape' of the enterprise can be examined. Thus, analysts can explore the collection and learn about the inherent structure of the corpus, i.e. identify relationships between documents and groups of documents.

4   Experiences

To study the use of document maps for cooperative analysis and exploration tasks we performed some scientific and industrial case studies. We briefly sketch two of them: A first study was concerned with analyzing informal requirement scenarios in an international software engineering project (a detailed report can be found in [1]). In the project, experts and researchers from the chemical industries, software vendors and universities defined standards for chemical process engineering simulators. So-called 'use cases' were collaboratively designed to describe the functionality of simulator objects – with the danger of redundancies, inconsistencies and lack of overview of the created collection. A document map of these textual scenarios has shown a grouping similar to that of a hand-crafted expert structure, which has been generated independently – a good validation of the approach. Furthermore, the map was used as a basis for discussion between some project members, aiming at refining the given structure. As a result, additional information about the sub-groups themselves and their interrelations could be derived and a refined hierarchy could be proposed. Thus the map approach turned out to be a valuable tool for cooperative software engineering.

A second study, which is currently performed, addresses the problem of structuring technical documentation of steel casting process simulators in order to support the definition of 'single knowledge sources' (i.e. knowledge units which identify basic pieces of knowledge and are reusable in different contexts). The complete collection of product documentation has been divided into 679 sub-documents regarding thematic sections of the original manuals; the corresponding map is shown in figure 1. Each icon on the map identifies a given class of documents: manuals, tutorial, and online help text (cf. legend at the right hand side of the main window). Consider the distribution of the different document icons. Obviously, for some topics (i.e. document groups) only few tutorial texts exist. When it comes to extending the tutorial's content the map can indicate 'neglected' topic areas. For defining single sources we use the map as a basis to discuss possible starting points for condensing textual knowledge assets in cooperation with the technical writers of the documentation. Therefore, we focus on documents which are located very close together and figure out whether one could derive a 'basic piece of knowledge'.

To conclude, our document map approach visualizes fine-granular relationships between single documents and allows the application of different document analysis methods. Case studies have shown that the method is applicable to real-world document collections and analysis tasks which involve cooperation between the analysts.

Acknowledgements. This work was supported by the Deutsche Forschungsgemeinschaft (DFG) in its focused doctoral programme on Informatics and Engineering at RWTH Aachen.

References

1. Becks, A., Köller, J. Automatically Structuring Textual Requirement Scenarios. Proc. of the 14th IEEE Conf. on Automated Software Engineering, Cocoa Beach, Florida, USA, 1999
2. Becks, A., Sklorz, S., Tresp, C. Semantic Structuring and Visual Querying of Document Abstracts in Digital Libraries. In Proc. of the Second European Conference on Research and Advanced Technology for Digital Libraries (LNCS 1513), Crete, Greece, 1998, 443-458
3. Chalmers, M., Chitson, P.. Bead: Explorations in Information Visualization. In Proc. of the 15th Annual International ACM SIGIR Conference on Research and Development in Information Retrieval, Copenhagen, 1992, 330-337
4. Chen, H., Schuffels, Ch., Orwig, R.. Internet Categorization and Search: A Self-Organizing Approach. Journal of Visual Communication and Image Representation, 7 (1), 1996, 88-102
5. Davidson, G. S., Hendrickson, B., Johnson, D. K., Meyers, Ch. E., Wylie, B. N. Knowledge Mining With VxInside: Discovery Through Interaction. Journal of Intelligent Information Systems, Vol. 11, No. 3, 1998, 259-285
6. Faloutsos, C., Lin, D.: Fastmap: A Fast Algorithm for Indexing, Data-Mining and Vizualization of Traditional and Multimedia Datasets. Proc. of the Int. Conf. on Management of Data (SIGMOD'95); 2(24), 1995
7. Kohonen, T.: Self-Organizing Maps. Springer, Berlin, 2nd Edition, 1995
8. Lagus, K., Honkela, T., Kaski, S., Kohonen, T.: Self-Organizing Maps of Document Collections: A New Approach to Interactive Exploration. Proc. of the 2nd International Conference on Knowledge Discovery and Data Mining, AAAI Press, California, 1996
9. Lenz, M.. Managing the Knowledge Contained in Technical Documents. Proc. of the 2nd International Conference on Practical Aspects of Knowledge Management (PAKM98), Basel, Switzerland, 1998
10. Lin, X., Soergel, D., Marchionini, G.: A Self-Organizing Map for Information Retrieval. SIGIR 91, Conf. on Research and Development in Information Retrieval, Chicago, 1991
11. Risch, J., May, R., Dowson, S., Thomas, J. A Virtual Environment for Multimedia Intelligence Data Analysis. IEEE Computer Graphics and Applications, 1996, 33–41
12. Salton, G. (Ed.): The SMART Retrieval System – Experiments in Automatic Document Processing. Prentice Hall, New Jersey, 1971
13. Sklorz, S. Becks, A. Jarke, M. MIDAS: ein Multistrategiesystem zum explorativen Data Mining (in German). 2. Workshop Data Mining und Data Warehousing als Grundlage moderner entscheidungsunterstützender Systeme, LWA'99 Sammelbd., Univ. Magdeburg, 1999
14. Sklorz, S.: A Method for Data Analysis based on Self Organizing Feature Maps, World Automation Congress (WAC '96), Albuquerque, USA, 1996, 611-616
15. Wise, J.A., Thomas, J.J., Pennock, K., Lantrip, D., Pottier, M., Schur, A., Crow, V. Visualizing the non-visual: Spatial analysis and interaction with information from text documents. In Proc. of IEEE Information Visualization 95 (InfoViz'95), 1995, 51–58

Organized Distributed Systems
(Extended Abstract)

Gil Tidhar[1]* and Elizabeth A. Sonenberg[2]*

[1] KESEM International
42 Zeela Street
Maccabim, Israel
gil@kesem.com
[2] Department of Information Systems
University of Melbourne
Melbourne, Australia
l.sonenberg@dis.unimelb.edu.au

Abstract. We describe an approach to the specification of distributed systems that exhibit complex behavior in dynamic environments. We present a model of decision making in artificial organizations that derives inspiration from Organization and Management Theory and from Multi-Agent Systems research. We argue that this approach aids the system designer by supporting a suitably high level of abstraction in the design process.

1 Introduction

Our main objective is to facilitate the design of distributed computer systems that can exhibit different types of complex behavior in a dynamic environment. The work adapts concepts and ideas from Organization and Management Theory (OMT) and shows how such ideas can be used in designing artificial organizations, i.e. organizations of artificial agents. The work also builds on prior research in multi-agent systems (MAS) dealing with teams (i.e., collectives with a common goal) by introducing explicit support for specifications of richer relationships than team membership.

In brief, by separating out generic aspects of organizational behavior and by providing domain specific component specifications, one can allow the organization to reason not only about what to do next, but to draw on a rich representation, including alternative social structures, and reason about the way decisions are made and execution is coordinated.

The structure of this paper is as follows: we present background material from OMT and MAS; then introduce a model of artificial organizations that derives inspiration from OMT; and finally describe a model of organizational decision making that extends approaches available in MAS.

---

* This work was completed while both authors were in the Department of Computer Science and Software Engineering at the University of Melbourne, Australia.

2   Background Theory and Limitations

According to the Systems Model of human organizations [3, 7] the reason for the emergence of organizational structures in human organizations is that they are more effective in achieving the goals of large groups. The loss in effectiveness when structure is absent is primarily due to the limited abilities of humans that make up the group. Although from some perspectives computer systems do not have human limitations, such constraints do apply when dealing with tasks that require decisions in limited time and information.

One model of organizations and inter-organization relationships which at least partly addresses this issue is the Command, Control, and Communication (C3) model [1]. This model has primarily been used to describe organizations that operate under mission critical circumstances and, in particular, to describe military organizations. Due to the critical nature of the tasks to be executed, such organizations tend to adhere to a formal organizational structure and attempt to eliminate (through training and discipline) informal aspects associated with natural human behavior. As such, they present a good candidate as a basis for developing a model of a distributed computer system.

In his work on defining the structure of organizations Mintzberg states that "the parts of an organization are joined together by different flows"... [4, page 35]. These flows are identified as the *operating flows* (namely *Authority* and *Decision*) and the *regulating flows* (namely *Performance Information* and *Staff Information*). For the purpose of our investigation, Mintzberg's description of flows can be seen to correspond to the theory of C3. Command is associated with authority flow and control is associated with decision flow. Both types of information flows are considered here as communication.[1]

A limitation in seeking to apply OMT to the problem of distributed system design, is the level of formality in which the models are described. A computer system requires information and instructions using a precise and formal language. The description of the model can not be in vague or general terms. Furthermore, a model of a real-time embedded distributed system performing a mission critical role should be validated and verified before it becomes operational. Such validation and verification can only be done with a formal specification.

Previous work on distributed real-time systems includes work on rational agents [6]. A rational agent is completely specified by its mental attitudes: its *beliefs, goals*, and *intentions*. Agents are provided with a library of useful procedures (*plans*) that can be invoked in a context sensitive way during execution. The single-agent view has been extended to a team-based one, using joint mental attitudes (*mutual beliefs, joint goals*, and *joint intentions*) and *team plans* [2, 8]. When a team plan is adopted by a number of agents, the actions and sub-goals of the plan are allocated to different *roles:* each team member is assigned to a particular role and executes the actions/sub-goals of that role as part of its commitment to the team plan. Importantly, each team member remains committed to the achievement of the *whole* plan.

---

[1] The distinction is significant when considering the operational semantics [9].

Team-oriented models focus on the interconnections between a team and its members and (social) relationships that reflect the decision-making context, such as authority and dependency relationships, are hard-wired into the behavior of the members of the team. The designer of such a system determines the social behavior and structure that is required and then "translates" it into the required individual behavior of each of the agents. The implemented specification describes details of single agent behavior.

In the resulting system notions of social behavior and structure emerge from the behavior of the individual agents. These abstract notions are more apparent in the eye of the beholder than they are in the code that generated this behavior. In this "bottom-up approach" there is no way to explicitly specify the behavior of the distributed system as a whole or the behavior of any of its sub-systems without explicitly specifying the behavior of the single agents. Furthermore, allowing for dynamic changes to the structure is very difficult. Our approach to organization design provides explicit support for such abstractions.

3   Representing Organizations

We introduce a language for specifying an organization that includes the notion of an organizational structure adopted. Such a definition allows the developer to specify the sub-organizations that are part of an organization (i.e., *Team Structure*), inter-organization relationships (i.e., *Social Structure*), the function assigned to each sub-team (i.e., *Responsibilities*), and the way the organization can be referred to or represented by other organization (i.e., *Identification*). Furthermore the notions of the beliefs of an organization (i.e., *Mutual Beliefs*), the goal states desired by an organization (i.e., *Joint Goals*), and the organizations intention towards achieving these goals (i.e., *Joint Intentions*) are also included. The language allows for the specification of beliefs and knowledge available to one organization about other organizations (i.e., *Social Mental Attitudes*).

The behavior of an organization depends on the social mental attitudes it has involving other organizations. We also consider the interactions between social mental attitudes and: (1) joint mental attitudes; (2) team structure; and (3) other social mental attitudes. We consider the rationality of an organization to be one particular interaction between these three aspects of an organization. Different types of rationality can be modelled using different interactions. Furthermore, this approach enables a form of abstraction suitable for "top-down" specifications of decision making in a distributed system.

Despite their relative simplicity there are many definitions of C3 relationships [9]. An example of a C3 model is captured in the following relationship between the C3 attitudes and the joint mental attitudes: (1) *Command* is the authority (and responsibility) that one organization has to determine the adoption of a joint goal by another organization; (2) *Control* is the authority (and responsibility) that one organization has to make decisions for another organization as to the various possible ways in which the other organization manages the joint intention to achieve an adopted joint goal; and (3) *Communication* is

Organization

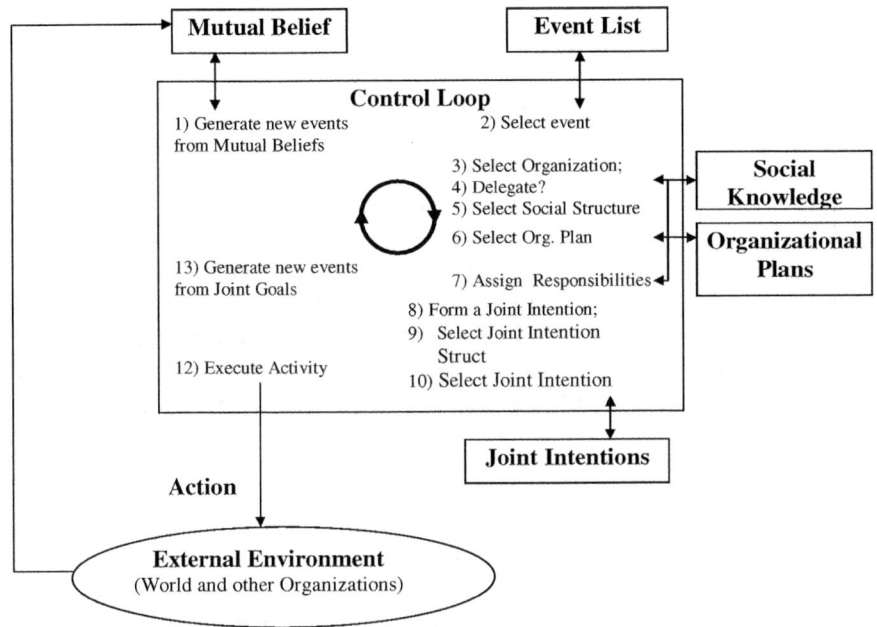

Fig. 1. Control Loop of an Organization.

the authority (and responsibility) that one organization has in communicating its own mutual beliefs to another organization.

A formal definition in a suitable logic language and additional examples of C3 models can be found elsewhere [10]. We now provide a description of how system behavior can be generated from a specification in this framework.

4   Operational Semantics for Organizational Decision Making

Our approach to organizational decision making is an extension of ideas from single agent decision making [5]. Decision making is taken to include three major processes: means-end reasoning, deliberation, and reconsideration. Means-end reasoning involves the processing of percepts from the external environment and internal goals and generating possible means for responding to the external percepts or achieving goals.

The main objective of an organization is to achieve joint goals or to react to environmental changes. Each such event is referred to as a triggering event. The main control loop includes the following main steps: (1) observe the environment and determine the goals (i.e., the "ends"); (2) decide on the means for achieving the ends (i.e., "means-end reasoning"); (3) synchronize the mental attitudes of the sub-organizations (i.e., "mind-set synchronization"); and (4) execute actions which affect the environment or the internal mental state (i.e., "act"). This is described in Figure 1. There are substantial details that are hidden in each of the above steps. Such details can be found elsewhere [10].

An *organizational plan* describes the domain specific procedures by which an organization can achieve joint goals or react to situations. In the *organization-oriented* approach the means of achieving a goal include the set of sub-organizations and the possible allocation of tasks to these sub-organizations. That is, the organization can modify its set of sub-organizations so that the new set has the capability of achieving the goals of the organization. Furthermore, one also considers the way the sub-organizations are organized in determining goals, making decisions, and communicating information. For each organization, the specification of the behavior of an organization is based on the knowledge available to the organization. Such knowledge includes: (1) possible social relationships; (2) organizational plans; and (3) other organizations in the system.

Each organization executes separately. The key to the coordinated behavior of the organization and its sub-organizations is to include relationships between the mental attitudes of an organization as constraints in the execution model. That is, when an organization attempts to adopt a mental attitude all relevant constraints are checked and enforced. Performing an activity may involve executing an action, adopting a new goal, or adopting a new belief. A goal can be adopted *only if* all the constraints imposed by the sub-organizations relationships can be maintained. Similarly for adopting a belief or executing an action. In the above example C3 model the social mental attitudes can affect the behavior of the organization in the following ways:

- an organization will accept a joint goal only from organizations that command it;
- an organization will communicate to its controlling organizations the possible choices available to it;
- the selection of social structure, organizational plan, joint intention structure, and joint intention, are all done by the controlling organizations;
- an organization will communicate the successful or failed execution of a joint intention to its controlling organizations;
- an organization will communicate the successful or failed attempt to achieve a joint goal to its commanding organizations.
- an organization will communicate changes to its mutual beliefs to the organizations it has a relevant communication relationships with.

Given that the organization is operating in an uncertain environment, failure can occur at a number of stages. The principle in responding to failure is to mark the option as failed, return to the last decision point, and seek an alternative option that has not been marked as failed.

5   Discussion

In a distributed system the activities of making decisions, evaluating options, and sharing information are not trivial. Furthermore, the way these are performed may affect the performance of the system and its ability to achieve its goals. In existing approaches, the designer of the system cannot explicitly specify the way decisions are being made, multiple options evaluated, or information shared between system components.

The organization-oriented approach described above is intended to support the design of distributed systems. The resulting design could have been developed using an agent-oriented approach, object-oriented approach, or a structured approach. The issue is not the ability to implement a system but rather how easy it is to do so using a particular model.

We argue that by explicitly representing organizational structures we simplify the designer's task by supporting *abstraction*, and *re-usability*. Abstraction, in that a system designer can reason about an organization as a unit without considering its components until such information is required. Re-usability, by separating generic features of organizational decision making from domain specific properties, as represented in organizational plans, social structures, etc.

Acknowledgements We thank Anand Rao for many stimulating conversations on the topic of this paper.

References

[1] C. J. Harris and I. White, editors. *Advances in Command, Control & Communication Systems*, pages xi–xvi. Peter Peregrinus, London, UK, 1987.

[2] D. Kinny, M. Ljungberg, A. Rao, E. Sonenberg, G. Tidhar, and E. Werner. Planned team activity. In C. Castelfranchi and E. Werner, editors, *Artificial Social Systems*, volume 830 of *LNCS*, pages 227–256. Springer Verlag, 1994.

[3] A. Kuhn. *The Logic of Organization*. The Jossey-Bass Social and Behavioral Science. Jossey-Bass Inc., San Francisco, CA, 1982. Completed by R. D. Beam.

[4] H. Mintzberg. *The Structuring of Organizations: A Synthesis of the Research*. Prentice Hall, Englewood Cliffs, N.J., USA, 1979.

[5] A. Rao. A unified view of plans as recipes. In G. Holmstrom-Hintikka and R. Tuomela, editors, *Contemporary Action Theory*. Kluwer Academic Pub., 1997.

[6] A. S. Rao and M. P. Georgeff. Modeling rational agents within a BDI-architecture. In J. Allen, R. Fikes, and E. Sandewall, editors, *Proceedings of the 2nd International Conference on Principles of KRR*, pages 473–484. Morgan Kaufmann Publishers, San Mateo, CA, 1991.

[7] W. R. Scott. *Organization: Rational, Natural, and Open Systems*. Prentice-Hall, Inc., 3rd edition, 1992. Originally published in 1981.

[8] M. Tambe. Implementing agent teams in dynamic multi-agent environments. *Applied Artificial Intelligence*, 12, 1998.

[9] G. Tidhar. *Organization-Oriented Systems: Theory and Practice*. PhD thesis, Department of Computer Science, University of Melbourne, Australia, 1999.

[10] G. Tidhar and E. A. Sonenberg. Organized distributed systems. Technical report, The University of Melbourne, Melbourne, Australia, June 2000.

Managing Aging Data Using Persistent Views
(extended abstract)

Janne Skyt   Christian S. Jensen

Department of Computer Science, Aalborg University
www.cs.auc.dk/~{skyt|csj}

Abstract. Enabled by the continued advances in storage technologies, the amounts of on-line data grow at a rapidly increasing pace. For example, this development is witnessed in the so-called data webhouses that accumulate data derived from clickstreams. The presence of very large and continuously growing amounts of data introduces new challenges, one of them being the need for effectively managing aging data that is perhaps inaccurate, partly outdated, and of reduced interest. This paper describes a new mechanism, persistent views, that aids in flexibly reducing the volume of data, e.g., by enabling the replacement of such "low-interest," detailed data with aggregated data; and it outlines a strategy for implementing persistent views.

1 Introduction

The developments in data storage technologies continue to obey Moore's Law and thus advance at a rapidly increasing pace. As a consequence, in his recent Turing Award lecture, Jim Gray predicted that there will be sold more disk storage in the 18 months following his lecture than had been sold previously in all of history.

Data storage will be exploited to store increasing amounts of data as soon as it becomes available. The increasing amounts introduce new complexity in data management and offer new challenges to database technology. This paper presents a new mechanism, termed *persistent views* (P-views), that is useful when weeding out data that are no longer desired—e.g., because they are out of date, inaccurate, or are just not needed by any applications—while retaining the data that are still desired.

Consider a sample e-commerce scenario where customer data are accumulated along with web-usage data extracted from clickstreams. The resulting database is effectively append only. The most recent addresses of current customers are used for billing; and geo-coded addresses, recent as well as past, and for current as well as previous customers, are used for data mining. However, only ZIP codes are used in data mining—street names and numbers are of no interest for this task. It is thus desirable to be able to physically delete detailed street data that is not current, or not for current customers. With P-views, one

O. Etzion and P. Scheuermann (Eds.): CoopIS 2000, LNCS 1901, pp. 132–137, 2000.

may specify the current, detailed addresses for current customers as a P-view. This ensures that this data is available in the database, even if all address data is deleted from the base relations. As another example, it may be desirable to retain only a high-granularity summary of the web-usage data when this becomes more than one year old. This summary data may be specified as one or several P-views, upon which the detailed access data more than one year old may be physically deleted.

As the context for P-views, the append-only nature of many applications is formalized by introducing relations with transaction-time support [6], for which conventional deletion has only a logical effect. A new mechanism is then needed for physical deletion: we employ vacuuming, which is a particular approach to physical deletion [8]. P-views, views immune to physical deletions on the underlying base relations, are defined in this context. These views enable, in a flexible and user-friendly manner, the retention of, e.g., select, aggregate, or summary data, while also enabling the deletion of detailed data. When data is physically deleted from base relations on which P-views are defined, the base data that is necessary to compute the P-views must be extracted and retained automatically and transparently. A provably correct foundation for accomplishing this extraction has been devised.

The notion of vacuuming was previously presented in [8], which extends and formalizes earlier work by the authors. P-views offer substantial benefits over vacuuming. Next, conventional views, i.e., named and stored query expressions, have been the topic of a multitude of papers. The notion of snapshot, a type of materialized and detached view, was originally advanced by Adiba and Lindsay [1]. In contrast to views, P-views are insensitive to physical deletions, and in contrast to snapshots, P-views are sensitive to insertions and logical deletions. Finally, some work has studied various notions of derived data, often in the context of data warehousing and materialized views [3], [4], [9]. In the most closely related of this work, Garcia-Molina et al. [3] explore how to "expire" (delete) data from materialized views so that a set of predefined, regular views on these materialized views are unaffected and can be maintained consistently with future updates. P-views solve a quite different problem and, e.g., do not involve two levels of views and does not assume a static set of predefined views.

The next section describes the context for this paper. Section 3 defines and characterizes the notion of P-views in general and in relation to vacuuming. Section 4 outlines the implementation of P-views and illustrates their use. Finally, Section 5 summarizes and offers research directions.

2   Context

Many real-world database applications rely on databases that exhibit an append-only behavior. This type of behavior is perhaps best formalized in the notion of a transaction-time database. Consequently, P-views are defined in the context of this type of database, where there are two mechanisms for deleting data, namely logical and physical deletion. Specifically, each tuple has attached two timestamp values, namely a start and an end time. A tuple is part of the current database state at all times in-between its pair of time values.

The interval of a tuple that is currently current extends from some time in the past until the changing current time, which is captured by the variable *now* [2]. A current tuple is logically deleted by replacing its end time of *now* with a fixed value. In contrast, physical deletion of a tuple entails the removal of the tuple from the database.

Consider the following transaction-time relation schema *Person*, recording the states in which people live.

$$Person = \{Name, State\_of\_Residence, Date\_of\_Birth, TT^\vdash, TT^\dashv\} \tag{1}$$

For simplicity, we use the numbers $1 \ldots 30$ as timestamp values. These may be thought of as days during some specific month. Assuming that three tuples are inserted in the relation at times 2, 5, and 7, we obtain the following relation instance.

$$\{(Jill, DC, 7/6/68, 2, now), (Jim, CA, 1/2/58, 5, now), (Joe, CA, 4/5/63, 7, now)\} \tag{2}$$

Next, at time 12, *Joe* is logically deleted, and *Jill* and *Jim* are physically deleted at times 13 and 16, respectively. Relation $\{(Joe, CA, 4/5/63, 7, 12)\}$ results.

The view below collects the birthday of the youngest person per state, using the aggregation formation operator [5].

$$Young\_pr\_State = \text{AGG}_{\{State\_of\_Residence, \text{MAX}(Date\_of\_Birth) \text{ AS } Date\_of\_Birth\}}(Person) \tag{3}$$

This view returns the relation $\{(CA, 4/5/63), (DC, 7/6/68)\}$ from time 7 to 13 and the relation $\{(CA, 4/5/63)\}$ after time 13. The view is affected by the physical deletion; as we shall see next, P-views are not.

3   Persistent Views

The P-view mechanism aims to ease the preservation of summaries of data from a transaction-time database, including data that has been physically deleted, logically deleted, or is current. We define P-views as follows (see reference [7] for a formal definition.)

DEFINITION   A P-view, defined at time t on a transaction-time database with physical and logical deletion, evaluates as if no physical deletion had happened at or after time t.   □

As a result, even though physical deletion is applied to the base relations, a P-view will always reflect all the data present in the database at any time at or after its definition.

To make the notion of P-views somewhat more specific, we relate it to a particular type of physical deletion, termed vacuuming [8]. Specifically, consider the sample vacuuming specification $\sigma_{TT^{\vdash} < now-10}(Person)$, entered at time 0, which removes tuples inserted into *Person* more than 10 time units ago. At times 13, 16, and 18, it causes the removal of *Jill*, *Jim*, and *Joe*, respectively.

The view *Young_pr_State* from Section 2, if defined as a P-view at time 12, will evaluate as if all vacuuming on the relation is stopped at this time, i.e., as if the specification is defined as "remove data inserted before time 2."

Therefore the P-view will evaluate to $\{(CA, 1/2/58), (DC, 7/6/68)\}$ even after *Jill* and *Jim* are physically deleted from *Person* at times 13 and 16.

4   Implementation Strategy

The implementation strategy for P-views must incorporate two aspects. First, it must ensure data reduction, meaning that the presence of P-views should not unnecessarily hinder the physical removal of data. Second, the strategy must ensure that P-views remain unaffected by physical removals.

This leads to the question of what data must be preserved and what data must be retained in the system even if it is physically removed from the database. Figure 1 illustrates the implementation strategy we propose. With this strategy,

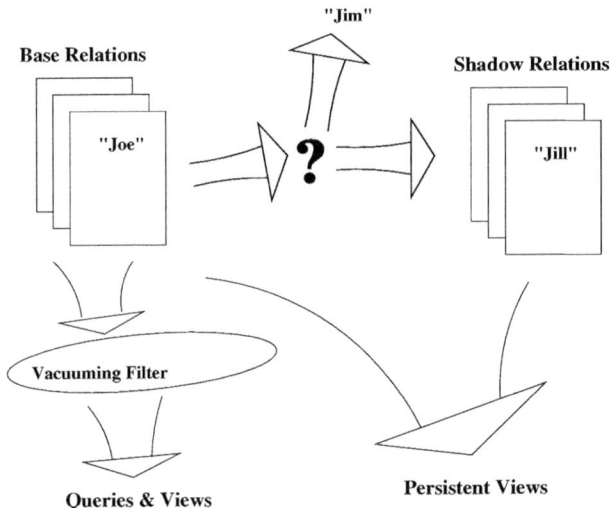

Fig. 1. Implementation Strategy

each base relation is equipped with a shadow relation that has the same schema. The shadow relation retains the tuples that are physically removed from its base relation, but necessary for evaluating a P-view. Further, P-views, unlike regular views and queries, are evaluated on both base and shadow relations.

More specifically, vacuuming separates the logical physical removal of tuples from the actual physical removal by reflecting the vacuuming specifications in a filter. This filter ensures that queries and views do not see tuples that are not yet physically removed, although they should have been so according to the vacuuming specifications. This approach makes it possible to perform the actual physical removal periodically without affecting correctness.

Continuing the *Person* example, the tuples for *Jim* and *Jill* will both qualify for physical removal at time 16. If they have not actually been removed from *Person*, the vacuuming filter will "catch" them so that they appear as physically removed. So with *Young_pr_State* defined as a regular view, the result will correctly be $\{(CA, 4/5/63)\}$.

Next, assume instead that *Young_pr_State* is defined as a P-view. When the tuples for *Jim* and *Jill* are being removed from *Person*, we must decide if the tuples must be retained in order to be able to correctly evaluate the P-view (see the "?" in Figure 1). We determine that the tuple for *Jill* is to be retained in the shadow relation because its absence will affect the P-view result, and that removing the tuple for *Jim* does not affect the result. The order in which the tuples are examined is not significant.

The algorithm given below performs the physical removal and migration to the shadow relation of a set r of tuples.

$NewDelete(r, R)$
[**if** $r \neq \emptyset$
   then [**select some** $u \in r$
         if $\sigma_{PR}(R \cup R^S) = \sigma_{PR}((R \cup R^S) - \{u\})$
         then $Delete(u, R)$;
         else [$Insert(u, R^S)$; $Delete(u, R)$;]
         $NewDelete(r - \{u\}, R)$;]]

Each tuple in r is moved to the shadow relation R^S if its removal affects any P-view; otherwise, the tuple is removed. The second **if**-statement's condition includes a predicate P^R that reflects all existing P-views (reference [7] gives the details).

The implementation strategy outlined above ensures that all views and P-views are always evaluated correctly. Other strategies, e.g., based on materialized views [4], [9], may also be used. The different strategies each have their strengths in different situations.

5   Summary and Research Directions

Motivated by the need for flexible mechanisms to manage the growing amounts of aging data from databases that effectively are append-only, the paper describes a new kind of view, termed *persistent views*, or P-views for short. P-views are similar to conventional views, with the exception that physical deletions on the underlying base relations have no effect on P-views. Although the difference between regular views and P-views is small definition-wise, the implications of this difference are profound. P-views turn out to be quite useful when it is desirable to eliminate bulks of detailed, old, and inaccurate data from the base relations, while preserving only select or aggregate data. In addition, P-views is a general mechanism with applications beyond this paper's focus.

When physically deleting base data, it is generally necessary to retain some of this data transparently to the user in order to be able to compute the P-views. The paper outlines a mechanism for accomplishing this retention using so-called shadow relations.

An extended version of this paper exists [7]. It offers significantly more in-depth coverage of the issues touched upon here.

In future research, it would be of interest to refine the strategy for implementing P-views, so that it retains less data in its shadow relations. This may most prominently be achieved by exploiting projections and, possibly, by introducing multiple shadow relations per base relation. A more radical change would be to abolish the shadow relations altogether and instead use relations that are tied to the individual P-views or subexpressions in P-views. In addition, it would be of interest to prototype the strategy.

Acknowledgments

This research was supported in part by the Danish Technical Research Council through grant 9700780 and by a grant from the Nykredit Corporation.

References

1. M. E. Adiba and B. G. Lindsay. Database Snapshots. In *Proc. VLDB*, pp. 86–91, 1980.
2. J. Clifford, C. Dyreson, T. Isakowitz, C. S. Jensen, and R. T. Snodgrass. On the Semantics of "Now" in Databases. *ACM TODS*, 22(2):171–214, June 1997.
3. H. Garcia-Molina, W. Labio, and J. Yang. Expiring Data in a Warehouse. In *Proc. VLDB*, pp. 500–511, 1998.
4. A. Gupta and I. S. Mumick (editors). *Materialized Views—Techniques, Implementations, and Applications*. The MIT Press, 1999.
5. A. Klug. Equivalence of Relational Algebra And Relational Calculus Query Languages Having Aggregate Functions. *JACM*, 29(3):699–717, July 1982.
6. R. T. Snodgrass and I. Ahn. Temporal databases. *IEEE Computer*, 19(9):35–42, September 1986.
7. J. Skyt and C. S. Jensen. Persistent Views—A Mechanism for Managing Aging Data. TR, Department of Computer Science, Aalborg University, March 2000.
8. J. Skyt, C. S. Jensen, and L. Mark. A Foundation for Vacuuming Temporal Databases. Manuscript under submission.
9. J. Widom (editor). Special Issue on Materialized Views and Data Warehousing. *IEEE Data Engineering Bulletin*, 18(2), June 1995.

A Workflow System through Cooperating Agents for Control and Document Flow over the Internet *

A. Dogac[1], Y. Tambag[1], A. Tumer[1], M. Ezbiderli[1], N. Tatbul[1], N. Hamali[1], C. Icdem[1] and C. Beeri[2]

[1] Software Research and Development Center
Middle East Technical University (METU), 06531 Ankara Turkiye
asuman@srdc.metu.edu.tr
[2] Hebrew University, Jerusalem, Israel
beeri@cs.huji.ac.il

Abstract. In this paper we describe an architecture that provides for automating and monitoring the flow of control and document over the Internet among different organizations, thereby creating a platform necessary to describe higher order processes involving several organizations and companies. The higher order process is designed through a graphical user interface and is executed through cooperating agents that are automatically initialized at each site that the process executes. Agents handle the activities at their site, provide for coordination with other agents in the system by routing the documents in electronic form according to the process description. The system is capable of activating external applications (which may be inside the company firewall) when necessary, keeping track of process information, and providing for the security and authentication of documents as well as comprehensive monitoring facilities. The architecture is general enough to be applied to any business practice where data flow and invocation of activities among different industries and cooperations follow a pattern that can be described through a process definition, however since the project is on maritime industry, some of the graphical user interfaces are customized accordingly. The system is fully operational for industrial use.

1   Introduction

In the MARIFlow system described in this paper, the higher order process is defined through a graphical user interface which is then mapped to a textual language called FlowDL. FlowDL is a block structured language encapsulating the six primitives defined by the Workflow Management Coalition through its blocks with which it is possible to describe flows and hence construct a workflow

* This work is being supported by the European Commission Project Number: INCO-DC 97-2496 MARIFlow, by the Middle East Technical University Project Number: AFP-97-07-02-08, and by the Scientific and Technical Research Council of Turkey, Project Number:197E038

O. Etzion and P. Scheuermann (Eds.): CoopIS 2000, LNCS 1901, pp. 138–143, 2000.
© Springer-Verlag Berlin Heidelberg 2000

specification [3]. FlowDL allows to indicate the source of the documents, their control flow and the activities that make use of these documents.

A MARIFlow process is executed through cooperating agents, called MAR-CAs (MARIFlow Cooperating Agents) that are automatically initialized at each site that the process executes. MARCAs handle the activities at their site, provide for coordination with other MARCAs in the system by routing the documents in electronic form according to the process description, keeping track of process information, and providing for the security and authentication of documents as well as comprehensive monitoring facilities.

The responsibilities of the agents (MARCAs) in our architecture are as follows:

- A MARCA receives messages through a persistent queue and evaluates them to decide what specific action to take.
- It persistently stores the documents it receives. It should be noted that the organizations may be reluctant to grant access inside the corporate firewall. In such cases when the need arises, the MARCA passes these documents to an in-house system by properly acknowledging the in-house system on further processing that may be necessary on the documents. The MARCA is also responsible for getting the documents from the in-house system and forwarding them to the related agents as specified in the process definition.
- Process related information also needs to be stored persistently for monitoring purposes. In our system MARCAs store the information related with monitoring to any JDBC compliant database to be accessed through a JDBC interface.
- There is a single MARCA at each site that handles all the activities of all workflow definitions and their instances related with that site. Therefore a new MARCA is generated only for a site participating to the system for the first time.

If we summarize, the functionality provided by the system developed is as follows:

- A declarative means to specify the control and document flow over the Internet where it is possible to define the source of data, its control flow and the activities that make use of this data.
- Invoking external applications (which may be inside the company domain) when necessary.
- Authentication and security of documents and the process related information.
- A monitoring mechanism for keeping track of the documents and/or for providing detailed account of the current status of a process instance within the system.
- Measures for failure recovery and exception handling.

In the following the system is described very briefly due to space limitations. Interested reader is referred to [2] where full design and implementation details are presented.

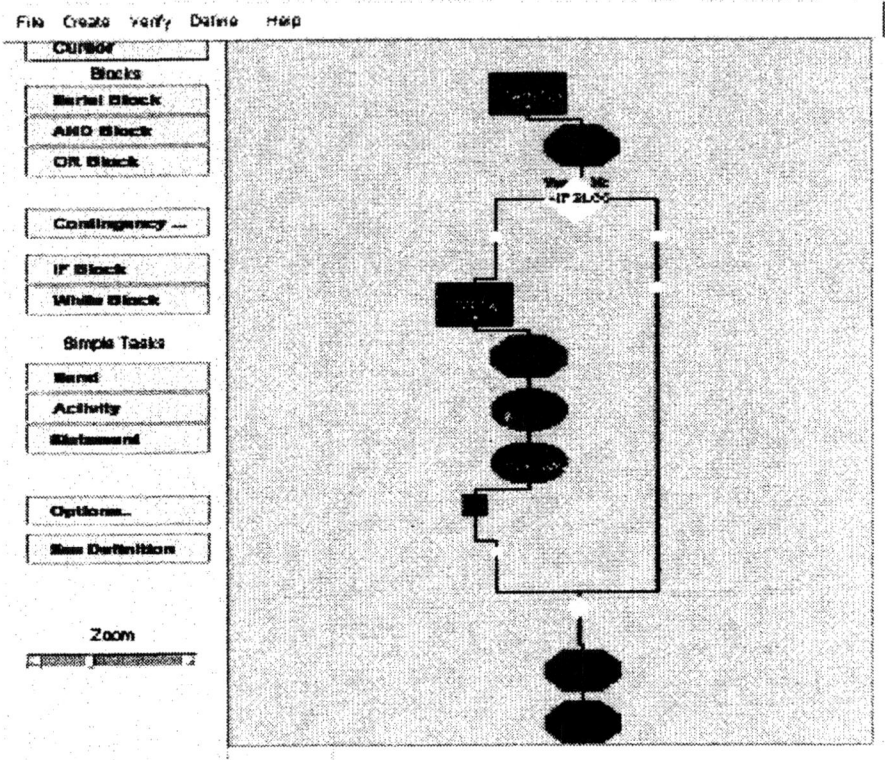

Fig. 1. The Graphical User Interface for Process Definition in MARIFlow

2   The Architecture of the System

In MARIFlow system each organization may have in-house applications inside a firewall protected from unauthorized accesses. MARCAs exist outside the firewall and inform in house applications when necessary through a User MARCA Interfacing Application (UMIA).

An inter enterprise workflow is defined graphically as shown in Figure 1. This tool allows the workflow designer to specify domains, tasks and process information which are then used in building the process definition graphically. This definition is mapped to the textual FlowDL language. The information on sites at which a MARCA should be installed are obtained from the domain definition in the process specification. These sites download a generic MARCA from a given URL. At compilation time the guards of activities within the responsibility of a MARCA are also determined according to the process definition and the MARCAs are initialized with these guards through the Workflow Definition Tool.

Guards are logical expressions for significant events of activities of a MARCA like "start" and "terminate". MARCAs evaluate these guards with the messages that they receive to decide on their actions. As an example, the start guard of an activity handled by a MARCA can be the arrival of a document, say, "doc1" from site "S1" and a document "doc2" from site "S2". In this case, MARCA will start execution of this activity when this AND expression evaluates to true by the arrival of the mentioned documents. Clearly the guards are generated from the information given in the process specification. Similarly "terminate" guard of an activity handled by MARCA may require the transmission of a document, say, obtained from the in-house system to another MARCA. It should be noted that this transmission is realized through persistent queues to survive through crashes.

3   MARIFlow Security Services

Within the life cycle of a process definition an application in the company domain may prepare a message, then may pass it to local UMIA. UMIA, in turn, passes it to the corresponding MARCA. The MARCA sends the message to one or more other MARCAs according to the process definition. The receiver MARCAs pass the messages to their corresponding UMIAs, which pass them to the local applications. Thus, inter/intra company communications basically consists of communication sessions between MARCAs and between a MARCA and its UMIA.

The security requirements of the system can therefore be summarized as follows:

- Confidentiality of data transfer between MARCAs: The contents of a message, including the process description fields, should not be visible to anybody except the sender and the receiver.
- Confidentiality of data transfer between a MARCA and the corresponding UMIA, as above.
- Authentication and integrity for both levels.
- Signatures for some of the inter/intra-company messages, such as certain types of test and certification documents. Here, a message consists of a document that is passed in order to be stored.

A comprehensive set of security services has been developed and integrated into the system which are described in [2].

4   Failure and Exception Handling

MARIFlow system provides comprehensive set of measures for failure recovery and exception handling.

4.1   Recovery of MARCAs

When a site goes down, restarting the MARCA is under the responsibility of the Operating System's start up control. The site's start up control analyzes the persistent logs of the MARCA and start a new instance using these stable logs created before the site crash. However, there is need for a further mechanism to prevent any Operating System related problem.

In Mariflow, for each MARCA installed there is a background process at that site, called the "rescue process". The rescue process is responsible for monitoring the life time of the agent and checks the MARCA at specific time intervals through a predetermined socket. A thread of the MARCA listens to this socket and responds to the signals. If the MARCA does not respond to this process for a given period of time, the process starts sending signals more frequently. If the MARCA still does not respond, after sending a bunch of signals the process assumes that the MARCA is not functional. The two possibilities in this case are: the MARCA could be blocked or it could be dead. When the rescue process is unable to find the OS process that belongs to this MARCA (i.e., it is dead), it instantiates a new MARCA by the help of the persistent logs related with the state of the agent.

Otherwise if the MARCA is blocked, it is necessary to kill the old instance prior to installation of a new instance. Since the logs are persistent it is possible to recover the state of the MARCA killed and hence the site does not suffer from any inconsistencies.

For the described mechanism to work correctly it is necessary to make sure that rescue process stays alive. Therefore, just as the rescue process checks to see that the MARCA stays alive, the MARCA also checks to ensure that the rescue process stays alive by signalling the rescue process at predefined time intervals. It is MARCA who reinstantiates the rescue process when it dies.

4.2   Failure Handling

The hierarchical approach to failure handling described in [1] is implemented in MARIFlow system which allows for partially rolling back the workflow instance to the nearest point in process history tree where it is possible to restart the execution. When a sub-activity T fails, it is necessary to determine the impact of that failure on the ancestors of T by finding out the highest level ancestor that should be aborted. The details of this technique is given in [1].

4.3   Exception Handling

The MARIFlow system handles the following types of exceptions:

- Semantic exceptions occur when a deviation from the expected behaviour in the program logic is encountered. These are handled through the IF block.

- Exceptions Raised by the Communication Infrastructure: Various types of errors can be encountered during communication between two agents, or communication with a database system or a mail server. The communication system recovers from possible failures by retrying the operation when possible and informing the user program if the request cannot be issued.
- Exceptions caused by NON-VITAL Activities: It should be noted that when document flow is a part of a workflow system, more often than not, there will be a need to archive the documents. The transfer and archival of the documents may take considerable amount of time. Therefore a mechanism which allows the other activities in the system (that does not use these documents) to proceed without waiting these archival activities provides for better performance. Yet there should also be mechanisms to guarantee that the workflow instance will not terminate before the successful termination of all such activities. We use NON-VITAL activities suggested in [1] with some modification. Originally the NON-VITAL activities are defined to be those, whose failure does not effect the flow of the process. On the other hand we say that NON-VITAL activities are those that can be assumed to terminate as soon as they start but raise an exception when they fail. In this way a NON-VITAL activity does not delay the execution of other activities unnecessarily; yet their successful termination is guaranteed by the exception handling mechanism.

5   Conclusions

MARIFlow system implements a fully distributed inter-enterprise workflow system through cooperating agents. The system is developed within the scope of the European Commission supported INCO-DC 97 2496 MARIFlow project and is fully operational for industrial use.

References

1. Q. Chen, U. Dayal, "A Transactional Nested Process Management System", in Proc. 12th International Conference on Data Engineering, New Orleans, 1996.
2. A. Dogac, Y. Tambag, A. Tumer, M. Ezbiderli, N. Tatbul, N. Hamali, C. Icdem and C. Beeri, "A Workflow System through Cooperating Agents for Control and Document Flow over the Internet", Technical Report, Software Research and Development Center, METU, March 2000, http://www.srdc.metu.edu.tr/publications.html.
3. D. Hollingsworth, "The Workflow Reference Model", Technical Report TC00-1003, Workflow Management Coalition, December 1996.

Distributed View Expansion in Composable Mediators

Timour Katchaounov, Vanja Josifovski and Tore Risch

Uppsala Database Laboratory,
Uppsala University, Sweden
$first\_name.last\_name$@dis.uu.se

Abstract. Data integration on a large scale poses complexity and performance problems. To alleviate the complexity problem we use a modular approach where many heterogeneous and distributed data sources are integrated through composable mediators. Distributed mediators are defined as object-oriented (OO) views defined in terms of views in other sub-mediators or data sources. In order to minimize the performance penalty of the modular approach we have developed a distributed expansion strategy for OO views where view definitions are selectively imported from sub-mediators. Our performance analysis has shown that the distributed view expansion can support modularity through distributed and composable mediators with little overhead.

1 Introduction

There has been substantial interest in using the mediator/wrapper approach for integrating heterogeneous data [9, 21, 7, 19, 4]. Most mediator systems integrate data through a single mediator server accessing one or several data sources through a number of 'wrapper' interfaces that translate data to a common data model (CDM). However, one of the original goals for mediator architectures [22] was that each mediator should be a relatively simple modular abstraction of the integration of some particular kind of data. Larger systems of mediators would then be defined through these primitive mediators by composing new mediators in terms of other mediators and data sources. Different mediator servers distributed on the network would define different logical views of data. Such a modular logical composition of mediators allows to overcome complexity problems of data integration on a large scale with many data sources and mediators involved. However, very few projects have used a distributed mediator architecture, e.g. [15], and there is little work on implementation issues of distributed mediators.

This paper investigates query processing in a distributed mediator system, AMOS II [20], where distributed mediators are composed as object-oriented (OO) views in terms of views in other sub-mediators or data sources. The views make the distributed mediators appear to the user as a single virtual database consisting of a number of types (classes) and functions (methods, attributes). However, unlike regular OO systems the extents of these types and functions

O. Etzion and P. Scheuermann (Eds.): CoopIS 2000, LNCS 1901, pp. 144–149, 2000.

are not explicitly stored in a database but are derived, through an OO multi-database query language, from data in the underlying data sources and other OO mediators [5, 10, 12]. Even though such an architecture addresses the complexity problems of data integration it also has some performance problems. Unlike distributed databases, the distributed mediators do not have any central schema and each mediator server has only limited knowledge about the structure of other mediators. This makes it difficult to find an optimal distributed query execution plan. In our approach the distributed mediator servers communicate with other known mediator servers to import some of the schema information, such as some OO view definitions. Exchanging OO view definitions in a composable mediator framework poses new problems compared to relational distributed databases as information about unknown user-defined types has to pass through intermediate servers. In order to deal with this problem we have developed a technique to process queries when incomplete type information is available, to be described in an upcoming work.

In [11] we described how to decompose distributed queries and then re-balance the decomposed query execution plans to minimize the communication overhead by generating an optimized data flow pattern between the distributed mediator servers. In that strategy the sub-mediators did not export their view definitions but only executed queries and provided query costing information. Such a strategy can be suboptimal when there are more than two distributed mediator layers. In this paper the importance is analyzed of a method based on distributed selective view expansion (DSVE) to minimize the penalty of several mediator server levels. The combination of DSVE, query decomposition and re-balancing is shown to significantly improve query performance. The method can drastically reduce query execution time when information from several hidden sub-mediators can be combined. A performance study of this case shows execution time improvement between 20 and 144 times for a test query selectivity varying between 1 and 0.01 [13]. Our measurements also show that savings in time are achieved in every component of the mediator composition (mediators, network, datasources). The performance improvements are due to more selective queries, smaller data flows between the servers, and fewer servers involved in the data exchange.

As our research platform we use the AMOS II mediator database system [20]. The core of AMOS II is an extensible and distributed main-memory OO DBMS. For more details about the architecture, query language and data integration capabilities the interested reader is referred to [5, 10, 12, 20]

2   Distributed Selective View Expansion

The following two subsections first describe the mechanism for view definition exchange and expansion in a hierarchy of AMOS II servers. After that a new heuristic based approach to selectively perform view expansion is proposed. Due to space limitations only an outline of the algorithms is given, while a detailed description can be found in [13].

2.1   Basic View Expansion Algorithm

Distributed view expansion is implemented as an extension to the query processor of AMOS II. Figure 1 illustrates the extended query processing with distributed view expansion. The view expansion is placed after the original query has been decomposed into distributed subqueries over the participating mediators. This improves query compilation time by minimizing the sizes of the query expressions. The grouped predicates are compiled and rewritten together at the coordinating mediator. In the distributed view expansion phase (the grayshaded boxes in Figure 1) the client mediator sends a view expansion request to each server where a subquery is to be executed and an expanded view definition of the subquery is retrieved. The subqueries are communicated between the servers in the form of declarative expressions [14]. At the server accepting the subquery expansion request, the subquery processing starts with query transformations and continues in the same manner as with other queries until the distributed selective view expansion phase. In this phase subqueries that contain themselves subqueries to other AMOS II mediators are selectively expanded. The process might span several levels of mediators, and, it terminates according to the strategy described in the next subsection.

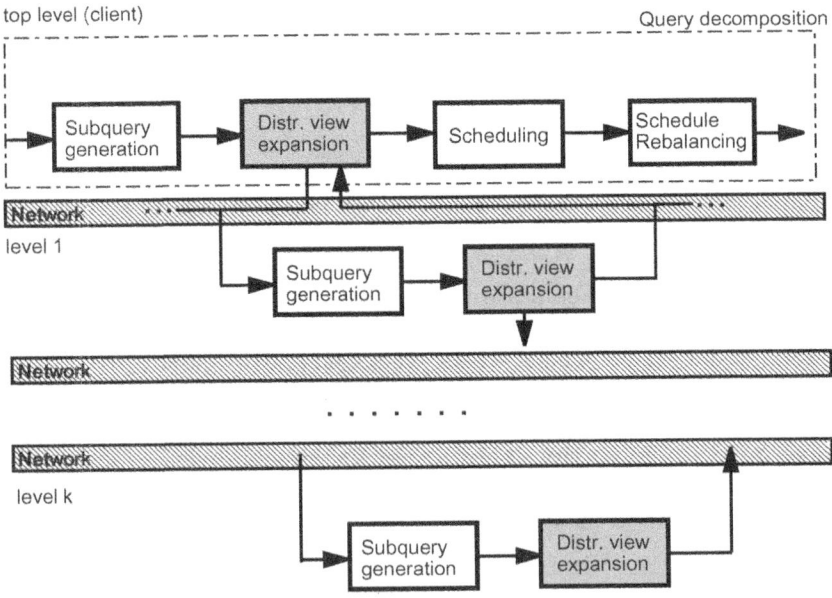

Fig. 1. Distributed selective view expansion process

After collecting the definitions of the remote subqueries selected for expansion, the next phase in the DSVE combines again all these expressions into one in order to be reoptimized by the subsequent optimization phases. Next a query scheduler generates distributed execution plan. In a final step this plan is rebalanced by a distributed algorithm [11].

The benefits of the proposed view expansion are the following:

1. Calculus based rewrites can be performed at the client to eliminate overlap in the calculation among the different servers.
2. Each subquery to be executed at another AMOS II server could be expanded into expressions derived from multiple AMOS II servers. These expressions might in turn have sub-expressions that are executed at a common AMOS II server. Putting them together in a single predicate may increase it's selectivity and allows for optimizations that eliminate overlap or achieve a better execution strategy.
3. The expanded expressions returned from the DSVE may contain predicates that could be combined/replicated with predicates at different data sources where they can act as selections, reducing the query execution time and the intermediate result sizes.
4. A richer space of data flow patterns will be considered by the query scheduler.

2.2   Controlling the view expansion process

While the view expansion can eliminate redundant computation and data shipment, it may also introduce extra costs in the optimization. Therefore we turn our attention to the problem of deciding when to perform expansion of the views and how to control the depth of DSVE.

An exhaustive cost-based algorithm determining which views to expand would need to fully compile the query for each combination of the views at the intermediate nodes, thus resulting in prohibitively long compilation times. To reduce the complexity of this problem each node makes a decision if a view is to be expanded based only on locally available data - the number of sub-subqueries of each subquery.

Whenever a multidatabase (sub)query is to be processed by the query decomposer, before DSVE is performed, a budget based decision procedure is used to control the depth of view expansion. The main goal of this procedure is to favor view expansion in cases of deep mediator hierarchies, and prohibit view expansion explosion when the number of direct sub-mediators is too large.

The query site starts with some initial budget. Whenever a view expansion request is to be sent, part of the budget is sent along with that request. The receiving site starts it's compilation process with the received part of the initial budget and proceeds in the same manner. The view expansion process stops when all of the initial budget is distributed among some of the participating mediators.

3   Related Work

This work is related to work on query optimization in distributed databases and mediators. Distributed databases [18, 3, 8, 1] have complete global schemas describing on what sites different (fractions of) tables are located, while distributed mediators do not have complete knowledge of meta-data from all mediators and data sources. Full expansion of all possible views in a distributed system with many nodes may be very costly. By contrast selective view expansion allows compositions of very many servers. In [16] a view expansion strategy for the System R* distributed database is briefly mentioned but not evaluated.

Mediator systems are usually not distributed (e.g. [9, 21, 17]) and thus do not use our strategies. In [4] it is indicated that a distributed mediation framework is a promising research direction without reporting any results. The DIOM system [19] is also a distributed mediator system using distributed query scheduling similar to our decomposer. However, no distributed view expansion is reported.

To our knowledge no work has addressed problems related to the use of OO features and more specifically user-defined types in a distributed mediator system.

4   Summary and Future Work

We described a distributed view expansion technique in composable mediators. Our results show that even in a simple mediator composition this approach leads to significant performance improvements, compared to a "black-box" approach to distributed query optimization. The main contribution of this work is that it shows that OO mediators may be logically composed to solve integration problems with very little execution overhead.

Though not addressed in this paper, we have also investigated performance problems in more complex composition scenarios. Preliminary results show that DSVE will be beneficial to use to discover optimal data flow in a non-homogeneous network with different communication speeds between the mediator nodes.

An issue not addressed in our current work is compilation time of large distributed queries. Our current experience shows that while mediator compositions of less than 10 mediators works reasonable with our framework, larger systems of distributed mediators require scalable and distributed compilation techniques.

References

1. P. Apers, A. Hevner and S. Yao: Optimization Algorithms for Distributed Queries. *IEEE Transactions on Software Engineering*, 9(1), 1983
2. O. Bukhres, A. Elmagarmid (eds.): *Object-Oriented Multidatabase Systems*, Pretince Hall, 1996.
3. D. Daniels et al.: An Introduction to Distributed Query Compilation in R*. In H. Schneider (ed): *Distributed Data Bases*, North-Holland, 1982
4. W. Du and M. Shan: Query Processing in Pegasus, In O. Bukhres, A. Elmagarmid (eds.): *Object-Oriented Multidatabase Systems*, Pretince Hall, Englewood Cliffs, 1996.
5. G. Fahl, T. Risch: Query Processing over Object Views of Relational Data. *The VLDB Journal*, Springer, 6(4), November 1997.
6. S. Flodin, T. Risch: Processing Object-Oriented Queries with Invertible Late Bound Functions, *21st Conf. on Very Large Databases (VLDB'95)*, Zurich, Switzerland, 1995

7. H.Garcia-Molina, et al: The TSIMMIS Approach to Mediation: Data Models and Languages. *Intelligent Information Systems (JIIS)*, Kluwer, 8(2), 1997

8. N. Goodman, P. Bernstein, E. Wong, C. Reeve and J. Rothnie: Query Processing in SDD-1: A System for Distributed Databases. *ACM Transactions on Database Systems (TODS)*, 6(4), 1981

9. L. Haas, D. Kossmann, E. Wimmers, J. Yang: Optimizing Queries across Diverse Data Sources. *23th Intl. Conf. on Very Large Databases (VLDB'97)*, Athens, Greece, 1997

10. V.Josifovski and T.Risch: Functional Query Optimization over Object-Oriented Views for Data Integration, *Intelligent Information Systems (JIIS)* Vol. 12, No. 2/3, Kluwer, 1999.

11. V.Josifovski, T.Katchaounov, T.Risch: *Optimizing Queries in Distributed and Composable Mediators, 4th Conference on Cooperative Information Systems*, CoopIS'99, Edinburgh, Scotland, Sept. 1999.

12. V.Josifovski, T.Risch: Integrating Heterogeneous Overlapping Databases through Object-Oriented Transformations, *25th Conf. on Very Large Databases (VLDB'99)*, Edinburgh, Scotland, Sept. 1999.

13. T. Katchaounov, V. Josifovski, T. Risch: Distributed View Expansion in Composable Mediators, *Research Report 2000:2*, Uppsala University, Department of Information Science, 2000.

14. W. Litwin and T. Risch: Main Memory Oriented Optimization of OO Queries using Typed Datalog with Foreign Predicates. *IEEE Transactions on Knowledge and Data Engineering*, 4(6), 1992

15. L.Liu, C.Pu: An Adaptive Object-Oriented Approach to Integration and Access of Heterogeneous Information Sources, *Distributed and Parallel Databases*, Kluwer, 5(2), April 1997.

16. G.Lohman, C.Mohan, L.Haas, D.Daniels, B.Lindsay: Query Procesing in R*, in W.King, D.S.Reiner, D.S.Batory (eds.): *Query Processing in Database Systems*, Springer Verlag, 1985.

17. S. Nural, P. Koksal, F. Ozcan, A. Dogac: Query Decomposition and Processing in Multidatabase Systems. *OODBMS Symposium of the European Joint Conference on Engineering Systems Design and Analysis*, Montpellier, July 1996.

18. M.T.Özsu, P.Valduriez: *Principles of Distributed Database Systems*, Prentice Hall, 1999.

19. K.Richine: *Distributed Query Scheduling in DIOM*, Tech. report TR97-03, Computer Science Dept., University of Alberta, 1997.

20. T.Risch, V.Josifovski, T. Katchaounov: *AMOS II Concepts*, available at *http://www.dis.uu.se/~udbl/amos/doc/*, 2000.

21. A. Tomasic, L. Raschid, P. Valduriez: Scaling Access to Heterogeneous Data Sources with DISCO. *IEEE Transactions on Knowledge and Date Engineering*, 10(5), 1998

22. G. Wiederhold: Mediators in the Architecture of Future Information Systems, *IEEE Computer*, 25(3), Mar. 1992.

eResponder: Electronic Question Responder

David Carmel, Menachem Shtalhaim, Aya Soffer

IBM Haifa Research Laboratory
MATAM, Haifa 31905, Israel
{carmel,menachem,ayas}@il.ibm.com

Abstract. With the complexity of systems increasing, support centers are flooded with questions submitted by e-mail, by Web, or by phone. This paper describes eResponder, a system which provides an integrated solution for automatic responses to user questions. eResponder stores question and answer pairs that have previously been asked. These pairs can be used to either provide an immediate response to user questions, or to assist customer service representatives in drafting new responses to similar questions or to yet unanswered questions. Users submit free text questions to the system via one unified interface. When a new question arrives, the system searches its databases for similar questions as well as for relevant answers and finds the most relevant Q&A pair based on both these measures. eResponder provides a relevance feedback mechanism and an answer summarizer to assist CSR's in creating new responses. The results of an experiment conducted to evaluate the system performance show that the combination of independent question and answer scores yields high precision search results.

1 Introduction

With the complexity of systems increasing, and with user expectation for immediate assistance, support centers are flooded with a large number of questions submitted by e-mail, by Web, or by phone. Companies that attempt to answer all of these questions need to allocate substantial resources, in terms of customer service representatives (CSR). NationsBank, for example, learned just how daunting large quantities of email can be. In 1996, as it's electronic banking clientele grew from 50,000 to 250,00, the number of messages soared from a few hundred to 20,000 a month. The following year, the bank had to hire about 100 people to cope with the external load [2].

A large number of questions submitted to call centers, turn out to be repetitive and address common problems that can easily be resolved and have been answered several times before. In order to reduce the effort required to answer new questions, a company should be able to capitalize on previous work of its CSRs, which have already answered many similar questions before. The accumulated knowledge encapsulated in this collection of previous answers could thus be exploited for better customer support.

A simple solution for this problem, used by many companies (e.g. Microsoft [1]), is to provide a Web interface to a collection of frequently asked questions and answers (FAQ). This collection can be searched and browsed by customers to locate answers to frequent problems which have been faced by many customers before, with no manual intervention of an expert, thus, reducing significantly the load on their call center.

O. Etzion and P. Scheuermann (Eds.): CoopIS 2000, LNCS 1901, pp. 150–161, 2000.

In addition to company FAQ services, there are many Web sites which are used as forums for asking experts questions or for asking fellow users questions e.g., [3, 4]. These collections of questions and answers are usually stored in knowledge bases. A user with an unresolved problem may search these collections for previously asked questions of a similar nature. If she does not find a satisfactory answer, then she can post a new question to the community and a fellow community member will hopefully post a response. These knowledge bases are very large cooperative systems in which a geographically distributed community interested in common domains can assist others.

There are some drawbacks to these solutions. Users need to submit a query that is almost identical to the question stored in the FAQ or forum in order to receive the proper answer. A search for a slightly different query, which describes the user's problem in different terms, will probably fail. Moreover, if the user's problem has not been handled before, most of these systems will retrieve non-relevant answers, leaving an unsatisfied customer. Finally, if you do not find an answer in the knowledge base, you most likely need to email your question to a CSR. From a user-centered point of view, it is desirable to deal with only one entry point. Users should submit their questions and either receive an immediate response if one exists, or get an answer from a CSR by email later.

eResponder is a system that provides an integrated solution for automatic responses to user questions. The underlying idea is to store in a knowledge base question and answer pairs that have previously been asked. The past knowledge can then be used to either provide an immediate response to users questions, or to assist CSRs in drafting responses to yet unanswered questions.

eResponder can function in two modes. In the online mode, queries are submitted via a Web page. In the offline mode, the question is submitted via email. In both cases, the system searches its databases for similar questions as well as for relevant answers to this question. From these questions and answers, a confidence level is computed. eResponder will follow one of the following paths based on the range of the confidence level:

1. If level is high, automatically return answer to user (in browser when online and by email when offline).
2. If level is average, generate a draft answer based on similar questions and pass it to a CSR, who can edit it and email to the user.
3. If level is low, pass the question to a qualified CSR, who can answer this question and insert it into the Q&A knowledge base for future use.

The confidence level thresholds can be tuned upon request by the call center administrator.

eResponder is based on advanced information retrieval (IR) techniques for computing similarity of new questions to previously asked ones based on full text descriptions as well as for computing the relevance of previous answers to this new question. The goal is to avoid previous questions whose answers are not relevant or perhaps locate previous relevant answers although the original question is not similar to the new one.

The user's query is specified using free text. Query terms are stemmed and stop words are removed. The Q&A pairs with the most similar questions and most relevant answers are retrieved from the Q&A knowledge base. Each pair is assigned a confidence level, which reflects its relevance to the new question.

The CSR can employ a relevance feedback mechanism for query refinement and resubmit the query to the system. In addition, he can ask eResponder to create a draft response based on a few selected answers from a set of relevant pairs suggested by the system. The draft generator uses summarization techniques to identify the sentences which are most similar to the new question as well as the most significant sentences in the set of selected answers. The set of significant sentences can be used by the CSR to synthesize a reply to the user's question.

The rest of the paper is organized as follows. Section 2 presents a sample session using eResponder. Section 3 describes the eResponder architecture. Section 4 provides some experimental results. Section 5 concludes the paper.

2   eResponder Sample Session

In this section we present a sample session using eResponder in online mode with a database of 90 Q&A pairs concerning the Mapuccino software developed at IBM research lab in Haifa. Figure 1 is a screen shot of the user interface for choosing a knowledge base and submitting a query. The user is asking how to print a map (created by Mapuccino).

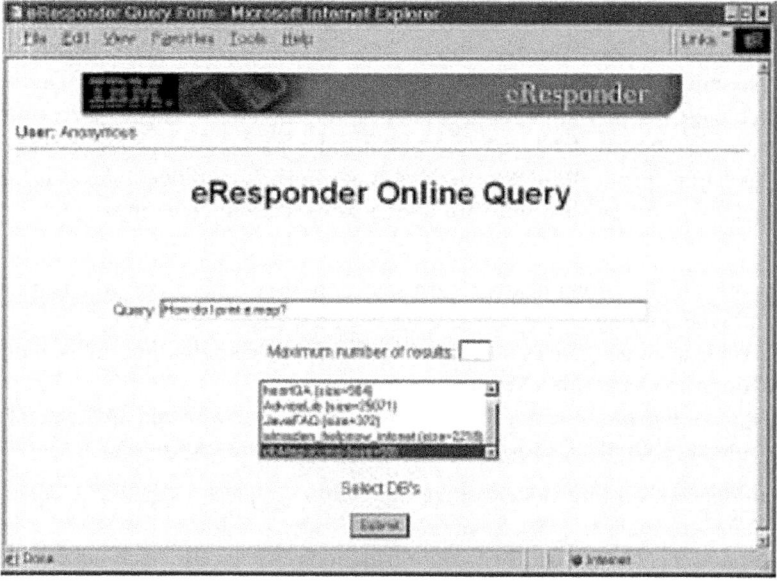

Fig. 1. eResponder user interface

In this case there are perfect matches to this query, and thus the system will return a list of solutions to consider as seen in Figure 2. The answers can be viewed by clicking on the relevant questions. If none of the answers are satisfactory, the user has an option to pass the query to a CSR by pressing the "Resubmit" button.

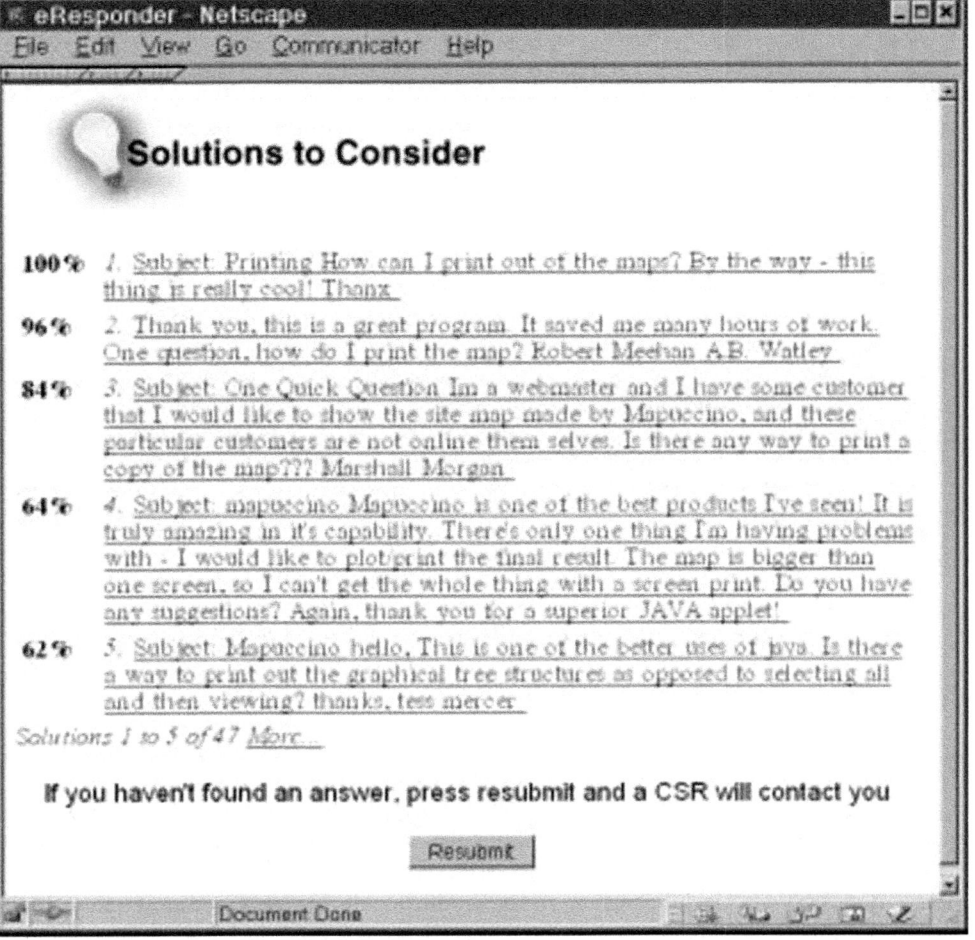

Fig. 2. The solutions returned by eResponder

Assuming that the user is unsatisfied, or that there were no perfect responses, the token would now be passed to a CSR. Figure 3 is the CSR view of the query results. The 10 top responses are presented with their associated question similarity (Q-similarity), answer relevance (A-relevance), and combined score (Total Score). The CSR could mark some of the questions as relevant or non-relevant using the left pane and resubmit the query by pressing the "Refine" button. In this example, this is not necessary, as there are several good answers. There are in fact 3 answers with an A-relevance of 100, and the CSR selects these three as the basis of the draft.

Note that the question in the third response chosen by the CSR is not very similar to the user's question (Q-similarity of 57.5), however the answer is judged to be very relevant (A-score 100). The CSR has thus selected it to be included in the new response.

Pressing the "Generate Draft" button, opens Netscape composer as seen in Figure

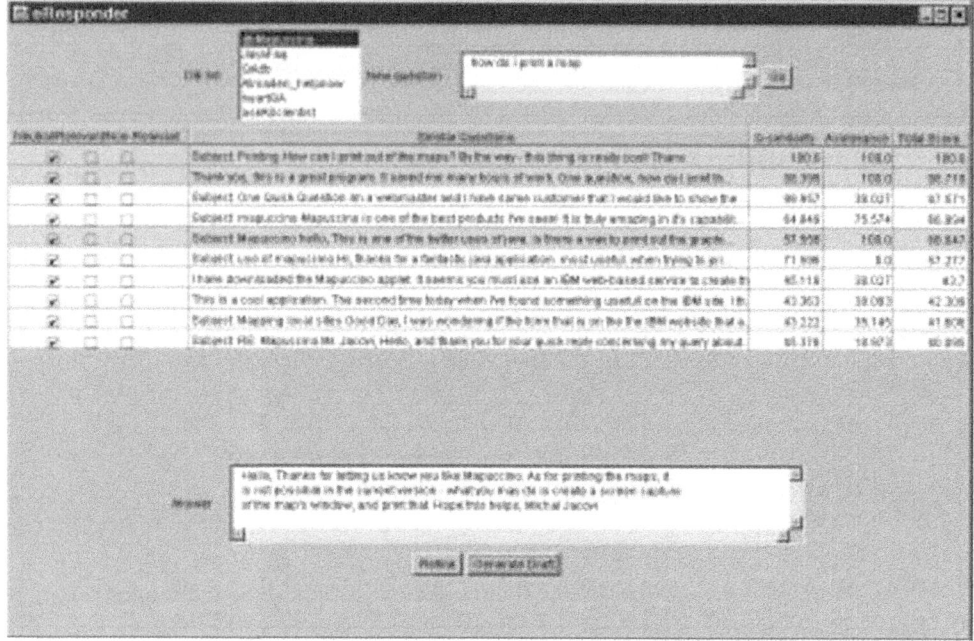

Fig. 3. The CSR view of the search results

4. The subject line contains the text of the user's new question. For each selected Q&A pair, first the overall score (confidence level) is displayed followed by the text of the original question and the answer. The terms that are common to the new question and the old question/answer are in bold face. Each sentence in the Q&A pair is either light gray, dark gray, or black according to its significance to the new question and to the answer. Light gray indicates that the sentence is not relevant, dark gray indicates that the sentence is somewhat relevant, and black indicates that the sentence is very relevant. The CSR can synthesize a new response by selecting the most significant sentences from the set of answers and tailoring it for the new question.

Note that in this case all of the sentences in black in fact discuss printing the Mapuccino map. In particular notice the answer to question 3. Even though the original question did not specifically ask about printing the map, the answer does include the proper instructions. Since eResponder evaluates the questions and answers separately it was able to find this answer and indicate this to the CSR for his consideration.

3   eResponder Architecture

eResponder is a Java-based system composed of the following components:

1. A validation tool that dynamically indexes question-answer pairs and incrementally adds them to one or more Q&A knowledge bases.

Fig. 4. Generate Draft page

2. A highly precise search engine that compares newly received questions to existing ones (as stored in the system knowledge bases), and returns a list of most related Q&A pairs ranked by degree of confidence.

3. A relevance feedback mechanism, which enables the CSR to provide feedback to the system by marking relevant and non-relevant Q&A responses. eResponder applies query refinement to transform the original query into a new query that reflects the CSR feedback [6]. The refined question is then resubmitted to the system.

4. A response draft generator, which assists in synthesizing a new answer from a given set of old relevant answers. The generator summarizes several answers marked as

relevant by the CSR by identifying the most significant sentences in each answer.

Figure 5 describes the components of system architecture. In the following these basic components are described in more detail.

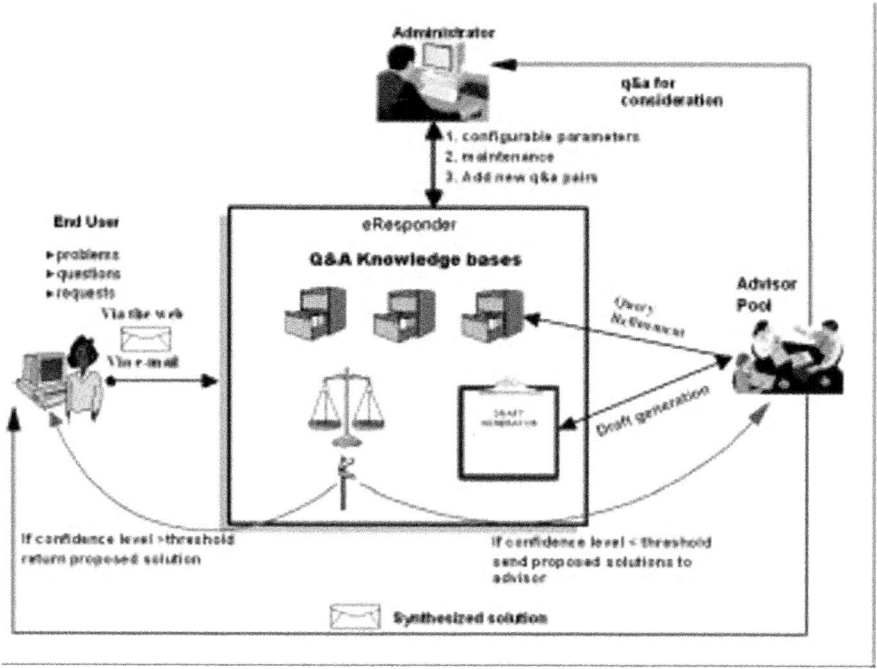

Fig. 5. eResponder architecture

3.1   Storage and Indexing

The storage and indexing component receives a Q&A pair and stores it for future retrieval in one or more Q&A knowledge bases. Each knowledge base contains a Q&A database, called Q&A dB, and two inverted indexes, one contains all of the question terms, while the other contains all of the answer terms. Each Q&A pair is associated with a unique identifier that is used as its key inside the Q&A dB. The unique identifier associated with the Q&A pair is used as the "filename" in the inverted indexes to identify the text of the associated question/answer. The Q&A database holds the Q&A pairs along with any additional information associated with these pairs such as a list of categories, a URL address of the answer, the date of submission, the email address of the submitter, etc.

eResponder uses Juru, a Java search engine developed at IBM research lab in Haifa, for indexing and searching the knowledge bases. Juru extracts for each question or answer a canonical representation, called a profile, which consists of a vector of indexing units of representative terms. The terms are stemmed and stop words are removed. Each knowledge base has its own stop word list of very frequent words to be filtered out from the text before storage. Juru indexes lemmatized words as well as lexical affinities, closely related terms frequently found in proximity to each other. It has been described elsewhere [5] how lexical affinities, when used as indexing units, improve precision of search results as compared to single words, especially in the context of IR systems.

3.2   Retrieval

The retrieval process treats new incoming questions as "free text queries" and retrieves a ranked list of the most relevant Q&A pairs from a set of predefined knowledge bases. Juru's inverted indexes and retrieval mechanism are used to find the questions that are most similar to the new question as well as the answers that are most relevant to it.

Unfortunately, there is no precise distinction between relevance and similarity in IR systems. While similarity among questions can be easily measured, it is not clear how to evaluate the relevance of answers to the query. In the current version, eResponder does not distinguish between relevance and similarity measures. The relevance of the answer is simply modeled by its similarity to the question.

eResponder first creates a profile for the new question using the same process used in the indexing process, and computes a textual similarity score for each question and each answer in the knowledge base with respect to this profile. Each term in the profile is associated with a weight w_i computed by a *tf-idf* formula as follows:

$$w_i = tf_i \cdot \log(\frac{1}{pr_i})$$

where tf_i is the frequency of term i in the profile, and pr_i is the probability of term i in the entire knowledge base.

The confidence of any question and answer is determined by measuring the cosine of the angel between the profile of the new question and the corresponding profile of the question or answer, respectively. The overall confidence value for the Q&A pair is a weighted linear combination of these two scores.

The result of the retrieval procedure is a ranked list of Q&A pairs. However, the order provided by ranking of results is insufficient for eResponder. Rather, an absolute measure which conveys the quality of the pair is necessary. To solve this, each Q&A pair is independently scored according to its similarity to the user's question. Juru's score is normalized by eResponder to a number between zero and 100. The zero value is assigned to absolutely non-relevant text (a question or an answer with no common terms with the query), while a score of 100 is assigned to a text that is identical to the query.

3.3   Relevance feedback

The user's query may often not be specific enough to enable retrieval of highly relevant answers, especially when the question is submitted via a form where users tend to type very little. Moreover, natural language ambiguity often causes people to describe concepts in their questions in a different manner than others have described the same concepts in their questions or answers. Therefore, in some cases, the Q&A pairs, which were identified by the system as most relevant, may not be judged as such by the CSR.

In eResponder the CSR has the option to refine the original question iteratively by marking some retrieved Q&A pairs as relevant or non-relevant. The original question is then modified by adding terms characterizing the relevant documents and subtracting terms characterizing the non-relevant documents. In addition, the weights of the query terms are modified to reflect their relative importance in the matching between the refined query and the marked documents. The refined query is resubmitted to the system.

3.4 Automatic Draft Generator

If there are no Q&A pairs with high enough scores, or if the user did not find a suitable response, then eResponder constructs a draft response which is to be edited by the CSR. The CSR first marks the most significant Q&A pairs for the new question. Next, eResponder estimates the significance of each sentence in these answers. Each sentence is assigned two scores. This first score indicates the relevance of this sentence to the problem (a similarity score between the sentence and the query). The second score indicates the relative significance of this sentence in the set of sentences in the marked answers. Using these scores eResponder indicates to the CSR which sentences are recommended for inclusion/exclusion in the response to the new question using different gray levels (see Figure 4). eResponder also highlights the original question terms in the retrieved questions and answers. This also assists the CSR in selecting the sentences to include in the new answer.

We compute the two sentence scores based on methods described in [7].

1. Similarity to the new question. The similarity between sentence s and query q is measured using a vector space model similarity function.

$$SQ(s,q) = \frac{\sum_{i=1}^{M} w_{i,s} w_{i,q}}{M}$$

where $w_{i,j} = tf_{i,j} \cdot log(\frac{N}{tf_{i,C}})$, $tf_{i,j}$ is the term frequency of term i in sentence j, $tf_{i,C}$, is the term frequency of term i in the corpus C, N is the number of terms in the corpus, and M is the number of terms in sentence s.

2. The internal weight of the sentence. The idea here is that sentences that contain terms that appear frequently within the entire set of selected answers are considered the most significant. The score of sentence s in answer a in answer set A is computed as follows:

$$SI(s,a,A) = \frac{\sum_{i=1}^{M} w_i}{M}$$

where $w_i = tf_{i,s} \cdot tf_{i,a} \cdot \overline{tf_{i,A}} \cdot log(\frac{N}{tf_{i,c}})$

$tf_{i,s}$ and $tf_{i,a}$ is the term frequency of term i in sentence s and answer a, respectively. $\overline{tf_{i,A}}$ is the average term frequency of i in the set of selected answers A. If a term appears in only one sentence, then its weight is set to zero. The weight of lexical affinities is boosted in order to increase their significance in the sentence score.

4   System Evaluation

In order to evaluate eResponder, it is necessary to have some benchmark for such systems. One option is the TREC question answering benchmark [9], which provides a set of fixed questions and the set of documents which best answer these questions. In this model, however, the questions are not part of the corpus of documents, and thus it is not suitable for a system that stores both questions and answers such as eResponder.

We are not aware of any existing benchmark for Q&A pairs. We thus used a set of Q&A pairs available on the NSF Ask a Scientist or Engineer Web site [3]. This is a collection of questions which youngsters have asked scientists along with their responses. The questions cover many areas of science including biology, chemistry, earth science and more. The Web site provides a search engine to search the Q&A database.

We downloaded the Q&A pairs from the NSF site and inserted them into the eResponder system. We compared the results of searching for the same information using the NSF search engine and eResponder. We submitted 30 queries to both systems and counted the number of relevant answers returned by each. Table 1 shows some examples of the questions submitted. We compared the number of relevant Q&A pairs which

| What happens to your body when you dream? |
| How do scientists clone animals? |
| How does the whale use its blubber? |
| How many trees are chopped down a year to make paper? |

Table 1. Some of the questions submitted to eResponder and NSF Ask a Scientist.

appeared in the first 3 responses (top@3), the first 5 responses (top@5), and the first 10 responses (top@10). Figure 6 shows the comparison of these parameters computed for the two systems.

The results show that eResponder is much more precise than the search engine used by the NSF site. When the query was almost identical to a question stored in the database, both systems had no problem locating the relevant Q&A pair. However, for free text queries, eResponder functioned much better. This can be attributed to several reasons. First, eResponder uses IR techniques for search which include term weights, lexical affinities, and an advanced ranking algorithm. On the other hand, the NSF site's search engine seems to be based on Boolean search techniques. Although the questions where submitted in free text form, we tried our best to translate them to comparable Boolean queries. The second reason for eResponder's success is the fact that we index and search the questions and answers independently of each other while the NSF engine seems to store the text of the Q&A pair as one indexing unit. Since the questions are usually much shorter than the answers, the NSF engine seemed to diverge into Q&A pairs that happened to contain the search terms in the text of the answer, although this was not the real topic of the question.

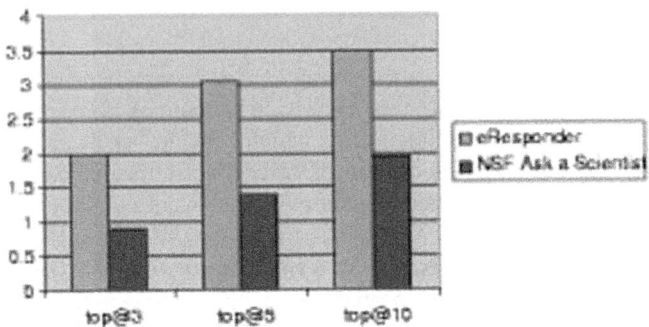

Fig. 6. The precision of eResponder and Ask a Scientist averaged over the same 30 questions

eResponder's method of computing the question similarity and the answer relevance as two separate scores and then combining them, contributes significantly to its high precision. The following example highlights this feature. For the question "what is photosynthesis?" eResponder returns the results shown in Table 2. Even though none

Similar Questions	Q-similarity	A-relevance	Total Score
Why are the leaves green?	0	100	50
Why is chlorophyll green?	0	91.2	45.6
What do trees use that we breathe out?	0	91.1	45.6

Table 2. eResponder results for the question: "what is photosynthesis?"'

of the questions in the database have common terms with the new question, the system found three relevant Q&A pairs by looking at the answers. The total score is a linear combination of the Q-similarity and the A-relevance. The system administrator can set the weights based on the nature of the Q&A knowledge base. In FAQ files, the question is usually a manually crafted title for the answer, and should thus receive a high weight. On the other hand, in collections of "real" questions and answers, the answer is usually as important as the question and the two should be assigned equal weights.

5   Concluding Remarks

eResponder, a system which provides an integrated solution for automatic responses to user questions, has been presented. eResponder stores in a Q&A knowledge base question and answer pairs that have previously been asked. These pairs are used to find the most relevant answers to a new question and either provide an immediate automatic response to user questions, or assist customer service representatives in drafting new responses to similar questions or to yet unanswered questions. eResponder also provides a relevance feedback mechanism and an answer summarizer to assist CSR's in creating new responses.

In the current version, eResponder does not distinguish between question similarity and answer relevance. The same measure is used to compute both, however they are each computed separately. We have already seen that even this distinction is beneficial and improves precision. Using a different measure to compute relevance may improve precision even further. This study is left for further research.

eResponder can use several knowledge bases of Q&A pairs. In order to work with eResponder effectively in this case, a new question must first be assigned to one or more domains using a categorization tool. eResponder will then use one or more domain specific knowledge bases in order to craft the response. The question categorization tool we intend to use is another IBM product [8] and is outside the scope of this paper.

Acknowledgments

We thank Pnina Vortman for initiating this line of research.

References

1. 2000 Microsoft   Corporation.   Microsoft   product   support   service. http://support.microsoft.com/directory.
2. Mark Fischetti. Ending Email overload. *IBM Research*, (1 @2):33 – 37, 1998.
3. The National Science Foundation. Ask a scientist or engineer. http://www.nsf.gov/nstw questions/start.html.
4. 2000 Electronic Arts Inc. Easports clubhouse. http://www.easports.com/clubhouse.cfm.
5. Yoelle Maarek and F. Smadja. Full text indexing based on lexical relations, an application: Software libraries. In N. Belkin and C. van Rijsbergen, editors, *Proceedings of the twelfth annual international ACM SIGIR conference on Research and development in information retrieval*, pages 198 – 206. ACM press, Cambridge MA, 1989.
6. J. J. Rocchio. Relevance feedback in information retrieval. In *The SMART Retrieval System: Experiments in Automatic Document Processing*, pages 313 – 323, Englewood Cliffs, NJ, 1971. Prentice-Hall Inc.
7. Mark Sanderson. Accurate user directed summarization from existing tools. In *Proceedings of the 1998 ACM 7th international conference on Information and knowledge management*, pages 45–51, Washington, United States, 1998.
8. Bruce Schechter. Driving eBuisiness. *IBM Research*, (4), 1999.
9. Ellen M. Voorhees and D. Tice. The TREC-8 question answering track evaluation. In *NIST Special Publication XXX-XXX: The Eighth Text REtrieval Conference (TREC 8)*. National Institute of Standards and Technology, August 1999.

Efficient matching for web-based publish/subscribe systems

João Pereira[1*], Françoise Fabret[1], François Llirbat[1], and Dennis Shasha[2**]

[1] INRIA Rocquencourt
{Joao.Pereira,Francoise.Fabret,Francoise.Llirbat}@inria.fr
[2] Courant Institute of Mathematical Sciences
New York University
shasha@cs.nyu.edu

Abstract. There is a need for systems being able to capture the dynamic aspect of the web information by notifying users of interesting events. Content-based publish/subscribe systems are an emerging type of publish/subscribe systems where events are filtered according to their attribute values, using filtering criteria defined by the subscribers, and then sent to the interested subscribers. Compared to traditional publish/subscribe systems, content-based systems offer more subscription expressiveness. The cost of this gain in expressiveness is an increase in the complexity of the matching process: the more sophisticated the constructs, the more complex the matching process. In this paper, we present an efficient and scalable solution to the matching problem. We also present a semi-structured event model which is well suited for the information published on the Web, and flexible enough to support easy integration of publishers.

1 Introduction

It is widely accepted that the majority of human information will be on the Web in ten years. As pointed out in [4], besides systems for searching, querying and retrieving information from the Web, there is a need for systems being able to capture the dynamic aspect of the web information by notifying users of interesting events. This functionality is crucial for web users (or applications) who want to exploit highly dynamic web information such as stock markets updates or auctions. A tool that implements this functionality must be scalable and efficient. Indeed, it should manage millions of user demands for notifications (i.e. subscriptions); It should handle high rates of events (several millions per day) and notify the interested users in a short delay. In addition, it should provide a simple and expressive subscription interface and efficiently cope with high volatility of web user demands (new subscriptions, new users and cancellations).

[*] Founded by "Instituto Superior Técnico" - Technical University of Lisbon and by a JNICT fellowship of Program PRAXIS XXI (Portugal)
[**] The work of D. Shasha was partly supported by grant IRI-9531554 of the United States National Science Foundation.

O. Etzion and P. Scheuermann (Eds.): CoopIS 2000, LNCS 1901, pp. 162–173, 2000.

Finally, it should facilitate integration of similar kinds of information issued by different publishers (e.g. new auctions coming from distinct auction sites).

The classical approach for query subscription is a mediator system where queries are periodically evaluated against static data. This static approach does not scale for high rate of events and a large number of volatile subscriptions, since it requires the storage of large event histories between two successive computations and requires repeated complex multi-query optimization. In this paper we propose a different approach where events are processed on-the-fly to discover matching subscriptions. Our main contributions are:

- A LDAP-like event model which is well suited for the information published on the Web, and flexible enough to support easy integration of publishers.
- A subscription language which is designed to be simple while supporting the most usual queries on event notifications.
- Efficient main memory matching algorithms for processing events in real time which can handle a large number of volatile subscriptions and support high event rates.
- We provide an experimental performance analysis of the algorithms using our "Le Subscribe" prototype[12]. Le Subscribe is a pub/sub system that permits publication and subscription on the web.

Apart this introduction the paper is structured as follows. In Section 2 we present our data model. Section 3 describes the algorithms for processing events. We provide experimental results and an analysis of the performances of these algorithms in Section 4. Finally, related work and conclusions are presented in Section 5.

2   Pub/sub system data model

In this section we present a data model for content-based pub/sub systems in a web context. This model, which is used in our prototype *Le Subscribe*, is in the spirit of the LDAP [8] data model. It consists of a set of attributes, and a set of event types. Each attribute has a domain that may be *numeric*, *string*, *enumerated* or *hierarchical*. The *hierarchical* domain is specific to our model: it is an *enumerated* domain where the elements are organized according to a hierarchy. Hierarchical domains are useful to depict categories and sub-categories. For example, a hierarchical domain ranging over furniture categories can be organized in bedroom, dining room, outdoor categories and sub-categories like table, chair, ⋯. An attribute A can be *multivalued* or *single valued*. In the former case, a value for A is a subset of the domain of A, while it is an element of the domain of A in the late case. An event type is always associated with a set of attributes each of them being either mandatory or optional. For example, a new auction item of type *antiques* is described by three mandatory attributes *price*, *period* and *quantity*. An item of type *furniture* can be described using three mandatory attributes: Attributes *price* and *quantity* are in common with the *antiques* event type; Attribute *furniture category* has a hierarchical domain ranging over furniture categories. Furniture description could be enriched with the optional attribute *material*.

An event instance can be associated with several event types. It is defined by a set of (attribute, set of values) pairs. Among these pairs there is always a pair of the form (*event type, T*) where *event type* is a distinguished attribute and *T* is a set of event types. An event instance definition has to include a non-empty set of values for each attribute that is a mandatory attribute of at least one event type in *T*, values for other attributes are optional. Let us point out that our model permits publishers to present a given event from several points of view by associating several event types with this event. For example, using event types *antiques* and *furniture*, a publisher can present a table of the Louis XVI period as furniture, as antique or as both. In the last case the event instance definition will associate two event types (*antiques* and *furniture*) to the distinguished attribute and will provide values for attributes *price, quantity, period* and *furniture category*, plus possibly for attribute *material*. Each event instance *e* published in the system is always automatically enriched with a pair of the form (*att set, A*) where *att set* is a distinguished attribute and *A* is the set of attribute names appearing in *e*. For example a published event of the form [((*event type, {antiques, furniture}*), (*price, 200*), (*period, Louis XV*), (*furniture category, table*), (*material, {rose-wood, marble}*]] is enriched with the pair (*att set, {* event type, price, period, furniture category, material*}*) The implicit attribute *att set* permits subscribers to express filters over the event schema.

2.1 Subscription language

A *subscription* is defined as a conjunction of predicates of the form $X\Theta y$, where X is an attribute name, y is an element belonging to the domain of X and Θ is an operator provided by the language. The language supports arithmetic comparison operators plus two specific operators *kind of* and *contains*. For semantics reasons it is not possible to associate any attribute with any operator. The operator *kind of* is used if the attribute is single valued and its domain is hierarchical. Comparison operators can be used only in predicates involving single valued attributes. Finally, the operator *contains* is used in predicates involving multi-valued attributes. The semantics of the predicates is as follows. Let $p = A\Theta y$ be a predicate, and v a valuation of attribute A. When Θ represents a comparison operator, the value of $p[v]$ is computed by comparing v and y wrt Θ. When Θ represents the *kind of* operator, $p[v]$ has the value *true* if v is located under y in the hierarchy defined by the domain of A, and otherwise $p[v]$ has the value *false*. Finally, if Θ represents the *contains* operator, $p[v]$ has the value *true* iff y is an element of v. For example, [(*event type contains antiques*); (*furniture category kind of dining table*); (*att set contains material*)] describes a subscription for all the events that concern any antique belonging to any sub-category of dining tables and include information over material.

An event instance *e* matches a subscription *s* if *e* provides a binding for every attribute occurring in *s* and all predicates of *s* are true with respect to this binding. A subscription is satisfied by any matching event instance.

3   Main Memory Matching algorithms

The matching problem can be formulated as the following question: Given an event e and a set S of subscriptions which are the subscriptions of S satisfied by e? We call *matching algorithm* an algorithm that intends to solve this problem.

With the emergence of computers having very large random access memory, more and more algorithms will run in main memory without any access to secondary memory. As pointed out by [13] the increasing size of the RAM has important consequences on the behavior of the algorithms whose performance are strongly dependent on the processor cache behavior. Processor cache memories are small fast static RAM memories which hold data that were recently referenced by running programs. Inside a cache memory, memory references can be proceeded at processor speed. References that are not satisfied by the cache, called misses, require the fetch of the corresponding cache block from the main memory at a much higher cost (several magnitude order). So cache misses severely impede the program performances. In order to cope with cache misses penalties, algorithms have to be aware of temporal and spatial locality. Spatial locality is reached when data that are used consecutively by the algorithm are placed in consecutive memory addresses. Temporal locality is reached when the same data is manipulated in consecutive instructions.

In this section we propose matching algorithms which are specifically designed to be cache conscious. A lot of matching algorithms have been proposed in the literature [7, 5, 1, 14]. Nevertheless, to our knowledge, none of them is aware of the cache behavior.

3.1   Algorithm overview

In what follows we suppose a **high predicate redundancy**: The number of predicates is small compared to the number of conditions occurring in the subscriptions. Given a set S of subscriptions, a set P of predicates occurring in S, a high predicate redundancy indicates that on the average each predicate of P occurs in a large number of subscriptions of S. The predicate redundancy ranges from 1 to $2^{|P-1|}$ where $\mid P \mid$ denotes the cardinality of P. The maximal value is reached when S consists in all the possible combinations of the predicates of P. In particular, a number of subscriptions very large compared to the size of attribute domains incurs in a high predicate redundancy. This assumption is realistic in the web context where many enumerated values are manipulated (e.g., categories, names, locations).

Given an event e and a set of subscriptions S, a naive solution for computing the subscriptions of S matching e consists of testing all subscriptions one-by-one against e. In the worst case, the time complexity of such an algorithm is $O(\sum_{s \in S} (\#(\text{ predicates of s })C_p)$, where C_p represents the cost of matching one predicate. This solution has several drawbacks. First there is a high redundancy in the evaluation of predicates (the same predicate can be evaluated as many times as it appears in the set of subscriptions). Second, the interdependency between predicates is not considered, leading to useless predicate testing (e.g.

input:
an event instance $e = (A_1, V_1), ..., (A_n, V_n)$
Body:
  $MatchingPreds := \emptyset$;
  for each attribute A_i in e {
    let F_i denote the set of predicate families having A_i as attribute
    for each family F_i^j in F_i {
      for each value v in V_i {
        $MatchingPreds \longleftarrow MatchingPreds + F_i^j.search(v)$ }}}
  return $MatchingPreds$;

Fig. 1. The predicate matching algorithm.

if e satisfies predicate $(price, \leq, 10)$, no test is needed to conclude that e also satisfies predicate $(price, \leq, 20)$). Finally, the locality of comparison instructions is very poor since a same predicate can appear in non-consecutive subscriptions.

To cope with these problems we propose algorithms running in two steps. The first step computes the predicates satisfied by the incoming event. The second step computes the matching subscriptions using the result of the first step.

3.2   Algorithm for predicate matching

Given a set S of subscriptions and the set P of predicates occurring in these subscriptions, the predicate matching algorithm uses a set of indexes over P in order to check in one step all the related predicates. More precisely, the predicates are logically grouped by predicate family puting together predicates having the same attribute and the same comparison operator. For example, suppose that S consists of three subscriptions $s_1 = [(price = 20), (quantity > 10)]$, $s_2 = [(price \leq 15), (quantity = 10)]$ $s_3 = [(price \leq 12)]$ then there are four families: $(price =)$, $(price \leq)$, $(quantity >)$, and $(quantity =)$. Fast access to the predicates belonging to a given family is achieved by using an index where the key values are the values used in the predicates belonging to the family. The nature of the indexes depends on the families. For example hashing provides fast access to equality predicates, but it is not usable for nonequality predicates. A lot of indexing techniques have been proposed in past years: binary search trees, T-trees, B+-trees, IBS-trees, KD-trees, and more recently a cache sensitive indexing technique, called CCS-tree[13], which is designed to cope with the cache behavior problem. In what concerns *contains* predicates, the techniques for equality predicates can be used, testing successively every value of the multivalued attribute. *Kind of* predicates require to design specific indexes (for example tree structures plus hash tables for accessing the elements). Our predicate matching algorithm is able to support any indexing technique, and it is possible to use two different techniques for two different families. In the current implementation we use an unique indexing technique. An index over a family F consists of an array of pairs <value, predicate identifier > sorted by values, so a look-up incurs a binary search in the index.

```
inputs :
nb cond[]: nb cond[] is vector of integer of size | S |
pred to subs[]: is an association table of size | P |
MatchingPreds[]: output of predicate matching algorithm
body:
1   matched ← {}
2   hitcount ←| S | #0
3   foreach p ∈ MatchingPreds
4       foreach s ∈ pred to subs[p]
5           hitcount[s] ← hitcount[s] + 1
6   for i = 1 to | S |
7       if hitcount[s] == nb cond[s] then matched ← matched ∪ {s} endif
8   return matched
```

Fig. 2. The counting algorithm.

Our algorithm for predicate matching is described in Figure 1. It considers successively the attributes A_1, ..., A_n. For each attribute A_i and for each predicate family F_i^j having A_i as attribute it performs one look-up of the corresponding index I_i^j to find the matching predicate positions. Then it cumulates these positions (if any) in the $MatchingPreds$ variable together with positions found in previous steps. So the per event instance cost of the algorithm is given by: $C(e) = \sum_{i=1}^{|e|}(\sum_{j=1}^{|F_i|} | V_i |\ search_{ij})$ where $| e |$ represents the number of attributes in event instance e, F_i and V_i represent respectively the set of predicate families and the set of values which are associated with the ith attribute in e, and $search_{ij}$ denotes the cost for a look-up in index I_i^j (i.e. the cost for computing what predicates belonging to the jth family of F_i match a given value of A_i). In our implementation, $search_{ij}$ represents the cost of a binary search in a sorted array, i.e. $search_{ij} = log(n) + 1$ where n represents the cardinality of family F_i^j.

3.3   Algorithms for subscription matching

Counting algorithm This algorithm is given in Figure 2. The algorithm uses the following global knowledge: S, P, $pred\ to\ subs$, $nb\ cond$. P is a vector of predicates. S is a vector of subscriptions. $pred\ to\ subs$ is a vector giving the correspondence between predicates and the subscriptions. This vector has one entry per predicate in P. The entry for predicate p gives the subscriptions containing p in the form of a list of entries over S. Finally, $nb\ cond$ is a vector having one entry per subscription of S, the entry for subscription s gives the number of predicates occurring in s. The algorithm takes as input $MatchingPreds$, the list of satisfied predicates computed by the predicate matching algorithm. It computes in variable $matched$ the set of matching subscriptions. To do that the algorithm first examines each satisfied predicate in $MatchingPreds$ and increments by one the number of satisfied predicates of each subscription associated to it. Finally it selects the subscriptions which have all their conditions satisfied. The complexity of this algorithm is $O(C_{add}P_{sat}N_p + C_{comp}(| S |))$, where C_{add} represents the cost of an addition, P_{sat} is the number of satisfied predicates by the event and N_p is the average number of predicates satisfied per subscription.

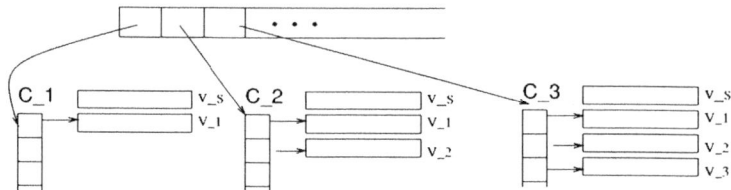

Fig. 3. Clusters Data Structure

C_{comp} represents the cost of a comparison and S is the set of subscriptions to match.

Propagation algorithm The counting algorithm is simple to implement nevertheless it performs useless work. Indeed, subscriptions are systematically considered even when some of their predicates are not satisfied. The goal of the propagation algorithm is to limit the number of subscriptions that have to be verified. The idea is as follows. The algorithm runs in two steps. The first step permits to eliminate a large number of subscriptions, the second step performs the matching solely over the remaining subscriptions. To do that the subscriptions are grouped in clusters in a such a way that for each cluster, C, (1) there exists a predicate, called the *characteristic predicate* of C, which is the most selective predicate of every subscription occurring in C, and (2) besides p all the subscriptions in C have the same number of predicates, this number is called the *size* of C.

The data structure for clusters is given in Figure 3. The main list contains the references to each cluster. A cluster c_n associated to subscriptions of length $n + 1$ is defined by: a vector v_s of subscription identifiers and n vectors $v_1, \cdots, v_n$ having the same length as v_s and where an element of the form $v_i[j]$ contains the predicate identifier associated to the $i + 1^{th}$ condition of subscription $v_s[j]$. Thus vector v_1 contains the second most selective conditions of each subscription (the most selective conditions are used in the first step of the propagation algorithm). Vector v_n contains the less selective conditions.

During the *elimination step*, the algorithm takes as input *MatchingPreds* the set of satisfied predicates computed by the predicate matching algorithm, and builds a vector, named *preds bitmap*, having one entry per predicate and indicating for each if the predicate is (or is not) satisfied. Then it uses an association table between the predicates and the clusters which gives for each predicate p the set of clusters having p as characteristic predicate. The result of this step is a set of clusters. Only subscriptions contained in selected clusters have to be verified. This done during the second step.

Selected clusters are verified one at a time using the algorithm for *cluster propagation* shown in Figure 4. The algorithm iteratively processes each vector v_i. At step i, the algorithm considers vector v_i and the set of subscriptions whose conditions contained in the previous vectors are verified. Then, the algorithm checks all the conditions in v_i that are associated to these subscriptions and eliminates the subscriptions whose condition is evaluated to false and propagates the reduced set to the next vector.

Cluster propagation
inputs
MatchingPreds: output of predicate matching algorithm
$c = (v_s, v_1, \cdots, v_n)$: a cluster of subscriptions of size n
preds bitmap: bitmap containing $| P |$ bits. *preds bitmap*$[p] = 1$
        if predicate p is verified 0 otherwise
initialmatch: indices of selected subscriptions in v_s
  body:
1   *match* ← *initialmatch*
2   **for** $i = 1$ **to** n {
3   *new* ← ∅
4   **foreach** $j \in$ *match* {
5   **if** *preds bitmap*$[v_i[j]]$ **then** *new* ← *new* ∪ j }
6   *match* ← *new* }
7 *matched* ← v_s[*match*]
8 **return** *matched*

Fig. 4. Cluster propagation

The algorithm's cost is $(C_{check} + C_{bitW})P_{sat} + \sum_{c \in S(C)} \sum_{i=1}^{i=|c|} C_{bitR} sv(c, i)$ where P_{sat} is the number of satisfied predicates, C_{check} is the cost of checking if a predicate is a characteristic predicate of a cluster, C_{bitW} is the cost of setting a bitmap item to 1, $S(C)$ is the set of selected clusters, $sv(c, i)$ is the number of subscriptions in cluster c that are still verified at step i of the Cluster propagation algorithm and C_{bitR} is the cost of checking if a bitmap item is equal to 1. The propagation algorithm ensures a good cache locality for two reasons: First the cluster data structure permits to group together subscriptions (and thus predicates to be verified) that have a high probability to match on the same event. Second, the propagation strategy permits to access only cache blocks that contains predicates of subscriptions selected at the previous steps.

4 Experimental results

In this section we evaluate the performance of both the counting and propagation algorithms described in Section 3. We implemented these algorithms in our prototype and run experiments under various simulated workloads. Our experimental results show that both algorithms are able to handle a large number of subscriptions (several millions). Our experiments also show that the propagation algorithm outperforms the counting algorithm in all situations and takes more advantage of the existence of selective predicates.

Experimental Setup: We ran our experiments on a single-CPU Pentium workstation with a i686 CPU at 500MHz and 1GB RAM having Linux as its operating system. Table 1 summarizes the workload parameters and their values for the experiments. In our workloads, all attributes have the same domain size (V) and all values in their domain have the same probability to appear ($1/V$). Moreover, each event published to the system have the same number (A) of attributes.

Generated subscriptions are described by the number of predicates (NP) they contain. Among these predicates, EQ predicates are equality predicates and NEQ are nonequality predicates. EQ and NEQ predicate are generated by as follows. Each predicate is associated to a distinct attribute and its value is chosen randomly over the attribute's domain using a uniform probability.

Name	Description	Range
S	number of subscriptions	15000 to 3000000
A	number of attributes per event	1 to 16
V	number of possible values per attribute	10 to 200
NP	number of predicates per subscription	1 to 16
EQ	number of equality predicates per subscription	0 to 16
NEQ	number of nonequality predicates per subscription	0 to 16

Table 1. Parameters definition and range values.

In our prototype, the matching module offers a Java interface. This interface receives events as Java objects and then translates them into a C structure that is submitted to the matching algorithm coded in K[10][1]. The identifiers of the matching subscriptions returned by the K program are then translated to Java objects. In our experiments both Java and K processes are running on the same machine. In our experiments we measured the total time of execution of both Java and K programs that includes communication between the Java and C processes.

Experimental Results: Experiments results are showed in Figure 5. In this Figure response time are given using a logarithmic scale. We first study the algorithm performance when subscriptions consist only of equality predicates ($NP = EQ$). Figure 5(a) shows the execution time of the matching algorithms when the number of subscriptions S varies and EQ, NP and V are respectively set to 4,4 and 35. Both algorithms show a linear dependency on S, and the propagation algorithm shows the best performance. For 15000 subscriptions, the propagation and counting algorithms are, respectively, able to process 2254 and 621 events per second. For one million (three millions) of subscriptions propagation algorithm can match 391 (117) events per second and the counting algorithm matches 7 (2) events per second. In this figure we also show the execution time of a third algorithm, designated as *no-propagation*. This algorithm first determines the predicates that are matched by the event. Next, it selects the subscriptions whose most selective predicate is verified by the event and verifies the remaining predicates of each of these subscriptions by consulting the predicate bitmap table. The propagation algorithm and the no-propagation algorithm perform a similar number of comparisons. However, the performance gap between the two algorithms increases with S. One explanation is the number of cache misses that are avoided by the propagation algorithm. Indeed as explained in the previ-

---

[1] The K language permits the implementation of very efficient C programs.

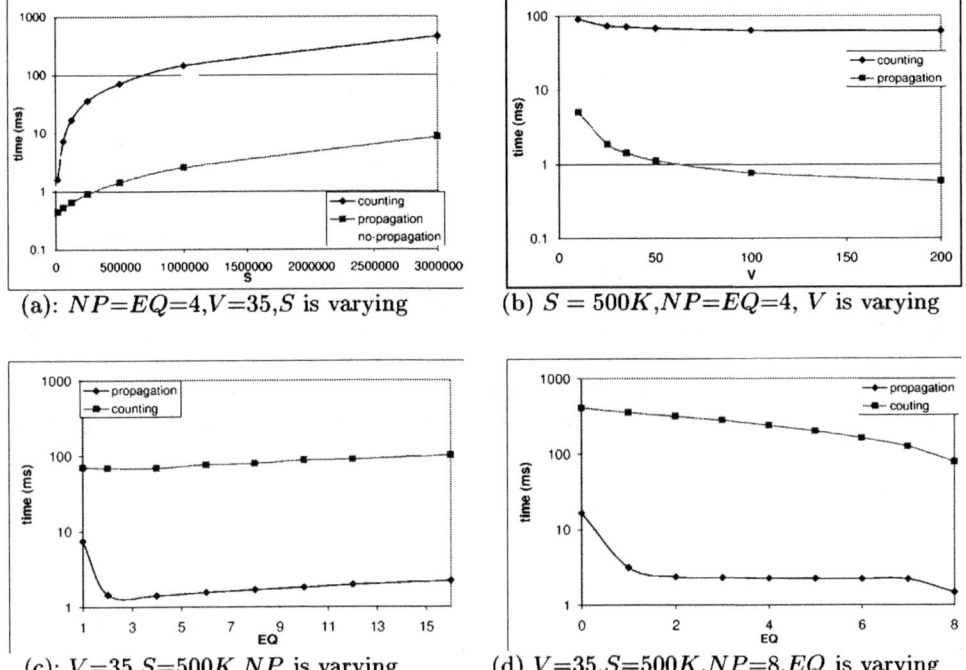

(a): $NP=EQ=4,V=35,S$ is varying

(b) $S=500K,NP=EQ=4,V$ is varying

(c): $V=35,S=500K,NP$ is varying

(d) $V=35,S=500K,NP=8,EQ$ is varying

Fig. 5. matching time per event (logarithmic scale)

ous section, the propagation algorithm avoids cache misses by increasing spatial locality.

In Figure 5(b) we measure the execution time when V is varying. EQ, NP and S and are respectively set to 4, 4, and 500000. Both algorithms are sensitive to this parameter, improving their execution time when V increases. For the counting algorithm, the total number of predicates matched by a given event decreases with V since the average number of subscriptions per predicate also decreases with V. However, the final number of comparisons made to determine the matched subscriptions remains constant. On the other hand, the propagation algorithm reduces the number of comparisons. Indeed, as V increases, the predicates become more selective and fewer subscriptions have to be considered in each step. This explain why the comparison algorithm is more sensitive to V.

In Figure 5(c) we measure the execution time when the number of subscription's predicates NP is varying. S and V are respectively set to 35 and 500000. Both algorithms are sensitive to NP. The cost of the counting algorithm increases linearly with the number of predicates since the average number of matched predicates per subscription increases linearly with NP. The execution time of the propagation algorithm also increases with NP since the size of each selected subscription cluster to verify in the second step of the cluster propagation algorithm is equal to NP.

Finally in Figure 5(d) we study the impact of having inequality predicates. In this experiment, the number of predicates per subscription is fixed ($NP = 8$), and the number of equality (EQ) and nonequality (NEQ) predicates per subscription respectively respectively vary from 0 to 8 and from 8 to 0. The other parameters, V and S are respectively set to 35 and 500000. As EQ increases, the performance of both algorithms improves (the propagation algorithms improves slightly), since the equality predicates are more selective than the nonequality predicates. Figure 5(d) shows that the counting algorithm is more sensitive to the number of nonequality predicates per subscription than the propagation algorithm. Indeed, when the number of nonequality predicates per subscription is high, there is a high probability for a subscription to have very selective nonequality predicates. Since the propagation algorithm takes strong advantage of the existence of at least one selective predicate, the impact of nonequality predicates is negligible as soon as subscriptions contains one equality predicate.

5   Related work and conclusions

To our knowledge we made the first proposal for using an event notification (or publish/subscribe) service on the web to deal with highly dynamic Web information. A lot of event notification services have been already developed as middleware for gluing together distributed applications or systems. These systems differentiate from each other by their filtering capabilities, the efficiency of their matching algorithm and additional features like QoS guarantees[2].

There are two kinds of publish/subscribe systems: *subject-based* and *content-based*. In subject-based systems, events are classified by groups and can be filtered only according to their group. Examples of such systems are OrbixTalk[9] and TIB/Rendezvous[3]. Content-based systems are an emerging type of pub/sub system where events are filtered according to their attribute values. Le Subscribe is a content-based system. We can cite other content-based systems, like Gryphon[2], NEONet[11], or READY[6] and publish/subscribe mechanisms integrated in commercial DBMS products like Oracle8i, SQL Server 7.0, or Sybase. Compared to subject-based systems, content-based systems offer more subscription expressiveness. The cost of this gain in expressiveness is an increase in the complexity of the matching process: the more sophisticated the constructs, the more complex the matching process. This complexity combined with a large number of subscriptions may severely degrade the matching efficiency. So, systems devoted to support a large number of subscriptions as our system does, have to face a tradeoff between the subscription language sophistication and matching efficiency. In our system we designed an expressive language that lends itself to very efficient matching.

The subscription languages of Gryphon and NEONet are quite similar to our language. Their matching algorithm do not exploit predicate redundancy nor dependencies (as Le Subscribe does). The READY system[6] has a more expressive

---

[2] In Le Subscribe we do not consider these additional features.

subscription language supporting grouping constructs, compound event matching and event aggregation. Its matching algorithm uses only local optimizations unlike Le Subscribe which intensively exploits global optimization opportunities and predicate redundancy. Commercial DBMS products use SQL as their subscription language, and these products are designed for contexts where the number of subscriptions is relatively small, as might occur in the context of enterprise application integration.

Hanson *et al* proposes a matching algorithm in [7]. During a pre-processing phase, the algorithm chooses the most selective predicate for each subscription and places it in an index (IBS tree) associated with the predicate's attribute. During the processing of an event, the algorithm first computes the set of subscriptions whose most selective predicate is verified and then checks the remaining predicates of each selected subscription in a naive way. Our propagation algorithm optimizes this second step by using a bitmap of predicates and a propagation strategy.

References

1. M. K. Aguilera, R. E. Strom, D. C. Sturman, M. Astley, and T. D. Chandra. Matching events in a content-based subscription system. In *Eighteenth ACM Symposium on Principles of Distributed Computing (PODC '99)*, 1999.
2. G. Banavar, T. D. Chandra, B. Mukherjee, J. Nagarajarao, R. E. Strom, and D. C. Sturman. An efficient multicast protocol for content-based publish-subscribe systems. In *International Conference on Distributed Computing Systems*, 1999.
3. A. Chan. Transactional publish/subscribe: The procative multicast of database-changes. In *SIGMOD'98*, 1998.
4. P. Bernstein et al. The asilomar report on database research. *ACM Sigmod record*, 27(4), 1998.
5. K. J. Gough and G. Smith. Efficient recognition of events in distributed systems. In *Proceedings of ACSC-18*, 1995.
6. R. E. Gruber, B. Krishnamurthy, and E. Panagos. The architecture of the ready event notification service. In *Proceedings of the 19th IEEE International Conference on Distributed Computing Systems Middleware Workshop*, 1999.
7. E. N. Hanson, M. Chaabouni, C. Kim, and Y. Wang. A predicate matching algorithm for database rule systems. In *SIGMOD'90*, 1990.
8. T. A. Howes, M. C. Smith, and G. S. Good. *Understanding and Deploying LDAP Directory Services*. Macmillan Technical Publishing, 1999.
9. IONA Technologies. *http://www.iona.com/products/messaging/index.html*.
10. KX SYSTEMS. *K USER MANUAL*, version 2.0 edition, 1998.
11. New Era of Networks Inc. *http://www.neonsoft.com/products/NEONet.html*.
12. J. Pereira, F. Fabret, F. Llirbat, R. Preotiuc-Pietro, K. A. Ross, and D. Shasha. Publish/subscribe on the web at extreme speed. In *Proccedings of the 26th VLDB Conference*, 2000.
13. J. Rao and K. A. Ross. Cache conscious indexing for decision-support in main memory. In *Proccedings of the 25th VLDB Conference*, 1999.
14. T. Yan and H. Garcia-Molina. The sift information dissemination system. In *ACM TODS 2000*, 2000.

A Software Retrieval Service based on Knowledge-Driven Agents*

E. Mena[1], A. Illarramendi[2], and A. Goñi[2]

[1] IIS depart., Univ. de Zaragoza. Spain. http://www.cps.unizar.es/~mena/
[2] LSI depart., UPV. San Sebastián. Spain. http://siul02.si.ehu.es/~jirgbdat/

Abstract. The ability of retrieving and installing software in an easy and efficient way confers competitive advantage on computer users in general, and even more especially on mobile computer users. In this paper we present a software retrieval service that allows mobile users to select, retrieve and install software anywhere and at any time. This service makes use of agents that allow 1) a browsing of a software ontology automatically customized to different kind of users and user computers; 2) an efficient retrieval of the selected software; and 3) an automatic update of the available software ontology. A software obtaining process based on agents, that manage semantic descriptions of available software, presents a qualitative advance with respect to existing solutions where users must know the location and access method of various remote software repositories.

1 Introduction

One of the most frequent tasks of computer users is to obtain new software, in order to improve the capabilities of their computers. Different kinds of users need different kinds of software. Nowadays a common procedure to obtain software is to visit some of the several websites that contain freeware, shareware and demos (such as Tucows [11], CNET Shareware.com [2], CNET Download.com [3]), games (such as Games Domain [1] and CNET Gamescenter.com[4]), java-related software (like Gamelan [5]) or many others. However, that procedure presents problems for many users because they must:

1. Know the different programs that fulfil their needs. Not only their names but also where to find them in the vast Web space. Web sites are moved and re-designed which makes that links and bookmarks become obsolete very frequently
2. Know the features of their computers, in order to select the most appropriate version for their computers. This task implies having technical knowledge, among other things, about her/his system (CPU, OS and version, free disk space available, RAM memory, etc.) and the software installed previously (to request a full version or just an update).

* This work has been supported by *CICYT (Comisión Interministerial de Ciencia y Tecnología*, Spain [TIC97-0962]), MoviStar (a spanish cellular phone company) and the University of the Basque Country.

O. Etzion and P. Scheuermann (Eds.): CoopIS 2000, LNCS 1901, pp. 174–185, 2000.

3. Be aware of new software and/or new releases of software of interest. Although few commercial programs currently alert about new releases, users need to keep an eye on the Web, or on other repositories, if they want to be informed about new software that could be of their interest.

Previous problems become even more important when users work with mobile computers using a wireless network media. Time expended in looking for the software, retrieving and installing it should be minimized as much as possible, in order to reduce communication cost and power consumed.

In this paper we present an alternative procedure: a Software Retrieval Service, based on the use of an ontology and the agent technology, that allows users to find, retrieve and install software in an easy and efficient way. Easy, because with the help of intelligent agents, users can browse the ontology that describes semantically the content of a set of data sources containing pieces of software, and so they can select from it the software (the service makes transparent for the users the location and access method of various remote software repositories); and efficient, because agents take care of reducing the wireless communication cost.

Concerning related work, to our knowledge, agents have not been widely used for software retrieval. In [6] they explain a mechanism to update several remote clients connected to a server taking advantage of mobile agents capability to deal with disconnections. However this work is more related to *push technology* than to services created to assist users in the task of updating the software on their computers.

In the rest of the paper, we present in Sect. 2 the cost model of software retrieval services based on webpages navigation. In Sect. 3 we explain the cost model of our proposal and present a comparison between the two approaches. A description of the different agents involved in the Software Retrieval Service is included in Sect. 4. Two of them, *Alfred* and the *Browser*, are described in detail in Sect. 5 and 6, respectively. Finally, conclusions can be found in Sect. 7.

2   Software Retrieval Based on HTML Pages Navigation

We said before that the most common way to obtain new software is by navigating HTML pages in (public or pay-per-download) software repositories. These repositories classify the different software in categories, in order to make easier the selection of the wanted piece of software. The user selects a category, browses the information, clicks on a link which involves a remote access, browses the information obtained, clicks again on another link and repeat this process until s/he requests a piece of software.

In the following we describe the cost model associated to this way of retrieving software. $C_{HTMLnav}$ is the cost to retrieve the software by interacting directly with the Web server that contains the software programs.

$$C_{HTMLnav} = [n \times (T_{newPage} + T_{readPage}) + T_{download}] \times C_{perSec}$$

where n is the number of links that the user has to navigate before finding the wanted program; $T_{newPage}$ is the time passed since the petition of a URL until the content of the new page arrives at the user computer; $T_{readPage}$ is the time spent by the user to check out a web page in order to find the link for the next software category or for the program to download; $T_{download}$ is the time passed since the petition of a URL that contains a software program until it is downloaded; and C_{perSec} is the cost of communication per second.

Notice that the above behaviour corresponds to the classical Client/Server (C/S) approach. $T_{newPage}$ and $T_{download}$ depend on the network transmission speed. Moreover, we cannot minimize $T_{readPage}$ as it depends on the kind of user (naive or expert). Thus, a system like this depends completely on the network and on the number of iterations needed to select the piece of software (i.e., n). The first problem is out of the scope of software system developers, and the second parameter is minimized by most common software repositories by classifying the enormous amount of available software in a hierarchy of categories.

A very important point is that users need several "clicks", more than five even when they perfectly know the software repository as well as what they are searching for[1]. Naive users that do not know neither the category of the software nor even the software itself could click a big number of times before finding the wanted software; some could even get lost in the taxonomy of categories. The system response to each click is fast when the network allows it. But the big disadvantage is that users need their computers to be connected continuously. This is an issue that we can improve by the use of mobile agents.

3   Our Proposal: the Software Retrieval Service

The procedure that our service supports for the software retrieval process is the following: first, the user receives the visit of an agent (the *Browser*) which helps the user to select the most appropriate software by browsing a catalog customized to that concrete user. The user can request more detailed information until s/he finally selects a piece of software. Then, a new agent arrives to the user computer (the *Salesman*) with the selected piece of software.

In the following we describe C_{SRS}, the cost model associated to the Software Retrieval Service:

$$C_{SRS} = [T_{BrowserCat}+T_{readCat}+m\times(T_{refine}+T_{readCat})+T_{SalesmanCat}]\times C_{perSec}$$

where $T_{BrowserCat}$ is the time passed since the petition of the software service until the Browser agent arrives to the user computer with the catalog; $T_{readCat}$ is the time spent by the user to check out a catalog in order to request a new refinement or select the program to download; m is the number of catalog refinements requested by the user; T_{refine} is the time passed since the petition of a new catalog refinement until the Browser presents the new catalog; and

---

[1] We are not considering the use of search engines available in some software repositories.

$T_{SalesmanCat}$ is the time passed since the selection of the wanted software is made until the Salesman agent arrives to the user computer with such a piece of program.

We refine the above expression considering the next properties:

1. $T_{BrowserCat} = T_{Browser} + T_{catalog}$, i.e., the time needed for the Browser to travel to the user computer and the time needed to carry a catalog to the user computer, respectively.
2. Similarly, $T_{SalesmanCat} = T_{Salesman} + T_{download}$, i.e., the time needed for the Salesman agent to travel to the user computer and the time needed to carry the selected piece of software to the user computer, respectively.
3. Concerning refinements requested by the user, we consider $m = k + l$, where k is the number of catalog refinements that can be answered by the Browser itself ($T_{localRefine}$), and l is the number of catalog refinements that imply that the Browser connects remotely to obtain such an information ($T_{remoteRefine}$).

Therefore, the cost expression for the Software Retrieval Service results as follows:

$$C_{SRS} = [T_{Browser} + T_{catalog} + T_{readCat} + k \times (T_{localRefine} + T_{readCat})$$
$$+ l \times (T_{remoteRefine} + T_{readCat}) + T_{Salesman} + T_{download}] \times C_{perSec}$$

Comparison of Costs of Both Procedures. We would like to know now when it is better each one of both possibilities, HTML navigation or our proposed Software Retrieval Service. We consider the following properties between the SRS and the HTML approach, and the resulting comparison:

– $T_{readCat}$ equivalent to $T_{readPage}$ (time spent by the user reading a catalog is similar to the one spent reading a web page with categories).
– $n = 1 + m$ (the first catalog retrieval and the m refinements in SRS are equivalent to n web pages in the HTML navigation approach). Thus, $n = 1 + k + l$.
– $T_{remoteRefine} = T_{newPage}$, since the information needed by the Browser to perform a new refinement is similar in size to a web page.
– $T_{localRefine} = 0$ (such an activity is performed by the Browser on the user computer without the need of being connected to the net).

$$C_{SRS} < C_{HTMLnav} \Longleftrightarrow$$
$$\Longleftrightarrow T_{Browser} + T_{catalog} + T_{Salesman} < (k+1) \times T_{newPage} \Longleftrightarrow$$
$$\Longleftrightarrow |Browser| + |catalog| + |Salesman| < (k+1) \times |newPage|$$

Notice that all the times are affected by the network speed, so we can rewrite the expressions in terms of size. We can observe here that, if we forget the size of the two agents which is small (in our prototype, the size of each agent is less than 10K), the keys of the success of our approach are the size of the catalog initially carried to the user computer and the number of refinements that the Browser is capable to perform without external help (k), which also depends directly on the size of the initial catalog as well as on the "intelligence" of the agents. The estimation of the relationship between the catalog size and k will be the goal of future papers.

In [8] we show an example of the different behaviour, from the point of view of network remote access, of a Client/Server (C/S) approach, like HTML navigation, and a mobile agent approach, like our proposed service.

4   Agents Involved in the System

In this section we present briefly all the agents that take part of the Software Retrieval Service [8]. This service is situated in a concrete server that we call GSN[2] and is one of the services provided by the ANTARCTICA system [12]. Agents are executed in contexts denominated *places* [10]. Mobile agents can travel from one place to another. The proposed service incorporates one place on the user computer called the *User place*, and other three places situated on the GSN, called the *Software Acquisition place*, the *Software place* and the *Broadcast place*, respectively (see Fig. 1).

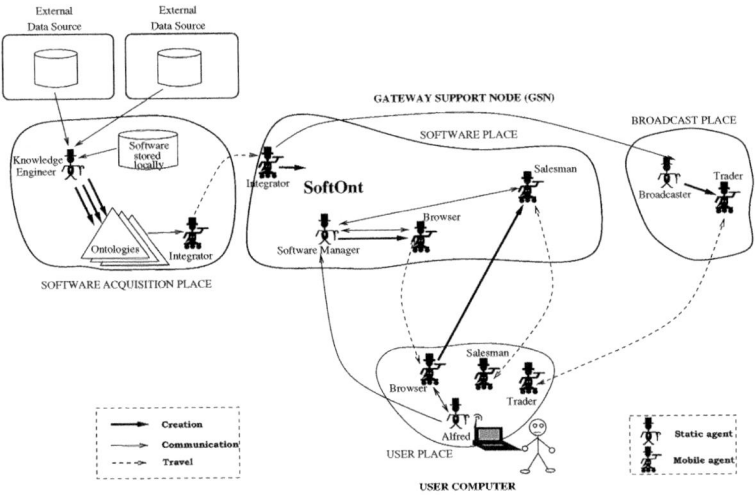

Fig. 1. Main architecture for the Software Retrieval Service

In the following we briefly describe such agents, grouped in three categories:

---

[2] The *Gateway Support Node (GSN)* is the proxy that provides services to computer users.

1. *The user agent.* **Alfred** is an efficient majordomo that serves the user and is on charge of storing as much information about the user computer, and the user her/himself, as possible. Although it helps the user in all the services provided by the GSN, we will stress its role in the Software Retrieval Service.

2. *SoftOnt ontology creation.* **The Knowledge Engineer** agent mines (local or remote) software repositories, with the help of specialized wrappers, in order to obtain a semantic description (an ontology) for each repository. Then, **the Integrator** agent performs the integration of all the ontologies obtained by the Knowledge Engineer with the goal of obtaining the ontology SoftOnt. During the integration process it uses a thesaurus for the automatic vocabulary problems resolution [7].

3. *SoftOnt ontology exploitation.* **The Software Manager** agent creates and provides **the Browser** agent with a catalog of the available software, according to the needs expressed by Alfred (on behalf of the user), i.e., it is capable to obtain customized metadata about the underlying software. For this task, the Software Manager consults the SoftOnt ontology. The software itself can be either stored locally on the GSN or accessible through the Web in external data sources. Thus, the GSN can have access to a great number of distinct software for different systems, with different availability, purpose etc. The goal of the Browser agent is to interact with the user in order to refine a catalog of software until the user finally chooses a concrete piece of software. When this is done, **the Salesman** agent carries the program selected by the user to her/his computer, performs any electronic commerce interaction needed (which depends on the concrete piece of software), and installs the program, whenever possible.

   The Broadcaster agent sends information of different nature to the users of any of the services provided by the GSN. Depending on the information, it can create **Trader** agents that carry non trivial information (demos, new releases, etc.) to users that manifested their interest in such an information.

Notice that we have only provided a description of the behaviour of the agents in the system, but we do not specify how the structure or state of such agents changes. In other words, how they *learn*, how its knowledge is structured. The reason is that the state of intelligent agents like these is too complex (ontologies, user preferences about many situations, etc.) to provide a brief description. A more detailed description of the *knowledge* managed by Alfred and the Browser, which are the core of the system, is included in the following sections.

5   Alfred: the User Majordomo

Alfred is an efficient majordomo that serves the user and is on charge of storing as much information about the user computer, and the user her/himself, as possible. Initially, Alfred is the only agent on the user computer that is able to interact directly with the user. When another agent wants to show/retrieve data to/from the user it has to communicate with Alfred who[3] will create the appropriate user interface for each case (other agents do not know how the user wants to be interacted). In the opposite way, anytime the user wants to perform any action or request some information, s/he communicates with Alfred who will perform such tasks by himself or by communicating with other agents in the system to achieve the requested task.

5.1   Alfred's Goal

We now explain the role of Alfred in the Software Retrieval Service. Let us start with the situation in which the user wants to retrieve some kind of software. Two cases can arise:

1. The user only knows some feature of the program, for example, its purpose. In this case, the user needs some kind of catalog concerning the software available, in order to navigate it and find the wanted program. With the help of a GUI, users can write a list of constraints, expressed as a list of pairs <*feature, value*>, in order to express their needs the best they can[4]. The system will try to match such a query with the semantic description of available software (i.e., the SoftOnt ontology). We propose the use of a (specialized) thesaurus in order to deal with the vocabulary problem. Moreover, the user can specify the level of detail (expressed as a percentage) that s/he wants in such a catalog, and select some pruning strategy. Advanced users could be interested in many features of software while naive users could only be interested in just a few, such as a brief description, the name of the program and the OS needed to install it.

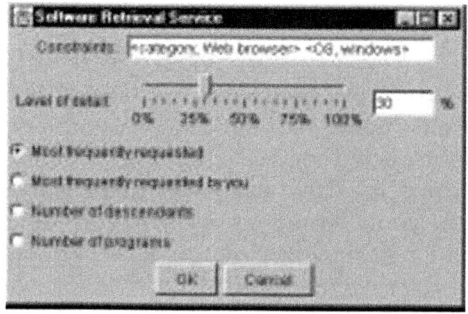

Fig. 2. Alfred's GUI for the Software Retrieval Service

---

[3] We denote Alfred as a person in an attempt of reflecting his role similar to a major-domo in the real world.

[4] The information provided can be imprecise. In Fig. 2, the user does not know neither the web browser name nor the concrete Windows version of her/his computer.

2. The user exactly knows which program s/he needs, for example, JDK1.2.2 for Win32, and also knows how to ask for it. This can happen because s/he is a usual client of this service. Thus, expert users could directly pose the request, with the help of a GUI, describing the software they need. The data entered is also represented as a (list of) pair(s), for example *[<name, JDK1.2.2>, <OS, Win32>]*.

All the information provided by the user is received and stored by Alfred. Thus, Alfred can add more useful information to users requests, taking previous executions as basis. This information is stored in the MU place and updated automatically by Alfred. Thus, with each user request, Alfred stores more information about the user computer and about the user. The information added by Alfred to the user request is also expressed as a list of pairs.

After the query is built, Alfred sends a request to the GSN, where the request is attended by a specialized agent, the *Software Manager* agent, which obtains a catalog with the kind of software that satisfies the user needs, according to the level of detail specified and the pruning strategy selected. Then, the Software Manager creates a specialized agent, the *Browser* agent, which travels to the User place in order to help the user to select the piece of software that fulfils her/his needs.

5.2 Alfred's Knowledge

As we said before, Alfred acts as a mediator between the user and all the services offered by the ANTARCTICA system. In the following we describe the kind of knowledge managed by Alfred, with a special stress in the knowledge involved in the Software Retrieval Service.

Basically we make a general distinction between the general knowledge of Alfred and the specialized knowledge related to concrete services:

1. Knowledge independent of the service: it is composed by technical knowledge related to the system, such as:
   - Hardware components available: RAM memory, sound and video card, CPU, type of network connection, and other periphericals installed.
   - Resource availability: free disk space, free memory, etc.
   - Software currently available: applications and software needed to install other software, such as Java, DirectX, etc.
   - General user preferences: common to all the services like GUI features, logging level, etc.

   Alfred obtains this information by consulting the OS. If the OS does not allow to automatically retrieve some data, Alfred would request such data to the user (only when needed).

2. Knowledge related to each service: the different kind of information that Alfred needs to deal with, when a service is requested by the user. The examples provided are related to the Software Retrieval Service:

- Technical knowledge concerning the service: information about other agents and places needed to achieve the goal of the service, such as residing nodes, names, services, etc. For example, Alfred needs to know how to communicate with the Software Manager agent residing on the GSN and any other coming agents like the Browser or the Salesman.
- Historical traces, with previous execution traces for such a service. This is a very important part of Alfred's "memory". The most important information of these traces are the interactions with the user, since we want to minimize them: all the information provided by the user is stored. In the same way, Alfred also saves the requests formulated to the user by other agents and the answers provided by her/him. This catalog of past interactions is updated every time that this concrete service is invoked.
- User preferences related with the concrete service, that have been extracted from the historical traces. For example, Alfred can detect that whenever the user needs a web navigator, s/he always selects the last version of Netscape. However, it is important to stress that these preferences can be time-changing, the user could like a different web navigator because of a new user interface or any other reason.

For the traces and the user preferences, Alfred manages probabilistic information of user's answers, in order to face the problem of different answers provided to the same question in different situations. For example, Alfred could store that the user selected Netscape as web browser the 85% of times. As we said before, the user can change her/his mind due to whatever reason. Thus, whenever Alfred can suggest different choices to the user, the most probable one will be selected taking into account the number of times that it was provided by the user as well as that recent answers could match better with current user preferences. Anyway, Alfred always reports to the user the reason of its proposal and the final decision depends on the user.

During the execution of the Software Retrieval Service, Alfred explains to the user some special situations that unable the system to satisfy the user, for example, "free disk space is not enough", "the requested software is not available for the current OS", etc. Hence, any refinement made on user requests, is communicated to the user for information purpose.

6   The Browser: a Specialist in Browsing Catalogs

We divide the explanation about the Browser agent into two subsections: 1) its creation, performed by the Software Manager agent; and 2) its main activity, when it helps the user to browse software catalogs.

6.1   The Software Manager and the SoftOnt Ontology

After receiving a request of Alfred (on behalf of the user), the Software Manager agent creates a new Browser agent which will be in charge of helping the user to select the most appropriate piece of software. The Browser agent manages an ontology (a subset of a bigger ontology that describes all the software available at the GSN) provided by the Software Manager right after the Browser is created.

We advocate using an ontology, called *SoftOnt*, to describe *semantically* the content of a set of data sources storing pieces of software. This ontology, which stores detailed information concerning the available software accessible from the GSN, is managed by the Software Manager. So, instead of users having to deal directly with different software repositories, the goal is that a system uses an ontology to help users to retrieve software.

In [7] we explain the translation step that permits obtaining ontologies from software repositories and the integration step that generates a global ontology by integrating the previously obtained ones, along with the explanation of how the previous process can be performed automatically and the justification about the use of only one ontology.

The SoftOnt ontology is pruned by considering the constraints, the level of detail and a pruning strategy, which have been provided by Alfred. The level of detail (which is a percentage) indicates the amount of data that should be included in the catalog; for example, a level of detail of 30% indicates that only the 30% of SoftOnt should be shown to the user. The pruning strategy indicates *which* nodes of the ontology will be selected, it is the selection criteria; for example, the most frequently requested or the most frequently requested by that user. Thus, we could obtain, for example, the most frequently requested nodes until completing the 30% of SoftOnt. Notice that, independently of the pruning strategy, a level of detail of 30% indicates that the user only wants to see the 30% of the ontology obtained after considering the constraints indicated by Alfred.

This pruning process is very important due to two reasons: 1) it avoids presenting the user categories and pieces of software that cannot be installed on the user computer (different OS, or other restrictions); and 2) it avoids presenting very specialized categories and pieces of software that could surely make naive users spend more time reading the catalog.

Therefore, *the SoftOnt ontology constitutes the main knowledge managed by the Software Manager agent and the pruned ontology (customized to each user) constitutes the main knowledge managed by the Browser agent.*

6.2   Catalog Browsing

Once on the user node, the Browser presents the pruned ontology as a graph (inner nodes are categories and leaves are programs), and the user can navigate it and ask for a bigger level of detail of the terms s/he is interested in. In that case, the Browser will request more information to the Software Manager, which resides on the GSN. In order to help users, each node in the ontology has associated a percentage (calculated when a view of SoftOnt is built) that indicates how much of the total information has been retrieved until then.

The following are the different refinements that a user can request by selecting a node of the current catalog:

1. Request of more detail for some node. Sometimes, the information can be on the GSN, so the Browser communicates with the Software Manager Agent or travel to the GSN, depending on the amount of information requested. However, the Browser could have such an information and no remote communication is needed.

2. Refinement by providing new constraints. The user could want to provide a new constraint (a new pair <*feature, value*>) instead of navigating the catalog. Then the catalog must be re-built again, taking into consideration the new constraint. If the Browser would have pruning capabilities, it could be done locally, on the user node without any remote connection. In other case, the Browser will request the new catalog to the Software Manager Agent or travel to the GSN if the resulting catalog may be very big.

Notice that the Browser can decide whether requesting remotely a certain information to the Software Manager or travelling to the GSN to request the information locally. In order to decide between those two strategies, the Browser evaluates the impact of new user refinements. If they only require a small amount of bytes, such an information will be requested remotely; in the case of refinements that affect to many categories, the Browser can request to the Software Manager the size in bytes of the needed information; for example: which is the size of all the information under the term 'HTML tools' ?.

In the case of travelling to the GSN, the Browser does not travel with the previous catalog: it is stored temporally on the user node and updated when the Browser comes back with the new information. Moreover, it can decide taking advantage of the trip and requesting to the Software Manager more information than what it was requested by the user (without compromising the efficiency). In this way, notice that the Browser upgrade its knowledge with each user refinement, making less frequent the need for remote connections. So, future refinements can be attended faster and avoiding remote connections.

The process of catalog browsing ends when the last catalog presented to the user cannot be refined as it is composed by a list of names of software that fit the user needs. The user can then click on one of the different choices which correspond to programs that fulfil her/his needs. As a consequence of that action, the Browser agent remotely creates a Salesman agent on the GSN. This agent will visit the user computer carrying the specified program. After this, the Browser Agent simply ends its execution. See [8] for a more detailed description of the task performed by the Salesman.

7   Conclusions and Future Work

Retrieving software is an activity that requires a particular effort to users and that must be done with a certain frequency. Therefore, it is widely accepted the interest of systems that help users with that task of software retrieval.

In this paper we have presented a Software Retrieval Service based on knowledge-driven agents that allows users to browse a catalog that contains semantic descriptions of available software, and to select and retrieve the wanted software in an efficient way. Although the service can be used by any kind of computer user it puts on a special emphasis on mobile users. Empirical results obtained through the implemented prototype and analytical tests [9] show the feasibility of the service.

As future work, we are studying the possibility of providing the Browser agent with the pruning capabilities of the Software Manager in order to make it more independent of the GSN and reduce dramatically the need of having an open network connection.

Acknowledgements

We would like to thank Daniel Fanjul and Ignacio García his valuable help in the implementation of the prototype.

References

1. Attitude Network Ltd., 1999. http://www.gamesdomain.com.
2. CNET Inc., 1999. http://www.shareware.com.
3. CNET Inc., 1999. http://www.download.com.
4. CNET Inc., 1999. http://www.gamecenter.com.
5. Earthweb & Sun Microsystems, 1999. http://www.gamelan.com.
6. IBM Corporation. TME 10 Software Distribution - Mobile Agents SG24-4854-00, January 1997. http://www.redbooks.ibm.com/abstracts/sg244854.html.
7. E. Mena, A. Illarramendi, and A. Goñi. Automatic Ontology Construction for a Multiagent-based Software Gathering Service. In *proceedings of the Fourth International ICMAS'2000 Workshop on Cooperative Information Agents (CIA'2000), Springer series of Lecture Notes on Artificial Intelligence (LNAI), Boston (USA)*, July 2000.
8. E. Mena, A. Illarramendi, and A. Goñi. Customizable Software Retrieval Facility for Mobile Computers using Agents. In *proceedings of the Seventh International Conference on Parallel and Distributed Systems (ICPADS'2000), workshop International Flexible Networking and Cooperative Distributed Agents (FNCDA'2000), IEEE Computer Society, Iwate (Japan)*, July 2000.
9. J. Merseguer, J. Campos, and E. Mena. Performance Evaluation for the Design of Agent-Based Systems: A Petri Net Approach. In *proceedings of the Software Engineering and Petri Nets (SEPN'2000) workshop within the 21st International Conference on Application and Theory of Petri Nets, Aarhus (Denmark)*, June 2000.
10. D. Milojicic, M. Breugst, I. Busse, J. Campbell, S. Covaci, B. Friedman, K. Kosaka, D. Lange, K. Ono, M. Oshima, C. Tham, S. Virdhagriswaran, and J. White. MASIF, the OMG mobile agent system interoperability facility. In *Proceedings of Mobile Agents '98*, September 1998.
11. Tucows.Com Inc., 1999. http://www.tucows.com.
12. Y. Villate, D. Gil, A. Goñi, and A. Illarramendi. Mobile agents for providing mobile computers with data services. In *Proceedings of the Ninth IFIP/IEEE International Workshop on Distributed Systems: Operations and Management (DSOM 98)*, 1998.

Benchmarking and Configuration of Workflow Management Systems

Michael Gillmann, Ralf Mindermann, Gerhard Weikum
University of the Saarland, Germany
e-mail: {gillmann,minderma,weikum}@cs.uni-sb.de
WWW: http://www-dbs.cs.uni-sb.de

Abstract. Workflow management systems (WFMS) are a cornerstone of mission-criticial, possibly cross-organizational business processes. For large-scale applications both their performance and availability are crucial factors, and the system needs to be properly configured to meet the application demands. Despite ample work on scalable system architectures for workflow management, the literature has neglected the important issues of how to systematically measure the performance of a given system configuration and how to determine viable configurations without resorting to expensive trial-and-error or guesswork. This paper proposes a synthetic benchmark for workflow management systems; based on the TPC-C order-entry benchmark, a complete e-commerce workflow is specified in a system-independent form. This workflow benchmark, which stresses all major components of a workflow system and is parameterized in a flexible manner, has been applied to two operational systems, the commercial system Staffware97 and our own prototype system Mentor-lite. The paper reports performance results from our measurements and discusses lessons learned. In particular, the results demonstrate the scalability of the Mentor-lite architecture. The measurements also underline the need for configuring systems intelligently, and the paper outlines an auto-configuration tool that we have been building to this end.

1 Introduction

1.1 Problem Statement

Workflow technology has penetrated into mission-critical, enterprise-wide or even cross-organizational, business applications. Typical examples are insurance claim processing, cargo shipping, or healt-care tracking and planning, and workflow technology is also embedded in many e-commerce services. Following the terminology of WfMC [32] (see also [5, 6, 8, 15, 18]), a workflow is a set of activities that belong together in order to achieve a certain business goal. Activities can be completely automated or based on interaction with a human user and intellectual decision-making. In particular, an activity can spawn requests to an arbitrary "invoked application" that is provided by some server independently of the current workflow. Workflow management systems (WFMS) orchestrate the control and data flow between a workflow's activities, based on a high-level specification of the intended behavior (e.g., using Petri-net variants, state charts, or some script language) with some leeway for exception handling and run-time improvisation (as needed, e.g., in medical applications).

Despite their business success, most WFMS products exhibit specific idiosyncracies and, by and large, significant deficiencies and limitations in terms of their performance. The current situation is probably comparable to that of relational database systems in the eighties. Also and similarly to database technology, configuring and tuning a WFMS for satisfactory performance falls more in the realm of black art (i.e., guesswork or expensive trial-and-error

O. Etzion and P. Scheuermann (Eds.): CoopIS 2000, LNCS 1901, pp. 186–197, 2000.
© Springer-Verlag Berlin Heidelberg 2000

experimentation) and sorely lacks scientific foundations. Even such mundane basics such as systematic benchmarks are still missing.

1.2   Contributions

This paper aims to improve the state of the art on the systematic assessment and judicious configuration of WFMSs by defining a simple yet powerful benchmark workflow, based on an e-commerce scenario. The benchmark specification takes the well-known TPC-C order-entry application as a starting point, combines the three major transactions of TPC-C into a workflow, and extends this setting to systematically stress all components of a WMFS architecture. The benchmark is parameterized for adaptation to different scales and application scopes. It is specified using the statechart formalism [13], and can be easily converted into the specification languages of most WFMSs.

To demonstrate the platform-independence and usefulness of the benchmark, we present performance measurements of two systems, the commercial product Staffware97 and our own prototype system Mentor-lite. These experiments have revealed limitations and system-specific bottlenecks with regard to scalability, thus underlining the need for such benchmarking. An additional, important lesson is that proper system configuration is a key issue, and that performance depends quite sensitively on subtle aspects of the configuration.

Out of the benchmarking efforts, we have started work towards an "intelligent" auto-configuration tool for WFMS architectures, with specific emphasis on the Mentor-lite architecture. In our prior work [9] we have focused on the analytical underpinnings for such a tool; in the current paper we present the architecture of the tool itself and its interaction with the various components of the WFMS environment. The implementation of the tool is close to completion and we plan on evaluating the quality of its recommendations using our e-commerce benchmark.

1.3   Related Work

Although the literature includes much work on scalable WFMS architectures [1, 5, 6, 8, 15, 19], there are only few research projects that have looked into the quantitative assessment of WFMS configurations. The work reported in [2, 3] presents several types of distributed WFMS architectures and discusses the influence of different load distribution methods on the network and workflow-server load, mostly using simulations. [28] presents heuristics for the allocation of workflow-type and workflow-instance data onto servers. Mechanisms for enhanced WFMS availability by replicating state data on a standby backup server have been studied in [11, 17]. [16] characterizes the workload of cross-organizational workflows by means of Markov models. None of this prior work has addressed the issue of how to systematically benchmark a WFMS and how to configure a WFMS for given performance goals.

Benchmarking is well established, with benchmark specifications gradually evolving, as a form of systematic performance assessment for processors and compilers [14], and also in the area of database and transaction processing systems [10, 25]. In particular, the suite of benchmarks published by the Transaction Performance Council (TPC) [30] has proven extremely useful for driving performance enhancements of commercial database systems over the last decade. On the other hand, the work of the TPC also shows that defining a systematic benchmark involves many subtle pitfalls and presents a quite challenge. In particular, finding a careful balance between making the benchmark realistic and functionally comprehensive and ensuring that it can be installed and run on many different platforms with affordable effort is all but trivial.

For the WFMS area and even for modern middleware in general, benchmarking is in its infancy. [20] presents a benchmark for a specific system, namely, Lotus Notes, but this effort solely focuses on Notes's use as a message/mail engine. [4] is even more specialized in its performance study of scientific lab processes in genome research. SAP has its product-specific benchmark suite [26] that stresses also the R/3-internal workflow engine, but this benchmark is completely tailored to the SAP environment, involves many issues of an ERP system that are not related to workflow technology, and would be difficult to port to another WFMS. The very recent TPC-W benchmark [31] considers Web-based e-commerce, but emphasizes the routing, multiplexing, load balancing, caching, and security capabilities of Web application servers (of the category such as Apache, IIS, etc.) and pays no attention to the workflow aspects of e-services. Finally, [7] has made a laudable effort to define a general benchmark for active database systems, but has indeed restricted itself to the core functions of an active rule engine and cannot be generalized to the richer spectrum of WFMS services.

1.4   Paper Outline

The rest of the paper is organized as follows. Section 2 discusses the general rationale for a systematic benchmark of advanced WFMS architectures. Section 3 presents the specification of the e-commerce benchmark. Section 4 briefly reviews the architecture of the two systems under test. Section 5 presents the setup of the experimental testbed. Section 6 shows the results of our measurements. Section 7 discusses major lessons learned. Section 8 presents the architecture of the auto-configuration tool that we are building.

2   Benchmark Rationale

2.1   Metrics for Performance Assessment

From a business perspective, the benefit of a WFMS should ideally be measured in terms of how smooth and cost-effective the system runs a company's business processes. This involves issues like how much the WFMS contributes to customer satisfaction, effectivity of office workers (e.g., call-center agents), meeting deadlines, reducing operational cost, and ultimately the company's success in the market. Obviously, despite some recent business research along these lines (e.g., [27]), such benefits are hard to quantify. Our goal is much more limited in scope, focusing on metrics that can be directly attributed to the computer-support infrastructure of business processes.

Similar to transaction-processing benchmarks, a key metric is obviously the **throughput** of the entire WFMS. Unlike OLTP, our notion of throughput has a much larger granularity and extension in time: we measure throughput in terms of completed workflows (i.e., instances of a given workflow type), and we have to collect these numbers separately for different workflow types. Note that it does not make sense to amalgate throughput figures for a complex workflow type that involves week-long activities (e.g., processing a credit request in a bank) and a simple, short workflow type that usually completes within a few minutes (e.g., opening a bank account) into a single, seemingly unified metric, which could, however, no longer be meaningfully interpreted.

When we know the number of clients that interact with the WFMS, the rates at which these initiate new workflows, and the relative frequencies of the different workflow types, then the throughput that the system can sustain must be at least as high as the aggregate load induced from all clients. In addition, it is equally crucial that the WFMS is sufficiently responsive. In the context of long-lived business processes, this entails the following two subgoals. (1) The **turnaround time** for an entire workflow must be acceptable. Obviously this depends also on the efficiency of the human users that process intellectual activities, but it is important that the WFMS does not incur any additional bottlenecks. Also, and importantly for benchmarking, the turnaround time from the initiation of a workflow to its completion, as perceived by the initiating user, is the key metric for fully automated workflows that contain no interactive activities. (2) For workflows that include interactive activities and could thus have an extended lifetime of several days or weeks, the critical units are the individual interactions between a user and the WFMS that occur during activities and, especially, at the start and end of an activity when role resolution and other worklist-handling tasks are performed. For the purpose of our benchmark definition we are thus interested in the **step response time**, where a step could be a specific type of user interaction or an entire activity.

2.2   Components under Test

A WFMS is a complex system that consists of a build-time component for specifying workflows, a run-time component with the actual **workflow engine** for the proper interpretation of control and data flow in between activities, and a suite of administration tools for monitoring etc. For our purpose, the run-time engine is the component that matters. In most WFMSs, the workflow engine is run as a multithreaded server process, or sometimes as a collection of processes on the same or different computers. This workflow server may have its own persistent storage system for tracking the states of long-lived workflows, or more typically relies on a **database server** for this purpose. In addition, it may interact with **application servers** for invoked applications that result from automated activities. Finally, the communication among these various servers may be based on other, lower-level, middleware that is itself implemented in the form of dedicated **communication servers**. The latter serve as a reliable request brokers, with TP monitors (MQ Series, MTS, etc.) or ORBs (e.g., Orbix) being prevalent examples.

With the workflow engine really being the heart of a WFMS, it is crucial for a benchmark to stress the entire functional spectrum of the engine. Therefore, one requirement is to exercise the different types of **control-flow constructs**, notably, conditional branching, fork-join parallelism, and also loops. These should be supported by all industrial-strength WFMSs, but it is widely open to what extent they are handled efficiently.

An equally important, orthogonal, aspect to be examined by the benchmark is the support for different types of activities. Fully **automated activities**, which may invoke an **external application** on an application server, and **interactive activities** that run on client machines pose fairly different requirements on the workflow engine, and some commercial WFMS are known to be particularly geared for one type of activities.

Our benchmark will include all major types of control-flow constructs and both types of activites. However, the benchmark will be designed such that different, restricted, levels of specialization can be derived when the interest is on specific application requirements or special-purpose WFMSs (e.g., for call-center applications or canonical, simple types of e-commerce). The components under test will include the workflow server as well as any underlying database or storage servers and also external application servers and communication servers if these are present in a given WFMS architecture. The actual external applications (e.g., the program for testing the authenticity of a hand-written or digital signature) will, however, only be emulated by a stub (i.e., a "dummy" program) inside the application server. Similar to the functional specializations, we will allow different scoping levels of the benchmark to either include or exclude such additional components. So, in the simplest case the benchmark solely examines the workflow engine, and in the most advanced case it takes the full suite of surrounding software and the corresponding servers into account.

3   Benchmark Specification

In this section we describe our benchmark specification. The benchmark reflects all previously described metrics and tests all interesting system components. Our proposal captures an e-commerce scenario. It is similar to the TPC-C benchmark for transaction systems [30], with the key difference that we combine multiple transaction types into a workflow and further enhance the functionality by control and data flow handling. Furthermore, we explicitly take application invocations into account.

The control flow specification is given in the form of state charts [12, 13]. This specification formalism has been adopted for the behavioral dimension of the UML industry standard, and it has been used for our own prototype system Mentor-lite [22, 33].

Figure 1 shows the top-level state chart for our e-commerce (EC) benchmark workflow. Each state corresponds to an activity or one (or multiple, parallel) subworkflow(s). We assume that for every activity *act* the condition *act*_DONE is set to true when *act* is finished. So, we are able to synchronize the control flow so that a state of the state chart is left when the corresponding activity terminates. For parallel subworkflows, the final states of the corresponding orthogonal components serve to synchronize the termination (i.e., join in the control flow).

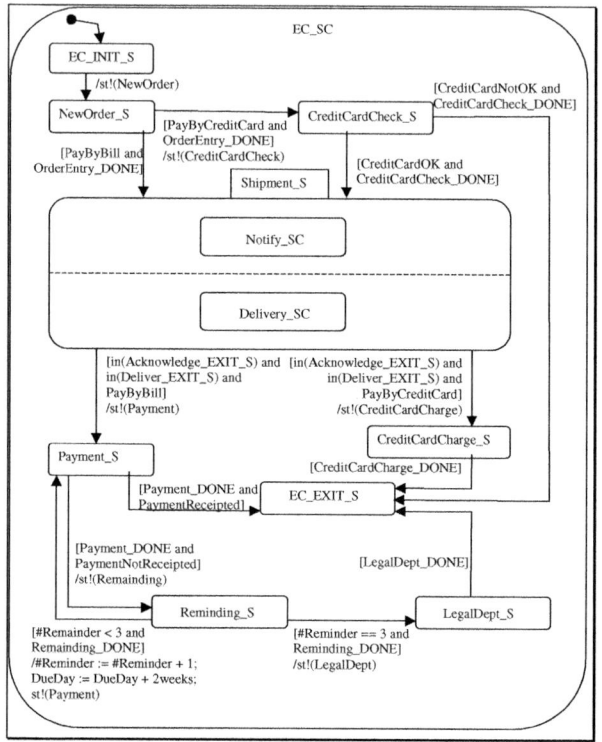

Figure 1 : State chart of the *electronic commerce (EC)* workflow example

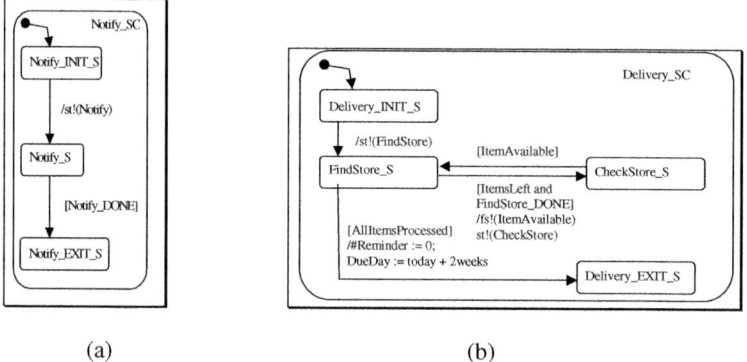

(a)   (b)
Figure 2 : State charts of the *Notify* and the *Delivery* subworkflows

The workflow behaves as follows. After the initialization of the workflow instance, the *NewOrder* activity is started. After the termination of *NewOrder*, the control flow is split. If the customer wants to pay by credit card, the condition *PayByCreditCard* is set and the *CreditCardCheck* activity checks the validity of the credit card. If there are any problems with the credit card, the workflow is terminated. Otherwise the shipment, represented by the nested top-level state *Shipment_S*, is initiated spawning two orthogonal/parallel subworkflows, specified in the state charts *Notify_SC* (Figure 2a) and *Delivery_SC* (Figure 2b), respectively. The first subworkflow *Notify* has only one activity that sends an acknowledgment mail. The delivery of goods is done by one or several external, eventual autonomous stores. So, the second subworkflow, *Delivery*, (sequentially) invokes for each ordered item an activity that identifies a store from which the item could be shipped. Then, a second activity instructs the store to deliver the item and waits for an acknowledgement. The both activities *FindStore* and *CheckStore* are repeated within a loop over all ordered items. If the customer wants to pay by bill, a reminder counter and the due day for the payment have to be initialized. After the termination of both subworkflows, the control flow is synchronized, and split again depending on the mode of payment. If the customer wants to pay by credit card, the credit card is now charged and the workflow terminates. If the customer wants to pay by bill, an activity is invoked that waits for the settlement of the invoice. If the payment is confirmed within the running period, the workflow also terminates. If the payment is not confirmed after two weeks, within a loop an activity is invoked that sends a reminder to the customer. Moreover, the reminder counter is increased and the due day initialized again. This is repeated at most three times. If the payment is not receipted within the period after the third reminder, an activity is invoked that inform the legal department and the workflow terminates. Note, that we have so far neglected the exception handling (e.g. if an item is not deliverable).

The EC workflow specification is straightforward to implement when the WFMS that is to be benchmarked uses state charts. In this case only the stubs for the simulated application programs have to be implemented, but this can be done with one generic stub with different parameter settings. Installing the benchmark on other WFMSs is still simple when the workflow specification language of the target WFMS is a well-founded "high-level" formalism such as Petri nets, event-process chains, etc. In fact, automatic conversion of state charts into other formalisms are largely feasible [22, 24].

4   Systems under Test

4.1   Mentor-lite

The core of our research prototype Mentor-lite [21] is an *interpreter* for state chart specifications. The interpreter performs a stepwise execution of the workflow specification according to its formal semantics [33]. For each step, the activities to be performed by the step are determined and started. Two additional components, the *communication manager* and the *log manager*, are closely integrated with the workflow interpreter. All three components together form the *workflow engine*. The execution of a workflow instance can be distributed over several workflow engines at different sites. A separate *workflow log* is used at each site where a Mentor-lite workflow engine is running. The communication manager is responsible for sending and receiving synchronization messages between the engines. These messages contain information about locally raised events, updates of state chart variables and state information of the local engine [23]. When a synchronization message is received, the corresponding updates at the receiving site are performed. In order to guarantee a consistent global state even in the presence of site or network failures, Mentor-lite uses the CORBA Object Transaction Services (OTS) to implement reliable message queues. The CORBA implementation Orbix provides the basic communication infrastructure for distributed execution. The workflow engine, comprising the three components interpreter, communication manager, and log manager, is implemented as an Orbix server. Its IDL interface provides a method to start a workflow instance and a method to set variables and conditions within the workflow instance.

Databases like the *workflow repository* (i.e., a repository of workflow specifications) or the *worklist database* can be shared by Mentor-lite workflow engines at different sites. In the current setup, the underlying DBMS is Oracle 7.

Communication interfaces to application programs are implemented by wrappers using the distributed computing environment CORBA. On top of these interfaces, protocols for complex interactions with application programs are specified in terms of state and activity charts. The workflow engine starts the wrappers asynchronously and uses the methods of the wrapper objects to read or set variables. The application wrappers can in turn use the workflow engine's method to set control flow variables.

In this paper, we consider two different versions of the Mentor-lite implementation. The difference between the two releases is in the handling of application invocations. The first version, referred to as *"ml-proc"*, starts a new process for each external application on the workflow-server site for the data exchange with the external application. The advantage of this approach is the increased availability of the system as only one workflow is affected when the communication with the application fails. However, the required main memory on the workflow server site increases significantly. The second version of Mentor-lite, referred to as *"ml-thr"*, uses threads within a single process, which is much more memory-efficient.

4.2   Staffware97

Staffware97 has a client-server architecture with a monolithic server. All components like log manager, worklist handler, etc. are implemented inside the *workflow engine*. The workflow engine can be run on multiple workflow servers, but each workflow instance is bound to one server and exclusively handled by this server throughout its lifetime. So Staffware97 does not support a partitioned and distributed workflow execution. The workflow engine manages several *work queues* that start application programs and can be polled by the user's clients.

A work queue schedules the work items of one or several users in a FIFO manner with priorities, i.e., FIFO among all processes with the same priority. The number of users per work queue as well as the number of parallel processes per user are system parameters. This is a critical issue especially for mostly automated workflows, i.e., workflows with mostly automated, non-interactive activities, because all such activities are scheduled in the work queue of a single user (i.e., dummy user "auto").

Staffware97 provides an interface to application programs based on Dynamic Data Exchange (DDE). External application programs are called via scripts that use DDE commands. Automated, non-interactive activities can also be started without the use of any scripts but only under the restriction that they run on the workflow engine's server machine.

The exchange of data between the workflow engine and the application programs is handled via the file system. Input data to the application as well as results from the application are stored in and read from temporary files. In an asynchronous application invocation, the calling script has to raise an *event* when the workflow engine is allowed to read the result data. Automated, non-interactive programs running on the server machine are able to communicate directly with the workflow engine also via *pipes*. In our measurements, we used both options for comparison. We refer to the file- and event-based as *"sw-ev"*, and to the pipe-based alternative as *"sw-pi"*.

Note that Staffware97 is no longer the current release of Staffware's workflow product, but the newer version Staffware2000 [29] became available only very recently.

5   Experimental Testbed

For every WFMS under test we must create its full-fledged system environment with all necessary servers, including middleware components (e.g. Corba or a TP-monitor), since even for simulated external applications the benchmark includes the invocation and completion steps. So the testbed is significantly more complex than for TPC-C-like benchmarks.

Our testbed consists of the following five modules. (1) A synthetic load generator starts new workflow instances with a given interarrival time distribution. In our case, we used a Poison arrival process with a given mean as a parameter. (2) A monitoring component observes and logs the start and stop times of the activities and entire workflows. (3) Stub applications simulate the external applications. These stubs simply read their input data, sleep for a specified time period, and return control-flow-relevant result data. The mean turnaround time of these stubs is a parameter of the experiments. (4) A dedicated SUN Sparc5 is used as an application server connected to the workflow-server machine with an Ethernet LAN. The use of a separate machine for the application server, as opposed to running applications on the workflow-server machine, was optional and varied in the experiments. (5) The workflow server itself runs on a dedicated SUN Sparc10 with all, WFMS-specific, additional components as described in following. In all experiments reported here, we limited ourselves to a single workflow server (i.e., did not make use of multiple workflow engines or even partitioned and distributed workflow execution).

Mentor-lite additionally needed the Oracle7 database system for its logging and recovery component and as a repository containing workflow specifications etc. The database was not dedicated for the WFMS and ran on a remote database server machine. For the communication interfaces of the workflow engine and the application wrappers we used Orbix 2.3.

Staffware97 offers a choice between logging in a database or to the file system. We chose the file system variant. In the experiments that involved a separate application server, the application invocation was done by a remote-shell call from a script on the workflow-engine machine.

In our baseline experiment, the system configuration consists of exactly one server machine. So, all components of the WFMS including the external application programs were run on the dedicated SUN Sparc10. The turnaround time of the activities was normally distributed with a mean of 10 seconds and a standard deviation of 4 seconds.

In the second series of measurements, we studied the impact of the system configuration. Specifically, we added a dedicated computer for the application server and the external applications.

As mentioned before, our e-commerce benchmark supports different test levels with regard to functionality and the scope of the benchmarking. For example, we can easily derive specialized, simplified variants that contain only automated activities or no loops. In the measurements presented here, we specialized the benchmark by using only the control flow path for the case of credit card payment, disregarding the reminder loops, and limiting the delivery loop to exactly one iteration. As a consequence, the workflow contained only automated activities, no interactive ones.

6   Experimental Results

As mentioned in Section 4, we benchmarked two versions of Mentor-lite, *ml-proc* and *ml-thr*, and two versions of Staffware97, *sw-ev* and *sw-pi*. In all measurements, we used an observation window of 8 hours.

The baseline experiment used one dedicated computer for all servers. The mean turnaround time of the activities was set to 10 seconds each.

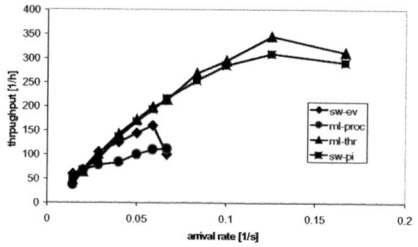 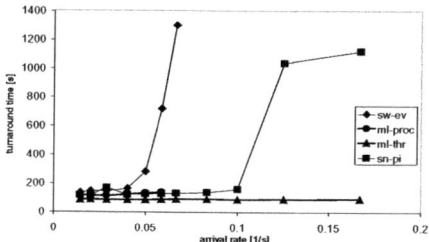

Figure 3 : Throughput and turnaround time of baseline experiment

Figure 3 shows the system throughput in completed workflow instances per hour as a function of the workflow arrival rate, and the mean turnaround time of workflow instances in seconds. As expected, the throughput increases linearly with the arrival rate until the system saturates. The maximum sustainable throughput of *ml-thr* is about 10% higher than that of *sw-pi*. The other two candidates under test performed poorly. *sw-ev* exhibited very high delays because of waiting for events to read result data from the file system. The low throughput of *ml-proc* resulted from hardware and operating-system bottlenecks, especially with regard to memory, for too many active processes (one per activity) had to be handled.

The turnaround time of Mentor-lite stays almost constant for all given arrival rates. Staffware97 is bounded by the number of workflow instances running in parallel. As the execution of invoked applications is carried out on behalf of a single, artificial "dummy" user (called the "auto" user in Staffware terminology), the work queue handling for this user caused congestion, which resulted in long waiting times. The major drawback of *sw-ev* is again its inefficient treatment of data that is returned from the application to the workflow engine.

As the *ml-proc* version of Mentor-lite performed much worse than *ml-thr* in all experiments, this architectural variant is no longer considered in the following experiment.

The impact of the system configuration was evaluated by adding a dedicated computer for the application server. Figure 4 shows the resulting system throughput and workflow turnaround time for the case of short activities with a mean duration of 10 seconds. Mentor-lite is able to fully exploit the additional hardware. Surprisingly, the throughput of Staffware97 dropped compared to the baseline experiment. So for Staffware97 the additional hardware turned out to be a penalty rather than an opportunity. The reason for this seemingly counterintuitive phenomenon lies in the peculiarity of Staffware97 that it needs remote-shell calls and thus dynamically spawns remote processes for applications that are invoked on a machine other than the workflow server. The turnaround time for Mentor-lite increases only marginally due to the remote application invocation.

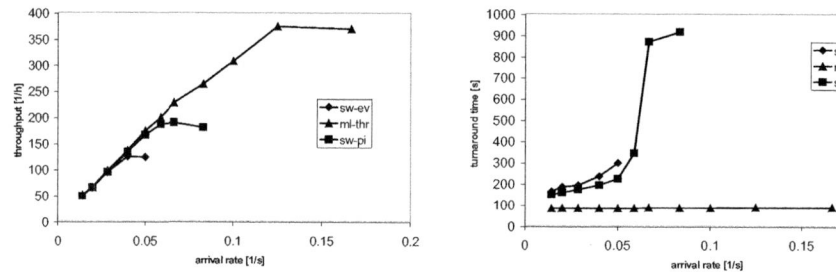

Figure 4 : System configuration impact on throughput and turnaround time

7   Lessons Learned

In addition to demonstrating the viability of the proposed benchmark, the experiments provided a number of important general insights:

- The Corba-based architecture of Mentor-lite proved to be reasonably scalable. In particular and unlike Staffware97, it was able to fully exploit the additional hardware resources of a dedicated application server machine.

- Multi-threading inside the workflow engine turned out to be crucial for bounding the memory consumption of the Mentor-lite workflow server. The version with a separate process for each activity performed very poorly and became unstable for higher load.

- Staffware97 did not scale as well as we expected. First, the file- and event-based version for the communication with invoked applications incurred high delays and resulted in long step response times, critically adding to the workflow turnaround times. Second and even more importantly, the architecture turned out to handle automated activities in a rather inefficient way. Remote invocations on a dedicated application server machine even resulted in decreasing throughput. So Staffware97 obviously is geared mostly for workflows with interactive activities running on client machines, with considerably less stress on the server side.

- Generally, the responsiveness of Staffware97 seems to be critically depending on the configuration of its work queues. For automated activities, all "work items" were assigned to a single queue, for the artificial user "auto", forming a response-time bottleneck. An alternative could be to add more artificial users with some intelligent assignment of activity types to these "auto"-type users, but this would entail a sophisticated load distribution problem and was beyond the scope of our experiments.

8   Architecture of an Auto-Configuration Tool for Mentor-lite

A distributed configuration of Mentor-lite consists of different workflow servers (i.e., instances of the workflow engine), application servers, and one communication server (i.e., ORB). Each server of the first two categories can be dedicated to a specified set of workflow activities and external applications, resp., on a per type basis. Each of these dedicated servers and also the communication server can be replicated across multiple computers for enhanced performance and availability. Given this flexibility (which is provided in similar ways also by some commercial WFMSs), it is a difficult problem to choose an appropriate configuration for the entire WFMS that meets all requirements with regard to throughput, interaction response time, and availability. Moreover, it may be necessary to adapt an initial configuration over time due to changes of the workflow load, e.g., upon adding new workflow types.

To this end, we have developed a suite of analytic models, using stochastic methods like continuous-time Markov chains and Markov reward models, to predict the performance, availability, and performability under a given load. The performance model estimates the maximum sustainable throughput in terms of workflow instances per time unit and the mean waiting time for service requests such as interactions upon starting an activity on the basis of a Markov chain model for the statistical behavior of the various workflow types. The availability model estimates the mean downtime of the entire system for given failure and restart rates for the various components. Finally, the performability model takes into account the performance degradation during transient failures and estimates the effective mean waiting time for service requests with explicit consideration of periods during which only a subset of a server type's replicas are running. These models, which are described in detail in [9], form the underpinnings of an auto-configuration tool for distributed WFMSs.

The auto-configuration tool is primarily driven by statistics on the workload from the monitoring tool of Mentor-lite. It can feed this information into its analytic models to a hypothetical configuration in a what-if analysis. By systematic variation of the parameters for such hypothetical configurations the tool is also able to derive the (analytically) best configuration, i.e., the minimum degree of replication of each of the involved server types to meet given availability and performance or performability goals, and recommend appropriate reconfigurations. The tool is largely independent of a specific WFMS, using product-specific stubs for its various components that need to interact with the WFMS.

The components of the configuration tool and its embedding into the overall system environment are illustrated in Figure 5. The tool consists of four main components: (1) the *mapping* of workflow specifications onto the tool's internal models, (2) the *calibration* of the internal models by means of statistics from monitoring the system, (3) the *evaluation* of the models for given input parameters, and (4) the computation of *recommendations* to system administrators and architects, with regard to specified goals.

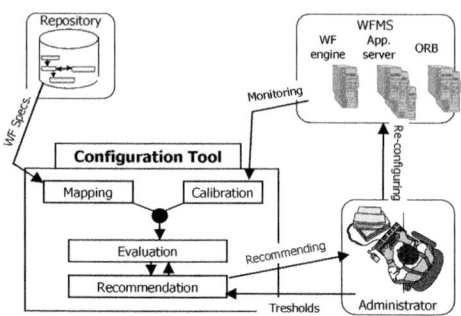

Figure 5 : Integration of the auto-configuration tool

9   Conclusion and Outlook

In this paper we have proposed the first systematic benchmark for WFMS architectures that we are aware of. We have demonstrated the viability and usefulness of the benchmark with measurements of two different WFMSs (each in two different versions). In particular, porting the benchmark, which is initially specified in terms of state and activity charts, to the specification language of Staffware was fairly easy and the installation of the entire setup for the measurements was relatively straightforward (albeit more time-consuming than we expected).

The measured results clearly show that the configuration of a WFMS architecture has a crucial impact on the achieved performance. For example, running an application server on a dedicated machine, as opposed to running it on the same machine as the workflow engine's server, can make a big difference in terms of throughput and turnaround time. To aid system administrators in finding a proper configuration, we have started working on an auto-configuration tool, which we have sketched in the paper. One important issue among the options of the tool is Mentor-lite's capability of having multiple workflow servers on different machines and running even single workflows in a distributed manner. Presumably, high-end commercial workflow systems have similar capabilities or will add such support in the near future. Our future work will include also additional performance measurements for this advanced type of system configuration.

References

[1] G. Alonso, D. Agrawal, A. Abbadi, C. Mohan: Functionality and Limitations of Current Workflow Management Systems, IEEE Expert Vol. 12, No. 5, 1997

[2] T. Bauer, P. Dadam: A Distributed Execution Environment for Large-Scale Workflow Management Systems with Subnets and Server Migration, IFCIS Int'l Conf. on Cooperative Information Systems (CoopIS), Kiawah Island, South Carolina, 1997

[3] T. Bauer, P. Dadam, Distribution Models for Workflow Management Systems - Classification and Simulation (in German), Technical Report, University of Ulm, Germany, 1999

[4] A. Bonner, A. Shrufi, S. Rozen: LabFlow-1: a Database Benchmark for High-Throughput Workflow Management, Int'l Conf. on Extending Database Technology (EDBT), Avignon, France, 1996

[5] A. Cichoki, A. Helal, M. Rusinkiewicz, D. Woelk: Workflow and Process Automation, Concepts and Technology, Kluwer, 1998

[6] A. Dogac, L. Kalinichenko, M. Tamer Ozsu, A. Sheth (Eds.), Workflow Management Systems and Interoperability, NATO Advanced Study Institute, Springer-Verlag, 1998

[7] A. Geppert, M. Berndtsson, D. Lieuwen, C. Roncancio: Performance Evaluation of Object-Oriented Active Database Management Systems Using the BEAST Benchmark, Theory and Practice of Object Systems (TAPOS), Vol. 4, No. 4, 1998

[8] D. Georgakopoulos, M. Hornick, A. Sheth: An Overview of Workflow Management: From Process Modeling to Workflow Automation Infrastructure, Distributed and Parallel Databases, Vol. 3, No. 2, 1995

[9] M. Gillmann, J. Weissenfels, G. Weikum, A. Kraiss: Performance and Availability Assessment for the Configuration of Distributed Workflow Management Systems, Int'l Conf. on Extending Database Technology (EDBT), Konstanz, Germany, 2000

[10] J Gray (ed.): The Benchmark Handbook, 2nd Edition, Morgan Kaufmann, 1993

[11] C. Hagen, G. Alonso: Flexible Exception Handling in the OPERA Process Support System, Int'l Conf. on Distributed Computing Systems (ICDCS), Amsterdam, The Netherlands, 1998

[12] D. Harel, State Charts: A Visual Formalism for Complex Systems, Science of Computer Programming, Vol. 8, 1987

[13] D. Harel, E. Gery: Executable Object Modeling with Statecharts, IEEE Computer, Vol. 30, No. 7, 1997

[14] R. Jain: The Art of Computer Systems Performance Analysis, John Wiley & Sons, 1991

[15] S. Jablonski, C. Bussler: Workflow-Management, Modeling Concepts, Architecture and Implementation, International Thomson Computer Press, 1996

[16] J. Klingemann, J. Waesch, K. Aberer, Deriving Service Models in Cross-Organizational Workflows, 9th Int'l Workshop on Reasearch Issues in Data Engineering (RIDE), Sydney, Australia, 1999

[17] M. Kamath, G. Alonso, R. Günthör, C. Mohan, Providing High Availability in Very Large Workflow Management Systems, 5th Int'l Conf. on Extending Database Technology (EDBT), Avignon, France, 1996

[18] F. Leymann, D. Roller, Production Workflow: Concepts and Techniques, Prentice Hall, 1999

[19] C. Mohan, Workflow Management in the Internet Age, Tutorial, http://www-rodin.inria.fr/~mohan

[20] K. Moore, M. Peterson: A Groupware Benchmark Based on Lotus Notes, Int'l Conf. on Data Engineering (ICDE), New Orleans, Louisiana, 1996

[21] P. Muth, J. Weissenfels, M. Gillmann, G. Weikum: Integrating Light-Weight Workflow Management Systems within Existing Business Environments, Int'l Conf. on Data Engineering (ICDE), Sydney, Australia, 1999

[22] P. Muth, D. Wodtke, J. Weissenfels, G. Weikum, A. Kotz Dittrich, Enterprise-wide Workflow Management based on State and Activity Charts, in [6]

[23] P. Muth, D. Wodtke, J. Weissenfels, A. Kotz Dittrich, G. Weikum: From Centralized Workflow Specification to Distributed Workflow Execution, Intelligent Information Systems, Special Issue on Workflow Management, Vol. 10, No. 2, 1998

[24] M. Nüttgens, T. Feld, V. Zimmermann: Business Process Modeling with EPC and UML: Transformation or Integration, in: M. Schader, A. Korthaus (eds.): The Unified Modeling Language - Technical Aspects and Applications, Workshop des Arbeitskreises "Grundlagen objektorientierter Modellierung" (GROOM), Heidelberg Germany, 1998

[25] P. O'Neil: Database Performance Measurement, in: A.B. Tucker (ed.): The Computer Science and Engineering Handbook, CRC Press, 1997

[26] SAP AG: SAP E-Business Solutions, http://www.sap-ag.de/solutions/technology/index.htm

[27] A.W. Scheer: Benchmarking Business Processes, in: Okino, N.; Tamura, H.; Fujii, S. (eds.): Advances in Production Management Systems, IFIP TC5/WG5.7 Int'l Conf. on Production Management Systems (APMS), Kyoto, Japan, 1996

[28] H. Schuster, J. Neeb, R. Schamburger, A Configuration Management Approach for Large Workflow Management Systems, Int'l Joint Conf. on Work Activities Coordination and Collaboration (WACC), San Francisco, California, 1999

[29] Staffware, http://www.staffware.com

[30] Transaction Processing Performance Council, http://www.tpc.org

[31] TPC-W Benchmark Specification, http://www.tpc.org/wspec.html

[32] Workflow Management Coalition, http://www.wfmc.org

[33] D. Wodtke, G. Weikum, A Formal Foundation For Distributed Workflow Execution Based on State Charts, Int'l Conf. on Database Theory (ICDT), Delphi, Greece, 1997

Workflow Modeling using Proclets

W.M.P. van der Aalst[1,2], P. Barthelmess[2], C.A. Ellis[2], and J. Wainer[2,3]

[1] Department of Technology Management, Eindhoven University of Technology, P.O. Box 513, NL-5600 MB, Eindhoven, The Netherlands. w.m.p.v.d.aalst@tm.tue.nl
[2] Department of Computer Science, University of Colorado at Boulder, Campus Box 430, Boulder, CO 80309-0430, USA. {barthelm,skip}@colorado.edu
[3] Department of Computer Science, State University of Campinas, Caixa Postal 6176, 13083-970, Campinas - SP, Brazil wainer@dcc.unicamp.br

Abstract. The focus of traditional workflow management systems is on control flow *within one* process definition, that describes how a single case (i.e., workflow instance) is handled in isolation. For many applications this paradigm is inadequate. Interaction between cases is at least as important. This paper introduces and advocates the use of interacting *proclets*, i.e., light-weight workflow processes. By promoting interactions to first-class citizens, it is possible to model complex workflows in a more natural manner, with improved expressive power and flexibility.

1   Introduction

Workflow Management Systems allow for the explicit representation and support of business processes. Available workflow management systems have difficulties dealing with the dynamic and inter-organizational nature of today's business processes [26]. We will argue that one of the core problems of current workflow languages is the focus on isolated case-based processes.

In traditional workflow management systems, the control-flow of a workflow is described by one *workflow process definition*, that specifies which tasks need to be executed and in what order. Workflow process definitions are instantiated for specific *cases*. Examples of cases are an insurance claim, or an order.

Today's workflow management systems assume that a workflow process can be modeled by specifying the *life-cycle of a single case in isolation*. For many real-life applications this assumption is too restrictive. As a result, the workflow process is changed to accommodate the workflow management system, the control-flow of several cases is artificially squeezed into one process definition, or the coordination amongst cases is hidden inside custom built applications. Consider for example an engineering process of a product consisting of multiple components. Some of the tasks in this engineering process are executed for the whole product, e.g., the task to specify product requirements. Other tasks are executed at the level of components, e.g., determine the power consumption of a component. Since a product can have a variable number of components and the components are engineered concurrently, it is typically not possible to squeeze this workflow into one process definition. In most workflow management systems, it is not possible to concurrently instantiate selected parts of the workflow process a variable number of times.

O. Etzion and P. Scheuermann (Eds.): CoopIS 2000, LNCS 1901, pp. 198–209, 2000.

To solve these problems, we propose an approach based on *proclets, performatives* and *channels*. Proclets are light-weight processes. The interaction between proclets is modeled explicitly, i.e., proclets can exchange structured messages, called *performatives*, through *channels*. By adopting this approach the problems related to purely case-based processes can be avoided.

The remainder of this paper is organized as follows. First, we motivate our approach by identifying the problems encountered when modeling the reviewing process of a conference. Then we present the framework, which is based on Petri nets [22, 23] and inspired by concepts originating from object-orientation [9, 24], agent-orientation [19], and the language/action perspective [15, 30–32]. Finally, we compare the framework with existing approaches and conclude with our plans for future research.

2   Motivating Example: Organizing a Conference

The process of selecting papers for a conference presents features that challenge existing modeling languages. The goal of this process is to select papers out of a larger set, based, e.g., on quality, minimum and maximum number of papers, and so on. After a set of people accepts to act as program committee members, a call for papers is issued. Authors submit papers that are then reviewed by peers (invited by pc members) and finally a selection is made. Such process is complicated by a series of factors:

- Prospective PC members and reviewers may accept or reject the invitation to join the committee and to review one or more papers, respectively. Replacements for those that rejected need to be found.
- Reviewers can fail to return reviews on time. As a result, some of the papers may lack enough reviews to allow their fair evaluation.
- For effective distribution, classification and matching, the set of papers needs to be considered as a whole, i.e., distribution can not be done only considering individual papers in isolation.
- For selection, paper quality needs to be gauged against the quality of remaining papers. Again, this requires that the set of papers be considered as a whole.

A modeler faces many problems translating these requirements. A first basic question is what is to be considered the case[1] - the submission, the review, the "empty slot" in the conference, that one wants to fill with a good quality paper, or is the case the whole set of slots?

The class diagram (Figure 1) shows that different tasks rely on information that is at different levels of aggregation - some of the tasks operate at the conference level, that groups all papers, others at the paper level, and others yet at the lower level of individual reviews. A major obstacle is, therefore, how to conciliate these multiple perspectives into one model.

Lacking the power to express differences in aggregation, most workflow management systems force one to depict the process at an arbitrarily chosen level. Important shortcomings result:

---

[1] Workflow instance.

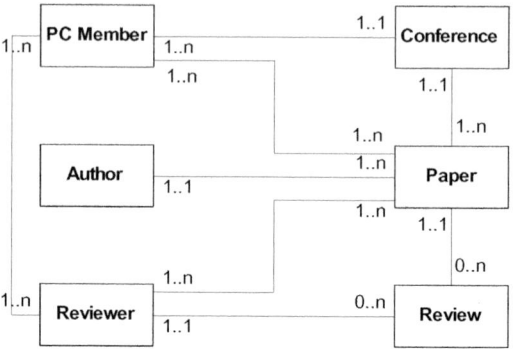

Fig. 1. Review process class diagram.

- Models are artificially flattened, being unable to account for the mix of different perspectives of the real process.
- Batch tasks are usually not supported. Batch tasks are those that require grouping sets of elements, e.g., the set of papers during distribution and selection.
- Launching and synchronizing variable numbers of tasks is also usually a problem, e.g., launching and synchronizing reviews from a paper centered case.
- Actors sometimes interact in complex ways. These interactions are usually not incorporated in process models.

Conference review is not an atypical example, in the sense that one encounters similar problems very frequently in other areas as well, for example:

- In software development: changes to one module may impact a variable number of other modules, making necessary the instantiation of a variable number of cascading tasks.
- Processing of insurance claims: some claims may refer to the same accident. At some point in time it is desirable that all related claims be merged so that a uniform decision can be reached.
- Hiring new people: candidates have to be evaluated and ranked with respect to each other. Again, the interactions between the applications are most relevant.

3   Framework

The examples given in the previous section show that today's workflow management systems typically have problems dealing with workflow processes that are not purely *case-oriented*

Inspired by these problems, we have developed a new framework for modeling workflows. This framework is based on *proclets*. A proclet can be seen as a lightweight workflow process equipped with a knowledge base containing information on previous interactions. One can think of proclets as objects equipped with an explicit life-cycle (in the object-oriented sense) [9, 24]. Proclets interact via *channels*. A channel is the medium to transport messages from one proclet to another. The channel can be used to send a message to a specific proclet or a group of proclets (i.e., multicast). Based on the properties of the channel, different kinds of interaction are supported, e.g., push/pull, synchronous/asynchronous, and verbal/non-verbal. In order for proclets to find each other, there is a *naming service*, that keeps track of registered proclets. The concepts *proclet*, *channel* and *naming service* constitute a framework for modeling workflow processes (see Figure 2).

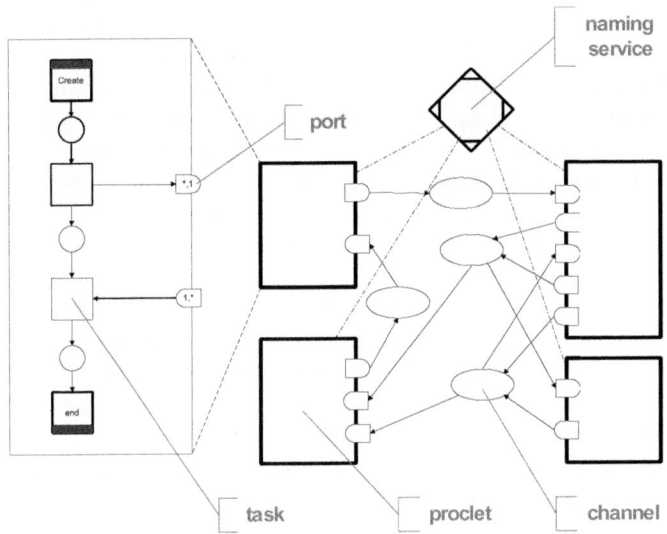

Fig. 2. Graphical representation of the framework.

Compared to existing workflow modeling languages, complex case-based workflow definitions describing the control flow of an entire process are broken up into smaller interacting proclets, i.e., there is a shift from control to communication. The framework is based on a solid process modeling technique (Petri nets [22, 23]) extended with concepts originating from object-orientation [9, 24], agent-orientation [19], and the language/action perspective [15, 30–32].

In the remainder of this section we present the four main components of our framework: *proclets, channels, naming service,* and *actors*.

3.1   Proclets

A *proclet class* describes the life-cycle of *proclet instances*. A proclet class can be compared to an ordinary workflow process definition or workflow type [18]. The class describes the order in which tasks can or need to be executed for individual instances of the class, i.e., it is the specification of a generic process. Proclet instances can be created and destroyed, and are executed according to a class specification. Proclet instances have a state.

To specify proclet classes, we use a graphical language based on *Petri nets*, an established tool for modeling workflow processes [1, 2, 6, 12, 13]. Powerful analysis techniques can be used to verify the correctness of Petri net models [22, 23].

In this paper, we use a specific subclass of Petri nets, the so-called class of sound WF-nets [1, 2].[2] A WF-net has source and sink transitions: A source transition has no input places and a sink transition has no output places. Every node (i.e., place or transition) is on a path from some source transition to some sink transition. Moreover, any WF-net is connected, i.e., the network structure cannot be partitioned in two unconnected parts. A WF-net becomes activated if one of the source transitions fires. In the remainder we assume that a WF-net becomes activated only once (single activation), and furthermore, that it is *sound* (see [1, 2] for a discussion of soundness).

Most workflow modeling languages primarily focus on control flow inside one process definition and (partly) abstract from the interaction between process definitions, i.e., coordination is limited to the scope of the process definition and communication and collaboration are treated as second-class citizens. Our framework explicitly models interactions between proclets. The explicit representation of interaction is inspired by the *language/action perspective* [32, 31] which is rooted in *speech act* theory [25]. The language/action perspective emphasizes how coordination is brought about by communication. The need for treating interaction as first-class citizens is also recognized in the agent community [19]. Emerging agent communication languages such as KQML [14] demonstrate this need.

Inspired by these different perspectives on interaction, we use *performatives* to specify communication and collaboration among proclets. A performative is a message exchanged between one sender proclet and one or more receiver proclets. A performative has the following attributes:

(1) *time*: the moment the performative was created/received.
(2) *channel*: the medium used to exchange the performative.
(3) *sender*: the identifier of the proclet creating the performative.
(4) *set of receivers*: list of identifiers of the proclets receiving the performative.
(5) *action*: the type of the performative.
(6) *content*: the actual information that is being exchanged.

The role of these attributes will be explained later. At this point, it is important to note the action attribute. This attribute can be used to specify the illocutionary point of the performative. Examples of typed performatives are request, offer, acknowledge, promise, decline, counter-offer or commit-to-commit [32]. In this paper, we do not restrict our model to any single classification of performatives (i.e., a fixed set of types). At the same time we stress the importance of using the experience and results reported by researchers working on the language/action perspective.

Proclets combine performatives and sound WF-nets. A *proclet class PC* is defined as follows:

---

[2] For the readers familiar with WF-nets: For notational convenience we omit the unique source and sink place used in [1, 2].

(1) *PC* has a *unique name*. This name serves as a unique identification of the class - the *class_id*.

(2) *PC* has a *process definition* defined in terms of a *sound WF-net*. The transitions correspond to *tasks* and the places correspond to *state conditions*.

(3) *PC* has *ports*. Ports are used to interact with other proclets. Every port is connected to one transition.

(4) Transitions can send and receive *performatives* via ports. Each port has two attributes: (a) its *cardinality* and (b) its *multiplicity*. The cardinality specifies the number of recipients of performatives exchanged via the port. The multiplicity specifies the number of performatives exchanged via the port during the lifetime of any instance of the class.

(5) *PC* has a *knowledge base* for storing these performatives: Every performative sent or received is stored in the knowledge base.

(6) Tasks can query the knowledge base. A task may have a *precondition* based on the knowledge base. A task is enabled if (a) the corresponding transition in the WF-net is enabled, (b) the precondition evaluates to true, and (c) each input port contains a performative.

(7) Tasks connected to ports have *post conditions*. The post condition specifies the outcome of the task in terms of performatives generated for its output ports.

A proclet class is a generic definition. Proclet instances are created by instantiating the proclet class and have a *unique identification* - the *proc_id*. Tokens in the WF-net specifying the process definition refer to one proclet instance, i.e., tokens of different proclet instances are *not* merged into one WF-net. Moreover, each proclet instance has its own knowledge base.

A performative has by definition one sender, but can have multiple recipients. The sender is always represented by a proc_id, i.e., by its identifier. The list of recipients can be a mixture of proc_id's and class_id's, i.e., one can send performatives to both proclet instances and proclet classes. A performative sent to a proclet class is received by all proclet instances of that class.

To illustrate the framework we use the example shown in Figure 3. There are two proclet classes, used to organize meetings. Proclet class *Meeting* is instantiated once per meeting. Proclet class *Personal entry* is instantiated for every potential participant of a specific meeting. The instance of class *Meeting* first multicasts an invitation to all potential participants. Note that the cardinality of the port connected to task *Invite for meeting* is denoted by a star ∗. This star indicates that the invitation is sent to an arbitrary number of potential participants, i.e., the performative has multiple recipients. We will use ∗ to denote an arbitrary number of recipients, + to denote at least one recipient, 1 to denote precisely one recipient, and ? to denote no or just a single recipient. Performatives with no recipients are considered not to have occurred, and are not registered in the knowledge base. The multiplicity of the output port connected to task *Invite for meeting* is denoted by the number 1. This means that during the lifetime of an instance of class *Meeting* exactly one performative is sent via this port. The invitation performative is sent though the channel *E-mail* (details in Section 3.2). The performative creates a proclet for each recipient, i.e., creation task *Create entry* is triggered. Creation tasks are depicted by squares with a black top. The input port connected

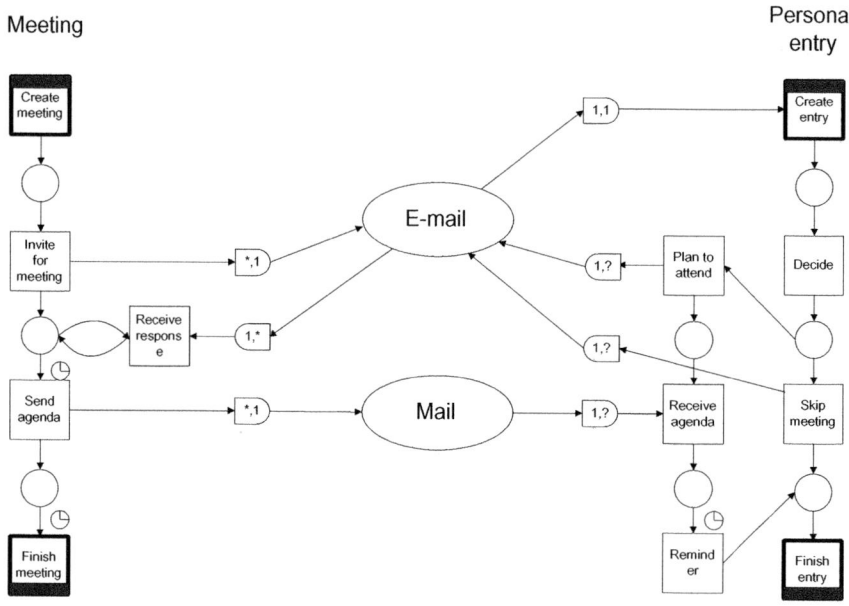

Fig. 3. Example of two proclet classes: *Meeting* and *Personal entry*.

to *Create entry* has cardinality 1 and multiplicity 1. Every input port has by definition cardinality 1, i.e., from the perspective of the receiving proclet there is only one proclet receiving the performative. Input ports connected to a creation task (i.e., a source transition) have by definition a multiplicity of 1 or ?: An instance can be created only once. Since there is just one creation task in *Personal entry*, the multiplicity is 1. After an instance of the class *Personal entry* is created, a decision is made (task *Decide*). Based on this decision either task *Skip meeting* or *Plan to attend* is executed. In both cases a performative is sent to the instance of the proclet class *Meeting*. The performative is either a confirmation (*Plan to attend*) or a notification of absence (*Skip meeting*). Note that each instance of the class *Personal entry* sends such a performative. These performatives are sent through channel *E-mail* Note that the ports connected to *Plan to attend* and *Skip meeting* both have cardinality 1 (i.e., one recipient) and multiplicity ? (one performative is sent via one of the two ports). Task *Receive response* is executed once for every "confirmation/notification of absence" performative. After some time, as indicated by the clock symbol [2], task *Send agenda* is executed. *Send agenda* generates one performative: the agenda of the meeting. This performative is sent to all proclets that confirmed the invitation (this information is in the knowledge base of the *Meeting* proclet). The proclets that confirmed the invitation receive the agenda (task *Receive agenda*) and a timer for the task *Reminder* is set. Finally, all proclets are destroyed by executing the finishing tasks *Finish meeting* and *Finish entry*. The finishing tasks (i.e., sink transitions) are depicted by squares with a black bottom.

3.2   Communication Channels

Communication channels are used to link proclets. Channels transmit messages containing performatives. There are many different categories of channels defined by channel properties such as medium type, reliability, security, synchronicity, closure, and formality. These properties are briefly explained:

— *Medium Type*
   This can be point-to-point or broadcast, or some form of limited multicast. Recall that performatives can be sent to an individual proclet instance (point-to-point), a set of proclets (multicast), or an entire proclet class (broadcast). Common media include postal mail, telephone, and electronic mail.
— *Reliability*
   Some channels are very reliable; some are unreliable. For some electronic channels, we assume that the technology is robust, and that error detection and retransmission are implemented at lower layers of the communication protocols. Sometimes channels are inherently unreliable (such as in data channels in some lesser developed countries).
— *Security*
   At times the content of a performative is considered to be quite valuable and secret. In such cases, the transmission should be via secure channels.
— *Synchronicity*
   Some channels are used for real time communications in which each party expects to get rather immediate feedback from recipient parties. This requires synchronous channels. Face-to-face spoken conversation falls into this category. In the case of an asynchronous channel, the sender usually is not waiting for an immediate response.
— *Closure*
   Channels can be classified as open or closed. When a channel is open, the sender does not know exactly who, and how many recipients are connected. When a channel is closed, the exact identity of all recipients is specified in advance. A radio broadcast, and a notice posted on a bulletin board are examples of open medium communications, in which the senders do not exactly know who are the recipients.
— *Formality*
   Some channels convey much more formality in the messages delivered than others. Performatives can be very formally specified, or can be informal and flexible. Generally, business letters are much more formal than chat rooms. A careful record is kept of formal channel transmissions, whereas informal channels are usually not recorded.

Clearly, channel properties and performative types are closely related, i.e., for a given performative certain properties are appropriate, others are not. For example, for the performative "You are fired!" a point-to-point, reliable, secure, synchronous, closed, and formal channel is most appropriate.

3.3   Naming service

All interaction is based on proclet identifiers (proc_id's) and class identifiers (class_id's). These identifiers provide the handles to route performatives. By sending a performative using a class_id, all instances of the corresponding class receive the performative. In many situations the sending proclet does not know the proc_id's of all receiving proclets. The naming service keeps track of all proclets and can be queried to obtain proc_id's. There are many ways to implement such a naming service. Consider, e.g., object request brokers developed in the context of CORBA. In this paper, we only consider the desired functionality and abstract from implementation details (e.g., distribution of the naming service over multiple domains).

The naming service provides the following main primitives: *register*, *unregister*, *update*, and *query*.

The function *register* is called by the proclet the moment it is created. The execution of one of the create tasks (i.e., source transitions) coincides with the execution of the *register* primitive.

The naming service stores a set of attributes for each proclet. These attributes are not fixed and may vary from one class to another. The function *update* with parameters *proc_id* and *attributes* can be used to change existing or add new attributes.

Based on the attributes, proclets can query the naming service using the function *query*. The function has one parameter describing a Boolean expression in terms of attributes and returns a set of proc_id's, i.e., all proclets satisfying the expression.

Entries in the naming service can be removed using the function *unregister*. Executing a finish task (i.e., a sink transition in the WF-net) results in a call to *unregister*.

3.4   Actors

Proclets have *owners*. Owners are the actors responsible for the proclet. Actors can be automated components, persons, organizations (e.g., shipping department), or even whole companies. Owners are specified at proclet registration time and this information is kept by the naming service (see Section 3.3). Ownership can be transferred by updating the naming service information.

Owners will sometimes be the executors of proclet tasks themselves - in the example of Figure 3, for instance, owners of each personal entry will most probably be the ones that will perform the tasks, essentially the decision of attending or skipping the meeting. Roles may be specified for each task, in which case the executor can be different from the owner. We assume then that the usual role resolution mechanisms [34] are employed.

We propose to model as *external proclets* those actors (in the broad sense of the word) that interact with proclets in a more complex way. *External proclets* are useful to model those interactions that go beyond the simple model assumed by the usual role mechanism, e.g., when a request for service may be either accepted, rejected or counter-proposed. *External proclets*, as the name implies, represent entities that are outside of the scope of the process proper, whereas *internal proclets* are those under the control of the workflow system's enactment service. Both types of proclets are modeled in a similar way - by describing expected interactions with other proclets. For more extensive examples of both *internal* and *external proclets*, see [5]. This technical report also describes the application of the approach to the example described in Section 2 (i.e., the workflow of organizing a conference).

4 Related work

Petri nets have been proposed for modeling workflow process definitions long before the term "workflow management" was coined and workflow management systems became readily available [12, 13]. Workflow models described in the literature focus on various aspects (cf. [26]) such as transactional concepts [16], flexibility [21], analysis [1, 2], and cross-organizational workflows [3, 4], etc. Any attempt to give a complete overview of these models is destined to fail. Therefore, we only acknowledge the work that extended workflow models to accommodate the problems identified in Section 2.

Zisman [33] presents a paper refereeing example that involves Petri-nets and allows multiple instantiation of the reviewer net.

Batch-oriented tasks were discussed in [8]. Creation of multiple instances of tasks have been proposed by some, e.g., Casati et al. [10] (multi-tasks); Regatta system by Fujitsu [27] (multi-stage); Spade-1 [7] (multiple active copies). The framework presented here is more generic. Multiple instantiation is just one aspect of a broader view of interactions as first-class citizens.

The idea to promote interaction to first-class citizens was proposed in different settings. In the context of language/action perspective [15, 30–32], Action Technologies developed a workflow tool [28]. Speech-acts also form the basis for performatives in agent interaction languages, e.g. KQML [14]. Agents are used to implement workflows, e.g., in the Bond multi-agent system [29] and others (e.g., [20, 11]). In the more systems-oriented domains there have also been some proposals for inter-process communication (e.g. in Opera [17]).

Some of the ideas presented in this section have been adopted by our framework: batch-oriented operation, multi-tasks, and inter-process communication can be handled easily by the framework. In addition, the framework employs concepts such as performatives, channels, ports, knowledge bases, naming services, and the rigor of a Petri-net basis which allows for various forms of analysis and a straightforward and efficient implementation.

5 Conclusion

In this paper, we presented a framework which advocates the use of interacting proclets, i.e., light-weight workflow processes communicating by exchanging performatives through channels. As was demonstrated in [5], the framework can solve many of the traditional modeling problems resulting from the case-oriented paradigm.

In the future, we plan to explore the relation between channels and performatives. We are also compiling a list of interaction patterns. In our view, the interaction between proclets typically follows a number of well-defined patterns, e.g., a request performative is followed by an accept or reject performative. Finally, we plan to build a prototype to support the framework. This prototype will be used to support the reviewing process of the ACM biannual Siggroup conference following the model described in this paper.

References

1. W.M.P. van der Aalst. Verification of Workflow Nets. In P. Azéma and G. Balbo, editors, *Application and Theory of Petri Nets 1997*, volume 1248 of *Lecture Notes in Computer Science*, pages 407–426. Springer-Verlag, Berlin, 1997.
2. W.M.P. van der Aalst. The Application of Petri Nets to Workflow Management. *The Journal of Circuits, Systems and Computers*, 8(1):21–66, 1998.
3. W.M.P. van der Aalst. Interorganizational Workflows: An Approach based on Message Sequence Charts and Petri Nets. *Systems Analysis - Modelling - Simulation*, 34(3):335–367, 1999.
4. W.M.P. van der Aalst. Process-oriented Architectures for Electronic Commerce and Interorganizational Workflow. *Information Systems*, 24(8):??–??, 2000.
5. W.M.P. van der Aalst, P. Barthelmess, C.A. Ellis, and J. Wainer. Workflow modeling using proclets. Technical report cu-cs-900-00, University Of Colorado at Boulder, February 2000. http://www.cs.colorado.edu/ skip/proclets.pdf.
6. N.R. Adam, V. Atluri, and W. Huang. Modeling and Analysis of Workflows using Petri Nets. *Journal of Intelligent Information Systems*, 10(2):131–158, 1998.
7. S. Bandinelli, M. Braga, A. Fuggetta, and L. Lavazza. Cooperation support in the spade environment: a case study. In *Proceedings of the Workshop on Computer Supported Cooperative Work, Petri nets, and Related Formalisms (14th International Conference on Application and Theory of Petri Nets)*, Chicago, June 1993. ftp://ftp-se.elet.polimi.it/dist/Papers/ProcessModeling/CSCWPN93.ps.
8. P. Barthelmess and J. Wainer. Workflow systems: a few definitions and a few suggestions. In N. Comstock and C.A. Ellis, editors, *Proceedings of the Conference on Organizational Computing Systems - COOCS'95*, pages 138–147, Milpitas, California, September 1995. ACM Press.
9. G. Booch, J. Rumbaugh, and I. Jacobson. *The Unified Modeling Language User Guide*. Addison Wesley, Reading, MA, USA, 1998.
10. F. Casati, S. Ceri, B. Pernici, and G. Pozzi. Conceptual modeling of workflows. In *Proceedings of the OOER International Conference*, Gold Cost, Australia, 1995.
11. J.W. Chang and C.T. Scott. Agent-based wrokflow: Trp support environment (tse). *Computer Networks and ISDN Systems*, 28(1501), 1996.
12. C.A. Ellis. Information Control Nets: A Mathematical Model of Office Information Flow. In *Proceedings of the Conference on Simulation, Measurement and Modeling of Computer Systems*, pages 225–240, Boulder, Colorado, 1979. ACM Press.
13. C.A. Ellis and G.J. Nutt. Modelling and Enactment of Workflow Systems. In M. Ajmone Marsan, editor, *Application and Theory of Petri Nets 1993*, volume 691 of *Lecture Notes in Computer Science*, pages 1–16. Springer-Verlag, Berlin, 1993.
14. T. Finin, J. Weber, G. Wiederhold, and et. al. Specification of the KQML Agent-Communication Language , 1993.
15. F. Flores and J.J. Ludlow. Doing and Speaking in the Office. In *Decision Support Systems: Issues and Challenges*, pages 95–118. Pergamon Press, New York, 1980.
16. D. Georgakopoulos, M. Hornick, and A. Sheth. An Overview of Workflow Management: From Process Modeling to Workflow Automation Infrastructure. *Distributed and Parallel Databases*, 3:119–153, 1995.
17. C. Hagen and G. Alonso. Beyond the black box: Event-based inter-process communication in process support systems (extended version). Technical report, ETH Zürich, July 1997. Technical Report No. 303. http://www.inf.ethz.ch/department/IS/iks/publications/files/ha98c.pdf.
18. S. Jablonski and C. Bussler. *Workflow Management: Modeling Concepts, Architecture, and Implementation*. International Thomson Computer Press, London, UK, 1996.

19. N. Jennings and M. Wooldridge, editors. *Agent Technology : Foundations, Applications, and Markets*. Springer-Verlag, Berlin, 1998.
20. M. Merz, B. Liberman, K. Muller-Jones, and W. Lamersdorf. Interorganisational Workflow Management with Mobile Agents in COSM. In *Proceedings of PAAM96 Conference on the Practical Application of Agents and Multiagent Systems*, 1996.
21. M. Reichert and P. Dadam. ADEPTflex: Supporting Dynamic Changes of Workflow without Loosing Control. *Journal of Intelligent Information Systems*, 10(2):93–129, 1998.
22. W. Reisig and G. Rozenberg, editors. *Lectures on Petri Nets I: Basic Models*, volume 1491 of *Lecture Notes in Computer Science*. Springer-Verlag, Berlin, 1998.
23. W. Reisig and G. Rozenberg, editors. *Lectures on Petri Nets II: Applications*, volume 1492 of *Lecture Notes in Computer Science*. Springer-Verlag, Berlin, 1998.
24. J. Rumbaugh, I. Jacobson, and G. Booch. *The Unified Modeling Language Reference Manual*. Addison Wesley, Reading, MA, USA, 1998.
25. J.R. Searle. *Speech Acts*. Cambridge University Press, Cambridge, 1969.
26. A.P. Sheth, W.M.P. van der Aalst, and I.B. Arpinar. Processes Driving the Networked Economy: ProcessPortals, ProcessVortex, and Dynamically Trading Processes. *IEEE Concurrency*, 7(3):18–31, 1999.
27. K. Swenson. Collaborative planning: Empowering the user in a process environment. *Collaborative Computing*, 1(1), 1994. ftp://ftp.ossi.com/pub/regatta/JournalCC.ps.
28. Action Technologies. *ActionWorkflow Enterprise Series 3.0 User Guide*. Action Technologies, Inc., Alameda, 1996.
29. Purdue University. Bond. the distributed object multi-agent system. http://bond.cs.purdue.edu, 2000.
30. E.M. Verharen, F. Dignum, and S. Bos. Implementation of a cooperative agent architecture based on the language-action perspective. In *Intelligent Agents*, volume 1365 of *Lecture Notes in Artificial Intelligence*, pages 31–44. Springer-Verlag, Berlin, 1998.
31. T. Winograd. Special Issue on the Language Action Perspective - Introduction. *ACM Transations on Office Information Systems*, 6(2):83–86, 1988.
32. T. Winograd and F. Flores. *Understanding Computers and Cognition: A New Foundation for Design*. Ablex, Norwood, 1986.
33. M. D. Zisman. Use of production systems for modeling asynchronous concurrent processes. *Pattern-Directed Inference Systems*, pages 53–68, 1978.
34. M. zur Mühlen. Evaluation of workflow management systems using meta models. In *Proceedings of the 32nd Hawaii International Conference on System Sciences - HICSS'99*, pages 1–11, 1999.

Dealing with Logical Failures for Collaborating Workflows[*]

R. Müller, E. Rahm

University of Leipzig, Germany

Abstract. Logical failures occurring during workflow execution require the dynamic adaptation of affected workflows. The consequences such a dynamic adaptation may have for collaborating workflows have not yet been investigated sufficiently. We propose a rule-based approach for dynamic workflow adaptation to deal with logical failures. In our approach, workflow collaboration is based on agreements specifying the delivery time and quality of objects a workflow expects from its collaboration partners. Our mechanisms decide which collaborating workflows have to be informed when a dynamic adaptation is performed. In particular, we estimate the temporal and qualitative implications a dynamic adaptation has for collaboration partners. Because of the automated handling of logical failures, we expect that our approach significantly improves the robustness and correctness of collaborating workflows. The approach has been developed in the context of collaborative workflow-based care for cancer patients.

1 Introduction

Failure situations during workflow execution are usually classified into *system* failures and *logical* failures [24]. System failures cover exceptional situations such as malfunctions of operating system components or database servers. Logical failures refer to application-specific exceptional situations for which the control and data flow of a workflow is not adequate anymore. For example, a workflow supporting a physician during a cancer chemotherapy may become inadequate because the patient suddenly shows a drug allergy. In this case, structural adaptations such as dropping a drug activity may become necessary to cope with the new situation. Previous work on dealing with system failures has often been based on advanced transactional models [13]. Logical failures have been addressed in the field of dynamic workflow management [23,12,4,7].

So far little work has dealt with logical failures affecting *collaborating workflows*. Workflow collaboration usually means that a workflow provides a result for another workflow within a specific time interval or quality range. Thus, a dynamic adaptation of the providing workflow may imply that this result cannot be delivered timely anymore or only with reduced quality. Generally, collaborating workflows are processed by *different* workflow systems located at separate organizational units so that one side usually has no detailed knowledge about logical failures and dynamic adaptations occurring to workflows at the other side. Therefore, a general mechanism is needed that informs collaboration partners in an appropriate way when a relevant dynamic adaptation has been performed for a workflow.

Collaborating workflows are necessary in many application domains, e.g. for e-business, banking or medical treatments. In Fig. 1 we illustrate an example that we will also refer to in subsequent sections. It originates from collaborative cancer treatment. In the shown example, we assume that a workflow system at the department of internal medicine supports the physicians w.r.t. the chemotherapy of a patient, while another workflow system at the radiotherapy department supports tasks such as the preparation, performance and aftercare of radiotherapy procedures. Both workflows depend on each other in order to allow for a coordinated treatment of a patient. For example, a treatment may consist of a two weeks che-

---
[*] Supported by the GERMAN RESEARCH ASSOCIATION (DFG) under grant number Ra 497/12-1

O. Etzion and P. Scheuermann (Eds.): CoopIS 2000, LNCS 1901, pp. 210–223, 2000.
© Springer-Verlag Berlin Heidelberg 2000

motherapy and parallel units of supporting radiotherapy every two days (for radiotherapy, the patient has ambulance appointments at the radiological department). If a logical failure such as an unexpected allergy w.r.t. the drug VINCRISTIN occurs, this may require dynamic adaptations of the chemotherapy workflow such as deleting the VINCRISTIN node (Fig. 1). This adaptation may impact the radiotherapy workflow. As a *temporal* implication the chemotherapy workflow may be finished earlier so that a radiotherapy unit may be started earlier. As a *qualitative* implication, additional radiotherapy units may become necessary to compensate the dropped drug being essential for tumor remission. Thus deletion of nodes in one workflow can make it necessary to insert additional nodes in a collaborating workflow.

To address logical failures and their impacts on collaborating workflows, we are currently developing the workflow management system AGENTWORK at the University of Leipzig. Main characteristics of AGENTWORK described in this paper are as follows:

First, AGENTWORK allows to specify at what time a workflow expects which results from other workflows. In particular, tolerance limits and constraints for delivery times and result qualities can be specified. Second, based on our previous work [21] we use a rule-based approach for dynamic workflow adaptation when logical failures occur.

Third, as a main contribution of this paper, we provide a model that enables a workflow system to decide which collaborating workflows have to be informed in what manner when a dynamic adaptation is performed. In particular, we propose a *predictive* strategy estimating whether constraints for delivery times or result qualities will be violated due to the dynamic adaptation. In this way we inform collaborating partners *in time* so that they can prepare themselves w.r.t. consequences of the logical failure. For example, if the chemotherapy adaptation in Fig. 1 implies that the required total amount of drug dosages cannot be applied anymore, we inform the radiological department as soon as possible and *before* the chemotherapy has finished. This allows preparing, for instance, additional radiotherapy units to compensate the reduced chemotherapy which would not have been possible without a predictive approach. *Temporal* implications of an adaptation are determined by estimating the duration that will be needed to execute the dynamically adapted workflow, and by compar-

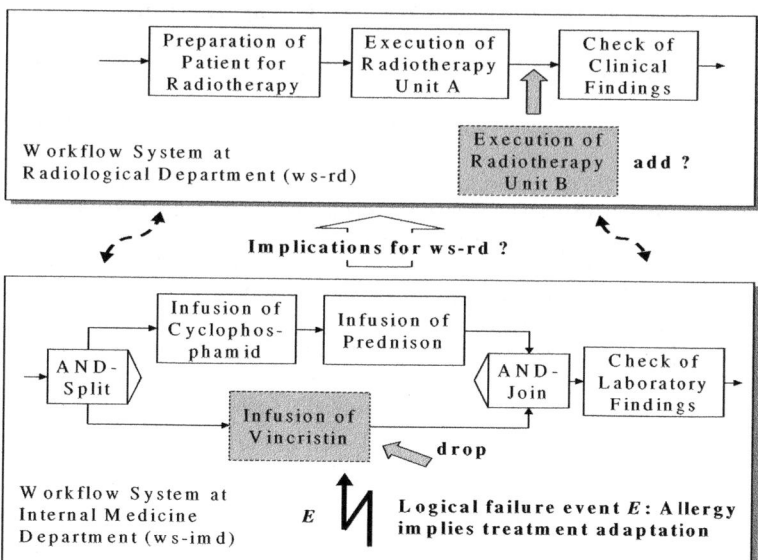

Fig. 1. Example of two collaborating workflows in a medical domain. CYCLOPHOSPHAMID, PREDNISON and VINCRISTIN are cancer drugs.

ing it with originally fixed time constraints. If time constraints are expected to be violated, affected collaboration partners are informed immediately. For determining *qualitative* implications we will introduce so-called *quality-measuring objects*. Such objects have already been used for quality control in data warehousing [15] but, to our knowledge, not yet in the workflow area. In our context, quality-measuring objects are numerical objects of a workflow's data flow that measure the quality of a result provided by a workflow. Such objects are used to decide whether an adaptation decreases the quality of a collaboration result below a specified tolerance limit so that collaboration partners have to be informed. In our medical example, the drug dosage applied to a patient can serve as a quality-measuring object as it is an important measure for the degree of tumor remission. In financial applications, price and credit limits may represent such quality objects.

Fourth, AGENTWORK aims at automating as much as possible of this process. This is desirable especially in large-scale workflow environments with many collaborating workflows running concurrently. By a high degree of automation, we expect to reduce the probability that collaboration partners are not informed timely about relevant logical failures and dynamic workflow adaptations.

The paper is organized as follows: After a discussion of related work in section 2, section 3 gives an overview of the AGENTWORK system. Sections 4 introduces our workflow and collaboration model; section 5 explains the rule-based approach for handling logical failures. In section 6 we outline the approach to determine the temporal and qualitative implications of workflow adaptation for collaborating workflows. Finally, we summarize and discuss future work.

2   Related Work

Collaborative workflow research has focussed on aspects such as interoperability frameworks, collaboration management infrastructures and workflow-oriented event notification systems [1,5,9]. However, not much work has been done so far to cope with failure management in inter-workflow collaboration scenarios.

For example, in [11] an approach is described for event-based communication between processes interacting in a consumer-producer relationship. A dependency graph maintains which processes have been triggered by which events. If a process P fails, the system derives from the dependency graph which processes depend on P and sends exception events to them. Notified processes then perform an abort or compensation-based partial rollback. The possibility that affected processes may continue after a dynamic adaptation is not investigated by the authors.

In WIDE [6], workflow collaboration is specified via SEND and RECEIVE nodes by which workflows synchronously can exchange information about results. Failures leading to a workflow starvation (i.e. a receiver workflow waits in vain for a result) or a deadlock (i.e. two workflows in vain wait for results from each other) are handled as follows: Either an alternative control flow path that already has been specified at definition time is executed when a waiting threshold expires, or the conflict is resolved manually in an ad-hoc manner. A more detailed communication protocol informing that because of a logical failure a result will be provided *later* or *with reduced quality* is not supported. In particular, it is not investigated how to adapt a receiver workflow dynamically so that it can better cope, for example, with a result of reduced quality.

In [18], unexpected terminations of workflows or workflow activities in e-commerce scenarios are addressed. In case of such a termination, a gateway protocol informs collaborating workflows about the termination reason and the state of the failed workflow or activity. Furthermore, collaborating workflows may be informed about a modification of an already agreed-on *price* for the service or product that is going to be provided by the workflow affected by the failure. To determine the price modification due to a termination, exception rules can be assigned to agreements specifying under which termination circumstances which price modifications shall be applied. However, the approach does not cover failures *not* leading to a workflow or activity termination but for example to the dynamic dropping or adding of activities. Furthermore, considering only price modifications is not appropriate for many non-commercial domains such as collaborative medical care.

Recently, also approaches from artificial intelligence have been proposed for workflow failure handling. For example, in [14] business processes are modeled in terms of *agents, services, (re-)negotiations* and *service failures*. In [17], exception handling agents detect and resolve workflow exceptions using the *heuristic classification* method [8]. However, both approaches do not address how failures are resolved in means of structural process adaptations and how the consequences for collaboration partners can automatically be derived. Other approaches addressing constraint violations during plan execution [3,22] also do not to the best of our knowledge, specifically address the temporal and qualitative consequences of plan adaptations for collaboration partners.

3   Layers and Components of AGENTWORK

We are currently developing the AGENTWORK prototype to support rule-based dynamic workflow adaptation in order to deal with logical failures. It consists of three architectural layers (Fig. 2). A *communication layer* based on CORBA is responsible for communication with other workflow systems, databases, users, etc. The *workflow definition and execution layer* supports the definition and execution of workflows. The *layer for logical failure handling* provides three agents to cope with logical failures:

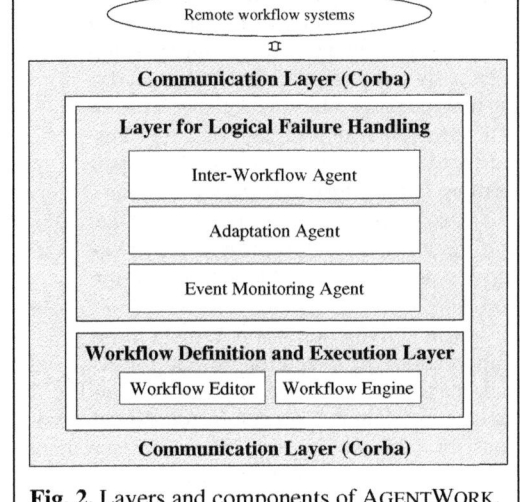

Fig. 2. Layers and components of AGENTWORK.

- The *event monitoring agent* decides which events in the workflow environment constitute logical failure events.
- The *adaptation agent* adapts affected workflows. For example, it removes or inserts activities so that the workflow can better cope with the new situation caused by the logical failure event.
- The *inter-workflow agent* determines whether a dynamic workflow adaptation has any implications for other workflows collaborating with this workflow.

How these tasks are achieved will be explained in the sequel. AGENTWORK is currently applied to the domain of cancer treatment within the HEMATOWORK project [19] at the University of Leipzig.

4   Workflow Model

We now briefly outline our approach for defining workflows and workflow collaboration. In particular we introduce temporal and qualitative collaboration agreements. AGENTWORK definitions are based on an object-oriented meta model mainly consisting of a class hierarchy for cases, events, activities and agents. A *Case* object represents a person or institution for which an enterprise or organization provides its services (such as a patient or a customer). Objects of class *Event* represent anything that occurs w.r.t. a case and therefore may impact workflows running for this case. The *Event* subclass *Activity* is used for events that do not only happen to a case but are actively performed (e.g. a drug infusion). Activities are performed by *Agent* objects, such as physicians, clerks or application programs. The agents of the layer for logical failure handling are also members of this class.

4.1 Workflows and Activities

Workflows are defined based on the sketched meta model. Activities of a workflow are represented by *activity nodes*; the control flow is specified by *edges* and *control nodes*. AGENT-WORK provides control node types for conditional branching (node types OR-SPLIT/OR-JOIN), for parallel execution (AND-SPLIT/AND-JOIN) and loops (LOOP-START/LOOP-END). For every split node or LOOP-START node there must be exactly one closing join node or LOOP-END node. The data flow is represented by data flow edges. Internal data flow edges specify the data flow between nodes within one workflow. External data flow edges specify the data flow between workflow nodes and external data sources such as databases or user interfaces.

An activity node has an associated *activity definition* to specify what has to be done when the control flow reaches this node. In Fig. 3 an activity definition using the *Activity* subclass *Drug-Infusion* has been assigned to an activity node specifying that the patient has to receive a VINCRISTIN infusion with a dosage of 2 mg. Furthermore, it is specified that the agent performing this activity must be a physician.

As a shorthand, we use the terms *A-activity* and *A-node* to denote an activity resp. activity node based on the activity definition *A*.

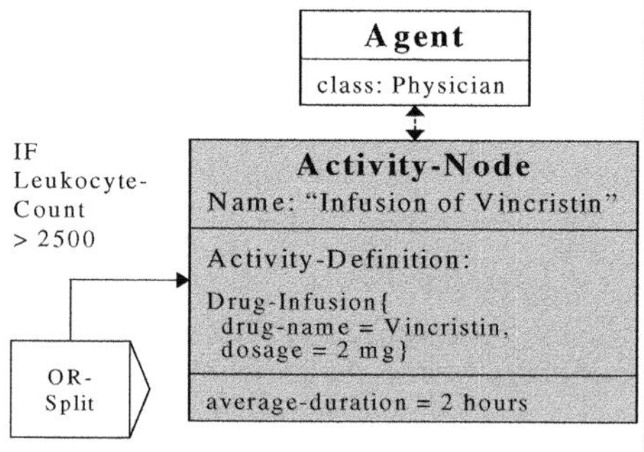

Fig. 3. Workflow definition part.

To an activity definition *A*, meta information about the execution duration of *A*-activities can be assigned. This may be the minimal, maximal or average duration (e.g. in Fig. 3 it is specified that the average duration of such an infusion is 2 hours). In addition, the workflow engine measures the execution durations for each activity type. These measurements are used to calculate and to continuously refine the *average, maximal* and *minimal* duration of activities of a specific type. These measurements allow restricting the use of pre-specified duration information to the first phase of an AGENTWORK installation.

As usual, the term workflow refers to an instantiation of a workflow definition executed by the workflow engine. In AGENTWORK, a workflow runs for exactly one case (e.g. patient or customer) but for one case several workflows may be executed concurrently.

4.2 Workflow Collaboration

In AGENTWORK, workflow collaboration is specified on a *communication level* by defining when a workflow has to exchange which information to which other workflow system. Note that we communicate with a *workflow system* and not directly with its *workflows*, as a workflow modeler at one site usually does not have knowledge about the structure of workflows at another site. Thus it is the task of the receiving workflow system as our collaboration partner to propagate information messages to those workflows that are affected.

Workflow communication is specified by COMM-OUT and COMM-IN nodes and inter-workflow objects. A COMM-OUT node specifies when information has to be send to some collaboration partner. A COMM-IN node specifies when information is expected to be received from some collaboration partner. The details are specified by *inter-workflow objects* assigned to these nodes. Such an inter-workflow object if of the structure *(ws, o: Class, cs)* where *ws* identifies the collaborating workflow system that shall receive or is expected to send information.

- *o* is an object of class *Class* which is exchanged between collaboration partners and which contains or describes a product or service.
- *cs* is a *Case* object and describes the case to which *o* belongs (e.g. a patient treated collaboratively or an industrial customer). The receiving workflow system uses *cs* to identify the affected workflows.

In Fig. 4 we extend the workflows of Fig. 1 with such communication nodes and inter-workflow objects. For the lower workflow, the COMM-OUT node and its associated inter-workflow object specify that a *Chemo-Report* object *c* has to be sent to the radiological workflow system *ws-rd* after the inspection of several laboratory findings. *imd-pat* identifies the patient to whom the report belongs. Vice versa, the upper workflow at *ws-rd* contains a COMM-IN node with an inter-workflow object stating that before the radiotherapy preparation a *Chemo-Report* object is expected from *ws-imd* w.r.t. the patient *rd-pat* treated by the radiotherapy workflow. Based on attribute values of *rd-pat*, *ws-rd* can determine which inter-workflow object received from *ws-imd* belongs to which of its workflows. To a COMM-IN or COMM-OUT node several inter-workflow objects can be assigned, and

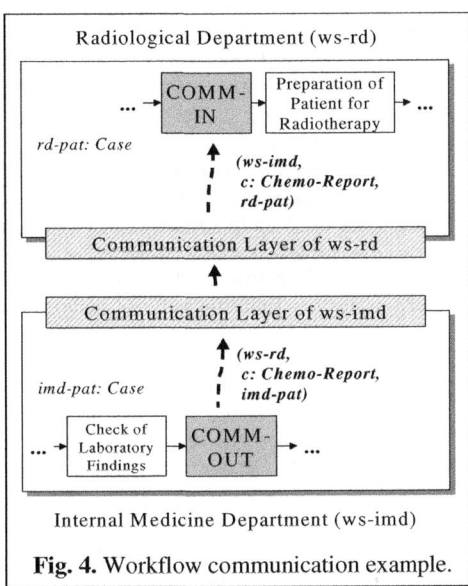

Fig. 4. Workflow communication example.

a workflow may contain an arbitrary number of COMM-IN or COMM-OUT nodes.

COMM-OUT and COMM-IN nodes are processed as follows:

- When a COMM-OUT node is reached, for each of its inter-workflow objects *(ws, o: Class, cs)* the tuple *(o: Class, cs)* is sent to *ws*. This is done asynchronously, i.e. the workflow is continued after the send operation. If the path with the COMM-OUT node shall not be continued until *ws* sends a reply, this can be specified by placing a COMM-IN node directly after the COMM-OUT node.
- Vice versa, when a COMM-IN node is reached with an inter-workflow object *(ws, o: Class, cs)*, the engine checks whether such an object *o* for case *cs* has already been received from *ws*. If yes, the engine forwards *o* to all activity nodes of the respective workflow that need *o*. If no, the engine waits for *o* until a deadline is exceeded and then sends a reminder to *ws*.

By default COMM-OUT and COMM-IN nodes are executed when they are reached during workflow execution. In addition, at workflow start time or during execution we can assign absolute (calendar) time points to them to specify when information has to be send *to* or when it is expected *from* a collaboration partner (e.g. send information on 20th July 2000, 6 p.m.). For example, for a long-term workflow covering two phases of a treatment it may be useful to dynamically assign absolute time points fixing the intended delivery times w.r.t. the remaining COMM-OUT nodes not before the second phase is entered. Such absolute (calendar) time points can be manually assigned or can automatically be derived by estimating the execution duration of the path(s) leading to the communication node and by adding this duration to the workflow's actual execution time point (similar to [10]). A combination could consist of a manual assignment and an automated check estimating whether this absolute time point is realistic w.r.t. the workflow definition. We describe such estimation algorithms in more detail in section 6 where they are used for determining temporal implications of workflow adaptations. Relative time points can also be assigned to a COMM-OUT node (e.g. send information 3 weeks after workflow start), but are converted to absolute time points by the system.

Furthermore, we assign so-called temporal and quality collaboration agreements to communication nodes in order to specify which deviations, e.g. caused by logical failures, are tolerable and which not.

Temporal collaboration agreements: To a COMM-OUT node two thresholds *acc-threshold* (*acc* for acceleration) and *delay-threshold* of the form *(v, time-unit)* can be assigned (with $v \geq 0$ and *time-unit* $\in$ {*sec, min, hour, day, week, ...*}). The semantics is:

- If *acc-threshold* or *delay-threshold* is left unspecified, an acceleration resp. delay is viewed as irrelevant.
- If an absolute time point *atp* (such as 20th July 2000, 6.00 p.m.) has been assigned to the COMM-OUT node, *acc-treshold* and *delay-threshold* specify that the workflow containing this COMM-OUT node should send its information within the interval
        [atp - acc-threshold, atp + delay-threshold]
  (e.g. within [20th July 2000 - 2 days, 20th July 2000 + 3 days]). Whenever a dynamic adaptation implies that this will not be possible anymore, the collaboration partner has to be informed.
- If *no* absolute time point has been assigned to the COMM-OUT node, *acc-treshold* and *delay-threshold* refer to the relative change in the execution time due to a workflow adaptation. Let d_{before} denote the execution time that would have been needed to reach the COMM-OUT *before* the adaptation, and d_{after} the execution time that will be needed to reach the COMM-OUT *after* the adaptation. The collaboration partner then has to be informed if:
  $d_{before} - d_{after} >$ *acc-threshold* (workflow accelerated by more than *acc-threshold*) or
  $d_{after} - d_{before} >$ *delay-threshold* (workflow delayed by more than *delay-threshold*).

We emphasize that the described semantics of these thresholds serve the specific purposes of logical failure handling. For handling deadlines and temporal thresholds for workflow execution not "disturbed" by dynamic adaptations we refer to [16,10].

Qualitative collaboration agreements: A collaboration partner often expects that a result provided by its partner will arrive not only in time but also with a certain quality. To express this AGENTWORK allows to assign *quality constraints* to inter-workflow objects. For example, the chemotherapy report object *c* of Fig. 4 may have different subsections for the applied drugs, for clinical findings and for laboratory findings. Then, by assigning a quality constraint to *c* such as

c.subsection-for-applied-drugs = Mandatory AND
c.subsection-for-laboratory-findings = Mandatory

both collaboration partners could fix the agreement that in the report at least the subsections for the applied drugs and the laboratory findings have to be filled out as otherwise the radiotherapy workflow cannot continue because important patient data are missing.

Even more, in many domains the quality of a result can be expressed by a numerical threshold value. For example, the weighted sum of the report's drug dosages describes the quality of the chemotherapy as it closely correlates to the degree of tumor remission[†]. The collaboration partners then could also assign a quality constraint such as

c.weighted-sum-of-drug-dosages > 100 mg

to the transferred report *c*. If this constraint is violated because some drugs had to be dynamically dropped from the chemotherapy workflow, the radiological department has to be informed as it may be necessary to dynamically add some radiotherapy units to compensate the reduced chemotherapy. Generally, we will refer to a numerical object that is used to mea-

---

[†] The sum is weighted as the different drugs have a different strength w.r.t. tumor remission.

sure the quality of a result as a so-called *quality-measuring object*. Non-medical examples for quality-measuring objects and constraints on them could be price ranges for e-business interactions or credit limits for banking applications.

Determining how dynamic adaptations may influence such a quality-measuring object requires additional quality-related meta knowledge w.r.t. workflow *activities*. Therefore, in AGENTWORK quality transformation rules can be assigned to an activity definition *A* stating how *A*-activities transform a quality-measuring object. For example, the activity definition of Fig. 3

$A := Drug\text{-}Infusion\{drug\text{-}name = VINCRISTIN, dosage = 2\ mg\}$

can be augmented by the quality transformation rule

c.weighted-sum-of-drug-dosages += 2 mg

to account for the respective drug dosage increase. Based on this meta knowledge, qualitative implications of adaptations can then be determined as we show in section 6.

5   Logical Failures and Intra-Workflow Adaptation

To handle logical failure events, we use *event-condition-action rules* of the structure

WHEN event WITH condition THEN control action

Such a rule specifies in its event-condition part which event constitutes a logical failure. The action part states which *control action* has to be performed for workflow activities to cope with the failure event. Table 1 lists the supported control actions. *A* and *B* denote activity definitions, *cs* again denotes a case (e.g. a patient or customer).

Control Action	Meaning
drop(A,cs)	For *cs*, *A*-activities must not be executed anymore.
replace(A,B,cs)	For *cs*, every *A*-activity execution is to be replaced by a *B*-activity.
check(A,cs)	For *cs*, every execution of an *A*-activity has to be checked by a user.
add(A,cs)	For *cs* an *A*-activity has *additionally* to be executed exactly *once*.

Table 1. AGENTWORK Control Actions

The *check(A,cs)* control action is used when there is not enough knowledge available to decide whether an *A*-activity has become inadequate or not for *cs*. When a *check(A,cs)* control action is triggered, control is shifted to a user who has to specify whether the activity should, e.g., be dropped or replaced.

An example for a rule triggering a control action is the following (*A* denotes the activity definition *Drug-Infusion{drug-name = VINCRISTIN}*, *Hemato-Findings(pat-id, parameter, value)* is a table collecting blood-related patient data):

WHEN INSERT ON Hemato-Findings REFERENCING NEW AS h   (*)
WITH   h.parameter = Leukocyte-Count AND h.value < 1000
THEN   drop(A, h.pat-id)

This rule expresses that if a patient has a leukocyte count less than 1000, VINCRISTIN infusions have to be dropped for this patient. With rules such as (*), AGENTWORK can monitor any application environment events that may impact workflows.

When a new event *E* occurs, the following steps are performed: First, the event monitoring agent checks whether *E* constitutes a logical failure. *E* is classified as failure event if at least one control action is triggered by rules such as (*). Second, if a control action *ca(A,cs)* has been triggered, affected workflows running for *cs* are determined. Concerning *drop, replace* and *check,* a workflow is affected if it contains at least one *A*-node in the remaining control flow. Concerning *add*, the workflow the user has selected for the new *A*-node is affected. An affected workflow then is interrupted. With N_E we denote the *interruption node set* which is the set of nodes which were either in execution or prepared for execution (i.e. the predeces-

218   R. Müller and E. Rahm

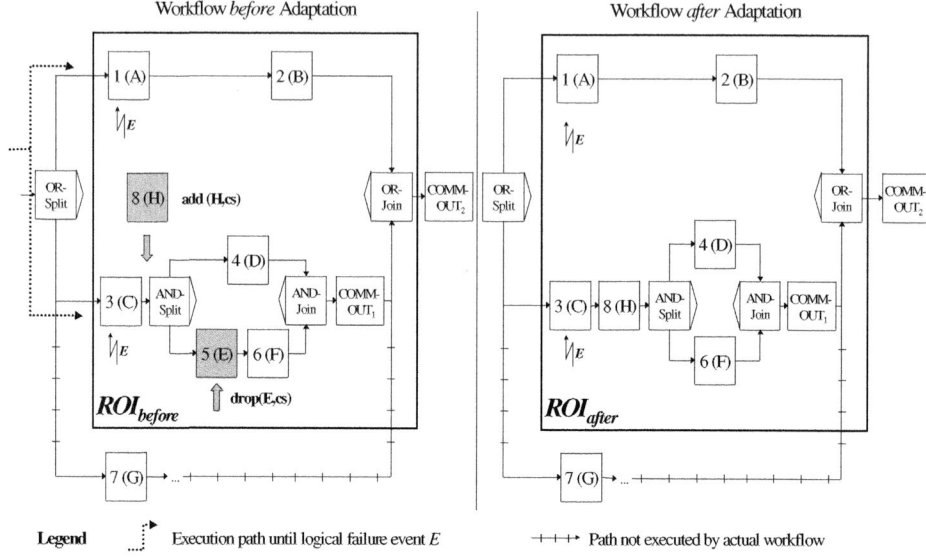

Fig. 5. The regions of interest ROI_{before} and ROI_{after}. Letters denote activity definitions.

sor nodes have already committed) at the interruption moment. The cardinality of N_E may be > 1, if the workflow is interrupted during parallel execution (i.e. after an AND-SPLIT or a non-exclusive OR-SPLIT). In Fig. 5, N_E consists of nodes 1 and 3.

Third, after the interruption the *adaptation agent* translates *ca(A,cs)* into node operators adapting the control and data flow. By default, *all* A-nodes in the remaining control flow are handled, e.g. all A-nodes would be dropped from the remaining control flow if *ca(A,cs) = drop(A,cs)*. If the adaptation shall be restricted only to a *part* of the remaining control flow, a user can graphically select the workflow part to which the adaptation operations shall be applied exclusively. A new node which has to be added because of an *add* control action is – by default – inserted directly after a node of N_E. If such a new node shall be inserted somewhere later in the control flow, this has to be specified by a user. In Fig. 5, the adaptation agent has dropped an E-node (5) from the control flow because of a *drop(E,cs)* control action and has added a new H-node (8) because of an *add(H,cs)* control action.

AGENTWORK also supports the *semi-automated* determination of an appropriate part to which the adaptation shall be restricted. This is mainly achieved by the possibility to assign a valid time interval to the action part of a failure rule, such as:

WHEN event WITH condition THEN drop(VINCRISTIN,cs)
VALID-TIME [now, now + 3 days]

stating that the drug VINCRISTIN shall be dropped only for the next three days (starting from "now" which is the moment when the control action was triggered). The adaptation agent estimates which part of the remaining control flow will be executed during the next three days, and applies the adaptations operation only to this part.

The *consistency* of adapted workflows is achieved as follows: First, the consistency of failure handling rules is ensured by rule consistency algorithms as proposed in [2]. This avoids that for example *drop(A,cs)* and *add(A,cs)* are triggered for the same workflow at the same time. Second, consistency constraints reject adaptations leading, for example, to an activity node for which input objects are not provided by data flow edges. Third, only authorized users such as senior physicians may contribute to adaptations.

As we want to concentrate on the *inter*-workflow aspects of workflow adaptation, we refer to [21] for further details w.r.t. our intra-workflow adaptation approach.

6   Managing Inter-Workflow Implications of Adaptations

Before an adapted workflow is continued, the *inter-workflow agent* is invoked if the workflow contains COMM-OUT nodes in its remaining control flow. This agent has to determine whether the adaptation affects any collaborating workflow. Principally, it operates as follows:

First, it determines the so-called **region of interest** *ROI* (Fig. 5). This is the workflow region which starts at the interruption node set N_E and contains *all* adapted workflow parts. If all adaptations from N_E occurred within a sequence of activities not belonging to a split/join region, *ROI* simply ends with the last node (having the largest distance to N_E) that was dropped, replaced or added. If the last adaptation took place within a split/join region (e.g. between an OR-SPLIT and an OR-JOIN node), *ROI* ends *beyond* these last adapted parts at the first AND-JOIN or OR-JOIN node *joining all reachable paths starting from nodes of N_E* even if one of these paths has not been adapted at all. This is necessary, as especially the *temporal* influence of an adaptation often can only be determined by considering *all reachable paths* starting at N_E up to this joining node. For example, in Fig. 5 for COMM-OUT$_2$ the temporal influence of the shown adaptation requires considering the path 1→2 although it has not been adapted. This is because the execution duration of path 1→2 may be longer than that of the adapted paths. Therefore, in Fig. 5 *both* paths starting at N_E have to be considered up to the closing OR-JOIN.

In the sequel, ROI_{before} and ROI_{after} denote the region of interest *before* resp. *after* the adaptation. They may cover the whole remaining control and data flow or only a part of it (e.g. if the user manually has restricted the adaptation to such a part). As the control actions of Table 1 only affect *activity* nodes, ROI_{before} resp. ROI_{after} contain the same set of communication nodes. We write *ROI* instead of ROI_{before} or ROI_{after} if the distinction between the region before and after the adaptation is irrelevant.

Second, the relevant **temporal and qualitative implications** of the adaptation are determined. This is mainly done by estimating and comparing the execution durations and "qualities" of the regions ROI_{before} and ROI_{after}. Whether the entire regions ROI_{before} and ROI_{after} are considered or only parts of them depends on the location of the COMM-OUT nodes. This will be discussed below. The *execution duration* of a workflow region is estimated on the base of several path duration algorithms of [20]. The *quality* of ROI_{before} and ROI_{after} is determined and measured by using quality constraints and quality-measuring objects (section 4.2). If temporal thresholds or qualitative constraints are violated for an inter-workflow object because of an adaptation, the affected collaborating workflow system is directly informed.

Third, when the workflow is continued, the **actual execution is monitored** by the inter-workflow agent. For example, unexpected delays of activity executions or external data accesses caused by system failures can be detected by this monitoring, and the inter-workflow agent can refine its estimations. If necessary, the collaboration partners are informed about such refined estimations.

A workflow system *ws* can handle temporal or qualitative effects about which it was informed as follows: It may itself have failure rules stating how to react on constraint violations caused by (remote) logical failures of a collaborating workflow system. Alternatively, users of both workflow systems together may decide how *ws* should react.

6.1   Determining Temporal Implications

We first sketch the principal algorithm of determining temporal implications. Then, we describe how execution durations are estimated.
The principal algorithm is as follows (Fig. 6):

1. *Handling nodes <u>within</u> ROI*: For each COMM-OUT node within *ROI* the subregion $SROI_{after}$ is determined leading from the interruption node set to the COMM-OUT node. For example, for COMM-OUT$_1$ in Fig. 5 $SROI_{after}$ consists of nodes 3, 8, 4, 6 and the AND-SPLIT/AND-JOIN nodes. After this, it is estimated how long it will take to execute $SROI_{after}$.

If an absolute calendar time point is assigned to the COMM-OUT node, it is then checked whether the estimated execution duration of $SROI_{after}$ violates a temporal threshold for any inter-workflow object *(ws, o: Class, cs)* of the COMM-OUT node. If yes, *ws* is informed (left branch of Fig. 6). If *no* absolute time point is assigned to the COMM-OUT node, the duration that would have been needed to execute $SROI_{before}$ has to be estimated, too. Then, it is checked whether there is a mismatch between the durations of $SROI_{before}$ and $SROI_{after}$ violating any temporal thresholds of an inter-workflow object *(ws, o: Class, cs)* of the COMM-OUT node. If yes, *ws* is informed (middle branch of Fig. 6).

2. *Handling nodes <u>beyond</u> ROI*: For COMM-OUT nodes beyond *ROI*[‡] – such as COMM-OUT$_2$ in Fig. 5 – the same procedure is performed as for COMM-OUT nodes within *ROI* with the only difference that we now consider the entire region *ROI* instead of a subregion *SROI* (right branch of Fig. 6). In particular, it is estimated how long it will take to execute ROI_{after}. Then, for every inter-workflow object of one of the COMM-OUT nodes beyond *ROI* we check whether any temporal constraints are violated. For example, if an absolute time point *atp* has been assigned to a COMM-OUT node beyond *ROI* it may be that already the duration of ROI_{after} makes it impossible to reach the node before *atp + delay-threshold*. If such a constraint is violated, the affected workflow systems are immediately informed. Obviously, for the duration estimations w.r.t. $ROI_{after/before}$ the results w.r.t. $SROI_{after/before}$ can be re-used.

Note that estimating the time duration of *ROI* does not take into account the execution time of nodes that have to be executed between the end of *ROI* and the COMM-OUT node.

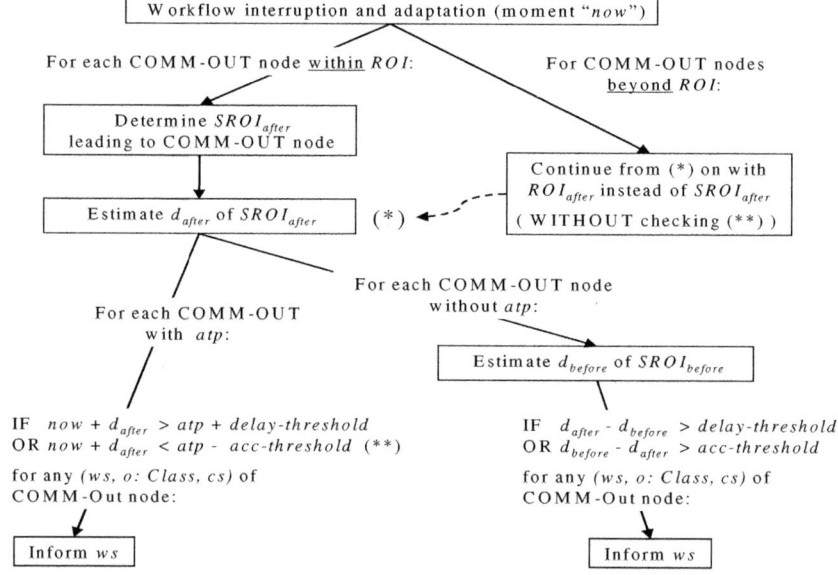

Fig. 6. Algorithm checking temporal implications for collaborating workflows (*atp* = absolute time point, $d_{before/after}$ = execution duration before/after adaptation). The acceleration check (**) is not done for a COMM-OUT node beyond *ROI* as there may be further nodes between *ROI* and the COMM-OUT node.

[‡] Note that ROI_{before} and ROI_{after} do not differ w.r.t. communication nodes.

For a COMM-OUT node with *no* absolute time point this is irrelevant as the algorithm then only has to check whether there is a relative temporal mismatch w.r.t. the durations *before* and *after* the adaptation. As nodes beyond *ROI* have *not* been adapted, this mismatch is entirely determined by *ROI*. For a COMM-OUT node with an absolute time point the nodes between it and *ROI* are relevant, but the COMM-OUT node may be far away from *ROI* so that estimating the time durations between *ROI* and such a node would be inherently imprecise. Yet, by considering the changed duration of *ROI* we already enable an early notification for workflow adaptations with significant impact on execution times (e.g. we detect if already the duration of ROI_{after} makes it impossible to reach the COMM-OUT node in time). For those COMM-OUT nodes outside *ROI* not affected by the change of the *ROI* execution time, we switch to a continuous monitoring approach. That is, after the workflow adaptation it is continuously checked for these COMM-OUT nodes whether their timing constraints can still be met. By combining the predictive approach with continuous monitoring we achieve early notifications even when only partial or imprecise execution time estimates are possible. The overhead for the additional checks is considered acceptable because first the number of affected COMM-OUT nodes is limited and second workflow adaptations due to logical failures should be relatively rare.

We now sketch how the execution duration of workflow regions is estimated. In the current implementation, estimations are based on the *average* duration of activity executions. *Worst*-case durations using the *maximal* activity duration are viewed as too pessimistic, as too often delays would be predicted which would not really occur.

The duration of a **sequence** is estimated by iteratively summing up the average activity durations. Control edges are assumed to have a *negligible* duration. The duration of an **AND-SPLIT/AND-JOIN region** (such as nodes 4, 5, 6 in ROI_{before} in Fig. 5) is the maximum of the estimated durations of all its paths.

If an **OR-SPLIT/OR-JOIN region** is discovered, it is tried either to predict which of the paths starting at the OR-SPLIT will qualify for execution when the workflow will be continued, or the maximum of all paths is taken as a worst-case estimation (as not all paths may be executed actually). A prediction may be possible if the workflow interruption has occurred close to the OR-SPLIT, e.g. when data needed for the decision which paths will qualify for execution is already available. For example, at an OR-SPLIT one path may qualify for execution if the patient has liver metastases, the other one if the patient has *no* liver metastases. If it is definitely known at adaptation time that the patient has liver metastases, then only the duration of the metastases path would have to be taken into account. Furthermore, instead of worst-case estimations one could also determine (and later on execute) the path with the *smallest* duration or *highest* quality, if constraints otherwise would be violated. However, as OR splits usually contain data-related conditions (such as *IF Leukocyte-Count > 2500* in Fig. 3), this often is not appropriate or at least requires some user intervention.

The duration of a **loop** is estimated by determining the duration of the loop's body sequence and then by trying to estimate how often the loop will be iterated. AGENTWORK supports three principal ways for the latter (used with decreasing priority): First, the engine records all loop executions and calculates an average number of iterations for every loop (analogously to the monitoring of activity executions). Second, at workflow definition time heuristic information about the average number of iterations can be specified (such as "On average, the radiotherapy unit of type *A* has to be repeated three times until the tumor vanishes"). Third, it is tried to resolve the loop's termination condition in a similar way as it is done w.r.t. OR splits (i.e. by inspecting whether necessary data is already available).

Duration information w.r.t. **data flow edges** (e.g. for accessing external data sources) is obtained by measuring the average duration of such data accesses.

The described mechanisms estimate the duration of workflow regions in a primarily *average*-based manner. If an OR-SPLIT can not be resolved and therefore the maximum of all (average) path durations has to be taken, this estimation *locally* becomes a worst-case estimation (but not as much as it would be the case when using the maximal duration for *all* workflow activities). In case nothing can be said about a loop, the region estimation remains incomplete but may nevertheless be helpful as, for example, relevant delays w.r.t. the rest of the region may still be predictable and can be communicated to collaboration partners.

6.2   Determining Qualitative Implications

For qualitative implications, the inter-workflow agent uses a modification of the temporal algorithm of Fig. 6 restricted to COMM-OUT nodes *within ROI*. Instead of estimating the *durations* of regions such as $SROI_{after}$ it determines the *qualitative* effects of the activities by using the quality transformation rules of section 4.2. Then, it checks whether the derived quality w.r.t. the adapted workflow violates any *quality* constraints (instead of temporal) of an inter-workflow object. The restriction to COMM-OUT nodes *within ROI* is made as AGENTWORK views qualitative estimations for COMM-OUT nodes far away from the adapted workflow region as being inherently imprecise.

If no qualitative implications can be determined because of missing quality-oriented meta knowledge, the inter-workflow agent at least informs the collaboration partners which activities have been dropped or added due to the dynamic adaptation. However, as this requires that the activities performed by one workflow are *meaningful* for the collaboration partner, AGENTWORK views this only as an "emergency solution".

The temporal and qualitative estimation approaches work if an AGENTWORK workflow is "well-formed" in the sense that an object o sent by a COMM-OUT node is only produced by predecessor nodes of this COMM-OUT node. For Fig. 5 this means that the objects sent by COMM-OUT$_1$ may only be provided by nodes 3, 5, 6, 4 (before adaptation) resp. 3, 8, 4, 6 (after adaptation) or predecessors of 3, but not by node 1 or 2. If, for example, node 2 would contribute to an object of COMM-OUT$_1$ (and therefore, for example, could delay the execution of COMM-OUT$_1$ or influence qualitative constraints) then COMM-OUT$_1$ would have to be placed behind the OR-JOIN node. However, the algorithm can easily be extended to cope also with "cross-over" data flow edges (e.g. a data flow edge transferring data from node 1 to COMM-OUT$_1$ in Fig. 5): For each COMM-OUT node within *ROI* the subregion $SROI_{after}$ has to be recursively extended by all nodes contributing to the objects send by the COMM-OUT node. Syntactically, these are the nodes from which internal data flow edge paths are leading to the COMM-OUT node.

7   Summary and Discussion

We have introduced a model to deal with logical failures and dynamic adaptations for collaborating workflows. If a workflow is adapted, the temporal and qualitative implications for collaborating workflows are automatically determined. Relevant failures causing agreed-on temporal and qualitative constraints to be violated are immediately communicated to affected collaborating workflow systems. By this approach, we expect that the frequency of failure situations inducing local workflow adaptations but *not* reported timely to affected collaboration partners can be reduced significantly.

Our approach is based on knowledge such as activity durations, quality-measuring objects and quality transformation rules. We expect that in many application domains – due to the increasing importance of quality management and quality assurance – the duration and quality transformation „behavior" of activities can be obtained quite exactly. In particular, in most real-world collaboration scenarios, there will be at least one object (such as a document) containing information which in some way measures the quality of products or results provided by the collaboration partners. Our approach does not need significantly more specifications than other workflow failure handling approaches where, for example, compensating activities have to be defined for every „normal" activity [13]. Of course, it is not possible to derive *all* implications of a logical failure automatically because the internal structure of workflows can be arbitrarily complex. If the most significant problem cases can be handled this would already be of great value.

Currently, we are completing the implementation of the sketched approach within the HEMATOWORK project. We are also evaluating the applicability of the approach in different application domains like electronic inter-business workflows. The approach shall also be extended by using additional activity meta information (such as the resources required to execute an activity) and by determining the respective implications of adaptations. Furthermore, we plan empirical studies on the quality of temporal estimations for real-world workflows.

References

1. Georgakopoulos, D., Schuster, H., Cichocki, A., Baker, D.: Managing Process and Service Fusion in Virtual Enterprises. Information Systems 24 (1999) 429-456
2. Baralis, E.: Rule Analysis. In: Paton, N. (ed.): Active Rules in Database Systems. Springer (1999) 51-67
3. Blum, A., Furst, M.L.: Fast Planning Through Planning Graph Analysis. Artificial Intelligence 90 (1997) 281-300
4. Borgida, A., Murata, T.: Tolerating Exceptions in Workflows: a Unified Framework for Data and Processes. WACC (1999) 59-68
5. Bussler, Ch.: Workflow Interoperability Classification and its Implication to Workflow Management System Architectures. EDBT Workflow Workshop (1998): 45-54
6. Casati, F.: Semantic Interoperability in Interorganizational Workflows. WACC Workshop on Cross-Organizational Workflows (1999)
7. Chiu, D.K.W., Li, Q., Karlapalem, K.: A Meta Modeling Approach to Workflow Management System Supporting Exception Handling. Information Systems 24 (1999) 159-184
8. Clancey, W.J.: Heuristic Classification. Artificial Intelligence 25 (1985) 289-350
9. Dogac, A., Kalinichenko, L., Özsu, T., Sheth, A. (eds.): Workflow Management Systems and Interoperability. Springer (1998)
10. Eder, J., Panagos, E., Rabinovich, M.: Time Constraints in Workflow Systems. CAiSE (1999) 286-300
11. Hagen, C., Alonso, G.: Beyond the Black Box: Event-based Inter-Process Communication in Process Support Systems. ICDCS (1999) 450-457
12. Heinl, P., Horn, S., Jablonksi, S., Neeb, J., Stein, K., Teschke, M.: A Comprehensive Approach to Flexibility in Workflow Management Systems. WACC (1999) 79-88
13. Jajodia, S., Kerschberg, L. (eds.): Advanced Transaction Models and Architectures. Kluwer (1997)
14. Jennings, N. R., Faratin, P., Norman, T. J., O'Brien, P., Odgers, B.: Autonomous Agents for Business Process Management. Journal of Applied Artificial Intelligence 14 (2000) 145-189
15. Jeusfeld, M.A., Quix, C., Jarke, M.: Design and Analysis of Quality Information for Data Warehouses. ER (1998) 349-362
16. Kafeza, K., Karlapalem, K: Temporally Constrained Workflows. ICSC (1999) 246-255
17. Klein M., Dellarocas C.: A Knowledge-Based Approach to Handling Exceptions in Workflow Systems. Journal of Computer-Supported Collaborative Work 9 (2000) 399-412
18. Ludwig, H: Termination Handling in Inter-Organisational Workflows - An Exception Management Approach. Workshop on Parallel and Distributed Processing (1999) 122 - 129
19. Müller, R., Heller, B.: A Petri Net-based Model for Knowledge-based Workflows in Distributed Cancer Therapy. EDBT Workflow Workshop (1998): 91-99
20. Marjanovic, O., Orlowska, M.E.: On Modeling and Verification of Temporal Constraints in Production Workflows. Knowledge and Information Systems 1 (1999) 157-192
21. Müller, R., Rahm, E.: Rule-Based Dynamic Modification of Workflows in a Medical Domain. German Database Conference (BTW). Springer (1999). http://dol.uni-leipzig.de
22. Schwalb, E., Dechter, R.: Processing Disjunctions in Temporal Constraint Networks. Artificial Intelligence 93 (1997) 29-61
23. Reichert, M., Dadam, P.: ADEPT$_{FLEX}$ - Supporting Dynamic Changes of Workflows Without Losing Control. Journal of Intelligent Information Systems 10 (1998) 93-129
24. Worah, D., Sheth, A.: Transactions in Transactional Workflows. In [13]: 3-34

A Negotiation Model for CSCW

Manuel Munier[1,2], Karim Baïna[1], and Khalid Benali[1]

[1] LORIA - INRIA - UMR 7503
BP 239, F-54506 Vandœuvre-lès-Nancy Cedex, France
{baina,benali}@loria.fr

[2] LIA - UPRES EA N°21.63
BP 1155, F-64013 Pau Cedex, France
munier@marsan.univ-pau.fr
(since september 1999)

Abstract The aim of this paper is to present our model for a generic and flexible negotiation service[1] and its implementation in Computer Supported Collaborative Work (CSCW) environments. Within a cooperative work environment, users naturally need negotiation support mechanisms to study possible alternatives in group decision making. The objective of our work is to build a negotiation model independent of any particular application field. Contrary to studied models, our model focuses on formalizing the negotiation from three points of view: exchanged information between the agents to negotiate (the language), the way this information is exchanged (the protocol), and the internal behavior of an agent (the tactics). In addition to a separation of the problems involved in each one of these three facets of the negotiation, this approach allows also a greater flexibility than traditional systems dedicated to one kind of problems. We chose to use a transactional approach based on speech acts to develop our axiom based negotiation model which has been implemented as a negotiation service in our CSCW environment *DisCOO* [1, 2]. After the tackled problem presentation, we will expose the state of the art, then the proposed negotiation formal model, and, finally, the implementation.

1 Introduction

Nowadays, the explosion of distributed applications for telecomuting, cooperative work, video-conference, electronic commerce,..., is giving an increasing importance to computer supported negotiation. Within a cooperative work environment, group decision making is among executive costliest tasks and users need some negotiation support to re-frame conflictual purposes, identify and structure different problems, propose, attack and defend solutions, and, finally, reach and confirm agreements [3, 4].

By integrating a negotiation support service within a cooperative work environment, we aim to increase cooperation among users by allowing each of them

---

1. This material is based upon work supported by the Xerox Research Center Europe in Grenoble and LORIA-INRIA.

O. Etzion and P. Scheuermann (Eds.): CoopIS 2000, LNCS 1901, pp. 224–235, 2000.
© Springer-Verlag Berlin Heidelberg 2000

to express his/her opinion inside the group decision. Such a negotiation service could offer, for instance, a comfortable framework to assist users in deciding which legacy tools to use for the elaboration of shared resources (ex: CAD applications, text editors, compiler and libraries versions), which resources to share with which partner, which cooperation schemas to share a resource, the final version for a shared resource (when modified by several users), how to merge two or more resources to obtain a common resource,...

Negotiation has been discussed by several research fields like psycho-sociology, game theory, economics, artificial intelligence. The objective of our work is to build a negotiation model independent of any particular application field: we do not want to produce yet another proprietary system, but to define a framework which can be configured to support various forms of negotiation.

This paper is organized as follows. After the tackled problem presentation, section 2 exposes the state of the art, section 3 describes the proposed negotiation formal model, finally, section 4 presents the implementation.

2   State of the art

There exists no universal negotiation model we can apply to every negotiation problem. The main reason is the multitude of parameters depending on culture of negotiators [5], language and vocabulary they use to negotiate, field of negotiation, and media of communication. The complexity of a negotiation process depends on negotiator number, negotiator coalition number, conflict nature, force relations between negotiators, perception of the conflict to resolve, purposes to reach,... Aiming to formalize a generic and flexible negotiation model and achieve a negotiation support service for a CSCW environment, we will discuss negotiation from the point of view of Distributed Artificial Intelligence, Speech Act theory and Group Decision Support Systems.

Distributed Artificial Intelligence (DAI) is the discipline that aims to design a system as a community of agents working together to resolve a problem. An agent is a particular computational unit which has a state, develops an expertise, and is able to react to external events. Negotiation techniques (based on theoretical frameworks like BDI[2] model [6, 7]) can be useful either in conflict resolution (to limit their effects by establishing compromises or by going beyond the nature of conflicts) or in service exchange situations (a service request may concern a failure diagnosis, a purchase of market parts, an allocation of a bandwidth for video-conference transmission,...). The *Contract Net Protocol* [8] dealing with the distribution of tasks between agents illustrates an example of service oriented negotiation. The *Commitment-Based Communication Model* [9] upgrades the Contract Net Protocol by allowing more interactivity and transparency between agents (possibility of compromising, arguing, counter-proposing,...). The negotiation process continues until one of the servers accepts a proposition.

Other works related to the communication between agents have proceeded from the point of view of negotiation language. While the use of natural lan-

---

2. BDI: Believes, Desires, and Intentions

guage is unlimited, the Speech Act theory [10–12] asserts that it is possible
to cluster terms in a finite number of verbal actions groups: *speech acts*. This
theory introduces the notion of communication protocol to represent different
social agents behaviors. As detailed in [13], the Speech Act theory has numerous applications in distributed systems, natural language processing, electronic
data exchange protocols,... Many DAI approaches use this theory to formalize
inter-agent communication protocols, especially to model the *illocutionary* aspect of speech acts (expected effect of messages). [13] proposes a classification
in seven categories: *assertive, expressive, declarative, promissive, permissive, directive* and *prohibitive* acts. [14,15] use speech-acts to model process centered
cooperation as a four-phase loop workflow (request, negotiation, performance,
satisfaction). In Speech Act theory, negotiation processes were modeled either
by state/transition diagrams where transitions are labeled by speech acts or by
sets of ECA rules [3] in which an event corresponds to the reception of a speech
act and an action describes the reaction to this act (sending of an other speech
act) (cf. Information Lens [16], SANP [4] [17]).

Finally, Negotiation Support Systems (NSS), which are a sub-class of Group
Decision Support Systems [5] [18], combine communication, computing and decision support techniques to assist people in their negotiation tasks. Within
conflictual situations, they can be used as a shared and common language for
mutual understanding. They traditionally support the process of negotiation
rather than model the decision-making aspects of the problem [19]. NSS can
provide either an automated or a semi-automated assistance to express the problem in a transparent and structured manner. Services ensured by GDSS/NSS
environments can be either synchronous or asynchronous. On the first hand, synchronous services develop rendez-vous mechanisms, requiring the "co-presence"
of different actors before the negotiation can begin (i.e. video-conference, electronic meeting systems,...). On the other hand, asynchronous services, offer a
more flexible negotiation framework in which actors can interact and work as
they do usually (eg: electronic mail, Computer-Mediated Communication, web-
based negotiation [5]).

While they propose a well defined framework to model negotiation process,
the negotiation models and techniques we have presented here suffer some drawbacks as far as our objective is concerned. For instance, many of DAI models
(including game theory) are based on heuristics and utility functions allowing
agents to estimate profits of proposed alternatives. Since, this approach ensures
the termination of a negotiation (each proposition is *better* than the previous,
negotiation by successive refinements,...), it assumes the existence of an order
relation (at least partial) on the set of possible propositions. This assumption
may be too strong in many application fields. Moreover, the design of most
of negotiation services do not distinguish the purpose of negotiation from the

---

3. ECA: event/condition/action
4. SANP: Speech-Act-based Negotiation Protocol
5. GDSS: Group Decision Support Systems is a discipline gathering technologies and
   methodologies helping groups of people to express and resolve unstructured problems

negotiation protocol (negotiation mechanisms are hard-coded among the other features of the application). Thus these negotiation services are very specific to the application field. While GDSS and NSS research provide rich notions to analyze and model negotiation process [20–22], they cannot be easily integrated within a CSCW environment. Either they give an informal expression framework which cannot be semantically usable inside a CSCW environment (electronic mail, video-conference, Computer-Mediated Communication, SANP), or they are adapted to the resolution of very specific problems (Information Lens [16], INSPIRE [5]).

Contrary to studied models, our approach distinguishes three different parts within negotiation mechanisms: data structures to be exchanged between agents, communication protocol between agents and their behaviors face to other negotiator acts. Such an approach provides us with a considerable flexibility since it will be possible to adapt negotiation mechanisms to take into account the negotiation context (topic of negotiation, agents roles,...). In such a way, several negotiation modes can be supported within a single CSCW environment. Finally, these interactions between agents can occur either in a synchronous or an asynchronous manner.

3 Axiom based negotiation model

We place ourselves within the framework of a distributed system composed of autonomous agents. An agent can be active (it reacts automatically or semi-automatically when it receives messages from the other agents) or passive (it acts under the control of a user who executes methods on the agent). Thus, the negotiation can be seen in the following way: *"An agent requires something from a second agent, and these two agents dialogue to find the best possible answer"*. The objective of our work is to build a negotiation model which is independent of any particular application field. It means defining **generic mechanisms for negotiation** that one can "instantiate" to negotiate the access rights to a particular service, or to define the cooperation rules to be respected when two agents share a resource, or to any situation requiring a negotiation process.

3.1 Overview

From the negotiation point of view, the two implied agents play different roles: *client* and *server*. The client is the agent having a problem to solve. For this purpose, it carries out a *request* to one of its partners (called server) to find a *solution* for its problem. It is the client which initiates the negotiation with the server. The request is the description of the problem that the client wants to solve. According to the application field, the problem may concern the use of a service, the sharing of a resource, the selection of a resource among those available,... The solution describes the alternative proposed by the server to satisfy the client's request. Depending on the application field, the solution may designate various concepts: access rights for the use of a service, cooperation rules to control the sharing of a resource, designation of a resource according to negotiated selection criterion,... A solution corresponds to a possible agreement between both agents. As we can note, the terms client and server only indicate roles played by the various agents during a given negotiation, and more particularly at the time of their connection. We are in fact in a peer-to-peer organization, i.e. an agent will be at the same time client and server according to whether it sends a request to an agent or it answers the request of one of its partners (i.e. it proposes a solution).

We can split the process of bilateral negotiation into three stages. First of all, the client establishes a connection with the server and announces its request. It is the **solicit** phase. Then the **negotiation** phase itself is held: the client and the server exchange messages to build the set of solutions acceptable by both the agents. Finally, the client chooses one solution among those resulting from the negotiation phase and informs the server. It is the **evaluate** phase. Another goal of this phase is to ensure that the client chooses at most one solution among those negotiated. The server can then performs actions corresponding to the selected solution (allocation of requested resource, allowing accesses to reach a service or to share data,...).

Our work focuses on the negotiation phase formalization. For that purpose, we chose to tackle the negotiation from three points of view for: the information exchanged between the agents to negotiate (the **language**), the way this information is exchanged (the **protocol**), and the "internal" behavior of an agent (the **tactics**). In other words, we distinguish the language in which are represented the decisions taken by the agents, the protocol allowing the agents to communicate their decisions, and the way in which an agent makes its decisions (own objectives, constraints to be checked, semi-automatic reactions to the decisions of the partner,...). More than a separation of the problems involved in each one of these three facets of the negotiation, this approach allows also a greater flexibility than traditional systems dedicated to one kind of problems (systems based on hard-coded negotiation protocols). Following our approach, one may combine various languages, protocols and tactics within a same community of agents, or even within a same agent if it simultaneously carries out several negotiations with several partners.

3.2   Using speech-acts to negotiate

As we already explained, we do not want to produce yet another proprietary system. On the contrary, our aim is to define a framework which can be parameterized to support various forms of negotiation. To achieve this goal, we chose to use a transactional approach based on speech acts: a negotiation is seen as being a transaction having a beginning (*solicit*), an end (*confirm* or *kill*), and having to respect certain criteria. We journalize (or log) some of events (in particular speech acts events via the invocation of *assert[speech_act]* operations) on the level of each agent (concept of local history), then we define properties which have to be checked on these histories (concept of correctness criterion). Some of these properties are dedicated to the coordination of the events between two agents (negotiation protocol), whereas some others relate to the control of the decisions taken by an agent (tactics implemented by this agent).

One should note that within this framework each agent has its own local history in which it only journalizes the events relating to itself, namely its own operations like its interactions with the other agents of the system. Once the properties are defined, each agent will be able to locally evaluate them according to its own history. Such an axiom based approach where axioms are locally checked by each agent according to a partial view of the system has several advantages:

- **Correctness**: The control of the negotiation process is based on the definition of properties on allowed sequences of decisions taken by the agents (correctness criterion) and not on predefined scenarios as with states/transitions diagrams. Axioms are viewed as pre-conditions on events invoked by agents.
- **Genericity**: The proposed formalism for defining these negotiation mechanisms is independent of any particular application field.
- **Distribution**: Each agent itself controls the "correct" executions of the negotiation process according to the information journalized (logged) in its local history (peer-to-peer organization between autonomous agents).
- **Scalability**: One can add new axioms without any risk of combinatory explosion as with the integration of numerous states/transitions diagrams.
- **Heterogeneity**: Within a single system, all the agents are not forced to negotiate according to a single model. Moreover, one agent can simultaneously lead in parallel several negotiations according to different models.

The originality of our approach is that controls made by the protocol and the tactics on the decision sequences are not founded on predefined negotiation scenarios (cf. state/transitions diagrams) but on the definition and the checking of invariants characterizing the decision sequences regarded as "correct". Using again the transactional systems vocabulary, one may say that we use negotiation correctness criteria. In order to illustrate our model, we will give two examples: the first one represents a negotiation protocol, the second one a negotiation tactic. Although these two examples were formally specified, we will only give a broad view of them, the objective of this article being the presentation of our approach rather than a formal and exhaustive definition of the operations and axioms of the model itself.

A Negotiation protocol sample The objective of a negotiation protocol is to control the interleaving of the *assert* operations invoked by both agents. That can be seen as a problem of access concurrency on the communication channel or as a problem of speech rights management: the rules controlling decision sequences, the possible decisions according to the context (current history), the actions to be undertaken according to the decisions taken by the partner,... do not relate to the negotiation protocol but to the negotiation tactics.

One example of negotiation protocol between two agents is the **turn-taking**. This one ensures that an agent will be able to make a decision, i.e. to invoke an *assert[speech_act]* operation, if and only if it has previously obtained the right to speak (*getTurn* event). Thus, in addition to the various *assert* operations invoked by it or by its negotiating partner, an agent will also journalize other events such as *getTurn* in his local history. The main axiom of the turn-taking protocol can then be schematized by the following invariant on the local history of each of both agents: *"an agent A can make a decision (assert$_A$[speech_act]) if and only if it acquired the right to speak (getTurn$_A$ appears in its local history) and if no other agent B ≠ A acquired this right since then (i.e. no getTurn$_B$ event was journalized since the last getTurn$_A$ event)"*. If the local history of agent A is denoted by H_A and if the relation of precedence between the events is denoted by →, this axiom can be written:

$$(assert_A[speech\_act] \in H_A) \Rightarrow$$
$$\begin{cases} getTurn_A \in H_A \\ \wedge \quad \forall B \neq A \quad \not\exists\, getTurn_B \in H_A \\ \qquad\qquad\qquad such\ that \quad LastOcc(getTurn_A) \to getTurn_B \end{cases}$$

A Tactical sample The concept of negotiation is not limited to agent communication aspects (language and protocol) nor to a single problem solving. It is also necessary to formalize the "internal" behavior of an agent, either from the point of view of the strategy adopted to negotiate with a partner (reactions, concessions, decision changes, ...) or from the point of view of the policy implemented to coordinate several negotiations. The objective of a negotiation tactical is to define the way an agent will make its decisions and/or will choose the solutions (*assert, reserve, confirm, kill,* ... operations) in terms of properties applied to its local history. Such a tactical enables us to describe:

– The **contextual behavior** of the agent, i.e. the decisions which can be taken relatively to the decisions which were previously taken by the various actors of the negotiation (journalized in its local history).

– The **reactive behavior** of the agent, i.e. the decisions which must be taken in reaction to the decisions taken by the partners.

– The **coordination** of the various negotiations carried out by an agent: when an agent is negotiating with several partners, these negotiations are not independent and the negotiated solutions are constrained one by the others (see an example in [23]).

– The **objective** of the agent, i.e. the constraints on its decisions: for example, if we use a utility/interest/cost/... function, a rule can be to always improve a certain coefficient in comparison to the preceding decisions aiming to ensure the convergence of the negotiation (cf. Operational Research, IAD).

A negotiation tactical can thus be seen as a set of behavior rules controlling the sequence of the operations invoked by an agent. To express these rules as axioms, the only available information is the events journalized in the local history of this agent.

One example of negotiation tactical is the **atomic negotiation**. A client agent takes part simultaneously in several negotiations with the constraint that either all the negotiations lead to the implementation of a solution, or no action is undertaken. This behavior is formalized by the both following axioms in which

RS (*RequestSet*) denotes the set of atomic negotiation requests. The first one indicates that an atomic negotiation solicited by an agent A is in fact made up of several elementary negotiations with agents $B_1, \ldots, B_n$.

$$(solicit\_atomic_A[RS] \in H_A) \Rightarrow \forall\, req_{B_i} \in RS \quad (solicit_A[req_{B_i}] \in H_A)$$

The second axiom affirms that if the agent A has confirmed a solution for one of the requests (with a agent B_i), then it must have also confirmed a solution for each other request (with agents B_j).

$$(solicit\_atomic_A[RS] \in H_A) \Rightarrow \forall\, req_{B_i} \in RS$$
$$(confirm_A[req_{B_i}] \in H_A) \Rightarrow (\forall\, req'_{B_j} \in RS \quad (confirm_A[req'_{B_j}] \in H_A))$$

This tactical corresponds to some extent to the two phases locking mechanism used in traditional transactional systems: a transaction requiring the use of several resources must first of all acquire a lock on each resource (first phase) before being able to use these resources (second phase). If, during the first phase, one of the resources cannot be locked, then all the already acquired locks are freed and the transaction is postponed and started again later on.

3.3   Expressiveness of our model

We think however that the negotiation between agents is not limited to the definition of a language, a protocol and tactics. In order to be able to support the various forms of negotiation, other concepts must be associated with these basic mechanisms. One example is the concept of **alternative branches** which represents the fact that both negotiator agents explore several parallel ways to find (different) solutions for the same problem. Another example is the concept of **delegation** which allows a server agent to bypass the control to a second server agent to continue the negotiation with a client agent. From this point of view, the fact that we check axioms on the local histories of each agent allows a greater flexibility than the classical approaches based on predefined explicit workflows. To integrate such new functionalities into our model we only need to define the new necessary events as well as the axioms controlling their use. If needed, it will be necessary to analyze the interactions of these new axioms with the existing ones in order to be sure that the coherence of the set of rules is preserved (for instance, we have to avoid any contradiction between axioms).

Alternative branches During negotiation, it may happen that it is no more possible to define any general solution to the whole problem. It is then necessary to make assumptions before being able to continue. These assumptions permit then to explore various alternatives, i.e. to continue the negotiation in parallel towards several different directions. Let us take an example in which an agent wants to access to the source code of a program developed by another agent. During the negotiation, the server agent proposes two choices to the client agent: the currently available public version, as well as a new version still under development, but access of which is subjected to the signature of Non-Disclosure Agreement. Before choosing, the client wishes to study both alternatives in parallel in order to evaluate benefits and drawbacks for each choice. If it decides to use the public version, it knows that it will have to migrate towards the new version as soon as available. On the contrary, if it chooses the new version under development, isn't the signature of the NDA likely to disturb its relations with other partners? Concerning the creation of a new branch of negotiation, we chose to represent this event by a particular decision, i.e. by a specific speech act which will appear in an *assert* operation. In this manner, it will be automatically journalized in the local history of the two negotiating agents.

Even if both agents can negotiate by simultaneously exploring several alternatives, one and only one solution can be finally chosen by the client. The controls carried out during the evaluation phase of a solution prohibit selection of multiple solutions on a given server for a same request, even if these solutions arise from different branches of negotiation.

Delegation Another classical concept in negotiation is the delegation. For an unexpected reason, the server cannot (or does not want any more) continue the negotiation with the client and decides to give the control to another server. This may concern a particular branch or all the branches of the negotiation. The delegation holds in two phases: the initial server must first of all stop its negotiation (or negotiation branch) in progress, then the client negotiates with the new server. However, it is not simply a *kill* operation followed by a *solicit* operation starting a new negotiation from zero. We consider this change of interlocutor as a "normal" decision in the negotiation process (*delegate* speech act).

3.4   Synthesis

The presented negotiation model allows to coordinate negotiations between agents, this coordination being based on invariants to be respected by negotiation histories. This coordination is definitively not constrained by a completely predefined scenario. This approach provides more freedom to agents: the model does not impose to take a decision, or to forbid a decision. It simply controls that the freely taken decisions are coherent. Nevertheless, helping agents in their decision making process is possible through the use of a negotiation tactical. Such a negotiation tactical may ensure convergence of negotiation process, or may forbid to cancel previously taken decisions,...

The following section presents implantation of this negotiation model on top of *DisCOO*, our CSCW environment. *DisCOO* kernel's aim is to coordinate exchanges of documents between several users. This coordination ensures that these exchanges respect certain cooperation schemas. Negotiation mechanisms have been added to assist users to resolve conflicts when sharing documents, or to simply assist them in the choice of the cooperation schema they agree to respect for sharing a specific document.

4   Implementation

We started this work on negotiation after the development of *DisCOO* [1, 24], our CSCW environment that allows geographically distributed agents (activities, driven by human operators) to cooperate by exchanging resources (mainly documents). Each agent having its own copy of the shared resources, the cooperation between agents is carried out through imports and exports of resources. When two agents connect together to share a resource, they must initially sign a contract indicating the cooperation mode that they chose ("cooperative-write" [6], "client/server" [7], and "writer/reviewer" [8]). Thus, it is indispensable to allow the agents to negotiate this cooperation mode according to their respective constraints. In addition, it can be useful to renegotiate a cooperation mode in runtime to solve a conflict between two modes or to soften the relations between two agents. Finally, these same negotiation mechanisms can be also used to assist the agents when they merge two versions of a same resource, typically in the final phase of a cooperative-write relation.

This implementation within *DisCOO* enabled us to validate the basic concepts of our model, namely the negotiation language and the negotiation protocol, about an example: the negotiation of the cooperation schema to be used for the sharing of a document. While the decision making lies with human operators supported by artificial agents, various informations are available in the local histories of each agent to provide more assistance, control and/or automation of the decision-making process. This will constitute the second stage of the implementation of our model within *DisCOO* via the definition and the implementation of negotiation tactics.

5   Conclusion

In this paper, we presented a brief description of the state of the art in negotiation systems. An analysis of current negotiation systems or approaches lead us to conclude that current systems/approaches are inflexible, lack any genericity across application field, and do not adequately answer to negotiation needs in Computer Supported Collaborative Work. This misfit between current solutions and negotiation needs in CSCW leads us to propose an original solution for a generic negotiation model for CSCW. This model focuses on formalizing the negotiation from three point of views: the language (negotiation information), the protocol (the way negotiation information is exchanged) and the tactics (the way a negotiator takes its decisions). From a modeling point of view, our approach provides an interesting alternative to current negotiation approaches and allows

---

6. Cooperative Write: two agents modify concurrently the same resource; both must reach a consensus on the final value of this resource.
7. Client/Server: an agent modifies a resource and another agent recovers, progressively, the different produced versions; this cooperation mode ensures that the customer will take well into account (at least) the last version produced by the server.
8. Writer/Reviewer: an agent A produces a document doc_1 and shared it with an agent B (B is client in a client/server relation with A); agent B uses doc_1 to produce a document doc_2 that it shares with agent A (B is server in a client/server relation with A); this cooperation mode guarantees that doc_1 and doc_2 will be coherent at the end of the process.

a greater flexibility than traditional systems. We formalized our axiom based approach upon a speech-act transactional approach. In our model, each negotiation information is represented as a speech act and a negotiation is seen as being a transaction which must respect certain criteria. Each negotiator agent journalizes (or log) the events relating to its own operations and to its interactions with the other agents. We defined and presented properties that have to be checked on these histories, some of the former being dedicated to control the negotiation protocol, whereas others are dedicated to control the taken decisions. The fact that we use axioms to model negotiation properties allows us to enrich our negotiation model with new axioms aiming to tackle classical negotiation need such alternatives or delegation. This enrichment can be pursued as long as the coherence of the set of rules is preserved and may be an interesting extension of our work. We validated our approach through the implementation on top of our CSCW environment (*DisCOO*) of an example using our model's basic concepts, namely the negotiation language and the negotiation protocol. Being mainly interested by human actors, we neglected the negotiation tactics assuming that the human actors will tackle this aspect without any help. Nevertheless, tackling this part of our negotiation model and implementing it will allow us, in the near future, to program reactive agents which can assist negotiators as long a s their tactics have been formally described. Another research direction in which we intend to use our results in negotiation modeling is dynamic federation of cooperative workflows. To allow cooperation and henceforth coordination of different workflows, various negotiation must hold between activities of different workflows (eg: rendezvous, contracts, results needed, exchanged services).

References

1. M. Munier, K. Benali, and C. Godart. A transactional Approach for Cross-Organizational Cooperation. In *GlobeComm99 (Enterprise Applications and Services Symposium)*, Rio de Janeiro, Brazil, december 1999.
2. M. Munier and C. Godart. Cooperation services for widely distributed applications. In *Tenth International Conference on Software Engineering and Knowledge Engineering (SEKE'98)*, San Francisco Bay, USA, 1998.
3. M. Stefik, G. Foster, D. G. Borrow, K. Kahn, S. Lanning, and L. Suchman. Beyond the chalkboard: Computer Support for Collaboration and Problem Solving in Meetings. *Communications of the ACM*, 30(1), January 1987.
4. L. L. Putnam and M. S. Poole. Conflict and negotiation. *In Handbook of Organizational Communication: An Interdisciplinary Perspective*, pages 344–369, 1987.
5. T. R. Madanmohan, G. E. Kersten, S. J. Noronha, M. Kersten, and D. Cray. *Decision Support Systems for Sustainable Development. A Resource Book of Methods and Applications*, chapter Learning Negotiations with Web-based Systems. Kluwer Academic, 1999.
6. S. Kraus, K. Sycara, and A. Evenchik. Reaching agreements through argumentation: a logical model and implementation. *Artificial Intelligence*, 104(1–2):1–69, 1998.
7. S. Parsons, C. Sierra, and N. R. Jennings. Agents that reason and negotiate by arguing. *Journal of Logic and Computation*, 8(3):261–292, 1998.

8. R. G. Smith. The contract net protocol: High level communication and control in a distributed problem solver. *IEEE Transactions on Computing*, 29(12):1104–1113, 1980.

9. C. C. Koo. A commitment–based communication model for distributed office environments. In *proc. of Conference on Office Information System*, pages 291–298, New York, 1988. ACM Press.

10. J. L. Austin. *How to Do Things with Words*. Oxford University Press, Oxford, England, 1962.

11. J. R. Searle. *Speech Acts: An Essay in the Philosophy of Language*. Cambridge University Press, New York, 1969.

12. J.R. Searle. A taxonomy of illocutionary acts. In K. Gunderson, editor, *Language, Mind and Knowldge*, volume 7 of *Minnesota Studies in the Philosophy of Science*, pages 344–369, Minneapolis, 1975. University of Minnesota Press.

13. M. P. Singh. A Semantics for Speech Acts. *Annals of Mathematics and Artificial Intelligence*, 8(I–II):47–71, 1993.

14. R. Medina-Mora, T. Winograd, R. Flores, and F. Flores. The actionworkflow approach to workflow management technology. In *Computer-Supported Coooperative Work, Toronto*, November 1992.

15. P. Denning. Work is a closed loop process. In *American Scientist*, volume 80, pages 314–317, July-August 1992.

16. T. W. Malone, K. R. Grant K. Lai, R. Rao, and D. A. Rosenblitt. The Information Lens:An Intelligent System for Information Sharing and Coordination. *Technical Support for Work Group Collaboration*, pages 65–88, 1989.

17. M. K. Chang and C. C. Woo. A speech-Act-Based Negotiation Protocol: Design, Implementation and Test Use. *ACM Transactions on Information Systems*, 12(4):360–382, October 1994.

18. M. T. Jelassi and A. Forroughi. Negotiation support systems: An overview of design issues and existing sorftware. *Decison Support Systems*, 5:167–181, 1989.

19. E. Bellucci and J. Zeleznikow. A comparative study of negotiation decision support systems. In *Proceedings of the 31st Hawaii International Conference on System Sciences (HICSS'98)*. the IEEE Computer Society. Copyright (c) 1998 Institute of Electrical and Electronics Engineers, Inc., 1998.

20. F. Ackerman and C. Eden. Issues in computer and non-computer supported GD-SSs. *Decision Support Systems*, 12(336):381–390, 1994.

21. I. Benbasat, F.J. Lim, and V.S. Rao. A framework for communication support in group work with special reference to negotiation systems. *Group Decision and Negotiation*, 4(371):135–158, 1995.

22. T. X. Bui and M. F. Shakun. Negotiation pocesses, evolutionary systems design, and NEGOTIATOR. *Group Decision and Negotiation*, 5(417):339–353, 1996.

23. J-M. Andreoli, D. Pagani, F. Pacull, and R. Pareschi. Multiparty negotiation for dynamic distributed object services. *Journal of Science of Computer Programming*, 31:179–203, 1998.

24. K. Benali, M. Munier, and C. Godart. Cooperation models in co-design. In *International Conference on Agile Manufacturing*, Minneapolis, USA, June 1998.

The Organizational Memory Information System PRINCE

Arndt Kuhlmann, Wolfgang Deiters

Fraunhofer Institute for Software- and Systems Engineering
P.O. Box 520 130, 44207 Dortmund, Germany
{deiters|kuhlmann}@do.isst.fhg.de

Abstract. Business process management has become an area of increasing interest in the last years. However, the acquisition of the information about business processes itself becomes a complex task since this information is spread over different people, quite often is inconsistent, and often is only available implicitly in the minds of the people involved in the processes. Within this paper we describe our work on a cooperative information system PRINCE serving as an organizational memory information system. The goal of the system is to support the systematic management of business processes capturing process information, structuring it, and preserving it in a way to be used during the different phases of a process management lifecycle. The system is able to manage information of different multimedia object types (such as text, audio and video documents). It can be used by different users giving dedicated access rights (both for filling and retrieving information). Since the information base is cooperatively filled by different users several mechanisms like consistency/ inconsistency indication, information abonements etc. have been introduced for managing the huge amount of information.

1 Introduction

Business process management has become an area of increasing interest in the last years [2]. This is partly because processes are seen more and more as the core of the business. In a business world where companies have to adapt to changing markets and growing competitors the organization and the IT support of the business processes heavily decides on the companies' success. Furthermore, new challenges like globalization of economics enforces companies to build more and more partnerships, resulting in even more complex business processes quite often spanning more than one organization.

This situation shows the importance of well designed and optimized business processes and its IT support. Workflow management is seen as one core technology for providing adequate IT support for business processes. One function of workflow management is to define the business processes in so called business process models [12]. These models are the basis for a guidance of the processes, i.e. the models are enacted, people are informed about the activities they have to perform, they are provided with appropriate tool support etc.

O. Etzion and P. Scheuermann (Eds.): CoopIS 2000, LNCS 1901, pp. 236–250, 2000.

However, for building up the process models first of all the knowledge about the processes is spread over various documents or is available in the heads of different people. For complex processes that - as discussed above - even span more than one organization or organizational unit it means that the information about the processes is distributed among different people residing at different places. Additionally, each person has its individual viewpoint onto a business process: managers responsible for organizing the processes view processes different from people who perform the actual process tasks. Thus, the capturing of process information itself is a complex task in an organization that has to be managed properly. Furthermore, taking into account a personal fluctuation where people either change teams or even leave the organization (e.g. due to retirement) the task of capturing the peoples' knowledge about the processes and the organization becomes extremely important. In the following we call this knowledge available in the peoples mind the *organizational memory* of an organization.

This organizational memory is the information source to be used when defining business processes in the resp. models. However, it is not the goal to see business process models as the externalization of an organizational memory. Business process models rather encompass the necessary information in order to drive the process, e.g. the definition of activities, activity schedules and responsibilities for activities. However, in knowledge intensive processes [6] there is many other information (e.g. context information, experiences, cross process information) that is available and used during the processes. Thus, the use of an organization's organizational memory is twofold, it provides the information source for building up process models and it serves as a background information pool to be exploited when performing the different activities during a business process.

Since the knowledge that builds up the organizational memory usually becomes quite complex and the knowledge is spread over many different minds of people it becomes interesting to build up IT support for organizational memories. In the following we call this IT support *organizational memory information system* (OMIS for short)[1]. In this paper we will describe our work on a concrete OMIS that we have build. Starting from a process management approach [7] and a number of experiences that we have gained from concrete process management projects [8] we have studied the problem of capturing information about business processes for mapping it onto process models and for making it available to different people during business processes. Based on these experiences we have designed the PRINCE system (process information center).

The remainder of this paper is structured as followed: In the following section we are going to sketch a process management lifecycle and discuss the role of an organizational memory information system within that lifecycle. In section 3 we collect different requirements onto an organizational memory information system that we have detected. For supporting these requirements we have designed and built the

---

[1] In this context we understand an OMIS as "an enterprise-internal application independent information and assistant system. It stores large amounts of data, information and knowledge from different sources of an enterprise. These are represented in various forms, such as databases, documents and formal knowledge-bases. The OMIS will be permanently extended to keep it up-to-date and can accessed enterprise-wide through an appropriate network infrastructure" [13].

system PRINCE (cf. section 4). Finally section 5 summarizes our work and concludes this paper.

2   The Role of an OMIS for Process Management

For developing process based IT applications based on the process management technology different activities have to be performed. The sequence of these activities is also called process model lifecycle.

Continuous engineering of systems usually takes place in running organizations. Thus, in a first activity the information about the processes has to be gathered. Within an *information acquisition* the information about the "as is processes" is collected. This can take place by different means: document analysis (e.g. using a ISO9000 documentation if it exists in the organization), structured interviews, workshops, etc.. This information that has been collected is, then, fixed in the process model in an activity that is called *process modelling*. This process model serves as a basis for documentation and discussion about the processes. Furthermore, in a *process model analysis* activity the model can be evaluated in order to detect deficiencies of the process. A typical analysis technique is the one of simulating the process. Results of the analysis usually are suggestions for improvement that result in changes of the process model. Iterating the modelling and analysis activities usually leads to "should be process models" which are an improvement of the "as is models". Once a "should be model" has been decided upon a *process model enaction* can take place. This takes place on the basis of a workflow application where the process is driven by the workflow engine, and different services are called supporting the different process activities. According to the process state the different persons involved in the process get informed about the activities they have to perform, and they are provided with the necessary process objects and services to work upon the objects according to the activity definitions. One further important activity is the *process evaluation* in order to detect further possible process improvements during the process or a posteriori, i.e. after the process has terminated.

Fig. 1 shows the control structure between the different activities during the process management lifecycle. Additionally an information flow view could be taken where a huge amount of information becomes available during the process acquisition phase when discussing with the various people about the processes. The information that is obtained comes in different types, usually in unstructured forms like (questionnaire reports, workshop protocols, personal notes or even audio records of interviews). Parts of this information is exploited in the process modelling phase. Thus, the result of this phase is a partial formalization of that information. During process model analysis additional information is obtained (e.g. analysis results such as critical paths). Based on this the process model is used by the workflow application and additional information is used by the workflow participants during process enaction. If an organizational memory information system is used as the information pool for all the various types of information it becomes a central repository that is used throughout the whole process management lifecycle (cf. Fig. 1).[2]

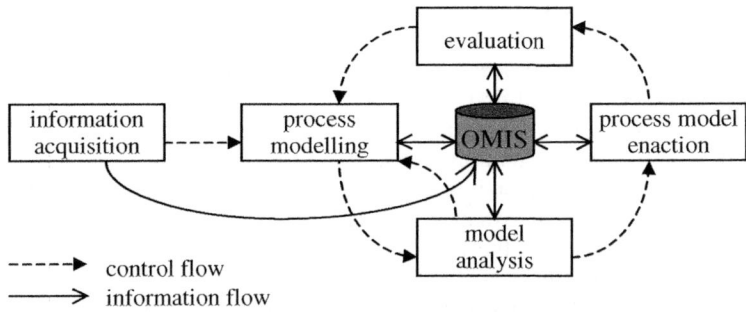

control flow

information flow

Fig. 1. The role of an OMIS in the process management lifecycle.

The information that is gained within the different phases of the process management lifecycle either contains facts about the process (e.g. descriptions of activities, tools to be used during activities, ..) or information about experts for certain process steps (in state x person y knows how to proceed). We call the former kind of knowledge codeable knowledge since it can be brought as information[3] into an organizational memory information system, the latter kind of knowledge we call personalized knowledge, knowledge that itself cannot be brought into an OMIS (only the information concerning the knowledge carrier, i.e. the expert person, should be stored into the system) (cf. [9]). We are convinced that an OMIS serving as a cooperative information system in the sense that has been sketched here has to encompass functionality supporting both codeable as well as personalized knowledge. However, for the rest of the paper we mainly concentrate on the codification issue, further thoughts on the personalization approach can be found in [15].

3   Requirements onto an Organizational Memory Information System Supporting the Management of Business Processes

As we have mentioned above one important phase during the systematic management of business processes is the information acquisition. Usually it is the goal of a process

---

[2] We do not give a complete list of requirements for OMIS here (cf. [13] or [17] for a discussion of general OMIS requirements.) Other work on concrete OMIS developments can be found e.g. in [1], [4], [14], [16] or [19].

[3] We use the terms knowledge and information in the following way. Knowledge in a narrower sense only exists in the mind of humans. We also use knowledge as the more general concept for implicit knowledge and documented knowledge (which is as a matter of fact information). On a software system level we use the term information. Knowledge can be represented by information which is stored, retrieved, presented etc. by information systems.

management project to improve and to support processes that are already being carried out in practice. Hence, only in rare cases processes are completely to be defined from anew. In most cases these processes have been carried out implicitly so far, i.e. the persons involved in the process knew their job (that means, that they have in mind what to do) but no (complete) explicit description of the processes existed so far. Thus, for building process models all relevant information concerning the processes has to be acquired first.

The acquisition of information about business processes is a complex process itself due to the fact that information about the processes is not concentrated in one information source but rather is distributed among different information sources of different types. Among information sources are written material e.g. handbooks of tools that are being used in the process so far, partial process descriptions that have been made so far (e.g. rule sets for handling certain activities, mission statements for certain processes, quality management information (e.g. ISO 9000), etc.). However most information about processes are available in the minds of the persons performing the processes that are to be supported. Different gathering techniques have to be adopted in order to capture this information. Among this techniques are document analysis, observation and inquiry, which means asking people about the information they have about the processes. This can take place by interviews (face to face or using telephone), workshops, questionnaires etc. As a result of applying these information acquisition techniques different documents (questionnaires, protocols, interview traces) exist the content of which has to be structured and put together in the organizational memory information system.

Additionally to the problem of having various sources and different types of information documents as a result of the information acquisition another fact has to be mentioned which makes the collection of information difficult - the process complexity. Industrial processes are quite often very complex, consisting of hundreds of activities, documents, persons involved, and tools that are used by the persons. For those processes the relevant information can not be collected in one step. It becomes necessary to start with an abstract process description identifying the process' scope and to refine the abstract description in a next step. One reason for doing so is that different persons usually have different type of information. Quite often managers know the processes on an abstract level, and know the interrelation of process parts while the persons that work in the process know the process details (e.g. how to perform activities, know why activities are performed in a certain sequence and so on).

Moreover since organizations that are involved in the process quite often are dispersed over different geographical locations it becomes impossible to bring all relevant persons together at one point in time for information acquisition since the relevant persons work at different places. Bringing all persons together would result in workshops the size of which would lead to unproductive work and the resulting information would be too complex and unstructured to be useful. Thus, information acquisition has to be performed in several steps, for example, starting with an initial workshop where the managers are interviewed about the process scope and the abstract process steps, followed by detailed interviews among the process experts, a review workshop after a first information integration, followed by interviews for refining and completing the information set, etc. For this it becomes necessary to collect information, integrate different information sources, to mark information as being relevant or irrelevant and consistent or inconsistent, to delete unnecessary information, etc.

Based on the aspects mentioned so far we point out requirements for the design of the organizational memory information system suitable to support the cooperative management of business process information:

1. According to what we addressed above the organizational memory information system has to be a storage of information objects of different type such as text, audio, video and graphics. The chosen information acquisition techniques result in different information objects such as, for example, hand-written protocols, audio tape traces of interviews or videos from process observation. This information has to be stored in the OMIS, it has to be possible to structure this information, to indicate relevant information areas in the objects, and to associate the information with appropriate meta information (e.g. date of gathering, author, etc.).

2. In most cases business processes are spread over different departments of an organization. Many people involved in a process use different tools and documents to edit or create the mass of documents during the many activities of the process. As mentioned above people do have different detailed information so that there is the need to structure process entities in an appropriate way.

3. Due to the process' complexity and the resulting huge amount of information it must be possible to associate information objects with each other for relating information objects that give information about the same process entities (e.g. a workshop protocol where a process activity is noted with an interview giving details about that activity). These associations have to be attributed in order to give certain semantics to the associations between the information objects that are linked to each others via these associations. By that it can, for example, be expressed that an object is needed for an activity (if an association is made between an information describing an activity and another one describing a document), that an activity is predecessor of another one (two information objects each one describing an activity), consistency or inconsistency of information can be denoted (two information objects describing the same entity), etc.

4. To serve the needs of different types of users the OMIS needs to support different kind of information supply. We distinguish between passive and active information supply, depending on whether the user selects the information (passive supply means the OMIS is passive) or whether the OMIS selects information and provides it to the user (active supply). In cases of a passive information supply a query interface as well as a navigation interface for information retrieval is needed. With the query interface the user can retrieve information by issuing queries like "give me all information about all process activities in a certain process step". The navigation interface allows to browse through the OMIS visiting information objects along the associations between the objects. In case of an active information provision the user gets information upon the occurrence of certain events he can specify. For example, if he specifies that he wants to be informed if new (or inconsistent) information concerning a certain process entity is put into the OMIS the system monitors this event and notifies the user upon its occurrence.

5. The OMIS has to be fit with a dedicated access right system in order to achieve an acceptance of the OMIS among the participants of the organisation. This requirement is based on the fact that for example in some cases process participants will not give all detail information how they behave in the process depending on

whether their superior or certain collegues get this information either. Thus, for each information object it must be possible to specify which persons are allowed to view or to change the information.

4   The Process Information Center PRINCE

The system PRINCE (PRocess INformation CEnter) is an OMIS for business process information. Based on the major requirements for such systems which we discussed above it has been designed and implemented. The system allows to store the results of the various methods of gathering process information namely different kind of multimedia objects and can be used to collect, structure and consolidate all information about business processes. It follows principles demanded in [5] namely to support hypertext, groupware and rethorical methods. Furthermore, it allows to manage different kinds of objects that are recognized as being important, e.g. forms [10] and it allows to build up hypertext structures among the information documents (cf. [3], [11]).

4.1   Structuring Process Information within PRINCE

Since information objects[4] usually give information about different process entities it makes it necessary not to store each information document as one coarse granulated object but rather to structure the document in different parts, thus, achieving a more fine grained document structure. For example, an interview protocol usually encompasses information about not only one process entity but rather a lot of different entities (e.g. the set of activities the interviewed person is involved in). This causes the need to focus not only onto the complete information object but rather onto the information about the individual process entities within this document which makes it necessary to divide the document into several parts (that we call information areas in the following).

The definition of information areas depends on the type of the multimedia object (e.g. areas on a photo or a hand-written note, time slots in an audio or video document). So each information document is a collection of information areas. Within each information area only information about one process entity is given (cf. Fig. 2). The information about the different process entities is structured according to the different entity types of the underlying process management approach. In our approach we base upon the entity types activities, documents, roles, tools. Each entity type is called an *information class* (e.g. "document") and a special item of a type is called an *information instance* of an information class (e.g. a concrete process entity "application form" is an information instance of the information class "document"). All instances and classes are structured in an *information tree* as shown in Fig. 2. Managing business process information in this way fulfills the first two requirements

---

[4]   In the following we use the terms information objects and information documents synonymously.

namely to store information of different source types and to support an appropriate structuring of process information in the organizational memory information system.

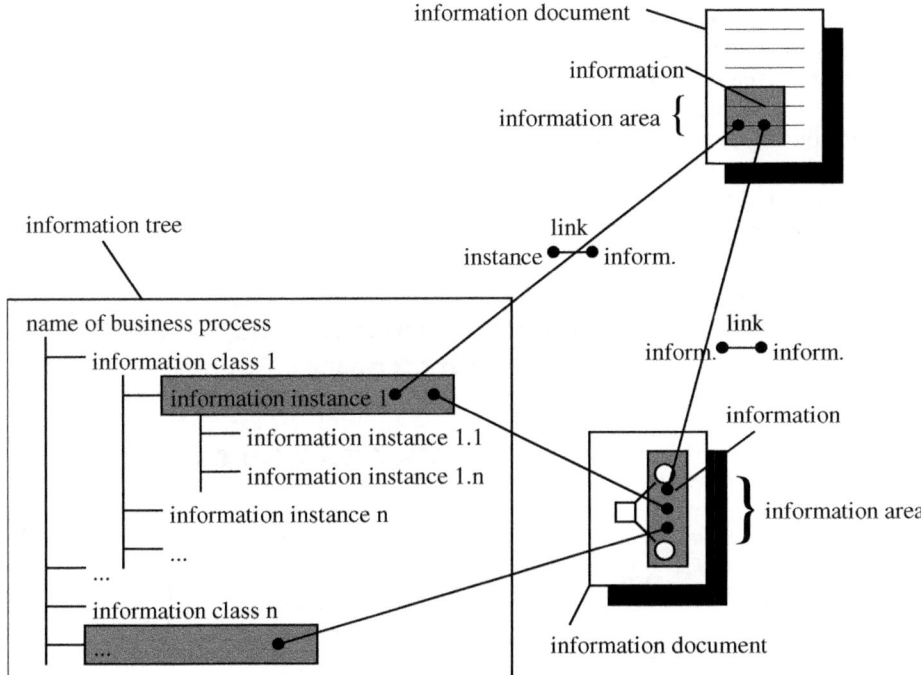

Fig. 2. Context representation of the user terms.

4.2   Filling PRINCE with Process Information

During information acquisition the information tree is build by identifying information instances according to the information within areas of information documents. For example, a generic term within an information area describes a collection of some basic activities which are mentioned in another information document in a more detailed way. In PRINCE the collection term is a father node and the detailed information are the sons (e.g a father node "activity" denotes one of the process entities, sons of this nodes are concrete process activities like "write_letter", "review_letter", etc., then). In this way an information tree is built up with the process name as the father node, the information classes (process entities) as direct sons and the information instances as direct sons of the information classes (see upper left part in Fig. 3).

Each of the information instances is linked to one or more area(s) in one or more document(s). As it has been demanded in requirement 3 this results in a network of linked information which makes it possible to retrieve information successfully just by selecting a special information instance. In addition to this Fig. 2 does not only show links between information areas and process entities but also between couples of information areas. These links are typed as consistent, inconsistent or variants meaning that the two information belonging to the same instance (= process entity) are consistent, inconsistent or variant to each other. Thus, bringing an information document into the organizational memory that encompasses information being inconsistent to the information that is stored already enables to mark the inconsistency so that the inconsistency can be revealed and discussed during the next workshop or interview during process information acquisition.

Fig. 3 illustrates the phase of bringing information into the organizational memory. In this screen dump an information document giving a hand written workshop protocol is shown (part A).

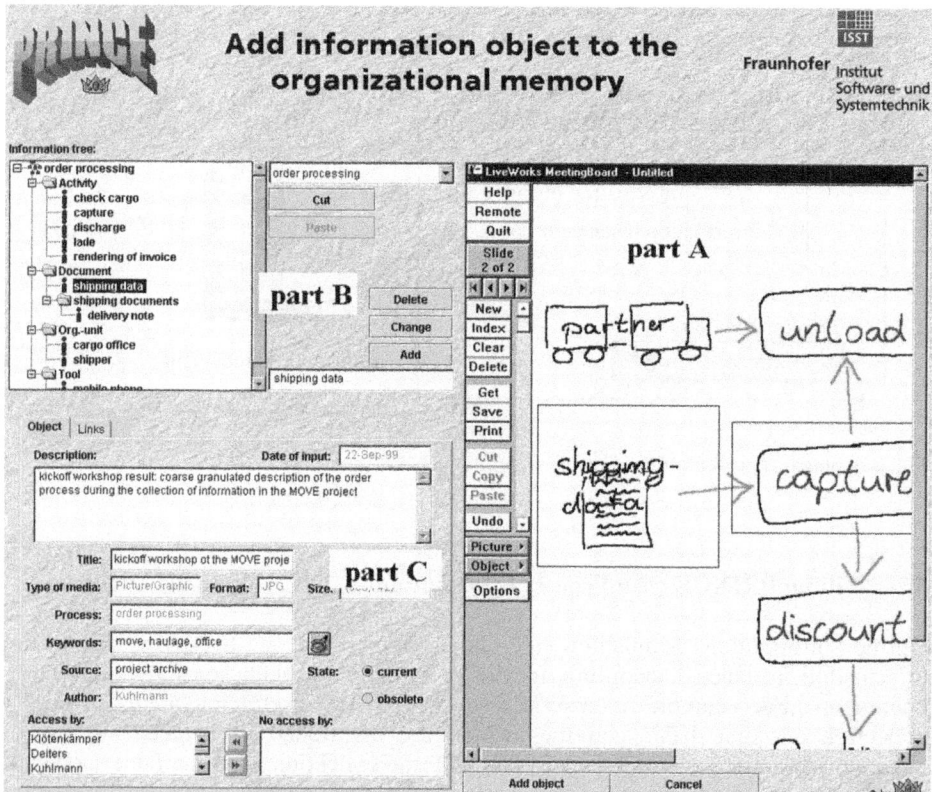

Fig. 3. Bringing information into the organizational memory PRINCE.

Two information areas one for a process document "shipping data" another for a process activity "capture" are defined. For these process entities instances are created (see for example the highlighted entry in part B of the screen dump which gives the information tree for all information instances for which information is available). Part C of the screen dump shows some meta information about the information document.

According to the discussed requirements the meta information is also used to control the access to the information document and the information itself. For each document as well as for each information area users will be named who are allowed or not allowed to access to the document or the specified areas.

4.3   Information Retrieval in PRINCE

PRINCE allows to retrieve information according to the requirements given above. The user can issue queries for obtaining certain information in three different ways:
- Retrieve information by using the information tree and selecting certain tree notes
- Retrieve information by querying certain meta information of links between information areas (e.g. for checking consistency/inconsistency of information within these areas)
- Retrieve information by querying certain meta information of documents

In all cases the user searches for specific information he can address by a query. Additionally, PRINCE provides another way to get information about business processes. The user can navigate through the graph of linked information documents given by the associations between the information areas. In Fig. 4 a screen dump showing how to browse through the information graph is illustrated.

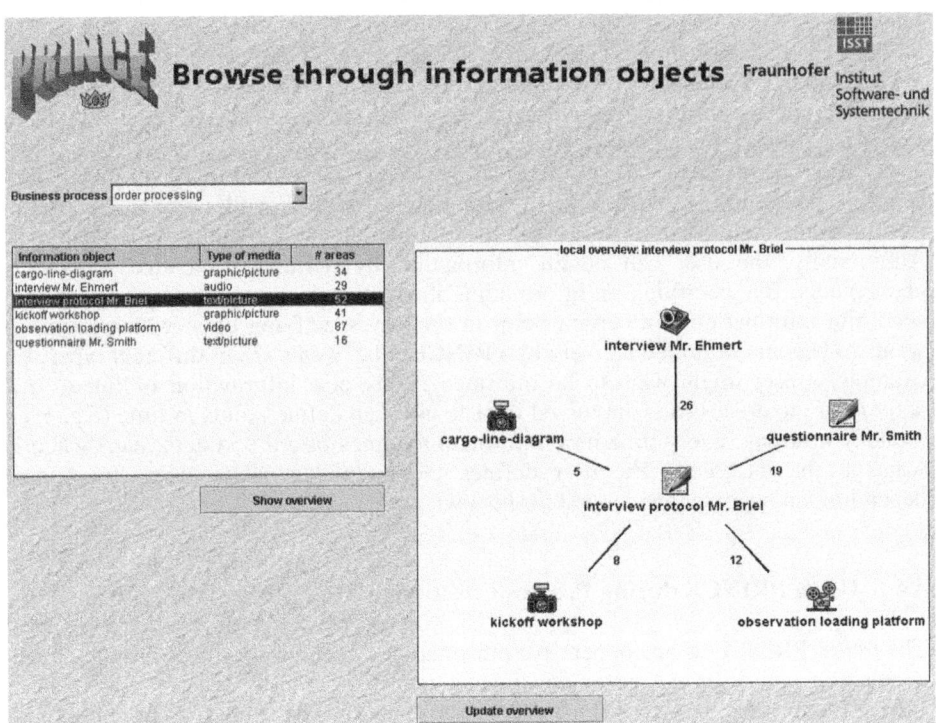

Fig. 4. Browsing through information objects in PRINCE.

By using so called local overview maps the information documents are presented. In normal case for each document exist associations to other documents. Two documents do have some couples of information areas where each area is linked to the same information instance in the information tree. That means the coupled information areas describe the same information instances. In Fig. 4 a central object is shown called "interview_protocol_Mr._Briel" on the right hand side. Around this central document other information documents stored in the system to which the central document is associated with are placed clockwise. The number at each line gives the information, how many couples of information areas exist in the central and the associated information document. The amount of couples decreases clockwise. On the left hand side of the screen dump all information documents encompassing information about a named business process are listed and for each one the number of information areas within the document is shown. This number and the number of the couples between two documents inform the user how many "new" information about the business process he can get, taking a look at an information document the central one is associated with. Thus, if the user knows the content information of the central document he is be able to get the most additional information about the same entities of the business process by selecting the document above or he gets many information about other entities when selecting an information document right to the central document (while he gets only few additional information when selecting a document left to the central one). The user now either can open the central document or he can select one of the associated ones. In this case this object becomes the selected one (i.e. moves to be the centred one) and the five documents with the most associated areas to the new central document will be placed around it. This feature of PRINCE allows the user to search for information without any special kind of query (i.e. the user is not forced to specify what he is looking for).

As mentioned above we distinguish between active and passive information supply. The described methods for information retrieval as well as for navigation on information documents is part of the system's passive information support. Additionally, the user can obtain information by defining so called knowledge abonements. By specifying an information abonement the user directs the system to send him information at a certain point in time by specifying upon which events he wants to become informed actively by PRINCE. The events are of different types. For example, a user might want to be informed if any new information is linked to an activity of the process he is involved in. The user can define points in time (e.g. every monday morning, every time new information comes into the system, etc.) when he wants to be informed. The user defines the knowledge abonements by himself depending on his own interest and for his own use.

4.4   Using PRINCE during Process Enaction

The use of PRINCE as an cooperative information system is not limited to the process acquisition phase during systematic management of business process management. PRINCE can also be used during process enaction. By this a user can request additional information (e.g. context information) from the OMIS when performing a certain activity, working on a certain document, or using a certain tool.

4.5   Access Rights in PRINCE

In PRINCE three user groups are defined. The user who uses the system to inform himself about business processes constitutes the normal (default) user that we call *process participant*. He is able to search for information but not to make any changes on stored information documents or meta information. The latter features are given to dedicated users that we call *process managers* in the following. Process managers are persons who are responsible for obtaining the business information during process acquisition using different techniques (questionnaires, protocols, interview tasks). They are allowed to bring information documents into the organizational memory information system and to identify process relevant information by creating information areas which are linked to process entities in the information tree (cf. Fig. 2). Moreover, they are responsible to keep the pool of information free from inconsistency by discussing detected inconsistencies with the relevant process participants. Users with utmost rights for the organizational memory information system are *administrators*. Additional to the rights of the process managers they have the right to administrate the system by adding, changing or deleting user accounts.

4.6   System Architecture of PRINCE

An organizational memory information system like PRINCE has the major function to store process relevant information and to place the information at the organization's disposal at the different places the information is needed. According to this requirement PRINCE has been implemented as a Web-based application in order to achieve a portable system that can be used at different user locations during the information acquisition phase.

   PRINCE is composed of a set of WWW pages including java applets. It's a frame based screen descriptor with one navigation frame and eleven content frames to bring information documents into PRINCE, to check and ensure information consistency, to edit user profiles etc. (e.g. cf. Fig. 3 or Fig. 4).

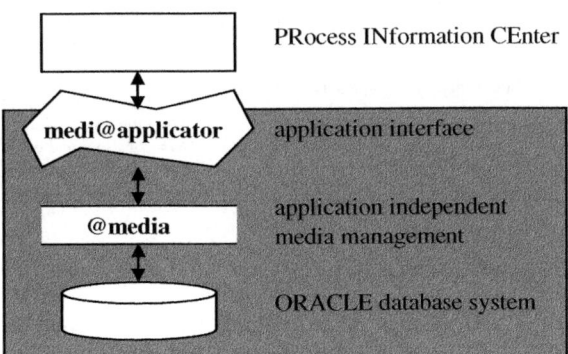

Fig. 5. The information storage architecture.

All process information as well as all meta information of the information documents and links are stored in an underlying ORACLE database system which is being upgraded to handle multimedia objects of different type [18]. PRINCE uses a database layer architecture composed of the database, an application independent media management tool and an application interface as illustrated in Fig. 5.

A more detailed description of the PRINCE's system architecture is shown in the following Fig. 6. As illustrated the database is the central unit. It stores all process information and provides it to the web-pages in pursuance of the query of the applets (A1-A8) within the pages. Furthermore, it receives all information from each applet to save it permanently.

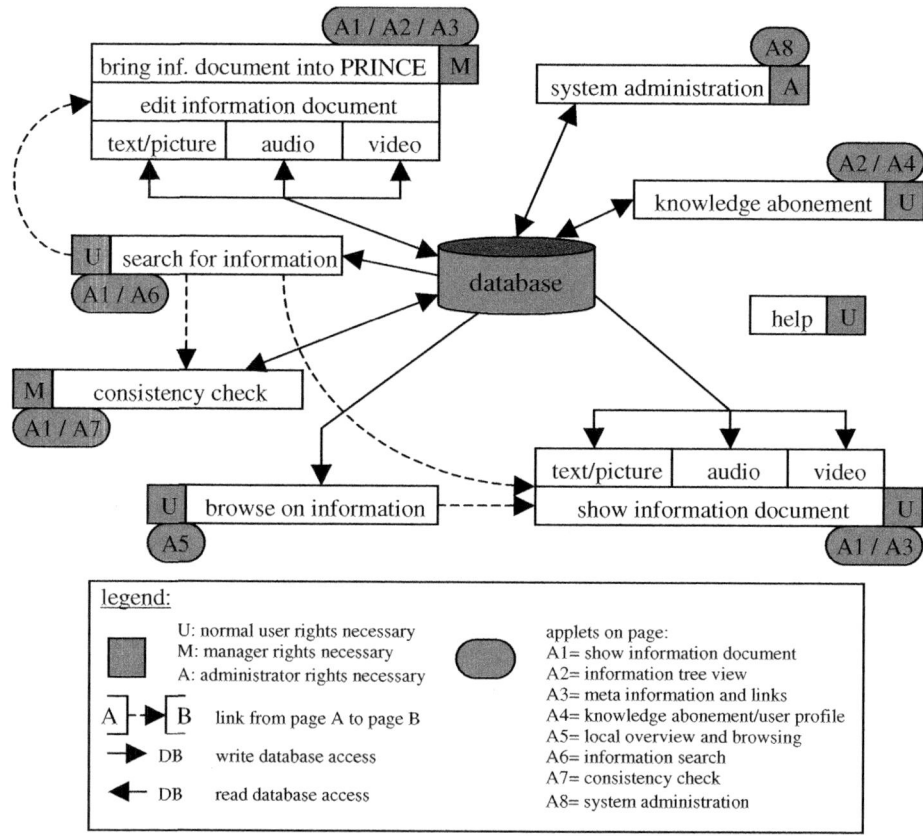

Fig. 6. System architecture of PRINCE.

The direction of the information flow is illustrated by the arrows between database and web-page. With the exception of the page "help" all pages get or save information in the database. On some pages the user can browse directly to another page of PRINCE without using the navigation unit, e.g. the web-page "search for information" allows to call the page "edit information document" as shown by the arrow in the figure. But editing information documents is only possible by users with process manager rights described by the "M" in the small upper right rectangle nearby the web-page symbol "bring inf. document into PRINCE/edit information document". Thus this link can only be used by process managers.

5   Summary

Within this paper we have described the cooperative information system PRINCE serving as an organizational memory information system. The goal of the system is to support the systematic management of business processes capturing process information that is yielded from the various people owning information about the processes, structuring it (such that it can be brought into process models) and preserving it in a way to be used during the different phases of a process management lifecycle. The system is able to manage information of different multimedia object types (such as text, audio and video documents). It can be used by different users giving dedicated access rights (both for filling and retrieving information). The users have several possibilities for information retrieval such as querying information browsing through an information landscape etc. Since the information base is cooperatively filled by different users several mechanisms like consistency/inconsistency indication, information abonements etc. have been introduced for managing the huge information amount.

So far a first version of PRINCE has been built implementing the majority of the OMIS requirements given above. We have applied the system in projects for e.g. modelling processes in the area of transportation logistics. The resulting information base has been the starting point for intensive discussions, reorganization efforts, and a process model definition for a workflow implementation. In that project PRINCE has proven its potential for a common information base streamlining the process of optimizing business processes. Future work on PRINCE will focus on extensions for automatically deriving a first process model skeleton from the structured set of information and on using PRINCE during process enaction phase (i.e. integrating it into a workflow application). Furthermore, we plan to extend PRINCE in order to support personalized knowledge (so far PRINCE captured coded knowledge, cf. section 2).

References

1. Abecker, A.; Bernardi, A.; Sintek, M.: Enterprise Information Infrastructures for Active, Context-Sensitive Knowledge Delivery. Proceedings of ECIS'99 (1999).
2. Aalst, W.v.d.; Desel, J.; Oberweis, A. (Eds.): Business Process Management: Models, Techniques and Empirical Studies, Lecture Notes on Computer Science, Springer, Berlin, Heidelberg, New York (2000).
3. Balasubramanian, V.: Hypermedia: An applications perspective. In: The X Journal, May-June, (1994), pp. 52-58.
4. Blumentahl, R.; Nutt, G. J.: Supporting unstructured workflow activities in the Bramble ICN system. Proceedings of the Conference on Organizational Computing Systems (COOCS'95), Milpitas, CA (1995), pp. 130-137.

5. Conklin, E. J.: Capturing Organizational Memory. In: Baecker, R.M. (Ed); Kaufmann, M.; Mateo, S.: Groupware and Computer-Supported Cooperative Work, California, (1996), pp. 561-565.
6. Deiters, W.; Goesmann, T.; Löffeler, T.: Flexibility in Workflow Management: Dimensions and Solutions, submitted for publication.
7. Deiters, W.; Gruhn, V.: Process management in practice - applying the FUNSOFT net approach to large scale processes, Automated Software Engineering, Vol. 5, Kluwer Academic Publishers, (1998), pp.7-25.
8. Deiters, W.; Gruhn, V.: The FUNSOFT Net Approach To Software Process Management, Int. Journal on Software Engineering and Knowledge Engineering, 4(2), June (1994).
9. Hansen, M. T.; Nohria, N.; Tierney, Th.: What's your strategy for managing knowledge? Harvard Business Review, 77(2), March/April (1999), pp. 106-116.
10. Hagemeyer, J.; Rolles, R.: Erhebung von Prozeßwissen für das Wissensmanagement. (in German) In: IM Information Management & Consulting, Vol. I (1998), pp. 46-50.
11. Isakowitz, T.: Hypermedia, information systems, and organizations: A research agenda. Proceedings of HICSS'93, CA: IEEE Press, (1993).
12. Jablonski, S.; Bussler, C.: Workflow Management, Modelling, Concepts Architecture and Implementation, Internaltional Thomson, London (1996).
13. Kühn, O.; Abecker, A: A Corporate Memory for Knowledge Management in Industrial Practice: Prospects and Challenges. In: Borghoff, U; Pareshi, R. (Eds.): Information Technology for Knowledge Management, Stringer, Berlin (1998), pp. 183-206.
14. van Kaathoven, R.; Jeusfeld, M. A.; Staudt, M.; Reimer, U.: Organizational Memory Supported Workflow Management. In: Scheer, A.-W.; Nüttgens, M. (Eds.): Electronic Business Engineering, 4. Int. Tagung Wirtschaftsinformatik, Physica-Verlag, Heidelberg (1999), pp. 543-563.
15. Lucas, R.; Weber T.: Skill Management: a building block for project management with flexible teams?, to appear: Proceedings of the Fourth International Baltic Workshop on DB and IS (BalticDB&IS'2000), Kluwer Academic Publishers (2000).
16. Maurer, F.; Holz, H.: Process-Oriented Knowledge Management For Learning Software Organizations. Proceedings of the 12th Knowledge Acquisition Workshop (KAW'99), Banff, Canada (1999).
17. Stein, E. W.; Zwass, V.: Actualizing Organizational Memory with Information Systems. Information Systems Research, 6 (2) (1995), pp. 85-117.
18. Wojciechowski, M.: Medientypklassifikation der MediaBase. (in German) Internal Paper, Fraunhofer Institute for Software and Systems Engineering. Berlin, Dortmund (1998).
19. Wargitsch, C.; Wewers, Th.; Theisinger, F.: An Organizational-Memory-Based Approach for an Evolutionary Workflow Management System - Concepts and Implementation. Proceedings of HICSS'31, Vol. I (1998), pp. 174-183.

An Extensible Business Communication Language

Hans Weigand & Wilhelm Hasselbring

Infolab, Dept. Information Management and Computer Science, Tilburg University,
PO Box 90153, NL-5000 LE Tilburg, Netherlands,
Email: {weigand|hasselbring}@kub.nl

Abstract. A main problem for electronic commerce, particularly for business-to-business applications, lies in the need for the involved information systems to *meaningfully* exchange information. Domain-specific standards may be used to define the semantics of common terms. However, in practice it is not easy to find those domain-specific standards that are detailed and stable enough to allow for real interoperability. Therefore, we propose an architecture that allows for incremental construction of a shared repository including a multilingual thesaurus, which is used in a business communication language. Communicating information systems then refer to the common thesaurus while exchanging messages. Our emphasis is be on separating semantics (in the thesaurus) and syntax (in XML). Therefore, our extensibility is not only that of XML, but also the extensibility of the semantics that is modeled in the shared repository.
The business communication language XLBC is presented and how it can be used in electronic commerce applications. XLBC message patterns and conversation protocols are stored in the shared repository as well.

1 Introduction

In spite of all the surrounding hype, it is becoming increasingly clear that electronic commerce is taking off on a global scale, not only in the consumer market but also in business-to-business and business-to-administration application areas. However, there are also many barriers that still need to be taken. One barrier is the standardization of the message formats for business communication. Although business-to-business electronic commerce has a longer tradition of electronic data interchange in the form of EDIFACT, it is generally recognized that EDI is too costly and not flexible enough to cope with the dynamics of the new economy [KM97,KL96,MG98]. However, traditional EDI is often being re-examined to define the *meaning* of the transferred data (semantics), and XML is employed as the practical foundation in which to structure this information (syntax). XML is a markup language for creating self-descriptive data; in contrast to HTML, it separates style and content and is extensible in the sense that new tags can be used as long as they are defined in the DTD (document type definition). For electronic commerce, it is especially interesting that one format can be used both for electronic messages (to be processed by computers) and for human interfaces; an XML document itself is already, to some extent, readable for humans (what an EDI document is not), but especially when it is accompanied by a style document (XSL), it can be presented by means of a web browser in any desired layout. This feature not only allows to have one

O. Etzion and P. Scheuermann (Eds.): CoopIS 2000, LNCS 1901, pp. 251–262, 2000.

single interface to application systems (for humans and for systems), but also enables hybrid set-ups in which humans and systems are involved in different stages of the process and the same format can be used throughout.

However, XML on itself will not do the job. The receiving party can recognize something as a valid XML document, and when it has the accompanying DTD, it can check whether it adheres to this DTD, but nothing is said yet about the meaning of the data elements. If every company were to develop its own DTDs, there would be no real interoperability. So, although XML is technically superior to EDI X.12, it does not solve the huge problem that EDIFACT has worked on for years, namely, how to define the contents of the messages. What elements should be there, how are they represented and what do they mean? If XML should be used in business-to-business electronic commerce, something equivalent to the EDIFACT standards must be in place. The standardization of messages can be at different levels: at the lexical level of character sets (data representation), the syntactical level of message structures, to a deeper semantic level of vocabulary and integrity constraints. If communicating parties want true communication, they must agree not only on the form but also on the meaning of the messages. It is not necessary and even undesirable to strive for explicit agreement on all semantics. All that is needed is that confusion is avoided and that messages can be processed automatically at both ends - which means that a mapping can be made to the local schema.

From an institutional point of view, standards are vehicles for facilitating coordination of economic activities [H+95]. Instead of repeated coordination between actors, a standard solves a number of dilemmas for actors in a situation where communication is required. A standard therefore diminishes the need for ad-hoc coordination. On the other hand, there is an increased need for concerted action when standards are created or changed. Normally, this concerted action is performed at the level of standardization committees. However, at present this often turns out to be infeasible, or only feasible to a very limited extent. In today's open and dynamic business environment, the partners have to take over part of the standardization process to themselves. This can involve two or more partners who intend to set up a business relationship on the spot, or an industrial platform/market owner who does this standardization for its members. For such a setting, a flexible system architecture that allows for dynamic evolution of the business communication language is required.

In this paper, we propose an architecture that allows for incremental construction of a shared repository, which is used in a business communication language. Our emphasis is on separating semantics (in the repository) and syntax (in XML). In this way, the architecture not only supports extensibility of message syntax (as offered by XML), but also the extensibility of the message semantics (by means of the shared repository).

2   Foundations for Formal Business Communication

Communication languages have been defined in several environments: KQML in the AI community, ACL in the FIPA agent consortium, and FLBC in the business communication field. In this section we give a short overview of FLBC that we take as our starting point. We also indicate at what points we have deviated from FLBC while developing XLBC.

2.1   FLBC

A number of researchers have investigated the possibility of developing general-purpose formal languages for business communication (FLBC), notably Kimbrough, Moore, Covington and Lee. The impetus for this research has been a common assessment of the fact that existing EDI standards leave much to be desired in flexibility, in expressivity, in clarity, etc. Kimbrough & Moore mention two assumptions of the FLBC approach [KM97]. The first assumption states that a properly designed FLBC should permit business messaging to begin and to proceed without the business partners having to come to a separate and specific agreement concerning the content, structure, and proper interpretation of the messages to be exchanged. This assumption is very close to the approach called Open-EDI [KL96]. It does not require that every message be based entirely on public lexicons. Exchange of particular vocabularies should certainly be allowed, as should 'linguistic bootstrapping' (agreement to define new expressions in terms of existing expressions). The second assumption calls for a semantic foundation of the language in First-Order Logic.

FLBC is based on speech act theory that makes a distinction between the illocutionary force of a message and the propositional content [KM97,Moo99]. By explicating the illocutionary force, FLBC makes clear that messages are not just pieces of data, but (intend to) have some social effects, such as creating an obligation. Moreover, the propositional content is represented in such a way that it contains indeed a proposition, that is, a statement that can be logically true or not (in the case of a assertive message), or an action to be taken (in the case of a directive message). This is in contrast to traditional EDIFACT messages where all the necessary data elements are present (otherwise it would not work, as a matter of course), but not structured in the form of a proposition or action. As a result, the syntax definitions of traditional EDI are somewhat arbitrary and unpredictable. In the FLBC approach proposed by Kimbrough & Moore, the basic structure of FLBC messages is defined once for all. Of course, different message types (also called patterns) can be defined on this basis, such as for ORDER, INVOICE, etc. These message patterns differ in the actions that they refer to and the arguments that these actions take. However, they can always be parsed, and interpreted to some extent; for the full interpretation, the receiver should know the meaning of the terms and predicates. In contrast to earlier languages such as EDIFACT, formal semantics are considered important in FLBC in order to arrive at rigorous definitions and facilitate automatic processing. FLBC uses First-Order Logic as much as possible. XLBC is based on communication semantics described in [WVD95] called Illocutionary Deontic Logic, which is a modal logic. The following subsections summarize our main extensions and adaptations to FLBC.

2.2   Conversation objects

Business messages that are exchanged typically occur in conversation patterns. For example, an order is followed by an acknowledgment, and together they form a transaction. It is not the order itself, but the order transaction that creates the obligation for the other party to deliver, as expressed in the legal definition of a purchase order as a "written authorization for a supplier to ship products at a specified price which becomes a legally binding contract once the supplier accepts it." In [WvH99], a pattern language is described that distinguishes different levels of conversations. Here, we do not repeat the details of this framework, but just assume that conversation objects at different aggregation levels can be defined.

2.3   Roles

In line with linguistic theory, Kimbrough takes a predication/argument structure as the basic representation of events [Kim98]. This means that events are thought of as a special kind of entity of a certain type (e.g., delivery) and the arguments are the entities that play a role in the event (who delivers, what is delivered, etc). The role names are taken from a controlled set. In line with Functional Grammar [Dik89], we allow a predication to have restrictors in addition to the role arguments. Restrictors further identify the entity or event denoted by the predication. Using restrictors, it is possible to add any attribute to the predication, as long as it is semantically coherent. Predication restrictors are the semantic equivalent of adverbial expressions in natural language.

2.4   Predicates

FLBC does not say much about the structure of the lexicon in which predicates are defined. With XLBC, the lexicon – or thesaurus as we call it – is set up in a linguistically motivated way and with support for multilinguality. Predicates can be nominal, adjectival or verbal. Verbal predicates denote some action or activity. Predicates with their roles and possible selection restrictions are called predicate frames and are stored in the multilingual thesaurus. Some are very general (e.g. deliver, arrive), and some will be domain-specific. The thesaurus entries specify lexical information with the representation in one or more languages and semantic information.

3   The Shared Repository

XLBC is based on a separation of syntax (XML messages) and semantics. The semantic definitions are stored in a shared repository. This could be made public, but it could as well be restricted in use for one market only. The shared repository contains two parts: a multilingual thesaurus, and an XLBC component library. The former defines the elements of which messages are composed, and the latter defines the messages and higher aggregation structures. We stress that the shared repository distinguishes several component levels, and is not just a large set of possible DTDs. We strongly believe that such a structure is necessary in order to obtain real extensibility.

3.1   The Multilingual Thesaurus

The different elements that make up a message refer to certain real-world entities, such as the parties involved, the products/goods that are exchanged, etc. Usually, these items will have different attributes such as location and price. Both the attributes themselves and the values of those attributes have a lexical representation, such as "company" or "product". These representations are basically words that denote some concepts. The thesaurus makes a distinction between words (or lexicals) and concepts, and supports a semantic network of concepts.

Figure 1 illustrates our general communication architecture, in which information systems communicate by means of a common business language (in our case XLBC messages that contain references to concepts in the multilingual thesaurus). The multilingual thesaurus for this language is managed by the vocabulary server, which allows for dynamic extension of the terms used in the business language. The communicating information systems are informed of changes to the common thesaurus by means of a notification service. The shared repository also manages the XLBC Document Type Definitions (see section 4).

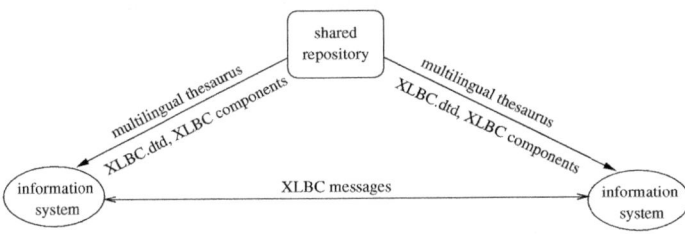

Fig. 1. The general communication architecture. The shared repository manages the common terms that are used in XLBC messages to be exchanged by the communicating information systems.

The thesaurus is built up around a semantic network of concepts. The concepts are defined through their relationships with words and other concepts. Words are the natural language representations of concepts. Multiple words can describe one concept (author and writer may be *synonyms*), and one word can be used to describe multiple concepts (company is a *homonym* that describes both an industrial organization or just a group of friends). We call the relation between a concept and a word a denotation. In addition, concepts are interrelated. For instance, the concept "author" may have as a generalizing parent (*hyperonym*) a concept that represents a person. This says something about the concept of author. A concept may have different types of relations with other concepts. As in typical object-oriented modeling techniques [Mey97], the parent relation (specialization/generalization), the part-of relation, and non-hierarchical relations between concepts (e.g., in the form of predicate frames) are used for defining concepts in the thesaurus. As can be seen in Figure 2, elements in the different message components that make up the conversation shall link to concepts which have been defined in the semantic network of the thesaurus.

Concepts are part of a semantic network but always organized in generalization hierarchies to facilitate top-down access. We have found it useful to distinguish three levels in this hierarchy. The *top level* contains categories such as Event, Physical Entity, Ge-

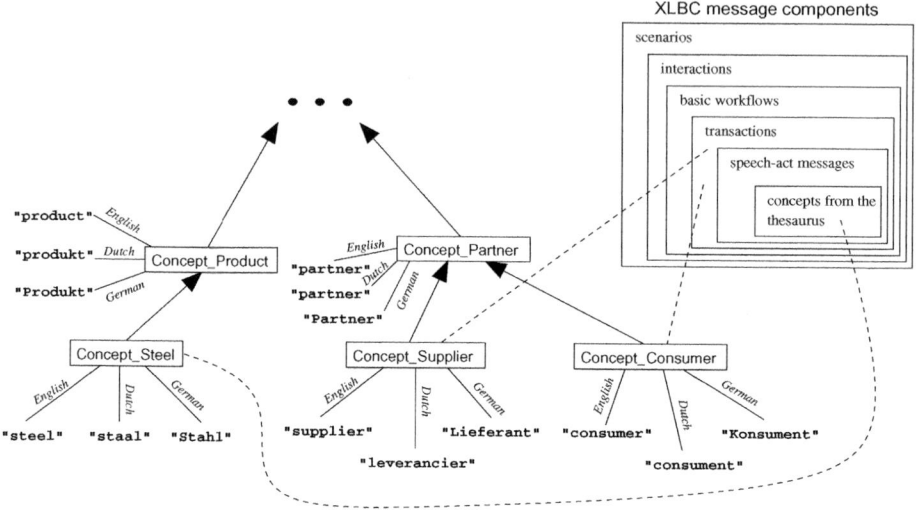

Fig. 2. Linking the XLBC components with the concepts in the semantic network of the multi-lingual thesaurus. Exemplary, translations of some concepts to English, Dutch and German are given.

ographical Entity, Measure Unit, Agent, and Time. It may also contain sub-categories, such as Transport Event, Transform Event, and Transfer Event. The middle level is called the *basic level* and it contains the concepts that are closest to human experience, such as Deliver (a Transport event), Pay (a Transfer event), Day, Month, City, etc. The *bottom level* is made up of sub-concepts, or specialized concepts, such as the many forms of delivery and payment. For retrieving information from the thesaurus, one usually starts at the basic level.

The thesaurus should also provide meaning definitions as far as these are relevant for the business application. Remember that we adhere to a minimalist approach as far as meaning definitions are concerned. We do not have one standard definition method because the relevance can differ and not all concepts are the same. Usually, real-world concepts (natural kinds) such as House, Horse, or Car, defy a formal definition but for the human interpreter, a verbal meaning definition (as in an ordinary dictionary) is usually sufficient, whereas the machine does not need to reason about them. For event types, it is often sufficient to specify the category (for example, Pay is a Transfer event) and the selection restrictions on the arguments (in this case, a Money theme). Sometimes, additional preconditions and postconditions are useful. For message types, the operational meaning typically depends heavily on the context. For example, an Invoice can be defined as a claim for payment in return for goods delivered or for a service provided. However, whether the Invoice causes an obligation to pay or presupposes it, is not so clear; in fact, different options can be chosen, leading to different trade scenarios. Trade scenarios are represented in the component library, and it is at this place where the operational semantics of message types such as Invoice are to be found (see the next subsection). In the thesaurus, a verbal definition is sufficient then. Although real-world concepts usually do not need a complete definition, sometimes quality regulations are relevant. For example, a product may only be called 'chocolate' if it contains at least a certain percentage of cocoa. Although this is not yet possible in the current implementation of the thesaurus, we intend to allow the inclusion of such regulations, but not as part of the definition, but as what they are: rules on the way concept names are applied to instances. In this way, we not only separate syntax and semantics, but also semantics and pragmatics. For the representation of rules, we need an expressive knowledge representation such as is used in logic-based ontologies (cf. [D+98]).

3.2   The XLBC Component Library

XLBC is based on speech act theory. Furthermore, the XLBC messages have been grouped into different aggregation levels of conversations, as illustrated in Figure 2. At each composition level, various patterns can be defined. As explained briefly in section 2.2 and in detail in [WvH99], speech acts typically go in pairs. The request/accept transaction is an example of a pattern at transaction level. Transactions can grouped into basic workflows, of which reciprocal interactions can be construed. It is possible to specify rules on, for instance, the sequence order in which elements of XLBC-patterns must occur.

The thesaurus and component library provide an architectural framework that is specifically aimed at extensibility. It is unrealistic to assume that any organization could arrive at an exhaustive repository of standard components and standard messages that any industry can adopt. This should not be the aim. Instead, what the repository should provide is a (well-structured) set of building blocks by means of which parties can develop new components with relative low effort. Given a shared repository with a certain content, users can develop new business processes top-down, by taking an existing business process and adapting it according to their needs, or bottom-up, by taking the basic terms of the Thesaurus - perhaps extended with newly defined ones - and compose them into messages etc. The advantage of the XLBC approach - and FLBC approaches in general - is that it supports compositional semantics. For example, if a new kind of business action has been defined - let's say, 'review' instead of 'deliver' - then it can be combined without further effort into a request for reviewing, a commit to reviewing, or a report on the reviewing being finished. When the Thesaurus is owned and managed by a professional community instead of one party, the procedures for updating and extending the shared repository is equally important. In the conclusions, we will have a few suggestions on this point, but the issue as such is beyond the scope of this paper.

4   The Extensible Language for Business Communication XLBC

Below, we introduce the language XLBC (Extensible Language for Business Communication). XLBC combines the semantic orientation of FLBC with the extensible syntax of XML. The Extensible Markup Language (XML) is *subset* of SGML that is designed to make it easy to interchange structured documents over the Internet [McG98]. The main role of XML (as opposed to HTML) in interoperable systems is likely to be for defining the structure of data to be exchanged between heterogeneous information systems. The syntactic structure of XML documents is specified by a Document Type Definition (DTD), which may be thought of as a schema of the document. Instances of XML documents can only be understood in relationship to their DTD. When we talk about XML documents we need to refer to explicit DTDs.

The top-level DTD for XLBC messages is defined as follows:

```
<!ELEMENT MESSAGE        (SPEECH-ACT+, CONTEXT) >
```

This definition defines a message as consisting of one or more speech acts and a context element. The attributes are omitted for reasons of space.

4.1   Speech Act and Propositional Content

Speech act and propositional content is then defined as follows:

```
<!ELEMENT SPEECH-ACT (CONTENT)>
<!ATTLIST SPEECH-ACT
                TYPE            CDATA                   #THESAURUS>

<!ELEMENT CONTENT (PREDICATION | COMPLEX-PRED)>

<!ELEMENT PREDICATION (ARG+, RESTRICTOR*)>
<!ATTLIST PREDICATION
                ID              CDATA                   #REQUIRED
                TYPE            CDATA                   #THESAURUS
                OPERATOR        ('NEG'|'POS')           #IMPLIED
                ASPECT    ('INTEND'|'START'|'CONTINUE'|
                          'STOP'|'DONE')                #IMPLIED>

<!ELEMENT ARG (TERM | PREDICATION | TIMEREF)>
<!ATTLIST ARG
                ROLE            CDATA                   #THESAURUS>
```

These definitions contain the basic structure of the speech acts. A speech act is divided into an illocution and a propositional content. The speaker and addressee of the speech act are already determined by the sender/receiver of the message. The propositional content consists of a number of predications, where a simple predication takes the form of a predicate (usually a verb, such as 'deliver') followed by one or more arguments. An argument consists of its identifying role and a term. We also allow for sub-clauses, and therefore instead of a term, it is also possible to fill an argument recursively with a predication. The ID of a predication is the identifier of the action occurrence, as it is used in event semantics. The TYPE attribute defines the message type taken from the controlled vocabulary in the multilingual thesaurus (specified via the keyword #THESAURUS). The predicate operator can be positive or negative (default: positive). The aspect operator can be used to indicate a phase of the event ('going to v', 'start v-ing', 'is v-ing', 'stop v-ing', 'has v-ed'). A complex predication allows for Boolean combinations of simple predications.

4.2   Context

The context of the message contains all kinds of pragmatic features, such as the session of which the message is a part, a link to a previous message, but also the thesaurus used or the preferred language setting. This definition is similar to the ones used in FLBC [Moo99] and FIPA [Fou].

4.3   Terms and References

A term is an expression by means of which the speaker refers to some entity [Dik89]. If the entity has a unique identifier, then the reference is simple, comparable to the reference by means of a personal name in natural language. However, this is not always the case. For example, when a customer orders 3 items of product X (identified by some EAN code), then the reference includes both a product type (identified by the EAN code) and a quantity. The situation becomes more complex when the product is not sold in discrete items. In that case, some unit-of-measure is needed, for example, 200 kg. The entity type can be uniquely identified by an EAN code, but it can also be described by means of a general entity type and a list of restrictors. For example, the entity type can be 'Toyota Carina Model 1432' and restrictors can specify the color, the transmission system, etc.

5   Related Work

In the absence of a complete and comprehensive set of document formats, as EDIFACT intended to provide, several attempts are made to set up repositories of components that can be taken out and used by business partners. XML.ORG, for instance, aims at being an independent industry portal for the standardization of XML applications in electronic commerce, whereby it serves as a reference for XML DTDs. BizTalk.ORG is a competing industry initiative started by Microsoft. Commerce One's CBL defines a set of building blocks. These building blocks are then pulled together to make the actual documents describing the interactions between two organizations. OASIS is a non-profit international consortium dedicated to accelerating the adoption of product-independent formats based on public standards, notably XML. Oasis could serve as a host for an XML registry and repository, including XLBC. The sister organization ON-TOLOGY.ORG has the objective to use ontologies to address the problems that impact the formation and sustainability of large electronic trading groups. In these initiatives, the goal is to put DTDs at the disposal for communication partners, but the dynamic, ad-hoc extension of common DTDs is usually not addressed.

[Lee98] suggests the use of a central repository in which formal trade procedures can be stored. Users can download these trade procedures — formally represented as Petri-Nets — adapt them if necessary, and then adopt them immediately for execution. The XLBC approach goes further by providing not only trade procedures (corresponding to XLBC components at the workflow level), but also term definitions and message types. [G+99] proposes a central repository of standard contracts that can be used by negotiating partners in the process of contract building. [Hue98] advocates a Trading

Partner Agreement in which business partners describe a new business process. The definition can be exchanged by means of EDIFACT meta messages. However, this scenario makes not clear yet how the definitions are managed. Moreover, it requires that the message formats are adapted each time a semantic change is made, such as the addition of a new action. In our approach, the message format can be kept unchanged.

A somewhat older approach that bears similarity to XLBC is the Basic Semantic Repository (BSR) [ISO] and the Business System Interoperation (BSI) project at the University of Melbourne [ICA]. This project was not based on XML, but also aimed at standardization of business terms for EDI in the form of repositories. The BSR was set up with multilinguality support. The semantics that it did provide (at least in the first prototype of which information is available) was limited; the main contribution was a structured way of describing EDI data elements. The idea behind BSI was that outgoing messages would be translated automatically to the standardized form at the sender's site and translated back to the in-house file of the receiver at the receiver's site. The translation in both cases is performed by an BSI server. Although we basically agree with this general idea, there are still many problems to be solved before this actually works. One is that a standard should be available that is sufficiently expressive - such as aimed at by XLBC and the multilingual thesaurus.

FIPA has taken the initiative of defining an Agent Communication Language [Fou]. The language is also based on Speech Act Theory and its semantics is specified in BDI logic. The FIPA language provides almost no support for conversation objects. The propositional content can be defined for different domains using a nested attribute/value scheme. The general message format is similar to XLBC; the main differences are that XLBC content is defined using predications and that the terminology is defined in a thesaurus (although FIPA also intends to set up directories where domain ontologies can be defined and published).

6   Conclusions and Future Work

The standardization process — defining a communication language and its semantics — is a process that is usually done by standardization committees, but if the users have to do it themselves, the question arises how it should be supported. We distinguish five aspects of this support:

Representation support: How to represent the syntax and semantics?
Accessibility support: How to store the definitions and make them available?
Methodological support: How to arrive at a definition of redefinition?
Process support: How to manage the standardization process?
Implementation support: How to implement the language in the context of existing legacy systems?

Drawing on FLBC, we introduced the XLBC language that defines the structure of messages. The meaning of the lexicals has to come from somewhere else. For this purpose, we have developed a multilingual thesaurus and a XLBC component library. By means of these techniques, the system is able to provide communication partners with representation and accessibility support, as mentioned above. Particularly, the specific (semantic) representation of business message components (in the shared repository) may incrementally evolve in our architecture. This would not be possible when relying only on prescribed XML DTD for message exchange. An important concern is the separation of the semantics in the repository and the concrete syntax in XML, as well as the separation of pragmatics (business rules on the application).

The other support aspects are not worked out in this paper, but we can make a few remarks. Process support is needed especially in the case that there are more than two stakeholders involved, for example, a business group or virtual community. In that case, the process should start by identifying all relevant stakeholders and ensure that everyone who wants to be involved has the possibility to do so. It is important that the process is legitimate so that the results are acceptable to all stakeholders. In [dM99], a method is described in which virtual professional communities can arrive at acceptable specifications. This method can be used also for a definition process.

Implementation support is especially important for the coupling of the standardized language with the legacy systems of the parties involved. Typically, the communication language is not identical to the language spoken by these legacy systems. A translation or mapping is needed to transform one representation into the other. This translation software is one of the major components of current EDI systems. [Has00] discusses the role of standards in the construction and mapping of global data models for cooperative information systems with different individual data models. The traditional bottom-up approach is to start with the data models to be integrated and then trying to define super-classes of which the original classes are specializations. The study shows that this can lead to very complex integrated models. A top-down approach starts with an available domain model, as the multilingual thesaurus may provide, and maps this to the situation at hand in the legacy systems. In the case of a message standard, a top-down approach could be followed if generic concepts, such as order, invoice but also product, buyer, seller, or transport medium are available. The top-down approach and the bottom-up approach can be combined in a so-called *yo-yo* approach. On the technical level, wrappers that provide unified interfaces are an established technique for accessing legacy systems [RS97].

Acknowledgments

XLBC and the associated Shared Repository are currently being developed and implemented in the context of the ESPRIT project MEMO (Mediating and Monitoring Electronic Commerce) with project code 26.895. The partners are: ABN-AMRO, Tilburg University (CentER Applied Research), RWTH Aachen, EURIDIS Rotterdam, IHK Aachen, EKD Spain, Sarenet Spain and Origin Spain. For more information, refer to `http://www.abnamro.com/memo`.

References

[D+98]   S. Decker et al. ONTOBROKER: Ontology based access to distributed and semi-structured information. In R. Meersman, Z. Tari, and S. Stevens, editors, *Proc. DS-8: Database Semantics - Semantic Issues in Multimedia Systems*. Kluwer Academic Publishers, 1998.

[Dik89]   S.C. Dik. *The theory of Functional Grammar*. Mouton-De Gruyter, 1989.

[dM99]   A. de Moor. *Empowering Communities: A Method for the Legitimate User-Driven Specification of Network Information Systems*. PhD thesis, Tilburg University, 1999.

[Fou]   Foundation for Intelligent Physical Agents. *FIPA*. (available from http://www.fipa.org/).

[G⁺99]   M. Gisler et al. Requirements on secure electronic contracts. Technical Report MCM-institute-1999-01, Univ. St. Gallen, 1999.

[H⁺95]   C.-F. Helgesson et al. Standards as institutions. problems with creating all-european standards for terminal equipment. In J. Groenewegen, C. Pitelis, and S.-E. Sjostrand, editors, *On Economic Institutions*, pages 162–184. Edward Edgar Publ., 1995.

[Has00]   W. Hasselbring. The role of standards for interoperating information systems. In K. Jakobs, editor, *Information Technology Standards and Standardization: A Global Perspective*, pages 116–130. Idea Group Publishing, 2000.

[Hue98]   C. Huemer. The growing need for meta messages in electronic data interchange. In *Proc. 6th ECIS*, Aix-en-Provence, France, 1998.

[ICA]   ICARIS. *Business System Interoperation (BSI) – a Generic Solution*. (available from http://www.cs.mu.oz.au/research/icaris/bsi.html).

[ISO]   ISO/UN-ECE. *The Basic Semantic Repository*. (available from http://www.cs.mu.oz.au/research/icaris/bsr.html).

[Kim98]   S. Kimbrough. On ESTheta Theory and the Logic of X12 Date/Time Qualifiers. In *Proc. HICSS'98*, 1998.

[KL96]   S.O. Kimbrough and R.M. Lee. On formal aspects of electronic commerce: examples of research issues and challenges. In *Proceedings HICSS'96*. IEEE Computer Society Press, 1996.

[KM97]   S.O. Kimbrough and S.A. Moore. On automated message processing in electronic commerce and work support systems: speech act theory and expressive felicity. *ACM Transactions on Information Systems*, 15(4):321–367, 1997.

[Lee98]   R. Lee. Towards open electronic contracting. *Electronic Markets*, 8(3), 1998.

[McG98]   S. McGrath. *XML by example: building e-commerce applications*. Prentice Hall, Upper Saddle River, NJ, 1998.

[Mey97]   B. Meyer. *Object-Oriented Software Construction*. Prentice Hall, Englewood Cliffs, NJ, second edition, 1997.

[MG98]   B. Meltzer and R. Glushko. XML and electronic commerce enabling the network economy. *SIGMOD Record*, 27(4):21–24, 1998.

[Moo99]   S.A. Moore. A foundation for flexible automated electronic communication. Working paper, University of Michigan Business School, 1999. (available from http://www-personal.umich.edu/~samoore/research/flbc/).

[RS97]   M.T. Roth and P.M. Schwarz. Don't scrap it, wrap it! a wrapper architecture for legacy data sources. In *Proc. 23rd International Conference on Very Large Data Bases (VLDB'97), August 1997, Athens, Greece*, pages 266–275. Morgan Kaufmann, 1997.

[WVD95]   H. Weigand, E. Verharen, and F. Dignum. Integrated semantics for information and communication systems. In R. Meersman and L. Mark, editors, *Proc. IFIP WG 2.6 Conf on Data Application Semantics*, pages 500–525. Chapman & Hall, 1995.

[WvH99]   H. Weigand and W.-J. vd Heuvel. Meta-patterns for electronic commerce. *International Journal on Electronic Commerce*, 3(2):45–66, 1999.

Exploiting the Features of Asymmetry for Query Processing in a Mobile Computing Environment

Wen-Chih Peng and Ming-Syan Chen
Department of Electrical Engineering
National Taiwan University
Taipei, Taiwan, ROC
E-mail:{mschen@cc.ee.ntu.edu.tw, wcpeng@arbor.ee.ntu.edu.tw}

Abstract With the cutting edge technology advance in wireless and mobile computers, the query processing in a mobile environment involves join processing among different sites which include static servers and mobile computers. Because of the need of energy saving and also the presence of asymmetric features in a mobile computing environment, the conventional query processing for a distributed database cannot be directly applied to a mobile computing system. In this paper, we first explore three asymmetric features of a mobile environment. Then, in light of these features, we devise query processing schemes. Performance of these query processing schemes is comparatively analyzed and sensitivity analysis on several parameters is conducted.

1 Introduction

In a mobile computing environment, a mobile user with a power-limited palm computer (or a mobile computer) can access various information via wireless communication. It is noted that mobile computers use small batteries for their operations without directly connecting to any power source and the bandwidth of wireless communication is in general limited. As a result, an important design issue in a mobile system is to conserve the energy of a mobile unit while allowing mobile users of the ability to access information from anywhere at anytime [3][9].

The query processing in a traditional distributed system has received a considerable amount of attention and been extensively studied in the literature [4][5][6][11]. The objective in distributed query processing is to reduce the amount of data transmission required. Note, however, that the cost models developed for query processing in a traditional distributed database do not reflect many important features in a mobile computing system. Explicitly, the prior studies in distributed query processing [5][6][11] did not fully explore the asymmetric features of a mobile environment, which are, as explained below, particularly important in devising the corresponding query processing schemes. Specifically, the energy consumption of mobile computers, the most important cost criterion, was not dealt with for the query processing in traditional distributed databases, making the corresponding distributed query processing schemes devised not applicable to a mobile computing environment. To remedy this, we shall

O. Etzion and P. Scheuermann (Eds.): CoopIS 2000, LNCS 1901, pp. 263–274, 2000.
© Springer-Verlag Berlin Heidelberg 2000

explore in this paper three important asymmetric features of a mobile computing system, and in light of these features, develop efficient query processing schemes for mobile computing systems. The three asymmetric features, which we shall explicitly address and reflect in the design of query processing schemes, are as follows.

1. **Asymmetric feature of computing capability between the server and a mobile computer:** Mobile computers use small batteries for their operations without directly connecting to any power source. In contrast, the server is not strictly constrained by energy consumption and thus possesses much more power than a mobile computer. Note that in traditional distributed query processing, the sites involved in a query processing are usually assumed to have the same level of processing capability. This feature distinguishes the query processing in a mobile environment from that in a traditional distributed system.

2. **Asymmetric feature of energy consumption between message sending and receiving:** The energy required for message sending is more than that required for message receiving at a mobile computer [8]. This feature also has to be modelled when the costs of the corresponding operations are evaluated.

3. **Asymmetric feature of energy consumption between activeness and idleness of a mobile computer:** The energy consumed by a mobile computer in its active mode is much more than that consumed in its idle mode [7][8]. In view of this, a mobile computer may be designed to stay in its idling mode by migrating its processing work to the server if so appropriate.

Consequently, we derive in this paper a cost model which considers these three asymmetric features of a mobile computing system. The cost model derived paves the way to the development of the query processing schemes in a mobile computing system. For ease of exposition, a semijoin which is initiated by the server and is beneficial to reduce the cost of a join operation is termed a *server-initiated*, or *SI profitable* semijoin. For query processing, judiciously applying SI profitable semijoin can reduce the amount of data transmission required and energy consumption. According to those asymmetric features of a mobile computing system, we devise some specific criteria to identify SI profitable semijoins. For query processing which refers to the processing of multi-join queries, we develop three query processing schemes. In particular, we formulate the query processing in a mobile computing system as a two-phase query processing procedure that can determine a join sequence and interleave that join sequence with SI profitable semijoins to reduce both the amounts of data transmission and energy consumption. Performance of these query schemes is comparatively analyzed and sensitivity analysis on several parameters is conducted. It is shown by our simulation results that by exploiting the three asymmetric features, the proposed two-phase query processing scheme is very powerful in reducing both the amounts of energy consumption and data transmission incurred.

This rest of this paper is organized as follows. Preliminaries are given in Section 2. In Section 3, we develop query processing schemes for multi-join queries. Performance studies on various query processing schemes are conducted in Section 4. This paper concludes with Section 5.

2   Preliminaries

To facilitate the presentation of this paper, some preliminaries are given in this section. The notation, definitions and assumptions required are described in Section 2.1. By taking the asymmetric features described above into consideration, a cost model for join and query processing in a mobile computing system is devised in Section 2.2.

2.1   Notation, Definition and Assumption

A join query graph can be denoted by a graph $G = (V, E)$, where V is the set of nodes and E is the set of edges. Each node in a join query graph represents a relation. Two nodes are connected by an edge if there exists a join predicate on some attribute of the two corresponding relations. We use $|R_i|$ to denote the cardinality of a relation R_i and $|A|$ to denote the cardinality of the domain of an attribute A. The notation $R_i \bowtie R_j$ is used to mean the join between R_i and R_j, and $|R_i \bowtie R_j|$ denotes cardinality of the result relation of $R_i \bowtie R_j$. To determine the effect of a join operation specified by a query graph, we employ the results stated in the theorem developed in [5].

Define the selectivity $\rho_{i,a}$ of attribute A in R_i as $\frac{|R_i(A)|}{|A|}$, where $R_i(A)$ is the set of distinct values for the attribute A in R_i. $R_i \Box A \to R_j$ means a semijoin from R_i to R_j on attribute A and $R_i \to R_j$ means a simple join from R_i to R_j. Note that the reduction of the relation R_j by the semijoin $R_i \Box A \to R_j$ is proportional to the reduction of $R_j(A)$. The estimation of the size of the relation reduced by a semijoin is thus similar to estimating the reduction of projection on the semijoin attributes. After the semijoin $R_i \Box A \to R_j$, the cardinality of R_j can be estimated as $|R_j| \rho_{i,a}$.

2.2   Cost Model for Query Processing in a Mobile Computing System

Table 1 shows the description of parameters in the cost model for a mobile computing system. Energy consumption in data receiving at a mobile computer, denoted by e_{RC}, refers to the energy consumed in receiving data via wireless communication. Energy consumption for receiving a relation R at a mobile computer, denoted by $e_{RC}(R)$, is formulated as $e_r \Box |R|$ where e_r is the receiving energy coefficient, representing the energy consumed in receiving one tuple of data. Also, energy consumption for sending a relation R out from a mobile computer, denoted by $e_{SD}(R)$, refers to the energy required in transmitting the

Description	Symbol
Processing ratio of server to mobile, i.e., server/mobile	r_{SM}
Energy consumption ratio of data sending to data receiving	r_E
Idling coefficient for a mobile computer	δ
Energy consumption in data receiving at a mobile computer	e_{RC}
Energy consumption in data sending at a mobile computer	e_{SD}
Processing time function at the server	T_S
Amount of data transmission for query processing	d_t
Amount of energy consumption for query processing	E_c

Table 1. Description of symbols for the cost model in a mobile computing system

relation R over wireless link. To capture the asymmetric feature of energy consumption between data sending and receiving of a mobile computer, we use the send-receive energy ratio r_E (i.e., $\frac{e_{SD}}{e_{RC}}$) to represent the ratio of the energy consumption of sending data to that of receiving data. The value of r_E is in general larger than one, and can more explicitly be approximated to a value between 2 and 10 [1]. Hence, $e_{SD}(R)$ is formulated as $r_E \cdot e_r \cdot |R|$ where $e_r \cdot r_E$ is the sending energy coefficient. Similarly to most relevant works [7], the processing time required to perform the given operations on the relation in a server is modeled as a function of the input relations involved. For example, the processing time of joining R_i and R_j in a server, denoted by $T_S(R_i \bowtie R_j)$, can then be expressed by $t_{tuple} \cdot (|R_i| + |R_j| + |R_i \bowtie R_j|)$, where t_{tuple} is the coefficient for the processing time required per tuple.

To capture the asymmetric feature of computing capability between the server and a mobile computer, the server-mobile processing ratio r_{SM} represents the ratio of the processing power of a server to that of a mobile computer. Clearly, the value of r_{SM} is larger than 1 and can be obtained empirically. Hence, the processing time of joining R_i and R_j at a mobile computer can be expressed by $r_{SM} \cdot T_S(R_i \bowtie R_j)$. To reflect the asymmetric feature of energy consumption between activeness and idleness of a mobile computer, we define the idling coefficient δ to be the ratio of the energy consumed by a mobile computer in its idle mode to that in its active mode. The idle coefficient δ of mobile computers can be approximated to a value between 0.02 and 0.5 and is in fact system dependent [7][8]. Consequently, the energy consumption at a mobile computer in its idle mode while a join is performed in a server can be estimated as $\delta \cdot T_S(R_i \bowtie R_j)$, whereas the energy consumed in processing the join between R_i and R_j at a mobile computer is approximated as $\frac{1}{\delta} \cdot r_{SM} \cdot T_S(R_i \bowtie R_j)$. Note that all these parameters can be estimated from the specifications of mobile computers [2][10]. Using the cost model developed, we are able to evaluate the energy consumption and data transmission costs (E_c and d_t, respectively) of the corresponding query processing schemes in a mobile computing system, and develop an efficient solution procedure for multi-join query processing accordingly.

3   Query Processing in a Mobile Computing System

In this section, we consider the processing of multi-join queries that involves one server and many mobile computers. The *destination mobile computer* refers to the mobile computer that issues the query and is expected to receive the query result. A *participating mobile computer* refers to the mobile computer that contains a relation involved in the query processing. Explicity, we first examine in Section 3.1 a query processing scheme (to be referred to as scheme QP$_C$). A two-phase query processing scheme which employs a simple join operation (to be referred to as scheme QP$_S$) is devised in Section 3.2. Next, we devise another two-phase query processing scheme that can determine a join sequence with SI profitable semijoins interleaved (to be referred to as scheme QP$_{SJ}$) to reduce both the amounts of data transmission and energy consumption in Section 3.3.

3.1   Query Processing at the Destination Mobile Computer (denoted by QP$_C$)

In scheme QP$_C$, all participating mobile computers and the server send their relations to the destination mobile computer for query processing. Clearly, though minimizing the energy consumption of participating mobile computers, scheme QP$_C$ results in a significant amount of energy consumption at the destination mobile computer (i.e., receiving relations from participating mobile computers and performing join operations). In our experimental studies in Section 4, scheme QP$_C$ will be implemented and evaluated for comparison purposes.

3.2   Query Processing at the Server (denoted by QP$_S$)

Clearly, despite its simplicity, scheme QP$_C$ does not exploit the asymmetric feature of computing capability between the server and mobile computers, and may thus consume much valuable processing power at the destination mobile computer. Explicitly, since the server is not strictly constrained by energy consumption, one can fully utilize the processing capability of the server. In view of this, we decompose the processing of a query into two phases, namely the *relation transfer phase,* denoted by RT, and *the final phase,* denoted by FP. In the relation transfer phase, each participating mobile computer sends its own relation to the server for a join operation. Thus, the server obtains the resulting relation of the multi-join query among the participating mobile computers. In the *final phase,* the join between the server and the destination mobile computer is performed.

Note that since the server in QP$_S$ takes over the query processing which costs much energy of the destination mobile computer in QP$_C$, the energy consumption of the destination mobile computer in QP$_S$ is significantly reduced. It can be seen that, in scheme QP$_S$, each participating mobile computer sends its own relation to the server without considering the use of semijoins. As can be seen in [5], judiciously interleaving a join sequence with semijoins is able to reduce the amount of data transmission required. Note, however, that without considering the asymmetric features and energy consumption, the algorithm in [5] is not applicable to the query processing in a mobile computing system. As a result, we will devise in the following subsection scheme QP_{SJ} to determine a proper join sequence with semijoins interleaved in the RT phase for further reducing both the amounts of data transmission and energy consumption.

3.3   Query Processing with SI Pro□table Semijoins (denoted by QP_{SJ})

In this subsection, we shall □rst derive a theorem to identify SI pro□table semijoins, and then, in light of the theorem derived, develop a solution procedure that can interleave a join sequence with SI pro□table semijoins for e□cient query processing.

De□nition 1: A semijoin $R_i \ \square \ A \rightarrow R_j$, where the server owns relation R_i and the mobile computer owns relation R_j, is called *SI pro□table* if its energy consumption of the mobile computer for performing this semijoin, i.e., $e_{RC}(\square_{i,a} \square |A|) + \frac{1}{\square} \square r_{SM} \square T_S(R_j \bowtie (\square_{i,a} \square |A|)) + e_{SD}(\square_{i,a}|R_j|)$, is smaller than that for sending R_j to the server, i.e., $e_{SD}(|R_j|)$. Note that energy consumption of an SI semijoin by the mobile computer consists of the energy consumed in performing the semijoin and that in sending the resulting relation of that semijoin to the server for a join operation.

With De□nition 1, we can derive the following theorem.

Theorem 1: A semijoin $R_i \ \square \ A \rightarrow R_j$ is *SI pro□table* if and only if $\square_{i,a}$ is less than $\frac{(r_E \square e_r \square \frac{1}{\square} \square r_{SM} \square t_{tuple})}{(r_E \square e_r + \frac{1}{\square} \square r_{SM} \square t_{tuple})}$.

Theorem 1 leads to the following corollary.

Corollary 1.1. An *SI pro□table* semijoin, $R_i \ \square \ A \rightarrow R_j$, implies that the amount of data transmission by performing this semijoin (i.e., $\square_{i,a}(|A| + |R_j|)$) is smaller than that of sending R_j to the server (i.e., $|R_j|$).

In the RT phase, by utilizing the server to perform the multi-join query, the server site contains the resulting relation. To facilitate our presentation, use $E_c^{d,j}$ to represent the energy consumption of a join operation between R_d and R_j, where d is the destination site. The energy consumption of an SI pro□table semijoin, $R_d \square A \rightarrow R_j$, can be expressed as $E_c^{d,j}(SJ)$ and the corresponding data transmission cost can be denoted by $d_t^{d,j}(SJ)$. The energy consumption of a join $R_j \rightarrow R_d$ can be expressed as $E_c^{d,j}(J)$ and the corresponding data transmission cost can be denoted by $d_t^{d,j}(J)$.

First, we develop a directed graph with proper weights in edges. Assume that the destination mobile computer in the query graph (V, E) is denoted by d and the set of edges of node d is represented as E_d. The destination mobile computer and its edges are omitted in the directed graph since they will not be involved in the RT phase. The resulting directed graph is thus (V-d, E-E_d). An edge connecting two nodes n_i and n_j is denoted by (n_i, n_j), and the weight of edge (n_i, n_j), denoted by $E_c^{i,j}$, can be set to either the value of $E_c^{i,j}(SJ)$ (meaning that an SI pro□table semijoin SJ will be performed) if $\square_i < \frac{(r_E \square e_r \square \frac{1}{\square} \square r_{SM} \square t_{tuple})}{(r_E \square e_r + \frac{1}{\square} \square r_{SM} \square t_{tuple})}$, or

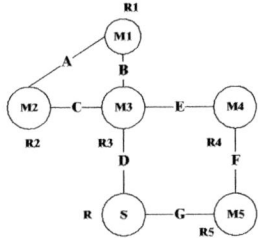

Fig 1. An illustrative query graph.

the value of $E_c^{i,j}(J)$ (meaning that a simple join J will be performed) otherwise. After constructing the directed graph, algorithm M is applied to determine a join sequence with SI profitable semijoins interleaved in the RT phase. Note that an edge (S,n_j) in a directed graph is being *shrunken* if (S,n_j) is removed from the graph and S and n_j are merged together. When a join operation between the two relations corresponding to nodes S and n_j in a given directed graph is carried out, we can obtain the resulting query graph by shrinking the edges between S and n_j. Algorithm M is outlined below.

Algorithm M: Determine the join sequence with SI profitable semijoins interleaved in the RT phase.

Input: A directed graph=$(V \cup d, E \cup E_d)$.

Output: SEQ /* SEQ contains the resulting sequence of joins semijoins */

1. **begin**
2. SEQ=ϕ;
3. **for** each vertex $w \in V \cup d$ **do**
4. **begin**
5. $w.mark$:=false;
6. $w.ct$:=∞; /* $w.ct$ is the cost of join operation from S to w. */
7. $w.op = J$; /* $w.op$ represents the join operation */
8. **end**
9. $S.ct$=0; /* The cost of join operation from S to itself is set to zero */
10. **while** $\exists$ an unmarked vertex **do**
11. **begin**
12. let w be an unmarked vertex such that w.ct is the minimal among all the corresponding costs of unmarked vertices;
13. **if** $(w.\square < \frac{(r_E \cup e_r \cup \frac{1}{\square} \cup r_{SM} \cup t_{tuple})}{(r_E \cup e_r + \frac{1}{\square} \cup r_{SM} \cup t_{tuple})})$
14. $w.op = SJ$;
15. SEQ=SEQ$\cup$ w;
16. $w.mark$:=true;
17. **for** all edges (w, z) with z is unmarked **do**
18. **begin**
19. **if** $w.ct$+weight$(w, z) < z.ct$ **then**
20. $z.ct := w.ct$+weight(w, z); /* Update the weight of the edge (w,z) */
21. **end**
22. **end**
23. **end**

W.-C. Peng and M.-S. Chen

Relation R_i	$|R_i|$	Attribute X	Selectivity $\rho_{i,x}$
R_1	107		0.8
			0.75
R_2	102		0.85
			0.75
R_i	106		0.8
		D	0.7
		E	0.4
R_4	100	E	0.8
		F	0.95
R_5	120	F	0.8
		G	0.85
R	1?1	D	0.9
		G	0.5

Table 2. profile for query here

$|\Box| = 19, |\Box| = 15, |\Box| = 17, |D| = 19, |E| = 16, |F| = 15, |G| = 18, r_{SM} = 5,$
$\delta = 0.5, e_r = 0.1, r_E = 5$ and $t_{tuple} = 0.001.$

Steps	M_2	M_i	M_4	M_5	Operation included into SEQ
0	∞	5.	∞	49.8	
1	∞	5.	99.8	49.8	R–G$\to R_5$, $R_5' \to R$
2	104.	5.	88.28	49.8	$R_i \to R^*$
.	104.	5.	88.28	49.8	R^{**}–E$\to R_4$, $R_4' \to R^{**}$
4	104.	5.	88.28	49.8	$R_2 \to R^{***}$

Table . an execution example of algorithm M.

To show the execution of algorithm M, consider the query graph in Figure 1 whose profile is given in Table 2. The corresponding directed graph is shown in Figure 2a. It can be verified that since $\Box_{R,G} = 0.5 < \frac{(r_E \Box e_r \Box \frac{1}{\Box} \Box r_{SM} \Box t_{tuple})}{(r_E \Box e_r + \frac{1}{\Box} \Box r_{SM} \Box t_{tuple})} = 0.6$, the weight of edge from S to M_5 in Figure 2a is $E_c^{S,5}(SJ) = 0.1 \Box 0.5 \Box 18 + \frac{1}{0.5} \Box 5 \Box 0.01 \Box (120 + 0.5 \Box 18 + 0.5 \Box 120) + 0.1 \Box 5 \Box 0.5 \Box 120 = 49.8$. Also, since $\Box_{R,D} = 0.9 > \frac{(r_E \Box e_r \Box \frac{1}{\Box} \Box r_{SM} \Box t_{tuple})}{(r_E \Box e_r + \frac{1}{\Box} \Box r_{SM} \Box t_{tuple})} = 0.6$, the weight of edge from S to M_3 is $E_c^{S,3}(J) = 0.1 \Box 5 \Box 106 = 53$. Similarly, the weights of other edges in the directed graph in Figure 2a can be obtained. Then, algorithm M is used to generate the proper join sequence with SI profitable semijoins interleaved in the RT phase. First, the costs from S to other vertices are evaluated in the directed graph for initialization (from line 3 to line 8 in algorithm M). The execution scenario of algorithm M is shown in Figure 2 where $R^\Box$, $R^{\Box\Box}$ and $R^{\Box\Box\Box}$ denote the resulting relations in the end of each step. Note that since the cost of (S, M_5) is the minimal (line 12 in algorithm M), as can be seen in Step 0 from Table 3, the vertex M_5 is selected first. Also, it can be verified that the semijoin operation R$\Box$G$\to R_5$ is SI profitable (line 13 in algorithm M) since the corresponding selectivity factor (i.e., 0.5) is smaller than $\frac{(r_E \Box e_r \Box \frac{1}{\Box} \Box r_{SM} \Box t_{tuple})}{(r_E \Box e_r + \frac{1}{\Box} \Box r_{SM} \Box t_{tuple})} = 0.6$. The semijoin $R \Box G \rightarrow R_5$ is thus performed. In Figure 2a, R_5 is selected for the semijoin and sends the resulting relation to the server. After the join with the relation at site M_5, the cost from S to M_4 is derived (from line 17 to line 21 in algorithm M). It can be seen that Figure 2a leads to the con□guration in Figure 2b in which the weight of the edge from S to M_4 becomes 99.8 (i.e., 49.8+50=99.8). Then, we shall determine the minimal cost among all the edges connecting to those unvisited vertices (line 12 in algorithm M) and perform the corresponding operations. This procedure repeats until all the vertices of the directed graph are visited (line 10 to in algorithm M). From Table 3, it can be seen that M_3 has the minimal cost in Step 1 and is next be selected. Since the semijoin $R^\Box \Box D \rightarrow R_3$ is not SI pro□table according to Theorem 1, the simple join from M_3 to S is executed in Figure 2b, leading to the con□guration in Figure 2c. Following the same procedure, the sequence of joins and semijoins can be derived. Note that while having the same cost as QP_S in the FP phase, scheme QP_{SJ} outperforms QP_S in the RT phase by incurring not only a smaller amount of energy consumption, i.e., 49.8+53+35.28+51=189.08 < 60+53+50+51=214, but also a smaller amount of data transmission, i.e., 69+106+46.4+102=323.4 < 120+106+100+102=428, showing the very advantage of employing proper SI pro□table semijoins in scheme QP_{SJ}.

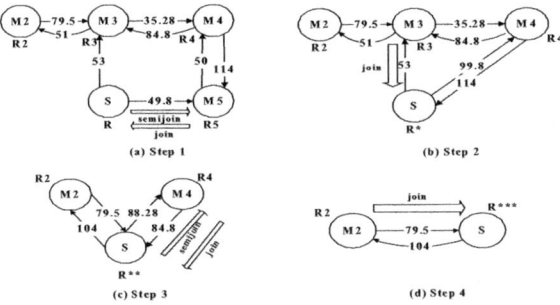

F□g□2□Exec□t□on scenar□□ of algor□t□m M□

4   □erformance E□al□at□□n

Extensive performance studies are conducted in this section. The simulation model built to evaluate the query processing in a mobile computing system is described in Section 4.1. Experimental results of query processing schemes, including those of QP_C, QP_S and QP_{SJ}, are presented in Section 4.2.

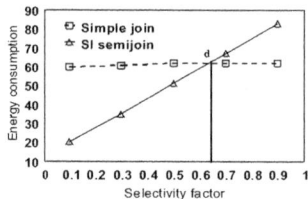
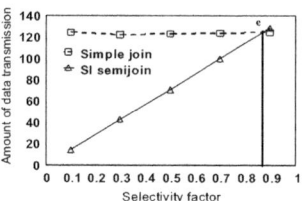

(a). The energy consumption of SI semijoin and simple join.

(b). The amount of data transmission of SI semijoin and simple join.

Fig. 3. The performance of SI semijoins and simple joins for $r_{SM} = 5$.

4.1   System Model

Simulations were performed to evaluate the effectiveness of query processing schemes. The simulation program was coded in C++, and input queries were generated as follows. The number of relations in a query was pre-determined. The occurrence of an edge between two relations in the query graph was determined according to a given probability. Without loss of generality, only queries with connected query graphs were deemed valid and used for our study. Based on the above, the cardinalities of relations and attributes were randomly generated from a uniform distribution within some reasonable ranges. These settings are similar to those prior works in query processing [5]. The values of related parameters employed in a mobile computing system will be given in each experiment separately. The number of relations involved in query processing, denoted by n, is chosen to be 4, 5, 6, 7 and 8, respectively.

4.2   Experimental Results of Query Processing

In this section, we first evaluate the performance of an SI profitable semijoin. Then, performance studies of QP_C, QP_S and QP_{SJ} are conducted.

Experiments of SI Profitable Semijoin In this experiment, we set the value of r_{SM} to 5, the value of δ to be 0.5, the value of t_{tuple} to 0.01, the value of e_r to 0.1, and the value of r_E to 5. The amounts of data transmissions and energy consumptions of an SI (server-initiated) semijoin and a simple join are examined with the selectivity factor varied. According to Definition 1, an SI semijoin is called profitable if the amount of energy consumed is reduced by including this semijoin. From Figure 3a, it can be seen that the amount of energy consumed by an SI profitable semijoin is smaller than that by a simple join when the value of the selectivity factor is smaller than the corresponding value at point d (i.e., 0.63). Thus, the corresponding value at point d can be used as a threshold to identify SI profitable semijoins. Note that according to

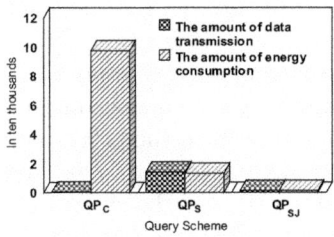

Fig. 4. The performance of QP_C, QP_S and QP_{SJ} when the number of relations is 5.

Theorem 1, the corresponding selectivity factor at point d can be estimated as
$\frac{(r_E \cdot e_r - \frac{1}{\rho} \cdot r_{SM} \cdot t_{tuple})}{(r_E \cdot e_r + \frac{1}{\rho} \cdot r_{SM} \cdot t_{tuple})} = \frac{5 \cdot 0.1 - \frac{1}{0.5} \cdot 5 \cdot 0.01}{5 \cdot 0.1 + \frac{1}{0.5} \cdot 5 \cdot 0.01} = 0.667$, which is very close to the value
of 0.63 at point d that is empirically determined from Figure 3a. It is shown in
Figure 3b the amount of data transmission incurred by an SI profitable semijoin
is much smaller than that by a simple join, and the corresponding selectivity
factor at point e is larger than that at point d, agreeing with Corollary 1.1.

Performance of QP$_S$ and QP$_{SJ}$ We now examine the performance of query
processing among one server and many mobile computers. The number of relations in a query is set to 5, and 300 queries are random generated. For each
query, the three query schemes, i.e., QP_C, QP_S and QP_{SJ} are performed. Without loss of generality, we set the value of r_{SM} to 5, the value of ρ to 0.5, the
value of e_r to 0.1, and the value of r_E to 5. Figure 4 shows the amounts of data
transmission and energy consumption incurred by QP_C, QP_S and QP_{SJ}.

From Figure 4, it can be seen that scheme QP_C incurs the largest amount of
energy consumption among all schemes. Also, as validated by the experimental
results, by exploiting the asymmetric feature of computing capability between
the server and mobile computers, scheme QP_S can save the energy consumption of the destination mobile computer and participating mobile computers.
Furthermore, though reducing the amount of energy consumption, scheme QP_S
increases the amount of data transmission required. Note that by employing SI
profitable semijoins, scheme QP_{SJ} can further reduce both the amounts of data
transmission of energy consumption, showing the very advantage of interleaving
a join sequence with SI profitable semijoins in the RT phase.

5   Conclusions

In this paper, we first explored three asymmetric features of a mobile environment. Then, in light of these features, we devised query processing schemes.
Explicitly, according to those asymmetric features of a mobile computing system, we devised some specific criteria to identify SI profitable semijoins. We also

proposed and investigated three query processing schemes for the processing of multi-join queries in a mobile computing system. In particular, we formulated the query processing in a mobile computing system as a two-phase query processing procedure that can determine a join sequence and interleave that join sequence with SI profitable semijoins to reduce the corresponding costs. Performance of these query schemes was comparatively analyzed and sensitivity analysis on selectivity factor was conducted. It was shown by our simulation results that by exploiting the three asymmetric features, the proposed query scheme, QP_{SJ}, is very powerful in reducing both the amounts of energy consumption and data transmission incurred.

Acknowledgment

The authors are supported in part by the Ministry of Education Project No. 89-E-FA06-2-4-7 and the National Science Council, Project No. NSC 89-2219-E-002-007 and NSC 89-2213-E-002-032, Taiwan, Republic of China.

References

1. R. Alonso and S. Ganguly. Query Optimization in Mobile Environments. In *Fifth Workshop on Foundations of Models and Languages for Data and Objects*, pages 1–17, September 1993.
2. Applications of mobile computing. http://www.nokia.com/g/index.html.
3. D. Barbara. Mobile Computing and Databases — A Survey. *IEEE Transactions on Knowledge and Data Engineering*, 11(1):108–117, January/February 1999.
4. S. Ceri and G. Pelagatti. *Distributed Databases Principles and Systems*. McGraw Hill.
5. M.S. Chen and P.S.Yu. Interleaving a Join Sequence with Semijoins in Distributed Query Processing. *IEEE Transactions on Parallel and Distributed Systems*, 3(5):611–621, September 1992.
6. M.J. Franklin, B.T. Jonsson, and D. Kossmann. Performance Tradeoffs for Client-Server Query Processing. In *Proceeding of ACM SIGMOD*, pages 149–160, June 1996.
7. R. Jain and N. Krishnakumar. Asymmetric Costs and Dynamic Query Processing in Mobile Computing Environments. In *Proceeding of fifth WINLAB Workshop*, April 1995.
8. R. Jain and N. Krishnakumar. An Asymmetric Cost Model for Query Processing in Mobile Computing Environments. Wireless Information Networks, J. Holtzman, Kluwer, 1996.
9. J. Jing, A. Helal, and A. Elmagarmid. Client-Server Computing in Mobile Environments. *ACM Computing Surveys*, 31(2):117–157, June 1999.
10. Palm Pilots of 3com. http://www.3com.com/palm/index.html.
11. C. Wang and M.S. Chen. On the Complexity of Distributed Query Optimization. *IEEE Transactions on Knowledge and Data Engineering*, 8(4):650–662, August 1996.

Data Lockers: Mobile-Agent Based Middleware for the Security and Availability of Roaming Users Data[*]

Yolanda Villate[**,1], Arantza Illarramendi[1], and Evaggelia Pitoura[2]

[1] Languages and Systems Department. University of the Basque Country.
Apdo. 649, 20080, Spain. {jibvipey, jipileca}@si.ehu.es
[2] Computer Science Department. University of Ioannina.
GR-45110 Ioannina, Greece. pitoura@cs.uoi.gr

Abstract. Accessing remote data anywhere and at anytime constitutes an important advantage in many business environments. However, when working with mobile devices, users face many problems related to: (1) device restrictions: mobile devices are resource-constrained, more vulnerable and fragile than stationary devices (*devise exposure problems*) and, (2) the communication media: wireless communications are often unstable, asymmetric and expensive (*media problems*). To alleviate these problems, we present a service, the *Lockers Rent Service*, for keeping the data of mobile users in a secure and safe space in a proxy at the fixed network, thus providing a solution to the device exposure problems. Data stored in data lockers are available even when the mobile device is disconnected. Furthermore, specific tasks are carried out at the fixed network on behalf of the mobile user, in this way relieving the media problems. The architecture of the *Locker Rent Service* is based on mobile agents.

1 Introduction

The sheer rapidity of the spread of wireless and Internet technologies is favoring a new telecommunication revolution. The possibility of accessing remote data anywhere and at anytime constitutes an important advantage in many business environments. However, when working with mobile devices, users face many obstacles related to the nature of the devices and the communication media used.

In [14], we introduced the preliminary version of ANTARCTICA[1] system. The main goal of this system is to provide a set of data services that enhance the

---

[*] This work is supported by *CICYT: Comisión Interministerial de Ciencia y Tecnología*, Spain. [TIC97-0962]; and MOVISTAR, a Spanish Cellular Phone Company.
[**] The work of this author was supported by a grant of the University of the Basque Country.
[1] ANTARCTICA: Autonomous ageNT bAsed aRChitecture for cusTomized mobIle Computing Assistance.

O. Etzion and P. Scheuermann (Eds.): CoopIS 2000, LNCS 1901, pp. 275–286, 2000.
© Springer-Verlag Berlin Heidelberg 2000

capabilities of Mobile Units (MU) and offer new possibilities to mobile users. The architecture of ANTARCTICA is based on the use of the *Client/Intercept/Server* model [11, 10] that incorporates modules and agents both at the mobile device and at an intermediary element, or proxy, situated at the fixed network called the *Gateway Support Node*[2] (GSN). In this paper, we consider a scenario in which a cellular phone company offers services that mobile users, clients of the company, can contract. In such a scenario, the GSNs belong to the cellular phone company. The number of GSNs in the network depends on the number of users.

The goal of this paper is to describe the design and implementation of a service central to ANTARCTICA: the *Rent of Lockers Service*, introduced in [15]. This service incorporates mechanisms that allow mobile users to rent storage space at the GSN. The service offers a variety of types of lockers so users can choose the one that better fits their needs and preferences. Independently of the specific type of locker, user or mobile computing device, the *Locker Rent Service* offers several advantages to the users of mobile units:

1. **Storage space:** The locker becomes an extension of the MU's disk at the fixed network.
2. **Data protection:** The mobile client is the owner of the data stored in the locker. The data stored in the locker are protected against unauthorized accesses and modifications as well as any unexpected failures.
3. **Battery power saving:** The mobile client can stay disconnected for longer periods of time, while the data obtained for it are sent to its locker and stored there until it reconnects or explicitly asks for them.
4. **Wireless communications optimizations:** The space in the locker can be used to store data until it is possible or desirable to send them to the MU. Before sending data to the MU, the data can be preprocessed, filtered or adapted to the needs of the mobile unit and its user. The locker can also be used to store data needed to perform tasks that can be developed and executed at the GSN, thus avoiding their transmission to the MU.
5. **Flexibility and adaptability:** The implementation of the locker service using mobile agents provides for the dynamic adjustment of the space allocated to each locker. It also provides for the easy adaptation of the locker, by facilitating the dynamic creation of lockers tailored to the users needs. Furthermore, it physically supports mobility of the locker to follow the movements of the MUs.

Lockers can be rented by individual users (*private locker*) or by groups of users (*shared locker*). A **private locker** is related to a single user; the data stored belongs to that particular user and can be accessed or modified only by authorized agents representing the user. A **shared locker** is a locker rented by a group of users. A shared locker distinguishes between data to be used by all users in the group and data for each particular user, by managing sub-lockers for each of them. Moreover, the space in the locker that is shared by all users

---

[2] The Gateway Support Node name is borrowed from the General Packet Radio Service (GPRS). We take GSM and GPRS as the cellular network model for our work.

of the group constitutes an encounter place for these users who are able to communicate, share data, interchange messages, write messages for the rest of the group in a blackboard service provided and collaborate together.

There are two lines of research related to our work. The first line includes research that relies on the idea of renting resources: in [2] the main focus is on accounting CPU cycles and communications consumption made by the hosted processes; Xdrive [16] is a commercial product that offers disk space located at safe hosts (situated at the X:drive company), accessible through the Internet using a Web browser, or a desktop application to make this space appear as a new disk partition in the user's computer. On the contrary, the main idea of the *Locker Rent Service* is to provide mechanisms that allow mobile users to use storage space that is external to their mobile computers but remains always as close as possible to their actual physical location. The space available in the ANTARCTICA lockers is intended to be used on behalf of the user by the agents working for him. Moreover, the locker is an autonomous and auto-managed extension of the MU, dynamically customizable to the user needs and network status, that gives the agents more autonomy to work for long periods of time even when the MU is disconnected. The second line of related research exploits the use of *proxies* and software agents [6, 4, 5, 3, 7, 9]. To our knowledge, our work is the first one to combine both aspects, by employing proxies and agents to provide users with storage external to their mobile computers. However, our work can benefit from other works, such as the CODA project [6], by implementing the ideas and techniques they propose for the maintenance of data consistency among copies stored in the MU cache, the GSN and the servers.

The rest of this paper is structured as follows. In Sect. 2, we present the main features of the agents that participate in the service. In Sect. 3, we introduce some advanced features related to the management of the space available and the data storage, the security and the mobility of the lockers. In Sect. 4, we present performance results. Finally, Sect. 5 offers conclusions.

2   Agents that Participate in the Service

The architecture of the *Locker Rent Service* is based on mobile agents. Agents are executed in execution environments called *places* [1]. Mobile agents can travel from one place to another. The proposed service incorporates one place on the user computer called the MU Place, and two places situated in the GSN, the *Inventory Place* and the *Locker Place*.

Mobile agents provide the means to improve performance by: using local resources and services offered at the proxy; supporting asynchronous communications; facilitating an efficient management of data transfer interruptions; and, allowing to reduce the traffic of data in the wireless network. Moreover, our autonomous agents are devoted to serve particular users and thus are customized according to the task they must develop, the preferences of the user they represent, the actual state and characteristics of the computer machine and the network used.

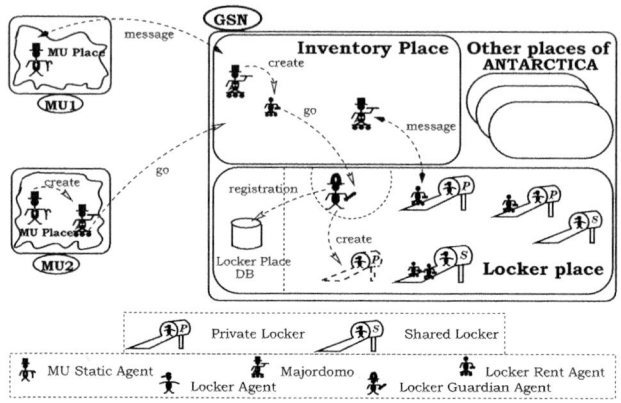

Fig. 1. Elements involved in the Locker Rent service

As shown in Fig. 1, there are five different kinds of agents involved in the *Locker Rent Service*. Each specific kind of agent has a different specialization area and a mission to perform, for which it may need to interact with other agents and places.

The MU Static Agent. At each MU there is a static agent running on a place in the MU, any time the MU is active. This static agent isolates the user's applications from network availability and the specific characteristics of the MU, and is responsible for the administration of the MU's resources.

The Majordomo Agent. The *majordomo* agent is created in the MU by the static agent and launched to a GSN at the fixed network. In each GSN, there is a place called *Inventory* where *majordomo* agents execute and can get the information they need about other GSNs, places and services in the system. Once launched, the majordomo agent remains in the GSN for the time period required, working on behalf of its MU even while the MU is disconnected.

Each mobile unit has its own *majordomo* agent with the aim of providing adequate services to its owner. Communications of the MU with the exterior are surveyed by both the static agent of the MU and its *majordomo* agent in the GSN. These two agents work together in order to adapt and optimize communications and use of the wireless media.

The Pair of Locker Agents. When the *majordomo* agent needs to use the *Locker Rent Service*, it creates an agent called *locker rent agent* and sends it to a *Locker Place*. The *Locker Place* is the place in the GSN that offers the *Locker Rent Service*. Although it would be possible for the majordomo agent to use directly the *Locker Rent Service*, we chose to create a special locker rent agent because it would be difficult for the majordomo agent to use efficiently all the different services offered by the ANTARCTICA system heeding at the same time the different user requirements.

Lockers are implemented using a new kind of static agents that we call *locker agents*. The *locker agents* are created by the *locker guardian agent* (we explain its features next) in the *Locker Place*, and each one of them is assigned to a specific user or group of users, i.e., to their *locker rent agents*. This pair of the *locker agent* and the *locker rent agent(s)* constitutes the locker and takes care of storing the user's data, saving email messages, processing results and communicating with the MU's *majordomo* agent. The fact that both agents have to communicate with each other and interchange data incurs some overhead. However, this interaction is local as both agents reside in the same place, the *Locker Place*. Furthermore, by having both kinds of agents, we can take advantage of specializing them.

The *locker agent* is specialized in interacting with the place and the available resources in order to store and recover data, and assure the privacy and security of its locker. So it makes the characteristics of the place and its resources transparent to the *locker rent agent* and to its user. Moreover, the *locker agent* of a shared locker interacts with a group of *locker rent agents*, acting as an intermediary and maintaining services such as a blackboard where the users can leave messages and data for other users. It also handles concurrent data accesses.

On the other hand, the *locker rent agent* is specialized on interacting with the user's *majordomo* agent. It has the knowledge about the user, as well as semantic knowledge about the data and how to utilize them. In that way, it makes transparent for the *locker agent* the characteristics of the specific user and its MU.

The Locker Guardian Agent. The *Locker Place* offers disk space for renting, so it has mechanisms to administer and monitor the available space, to assign spaces and survey their use, and to register data necessary for billing for the service. In order to get these functionalities, the *Locker Place* has associated a database and a *guardian agent*.

When the *Locker Place* is created a static agent is created within it, the *locker guardian* agent. The *locker guardian* agent is always active, its mission is to control the population of agents in the *Locker Place*, check the authorization and authentication of incoming agents, create and dispose *locker agents*, maintain a registry of the agents in the database (DB) and monitor the use of the resources.

3 Advanced Features

In this section, we introduce some advanced features of the *Locker Rent Service*.

3.1 Dynamic Management of Space

As mentioned in the previous section, lockers are implemented by a pair of agents collaborating together: the *locker rent agent* and the *locker agent*. The latter agent constitutes the locker itself. This solution allows us to manage the locker in a dynamic and flexible manner. There are no physically separated compartments to reserve, instead *locker agents* are created with space assigned in which they can store data. This means that lockers are created as they are rented by new users. Each *locker agent* occupies disk space according to its needs and limitations. When it needs more space, the agent occupies it, and when it needs less, the agent releases space. The space used by the locker is exactly the storage used by the data saved there. Although there is a limit in how much space the agent can use (by contract or specification), flexible policies can be used to optimize the use of space and improve the service provided.

3.2   Storage Management and Metadata

The data stored in a locker are actually text files that contain the raw data (files, e-mails, images, WWW pages, sql results) as well as metadata used to rebuild the object stored in the file to its original format. Metadata also provide summary information about the data stored such as their origin and content; and allow us to deal with large pieces of data, such as large files, images, sql results, by dividing them into smaller pieces that later can be reorganized and put together in order to rebuild the original. This feature can be very useful when considering for example the transmission of data from the MU to the GSN. Instead of sending the whole piece of data in a single message to the MU, the data can be broken into smaller pieces and then send each piece in an independent message. This way, if the communication is broken during the transmission or the MU has to disconnect, the transmission of the data can be resumed later, avoiding the retransmission of the pieces of the file that where already successfully sent and received at the MU.

3.3   Security

In the context of mobile agents, security is always a principal concern because generally agents can not trust the hosts they visit, and hosts can not trust the agents they receive. The protection of agents against malicious hosts is an open problem still without a completely satisfactory solution. The approach most commonly used is to rely on an organizational framework whose hosts can be trusted [13]. This is the case in our system, since the services offered by the GSN are provided within a trusted cellular phone company. Similarly, users are not unknown to the system, since they have signed a contract with the company for renting the services, and they have been assigned an ID and a set of passwords. Thus, the system can authenticate and validate authorized users and their agents.

In particular, the security of hosts against agents can be achieved satisfactorily by using existing techniques [13]. The central issue is to prevent uncontrolled access. In our system, the only agents that come from the outside, i.e. are created from classes unknown to the GSNs, are the *majordomos*. It must be ensured that such agents represent authorized users. To achieve this, credentials are associated with the agents. Credentials correspond to the identity of their user, access level and key. Such credentials are used for the authentication and authorization of the majordomo agents, and for controlling their access to services and data. This is achieved by checking their credentials against the information the system maintains about the registered users. When an agent creates another agent, it passes part of its identification information to the new born agent by issuing it a "passport" containing the necessary information to identify the agent and its creator. That "passport" is sensitive information that needs to be protected against copies, thieves and modifications.

Another important issue is preventing uncontrolled use of the host resources. The programming languages and the agent platforms used provide mechanisms to prevent agents and hosts to access the data or code of others such as separated memory address spaces for the host and each agent. Also, they provide authentication and authorization mechanisms, as well as mechanisms to avoid uncontrolled copying and cloning of agents. To authenticate code and its origins, cryptographic techniques can be used, as for example signatures [12].

Apart from the use of mobile agents, in the *Locker Rent Service*, data stored in a private locker belong to the user and are protected against unauthorized access from other users or their agents. In a shared locker, members of the group owning the locker are allowed to access the data that is specifically stored as common, while each user in the group has a private area where he can store information that nobody else has the right to access. This is achieved by not allowing the *locker agents* access any other disk space but their own. When a *locker rent agent* makes a request to a *locker agent*, the *locker agent* checks the authenticity of the *locker rent agent* and decides to which data it has access to.

3.4   Mobility of the Locker

Private lockers are typically created in the GSN under the coverage of which the MU is located. In our system, the *majordomo* agent is located as close as possible to the MU it belongs to. This means that when a MU moves to an area covered by a different GSN, its *majordomo* agent also moves to the new GSN carrying with it its data and (some of) the agents that are working for it. When deciding to occupy a locker, the user can specify whether he wants: (a) the locker to move following his movements, (b) the locker to remain stationary, or (c) the system to decide when to move the locker. When the user specifies that he wants the locker to follow his movement, there is a possibility that neither the corresponding GSN nor any GSN in the neighborhood can accommodate the locker. In this case, the system informs the user or his majordomo that the locker can not be moved.

The system decides on whether to move a locker or not based on the cost-benefit of the transmission. Prior to the computation of the cost of the transmission of the locker and its contents, the *Locker Place* must negotiate to find another *Locker Place*, located closer to the new GSN of the *majordomo*, which can accept the locker being transmitted. Briefly described, the cost of moving the locker (C_{Move}) consists of the cost of transferring all data stored in it (C_{Transf}) plus the cost of interacting with the *majordomo* in the second GSN ($C_{CloseInt}$).

The cost of not moving the locker is the cost of the interaction between the *majordomo* and the locker located at different GSNs ($C_{NotMove}$).

The following parameters are involved in the computation of $C_{CloseInt}$ and $C_{NotMove}$: (1) $T_{stay}(s)$: an estimation of the time the *majordomo* will stay in the new GSN. The *majordomo* can estimate this from the previous behavior of the user, or the user can explicitly provide such information. (2)$R_{Int}(Kb/s)$: an estimation of the rate of interaction between the *majordomo* and its locker that can also be induced from previous interactions. (3)$C_{FarCm}(s/Kb)$: the cost of communications between the *majordomo* in the new GSN and its locker in the current position. This can be calculated by the system. (4)$C_{NearCm}(s/Kb)$: similar to the previous cost but for the case of the locker being located in a position near to the new GSN.

To compute C_{Transf}, the following must be considered: (1) $T_{CrLAg}(s)$: the time to create a new *locker agent* in the new *Locker Place*, (2) $T_{Send}(s/Kb)$: the time to transmit to the new *Locker Place* the contents of size $S(Kb)$ stored in the locker, (3) $T_{UpdDB}(s)$: the time to update the DB of the new *Locker Place* with the N entries about the contents of the locker being transfered, (4) $T_{MoveLRAg}(s)$: the time to move the *locker rent agent* from the old *Locker Place* to the new one.

Without going into details and without considering the cost of interchanging few messages among the agents in order to coordinate the movement, as well as the deletion of what remains of the old locker, the two costs under consideration are:

$$C_{NotMove} = T_{stay} \times R_{Int} \times C_{FarCm} . \tag{1}$$

$$C_{Move} = C_{CloseInt} + C_{Transf} = (T_{stay} \times R_{Int} \times C_{NearCm}) + \\ + (T_{CrLAg} + S \times T_{Send} + N \times T_{UpdDB} + T_{MoveLRAg}) . \tag{2}$$

The locker is transferred if $C_{NotMove}$ is greater than C_{Move}. In general, moving the locker from one GSN to another is an expensive operation. Nevertheless, the possibility of moving a locker is useful since the system can choose to move a number of lockers from one GSN to another to balance the system load, while taking care of not deteriorating the interaction between the lockers and their *majordomos* by overly incrementing the cost of their communications.

The shared lockers are associated with a group of users whose movement is in general independent. Their location is the result of a decision of the group or of the representative of the group, so shared lockers do not necessarily move following their users.

4   Implementation and Performance Results

A prototype implementation of the *Locker Rent Service* using the platform "Aglets Workbench" [8] is under development. Currently, our prototype allows the creation of private lockers, the storage of files in the lockers, authorized access to the files, and the release of the lockers. Also, we have fully implemented the interaction among all components involved in the service: the agents (*MU static agent, majordomo, locker guardian agent, locker rent agent* and *locker agent*), the places (*MU, Inventory* and *Locker*) and the database in the *Locker Place*.

We have performed a number of experiments to validate our approach. In these experiments, the mobile device was a portable computer running Windows 98, equipped with a 233 MHz Pentium processor and 64 MB of RAM. We used a 9,600 bps GSM card as the communication device. For the GSN, we used a stationary computer running Linux Red Hat 6.1, equipped with a 400 MHz Pentium II processor, and 128 M of RAM. We have performed several experiments[3], in which we compared the time that the MU needs to be connected in order to get, for example, a file or a web page, according to three different approaches.

The first approach corresponds to the traditional Client/Server(CS) model: the MU opens a connection directly to the address where the file is located and the connection remains open until the file is downloaded. The second approach corresponds to the Client/Agent/Server(CAS) model: the MU sends a message to its *majordomo* agent located in the GSN, specifying the address of the file to be downloaded, and delegating the task of obtaining the file or web page to the *majordomo*. Then, the MU can close the connection. Once the file is obtained, the *majordomo* sends it to the MU in one message. Finally, the third approach corresponds to the Client/Agent/Locker (CAL) model: this is similar to the CAS model, except that the *majordomo* after obtaining the web page or file, sends it to the user's locker, where it is stored until the MU reconnects and the user asks for the file or web page.

Notice that we are only interested in the MU connection time and not in the total cost. That is, for the CAS and CAL approaches, we only have to consider the time needed to interchange the messages between the MU and the majordomo in the GSN. Saving connection time also means that the MU saves battery power and money. The CAS and CAL approaches make it possible to work in an asynchronous way, i.e., the MU submits a task to be performed and then disconnects or continues working on other tasks, while the submitted task is being executed in the GSN. When the task finishes, the MU receives the results.

Our experiments showed that when downloading a single file, the CS approach performs slightly better than the approaches using agents. The time the MU needs to be connected is determined by the time it takes to interchange data between the MU and the GSN. With the CS approach, this time is mostly the time it takes to send the file through the wireless media. However, in the CAS and CAL approaches there are some messages interchanged between the agents situated in the MU and in the GSN. Even if these messages are short, their transmission through the GSM media at 9,600 bps causes the small overhead of those approaches over the CS one. However, the bigger the size of the file, the more irrelevant the overhead. Nevertheless, these results do not constitute a proof against the use of the CAS and CAL approaches. Taking into account that the cost that influences the most the final cost is the one associated with the

---

[3] Each experiment has been performed more than 20 times.

low speed communication media, the approaches using the intermediary agent give the opportunity to reduce the communication cost by applying various optimizations such as (a) applying filters in the GSN that reduce the amount of data to be transmitted; (b) avoiding interactions between the MU and the GSN, i.e. the need of using the wireless media; and (c) performing tasks in the GSN that otherwise should be done in the MU (with the higher use of low speed communication media that this implies).

Experiments with such optimizations are reported in [15]. In one experiment, we applied *lossless compression* to the files before transmitting them to the MU. The results showed that even a small compression percentage suffices to make the approaches with agents perform better than the CS approach. In another experiment, to avoid interactions between the MU and its outside world, we run a test in which web pages (the .html file along with the files of the images incrusted in the page) were downloaded to the MU. The results demonstrated that the avoidance of interactions needed to download a single web page with few images is enough to make the approaches using agents perform better than the CS one.

These experiments show the benefits that the use of the approaches using intermediary elements can bring to the mobile computing framework. However, the performance of the CAL approach is slightly worse than the behavior of the CAS approach. This is because the use of the locker in the CAL approach introduces a time overhead due to the extra message sent from the MU to the *majordomo* in the GSN, once the MU reconnects. However, the ability of storing data for the MU in a persistent and safe way constitutes the strong point of the CAL approach over the CAS one. Moreover, we present an experiment that shows how the small overhead between the CAS and CAL is compensated and even inverted, by using a feature provided by the locker to facilitate dealing with complex requests, by storing their results in the locker for a period of time, and downloading them to the MU later.

For this test we assumed that the user requests, within a single *request message*, 4 different web pages to be obtained and stored in the locker. Table 1 shows the characteristics of the pages used. Later on, he requests (one *read message*) to download them together to the MU (one *answer message*). We compared this scenario with the following one in which the user request each page, one by one (one *request* and one *answer message* per page), to be obtained and downloaded to the MU. Notice that this last scenario corresponds to the case in which the user has not contracted a locker. Therefore, the *majordomo* agent can only keep the web pages with it for a short period of time before sending them to the MU.

In Fig. 2 we observe how the avoidance of messages between the MU and the GSN makes the CAL approach better than the CAS one. The total amount of data transmitted, belonging to the web pages, is the same in both cases, the only difference between both approaches is the number of messages interchanged. The analysis of the standard deviation also shows how the bigger the number of messages interchanged the bigger the instability.

Table 1. Characteristics of the set of web pages used

Page	No. of images	size of each image	No. of files to download	Data to download
Page 1	1	80 Kb	2	80 Kb
Page 2	4	20 Kb	5	80 Kb
Page 3	8	10 Kb	9	80 Kb
Page 4	16	5 Kb	17	80 Kb

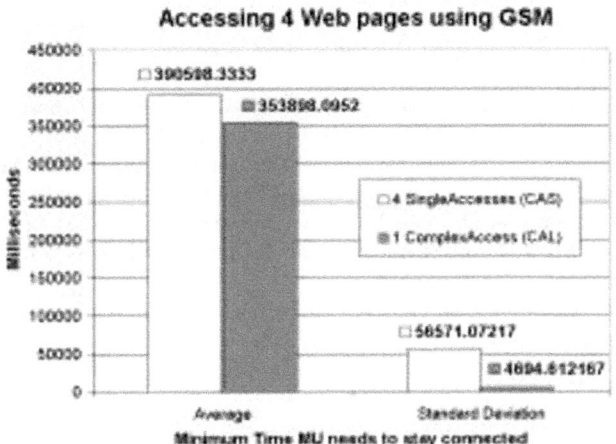

Fig. 2. Using GSM. Comparison of the minimum time the MU has to be connected in order to get 4 Web pages using the CAS and the CAL approaches

5   Conclusions

In this paper, we present a new data service for the mobile user: the *Locker Rent Service*. This service allows its users to use extra storage space located at the fixed network, outside of their mobile computer but close to them. Besides providing an extension of the storage space of the mobile computer, the service gives to its users more autonomy. Autonomy means that users can decide when to work disconnected or connected to the wireless network, since they can always count on the locker space for storing both the messages sent to them by other users and the results of their requests. Moreover, the use of lockers allows reducing data traffic in the wireless network, and provides an alternative for storing sensitive data.

For the implementation of the *Locker Rent Service* we use the agent technology. The induced overhead of using agents is greatly compensated by the advantages they provide with respect to performance, flexibility and adaptability. Our experiments show the feasibility of the implementation when compared to the traditional Client/Server approach. Furthermore, our experiments show how the performance of our approach is further improved when complex tasks are considered.

References

1. Milojicic et al. MASIF, the OMG Mobile Agent System Interoperability Facility. In *Proceedings of Mobile Agents '98*, September 1998.
2. Yair Amir, Baruch Awerbuch, and Ryan S. Borgstrom. A cost-benefit framework for online management of a metacomputing system. *The International Journal for Decision Support Systems, Elsevier Science. To appear.*
3. R. Gray, D. Rus, and D. Kotz. Agent TCL: Targeting de needs of mobile computers. *IEEE Internet Computing*, 1997.
4. A.D. Joseph, J.A. Tauber, and M.F. Kaashoek. Mobile computing with the Rover toolkit. *IEEE Transactions on Computers: Special Issue on Mobile Computing*, 46(3), March 1997.
5. A. Joshi, S. Weerawarana, and E. Houstis. On disconnected browsing of distributed information. In *IEEE RIDE97*, pages 101–107, 1997.
6. J.J. Kistler and M. Satyanarayanan. Disconnected operation in the Coda file system. *ACM Transactions on Computer Systems*, 10:3–25, 1992.
7. E. Kovacs, K. Röhrle, and M. Reich. Mobile agents OnTheMove – integrating an agent system into the mobile middleware. In *Acts Mobile Summit. Rhodos, Greece.*, June 1998.
8. IBM Aglets Workbench Home Page. http://www.trl.ibm.co.jp/aglets/.
9. S. Papastavrou, G. Samaras, and E. Pitoura. Mobile agents for WWW distributed database access. In *Proceedings of the International Conference on Data Engineering*, 1999.
10. E. Pitoura and G. Samaras. *Data Management for Mobile Computing*. Kluwer Academic Publishers, 1998.
11. G. Samaras and A. Pitsillides. Client/Intercept: a computational model for wireless environments. In *Proceedings of the 4th International Conference on Telecommunications (ICT'97)*, April 1997.
12. Bruce Schneier. *Applied Cryptography. Second Edition.* John Wiley & Sons, 1996.
13. Christian Tschudin. Mobile agent security. In *Intelligent Information Agents. Forthcoming LNCS.* M. Klusch.
14. Y. Villate, D. Gil, A. Goñi, and A. Illarramendi. Mobile agents for providing mobile computers with data services. In *Proceedings of the Ninth IFIP/IEEE International Workshop on Distributed Systems: Operations and Management (DSOM 98)*, 1998.
15. Yolanda Villate, Evaggelia Pitoura, Arantza Illarramendi, and Ahmed K. Elmagarmid. Extending the data services of mobile computers by external data lockers. In *Proceedings of the Third International Workshop on Mobility in Databases and Distributed Systems, MDDS'2000.* IEEE Computer Society Press, September 2000.
16. X:drive. http://www.xdrive.com/.

A Java Framework for Mobile Data Synchronization

Norman H. Cohen

IBM Thomas J. Watson Research Center
P.O. Box 704, Yorktown Heights, New York 10598, USA
ncohen@us.ibm.com

Abstract. An industry consortium has developed a Java framework for peer-to-peer synchronization of object stores on mobile devices. A device may issue or service requests for synchronization. Successful synchronization leaves replica stores in identical states. The framework is designed to accommodate memory-limited devices and unreliable and expensive connections. Stored objects belong to application classes with methods that are invoked by the framework during synchronization, for example to resolve update conflicts.

1   Introduction

The Mobile Network Computing Reference Specification, or MNCRS [15], defines a Java-based platform for communicating mobile devices. The specification, developed by an 18-company consortium, includes a framework for data synchronization. This paper describes version 1.1 of the framework, published in March 1999 and posted at http://www.mncrs.org.

The heart of the framework is a persistent synchronizable store, or *sync store*, containing Java objects. There may be *replicas* of a sync store on several usually disconnected devices. Replicas are peers. *Synchronization* brings two replicas into identical states. Synchronization may be initiated by an application, perhaps upon some action by the end user, or by a system utility that awakens at specified times or upon specified events, such as reestablishment of a network connection.

During synchronization, a sync store may receive an update that conflicts with its own most recent update to a given object. The sync store *reconciles* the conflict by invoking a method of the object. The object's class, and thus the reconciliation method, are provided by the application.

Section 2 explains the framework's notion of synchronization. Section 3 briefly addresses consistency among replicas. Section 4 presents the application programmer's view of the framework. Section 5 discusses the tracking of deletions. Section 6 reevaluates some of the assumptions underlying the design of the framework and discusses follow-on work. Other work on mobile data synchronization and distributed databases is compared with our approach throughout the paper. In [3], we discuss the design of the framework, and a reference implementation that we constructed at the IBM Watson Research Center, in greater detail.

O. Etzion and P. Scheuermann (Eds.): CoopIS 2000, LNCS 1901, pp. 287–298, 2000.
© Springer-Verlag Berlin Heidelberg 2000

2   Synchronization

A synchronization consists of some number of *phases*, each of which sends updates in one direction. Conflicting updates are detected and reconciled at the receiving sync store. A successfully completed phase leaves the receiving store at least as up-to-date as the sending store was at the start of the phase.

A complete synchronization, leaving two sync stores A and B with identical contents, can be achieved by a phase sending updates from A to B followed by a phase sending updates from B to A. The results of reconciling conflicts at B during the first phase are sent back to A during the second phase (along with any nonconflicting updates that were performed at B before synchronization started). A set of many sync stores can be completely synchronized by arranging the sync stores in a ring and performing a sequence of one-phase synchronizations that propagate updates around the ring, back to the starting point.

A device capable of accepting a synchronization request from another device is called a *synchronization server*. Such a request includes a URL identifying the protocol to be used, the synchronization server's host name, and a sync-store name. A *synchronization request handler* running on a synchronization server continuously listens for an incoming synchronization request and invokes a new synchronizer to handle it. A synchronization request handler might listen at a well-known TCP/IP port for a socket connection request, or monitor a message queue for incoming messages, or periodically check an e-mail in-box, for example.

While synchronizing with one replica, a sync store will pass on updates it received earlier from other replicas. Therefore, an update can be received from a sync store other than the one at which it was first applied. Updates to the same object from different replicas, received during different synchronizations, do not necessarily conflict. One update may have been applied at a sync store where the other update had already been known, in which case the intent of the later update was to supersede the earlier one, as illustrated in Fig. 1.

For every object in a store, there is a history of update actions that resulted in the object's current state. Every set of update actions corresponds to a *version* used to determine when one update history conflicts with or supersedes another. Versions are partially ordered by a relation *later than* such that version v_1 is later than version v_2 if and only if the set of update actions corresponding to v_1 properly includes the set corresponding to v_2. An update supersedes another update to the same object if its version is later. Two updates conflict if they have versions neither of which is later than the other.

During synchronization, the sender need send only those updates that are new to the receiver. To determine which updates to send, the sender first obtains the receiving store's *summary version*, a version corresponding to the set of all updates that have been applied to that store. The sender transmits the current contents of objects with versions later than or conflicting with the receiver's summary version. Since none of the updates already reflected by the receiving store has a version later than or in conflict with the receiving store's summary version, but each of the transmitted updates does, only updates not already reflected by the receiving store are transmitted. Conversely, if a current

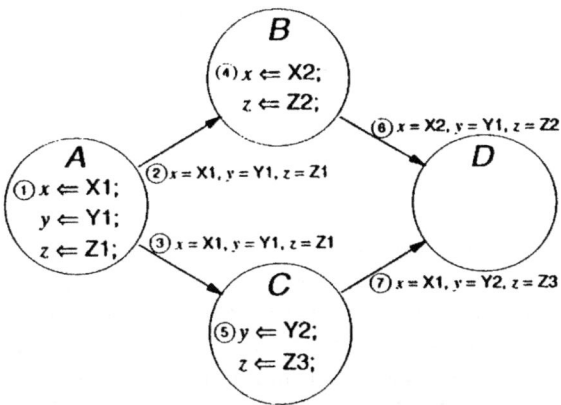

Fig. 1. The propagation of superseding and conflicting updates. Updates are applied at replica A and sent to replicas B and C during synchronization, where further updates are applied. Then B and C both synchronize with replica D. The update to object x that D receives from B supersedes the update to x that D receives from C. The update to object y that D receives from C supersedes the update to y that D receives from B. The updates to object z that D receives from B and C conflict.

update has not been reflected by a receiving store, its version is later than or in conflict with the receiving store's summary version, ensuring that the update is transmitted.

The framework requires that transmitted updates be applied to the receiving store, in *introduction order*—the order in which they were introduced to the sending store, either by an application running locally or by a previous synchronization session. Consequently, replicas obey what Petersen *et al.* [17] call the *prefix property*: If an update originally performed at some replica A is reflected in replica B, then so are any updates performed earlier at replica A.

The prefix property allows a version to be represented succinctly as a *version vector* [16]. Each replica assigns increasing integers to the updates originating there. The version vector corresponding to some set of updates specifies the last update originating at each replica that is a member of the set. In step 6 of Fig. 1, replica D receives version vectors $<A{:}1, B{:}1, C{:}0, D{:}0>$ for x (indicating that x was updated by update 1 at replica A, update 1 at replica B, and no updates at replicas C and D), $<A{:}2, B{:}0, C{:}0, D{:}0>$ for y, and $<A{:}3, B{:}2, C{:}0, D{:}0>$ for z; in step 7 it receives version vectors $<A{:}1, B{:}0, C{:}0, D{:}0>$ for x, $<A{:}2, B{:}0, C{:}1, D{:}0>$ for y, and $<A{:}3, B{:}0, C{:}2, D{:}0>$ for z. One version vector represents a later version than another, unequal version vector if each of its components is greater than or equal than the corresponding component of the other; two version vectors represent conflicting versions if each has some component greater than the corresponding component of the other.

The prefix property also ensures that if the transmission of updates is interrupted, so that only the selected updates preceding a certain point in the introduction order are received, the system remains in a normal state. The next synchronization can proceed as usual, selecting all updates with versions later than or conflicting with the receiver's new summary version. None of the updates successfully applied before the interruption will be retransmitted.

3   Consistency

Davidson, Garcia-Molina, and Skeen [4] classify database consistency strategies as *pessimistic* or *optimistic*. Pessimistic strategies prevent conflicts by limiting availability of data. Optimistic strategies allow replicas to be updated independently, detecting and resolving any resulting conflicts. It is widely agreed [8, 10, 13, 21] that pessimistic approaches are inappropriate in a network with many primarily disconnected mobile devices. Fischer and Michael [6] observe that there is an inherent conflict between serializability and availability in a distributed system, but that availability is a principal reason for deciding to replicate data in the first place. They assert that for applications such as appointment calendars, distributed e-mail in boxes, and distributed file systems, availability is more important than serializability.

Our framework is optimistic, and makes only weak consistency guarantees. Two replicas have identical contents after a complete synchronization with no intervening application updates. Repeated synchronization, propagating updates to all replicas, achieves eventual consistency. However, as we explain in [3], a phase interrupted by a communications failure can leave the store in a causally inconsistent state until the next synchronization.

The design of the framework anticipates transactional extensions. The update objects exchanged during synchronization may specify a *set* of operations on multiple objects, to be applied to a sync store atomically. Implementations may extend the framework's interfaces with methods for grouping operations into a single update object.

4   Application Programming

The fundamental components of the framework are *sync stores*, *synchronizers*, and a *store manager*. A sync store is a persistent store containing Java objects identified by keys called *sync IDs*. An application can provide its own classes for sync IDs that correspond to natural application keys, or let the framework generate sync IDs. Associated with each sync store is a registry of known replicas. An application accesses a sync store through the interface SyncStore. A *sync-store data collection* is the collection of data, stored persistently on a particular device, that can be accessed through a SyncStore object. The store manager administers sync-store data collections on the local device. A synchronizer obtains updates from a local sync store, exchanges updates with a synchronizer on another device, and applies remote updates. Different classes implementing the Synchronizer interface handle different transports and protocols.

The framework includes a cluster of classes and interfaces that form the implementation of sync stores, and another cluster of classes and interfaces that form the implementation of synchronizers. The two clusters, and the store manager, can be implemented independently of each other, and alternative implementations can be plugged into the framework.

A store-manager method named **open** constructs and returns a SyncStore object for a given sync-store data collection. A call on **open** may name an existing collection or request that a new, empty collection be created, to be populated by insertions or synchronization. Each call on **open** generates a reference to a distinct SyncStore object. However, several SyncStore objects may correspond to the same collection, as shown in Fig. 2, allowing multiple applications on a device to access the local sync-store data collection concurrently.

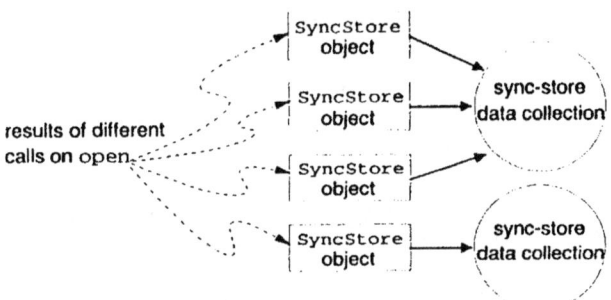

Fig. 2. Sharing of sync-store data collections through multiple SyncStore objects. Each call on open returns a reference to a new SyncStore object. Different SyncStore objects may refer to the same data collection or to different collections.

An object to be stored in a sync store belongs to an application class that implements the Reconcilable interface. This interface has methods to read and write byte-stream representations of the object's contents, plus three methods invoked during synchronization:

- a method to replace the object's contents, invoked when more up-to-date contents for the object are received
- a method invoked on an object in the local sync store when a local update to that object is found to conflict with a remote update, to set the local object to a state that resolves the conflict
- a method invoked to resolve a conflict between an update and a deletion, and either delete the local object or set it to a state that resolves the conflict

A Reconcilable object can be inserted in a sync store in association with some sync ID, retrieved using that sync ID, or deleted. The association established by an insertion can only be broken by a deletion. Until then, as long as the sync store remains open, the same object will always be associated with a given sync ID, although the *contents* of the object may change, and retrieval delivers the same object *reference* that was inserted with a given sync ID. When an application modifies the contents of an object in a sync store, it calls a method to inform the sync store of the change.

A sync-store data collection may be opened for *exclusive access*, or for *shared access* by multiple applications and synchronization request handlers. Since users of a collection share references to the same `Reconcilable` objects, race conditions can arise. Synchronization threads manipulate a `Reconcilable` object only within a `synchronized` block for that object. An application updating a `Reconcilable` object should perform the update, and mark the object as updated, in a `synchronized` block, to ensure that a synchronizer does not access the object after it has been updated, but before it has been marked. An application might also test, within this `synchronized` block, whether the object has been deleted from the store since the caller obtained a reference to it.

An application *closes* a `SyncStore` object when it no longer needs it. If other `SyncStore` objects for the same collection remain open, `Reconcilable` references obtained or inserted through the closed `SyncStore` object may still be shared by the holders of the other `SyncStore` objects; if no `SyncStore` objects remain open, then the in-memory representation of the sync store may be discarded, in which case the next `SyncStore` object constructed for that collection will yield references to *new* `Reconcilable` objects, freshly reconstructed from persistent storage. In either case, it is prudent for an application closing a `SyncStore` object to discard all `Reconcilable` references it obtained through that object.

Our framework implementation includes an interface for a *persistent-storage manager*. Our sync-store implementation is portable, accessing persistent storage through this interface and avoiding dependence on particular persistent-storage mechanisms. Framework implementations by other consortium members include similar interfaces, but members were unable to agree on a common definition, because of two apparently contradictory needs:

- There is an application-determined mapping between the contents of a `Reconcilable` object and data that is to be stored persistently. This mapping should be independent of the persistent-storage implementation.
- There is a mechanism determined by the persistent store for storing and retrieving representations of objects. It should be possible for the persistent-store implementation to implement this mechanism without any knowledge of the objects being written by particular applications.

In [3], we propose a standard intermediate representation to satisfy both needs. Application methods would map between the contents of `Reconcilable` objects and this intermediate representation; a persistent-store manager would map between the intermediate representation and persistent storage.

Using the JavaBeans event model [9], an application registers objects that *listen* for certain *events*. These objects can be used to track the progress of synchronization, or changes to a sync store by other applications or by synchronizers. There are three kinds of events:

- a *sync-object* event, reflecting the insertion, modification, or deletion of an object in the sync store
- a *sync-store* event, reflecting the opening or closing of a sync store, or the flushing of a sync store into persistent storage
- a *sync-status* event, reflecting the start, normal completion, or failure of a synchronization phase, or the completion of some portion of a phase

An application might, for example, listen for insertions during synchronization to accumulate a list of newly inserted objects, and listen for completion of the receiving phase to add these objects to a data structure; or it might update a graphical display of the current contents of a sync store after each change.

All SyncStore objects for a given collection share a single registry of sync-object-event listeners and a single registry of sync-store-event listeners. Each sync-object or sync-store event affecting the collection is reported to all registered listeners. The source of the event is the SyncStore object that triggered it. By examining the source, an application can distinguish events triggered through its SyncStore object from those triggered through other SyncStore objects.

A synchronizer performs a single synchronization between a particular local sync store and a particular remote replica. The local sync store is specified by a SyncStore object and the remote replica is specified by an object that specifies its URL and a schedule of synchronization phases. The Synchronizer interface has methods to start a synchronizer, or to request a synchronizer to stop; these methods return immediately. There is also a method that blocks until the synchronization has ended. For each of these methods, there is a corresponding method of a class named SynchronizerGroup, representing a set of synchronizers to be started, stopped, or waited for together.

The framework supports two styles for managing synchronization: The *synchronous style* entails calling a method that does not return until synchronization has completed, and then examining the synchronizer's final status. The *asynchronous style* entails obtaining a SynchronizerGroup object, registering listeners for sync-status events, then calling a method that starts a synchronizer or group of synchronizers and returns, so that the calling thread can continue in parallel with the synchronization. Synchronizer groups can be generated to synchronize one or more specified sync stores; each may be synchronized either with all it registered replicas or with a specified replica, which need not be registered.

Synchronizers are constructed using the *abstract factory* design pattern [7]. A *synchronizer-factory* interface has a method that attempts to create a synchronizer appropriate for a specified sync store, a specified replica URL, and current connectivity. For each class implementing the Synchronizer interface, there is a synchronizer-factory object constructing objects of that class. A new synchronizer is constructed by invoking each factory in turn, until one succeeds. If none succeeds, an object of a class named FailureSynchronizer (which implements the Synchronizer interface) is constructed. Any attempt to activate a FailureSynchronizer object immediately fails. The construction of a synchronizer group always succeeds, even if one or more of the synchronizers in the group fails upon activation or during synchronization.

A detailed tutorial on application programming with the MNCRS data-synchronization framework can be found in [2].

5   Deletion Tombstones

A classic problem in replicated databases, pointed out by Fischer and Michael [6], is that the presence of an item in one replica and its absence from another can mean that either an insertion or a deletion in one replica has not yet reached the other replica. Ratner, Popek, and Reiher [18] call this *the create/delete ambiguity*. The MNCRS data-synchronization framework addresses the ambiguity by maintaining a *sync entry* for each object in a sync store, retained as a *tombstone* when the object is deleted.

Tombstones cannot be allowed to accumulate indefinitely, especially on memory-constrained mobile devices. Once news of an object's deletion has reached every replica that was aware of the object's existence, its tombstone can be safely removed from all these replicas. However, the framework does not specify the distributed algorithms or protocols that synchronizers should use to reach this determination.

Without a central replica that participates in every synchronization, it is difficult to determine when tombstones can be removed. A two-phase distributed algorithm, analogous to those described by Sarin and Lynch [20] and by Ratner, Reiher, and Popek [19], can first determine the latest version earlier than or equal to the summary versions of all replicas, then inform all replicas that it is safe to discard tombstones with earlier versions. However, such algorithms are not well-suited to networks of weakly-connected mobile devices, because they generate high message volume over expensive links and depend on all nodes being reachable. Worse, the membership and topology of our network are defined dynamically, not by some recorded state, but by the act of synchronization.

We discuss the management of deletion tombstones in greater detail in [3].

6   Conclusions

Early in its deliberations, the MNCRS data-synchronization working group adopted several fundamental principles, which were accepted as axioms and constrained the design of the framework. Our specification and implementation experience validates some of these axioms, but call others into question.

- **Axiom: Synchronization should maintain sync stores as replicas.**
  Strict replication precludes an archiving function that deletes an object from a memory-constrained client without deleting it from the server. Furthermore, the user of a client device is often interested in only a subset of the objects in a server data store. A server could maintain separate mirror copies of each client sync store; alternatively, a server-based replica of a client sync store could store its contents in some larger, shared persistent store, as shown in Fig. 3. In [3], we discuss the semantic implications of several approaches for determining membership in the overlapping subsets of Fig. 3.

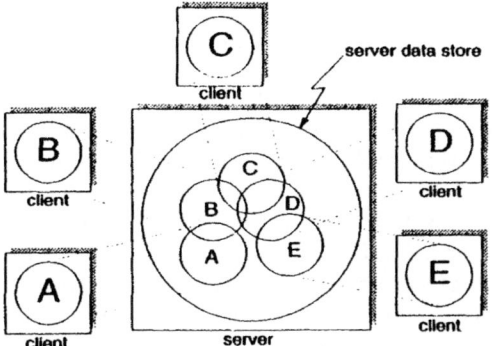

Fig. 3. Implementing server sync stores as subsets of some larger persistent store.

- <u>Axiom</u>: **An application marks an entire object rather than a particular field as updated, and a copy of the entire updated object is transmitted during the next synchronization.**
  Some applications require the exchange of transformations rather than the states resulting from those transformations. For example, when an application increments a shared count, the appropriate reconciliation of a conflict depends not on the resulting count, but the amount of the increment. Furthermore, transmitting differences between states, rather than entire states, usually requires less bandwidth. Early drafts of the framework included provisions for synchronization based on transformations, which were dropped because they were too complicated to specify and use. In [3], we describe simpler differential-update mechanisms, in which transformations are constrained to have certain algebraic properties.
- <u>Axiom</u>: **Peer-to-peer synchronization should be supported.**
  We expected that if we accommodated the most general synchronization topology, appropriate solutions for more restrictive topologies, such as star topologies, would fall out as a byproduct. Instead, we found that the best approaches for more restrictive topologies are fundamentally different from those required for peer-to-peer synchronization. We were hard pressed to come up with compelling applications for peer-to-peer synchronization. The developers of Ficus [18] and Bayou [5] envisioned mobile workgroups with devices disconnected from any fixed network, but able to communicate with each other wirelessly, or even by the exchange of diskettes. However, access to fixed networks has become ubiquitous since those scenarios were posited.
- <u>Axiom</u>: **Asynchronous synchronization phases should be supported.**
  Updates might trickle to a mobile device through a pager throughout the day, and updates from the device might be sent in a burst once a day over a phone line. However, as we explain in [3], there is a price for this flexibility. The need to accommodate asynchronous phases complicates version management, detection of communication errors, and error recovery.

– <u>Axiom</u>: **Updates are transmitted in introduction order.**
  This restriction allows versions to be represented by version vectors, and
  facilitates incremental progress when the transmission of updates is interrupted. However, it precludes application-managed delivery priorities. Objects with different priorities could be placed in different sync stores, synchronized in priority order, but this would complicate the application. An
  enhanced framework could relieve the application of some bookkeeping, implementing a single sync store internally with a separate summary version
  for each priority level. An application would be required to select an object's
  priority upon insertion, from among a few discrete priority levels.
– <u>Axiom</u>: **Conflicts consist of concurrent writes.**
  Bayou *dependency checks* [21] detect application-defined conflicts. A system that detects semantic conflicts can be programmed to detect concurrent
  writes. If applications requiring the detection of write conflicts are rare, it
  makes sense for the storage burden of version vectors to be borne only by
  those applications requiring them; if such applications are common, it makes
  sense for the data-synchronization framework to do the bookkeeping.
– <u>Axiom</u>: **Application code is trustworthy.**
  We trust an application to inform a sync store when it changes the contents of a Reconcilable object, to avoid race conditions, and to discard
  Reconcilable references when a sync store is closed. The application methods invoked to resolve conflicts and read or write byte-stream representations
  are trusted to do no harm, to terminate, and to produce correct results. In
  contrast, Bayou *merge procedures* [5] and Coda *application-specific resolvers*
  [11, 12] are untrusted. Bayou merge procedures are not allowed to have any
  side-effects other than writing the database. Coda resolvers are executed on
  client machines with user privileges, thus protecting servers from resolvers.
  Both systems abort conflict resolution if it runs too long.
– <u>Axiom</u>: **The framework should be Java-centric.**
  The single-reference model of object storage and retrieval relies on garbage
  collection. Once an application retrieves a reference to a stored object, the
  sync store loses the ability to count live references to the object. Neither the
  sync store nor the application program can safely free the object's storage.
  This precludes direct transliteration of the framework to a language like C.

Important lessons were learned from the specification and implementation
of the framework, and we expect the framework to inspire and influence future data-synchronization research. There have already been two spinoffs of the
MNCRS data-synchronization work at IBM: a state-machine model of data synchronization and the Mobile Data Synchronization Service.

The state-machine model is called the Co-Operative State Machine for Object
Synchronization, or COSMOS. It was a response to interest expressed in implementing a synchronization server with no application interface, and in specifying
protocols that enable non-MNCRS data stores to synchronize with MNCRS sync
stores. The framework specifies MNCRS data-synchronization semantics only in-
directly, in terms of Java methods. COSMOS specifies the set of synchronization

updates generated in a given state and the state transition that occurs when a synchronization or application-program update is applied to a given state. COSMOS does not define protocols, transports, or interfaces for application updates and queries. Work is underway on additional COSMOS models reflecting a variety of synchronization topologies and policies. These models will help us understand the performance implications of various policy decisions, catalog synchronization models to facilitate interoperability among independently developed products, and prove properties of synchronization protocols.

The Mobile Data Synchronization Service [1], or MDSS, allows a variety of clients, including a Java object store, to synchronize with a variety of central databases. MDSS platforms communicate through the *Mobile Data Synchronization Protocol*, which defines the form of an XML document for data exchange. Documents are encoded into WBXML [14], a succinct representation of XML, and transmitted by MQ Series Everywhere, a lightweight reliable message-queuing facility. We used our reference implementation of the MNCRS data-synchronization framework as the starting point for the MDSS Java object-store client, wrote a new pluggable synchronizer, and modified our implementation to exploit the restricted way in which MDSS clients use the framework.

Acknowledgments. This paper describes the results of a collaborative effort by the MNCRS data-synchronization working group. The group included Lonnie Hansen of Arkona; Henry Kings of Ericsson; Yoshifumi Miyata of Fujitsu; Yoshinori Kishimoto of Hitachi; Maria Butrico, Henry Chang, Jeremy Jones, Shinsuke Mitsuma, Hiroki Murata and Apratim Purakayastha of IBM and Lotus; Tetsuo Maeda of Matsushita; Seiji Fujii, John Howard, Masahiro Kuroda, Hideaki Okada, Ryoji Ono, Luosheng Peng, and Mariko Yoshida of Mitsubishi; Ken Chan of Nortel; Rafiul Ahad and Jiader Day of Oracle; Takao Ikoma of Sharp; Teck Yang Lee, Brian Raymor, and Roger Riggs of Sun; and Hidekazu Izumi, Satoshi Hoshina, and Tetsuro Muranaga of Toshiba. All members of the group could be considered coauthors of this paper; however, the opinions expressed about the strengths and shortcomings the framework are my own.

References

1. Butrico, M., Cohen, N., Givler, J., Mohindra, A., Purakayastha, A., Shea, D., Cheng, J., Clare, D., Fisher, G., Scott, R., Sun, Y., Wone, M., Zondervan, Q.: Enterprise data access from mobile computers: an end-to-end story. Proc. Tenth Intl. Workshop on Research Issues in Data Eng., February 27–28, 2000, San Diego, California. IEEE Computer Society, Los Alamitos, California (2000) 9–16
2. Cohen, N.H. Application programmer's guide to mobile network computing data synchronization. Mobile Network Computing Reference Specification Data Synchronization Working Group <URL: http://www.oadg.or.jp/activity/mncrs/dsync/pgmguide/tutorial-1_1.pdf> (1999)
3. Cohen, N.H.: Design and implementation of the MNCRS Java framework for mobile data synchronization. Research report RC-21774, IBM Thomas J. Watson Research Center, Yorktown Heights, New York (2000)
4. Davidson, S.B., Garcia-Molina, H., Skeen, D.: Consistency in partitioned networks. ACM Computing Surveys **17** (1985) 341–370

5. Demers, A., Petersen, K., Spreitzer, M., Terry, D., Theimer, M., Welch, B.: The Bayou architecture: support for data sharing among mobile users. In: Cabrera, L.-F., Satyanarayanan, M. (eds.): Workshop on Mobile Computing Systems and Applications, December 8-9, 1994, Santa Cruz, California. IEEE Computer Society Press, Los Alamitos, California (1995) 2-7

6. Fischer, M.J., Michael, A.: Sacrificing serializability to attain high availability of data in an unreliable network. Proc. ACM Symp. Principles of Database Systems, March 29-31, 1982, Los Angeles, California. (1982) 70-75

7. Gamma, E., Helm, R., Johnson, R., Vlissides, J.: Design Patterns. Addison-Wesley, Reading, Massachusetts (1995)

8. Guy, R.G., Heidemann, J.S., Mak, W., Page, T.W., Jr., Popek, G.J., Rothmeier, D.: Implementation of the Ficus replicated file system. Proc. Summer USENIX Conf., June 1990, Anaheim, California. 63-71

9. Hamilton, G. (ed.): JavaBeans, version 1.01. <URL: http://java.sun.com/ beans/docs/beans.101.pdf> Sun Microsystems (1997)

10. Kawell, L., Jr., Beckhardt, S., Halvorsen, T., Ozzie, R., Greif, I.: Replicated document management in a group communication system. In: Marca, D., Bock, G. (eds.): Groupware: Software for Computer-Supported Cooperative Work. IEEE Computer Society Press, Los Alamitos, California (1992) 226-235

11. Kumar, P., Satyanarayanan, M.: Supporting application-specific resolution in an optimistically replicated file system. Fourth Workshop on Workstation Operating Systems, October 14-15, 1993, Napa, California. IEEE Computer Society Press, Los Alamitos, California (1993) 66-70

12. Kumar, P., Satyanarayanan, M.: Flexible and safe resolution of file conflicts. Proc. USENIX 1995 Technical Conf. UNIX and Advanced Computing Systems, January 16-20 1995, New Orleans, Louisiana. n.p.

13. Lu, Q., Satyanarayanan, M.: Isolation-only transactions for mobile computing. Operating Systems Review 28 (1994) 81-87

14. Martin, B., Jano, B.: WAP binary XML content format. <URL: http: //www.w3.org/TR/wbxml/> W3C Note (1999)

15. Montenegro, G.: MNCRS: industry specifications for the mobile NC. IEEE Internet Computing 2 (1998) 73-77

16. Parker, D.S., Popek, G.J., Rudisin, G., Stoughton, A., Walker, B.J., Walton, E., Chow, J.M., Edwards, D., Kiser, S., Kline, C.: Detection of mutual inconsistency in distributed systems. IEEE Trans. Software Eng. SE-9 (1983) 240-247

17. Petersen, K., Spreitzer, M.J., Terry, D.B., Theimer, M.M., Demers, A.J.: Flexible update propagation for weakly consistent replication. SIGOPS '97: Proc. Sixteenth ACM Symp. Operating Systems Principles, October 5-8, 1997, Saint-Malo, France. 288-301

18. Ratner, D., Popek, G.J., Reiher, P.: Peer replication with selective control. UCLA Technical Report CSD-960031 (1996)

19. Ratner, D., Reiher, P., Popek, G.J.: Dynamic version vector maintenance. UCLA Technical Report CSD-970022 (1997)

20. Sarin, S.K., Lynch, N.A.: Discarding obsolete information in a replicated database system. IEEE Trans. Software Eng. SE-13 (1987) 39-47

21. Terry, D.B., Theimer, M.M., Petersen, K., Demers, A.J., Spreitzer, M.J., Hauser, C.H.: Managing update conflicts in Bayou, a weakly connected replicated storage system. SIGOPS '95: Proc. Fifteenth ACM Symp. Operating Systems Principles, December 3-6, 1995, Copper Mountain Resort, Colorado. 172-182

Dynamic Pricing with Limited Competitor Information in a Multi-Agent Economy

Prithviraj Dasgupta[1] and Rajarshi Das[2]

[1] Dept. of Electrical and Computer Engineering, University of California
Santa Barbara, CA 93106, USA,
pdg@alpha.ece.ucsb.edu,
[2] Institute for Advanced Commerce, IBM Research,
Hawthorne, NY 10532, USA,
rajarshi@us.ibm.com

Abstract. We study the price dynamics in a multi-agent economy consisting of buyers and competing sellers, where each seller has limited information about its competitors' prices. In this economy, buyers use *shopbots* while the sellers employ automated pricing agents or *pricebots*. A pricebot resets its seller's price at regular intervals with the objective of maximizing revenue in each time period. Derivative following provides a simple, albeit naive, strategy for dynamic pricing in such a scenario. In this paper, we refine the derivative following algorithm and introduce a model-optimizer algorithm that re-estimates the price-profit relationship for a seller in each period more efficiently. Simulations using the model-optimizer algorithm indicate that it outperforms derivative following even though it does not have any additional information about the market. Our results underscore the role machine learning and optimization can play in fostering competition (or cooperation) in a multi-agent economy where the agents have limited information about their environment.

Keywords: Electronic commerce, dynamic pricing, multi-agent systems, shopbots and pricebots.

1 Introduction

With the rapid growth of agent-mediated electronic commerce, it is becoming increasingly evident that in a few years the Internet will host large numbers of interacting software agents. A vast number of these agents will be economically motivated, and will exchange a variety of information goods and services. In this information economy, software agents will be economic decision makers and will play a fundamental role in many different aspects of electronic commerce, including negotiations, sales, and purchase. Compared to human agents, such software agents will have limited intelligence and rationality, and will need to take decisive actions without having complete information about the market. On the other hand, software agents will be adaptive, and will be able to think and act much faster than human agents. How will the dynamics of the collective behavior of such agents affect our economy? We believe that there

O. Etzion and P. Scheuermann (Eds.): CoopIS 2000, LNCS 1901, pp. 299–310, 2000.
© Springer-Verlag Berlin Heidelberg 2000

is the need to understand and anticipate the collective behavior of economically motivated software agents before employing them in the real world. With these issues as the underlying motivation for our work, this paper focuses on a particular model of an information economy involving groups of autonomous software agents employing *dynamic posted pricing*, i.e., take-it-or-leave-it pricing in which the seller may change the price at any time. Our particular emphasis is on the price dynamics engendered by small groups of myopic and selfish software agents trying to maximize their payoff from the market.

Typically, in determining its own pricing strategy, a seller uses available information about the market, such as the distribution of buyer preferences, or its competitor's prices. There has been recent work in the literature which attempt to address the question of automated dynamic pricing assuming more or less complete information about the market [6, 8, 12]. But what if the seller has only limited information about its environment? In our earlier work, we have explored how a monopolistic seller might dynamically set its price schedule to maximize profit in a market where it has to learn the buyer preferences [2, 7]. In this work, we study markets with multiple sellers competing for the largest market share, where each seller has no information about the buyer preferences or its competitors' prices.

In the traditional economy, obtaining a competitor's pricing information often involves considerable effort, and in certain situations such information may be unavailable (e.g., sealed-bid auctions) or it may be unethical and illegal to gather such data. In contrast, price-checks from competitors in electronic markets is fairly trivial and, indeed, is a common practice. However, there is no guarantee that online competitors will continue to maintain the price they have revealed. An intelligent seller might reset its price slightly at irregular intervals to leave an inquisitive competitor with outdated price information. Moreover, with a huge population of online sellers, price comparison with competitors can become an arduous burden in comparison to the actual task of selling goods. Our objective in this paper is to investigate strategies that enable profit maximizing sellers to identify price settings without having direct knowledge of the price charged by competitors.

Derivative following, which neither uses information about competitors' prices nor any information about buyers, offers one possible dynamic pricing strategy. We show that a naive derivative following approach is inefficient and in certain real world situations, it fails miserably. In this paper, we extend our earlier work in this area [4] by refining the derivative following algorithm and by introducing a model-optimizer algorithm which enables sellers to be more competitive in information-limited environments.

The paper is organized as follows. In Section 2, we describe the shopbot model of the multi-agent economy considered in this work, and outline previous work related to this model. Section 3 delineates the different non-negotiable dynamic price-setting algorithms, while Section 4 contrasts the interacting dynamics and the performance of agents employing the different pricing strategies through simulations. We conclude with an outline of the directions for future research.

2   Model

We study the price dynamics in a simple model of the shopbot economy proposed by
Kephart and Greenwald [6, 8, 9]. In this model, the market consists of S sellers who
compete to provide B buyers ($B \gg S$) with a single indivisible commodity, such as a
specific book.

Each buyer has a valuation p_m corresponding to the maximum unit price it is willing
to pay. Prior to purchase, each buyer samples the market price of the item by querying
the sellers at a rate ρ_b. Buyers are of two types depending on their selection criterion of
a seller:

- A *bargain-hunting buyer* employs a shopbot to select the seller that offers the lowest price and purchases the good if the price offered by the seller is below its valuation p_m. Price ties between multiple sellers are broken randomly.
- A *randomly-selecting buyer* chooses a seller at random and purchases the good if
  the price offered by the seller is below the valuation price p_m.

The model further assumes that a buyer's strategy in selecting a seller is uncorrelated
with its valuation p_m, and that it does not change with time.

Upon entering the market with an initial price p_0, sellers are allowed to reset their
price at time intervals $\tau_s = 1/\rho_s$. At any time interval t, a seller's goal is to maximize its
immediate profit by setting a price p_t for a single unit of the good, given its production
cost p_{co}.

If B_{BH} and B_{RS} respectively represent the number of bargain-hunting buyers and
the number of randomly-selecting buyers in the buyer population, then the profit of a
seller at time t is given by

$$\pi_t = p_t(B_{BH} + \frac{B_{RS}}{S})\frac{\rho_b}{\rho_s}$$

if the seller is charging the minimum price in the market at time t, and,

$$\pi_t = p_t(\frac{B_{RS}}{S})\frac{\rho_b}{\rho_s}$$

if the seller is not charging the minimum price in the market. The expression in paren-
theses in the above equations represent the expected number of times a seller is selected
by the buyers during the time interval t.

In [5, 6], Greenwald and Kephart view the price setting problem as a one-shot game,
and provide a detailed game theoretic analysis of the shopbot economy showing that
although there is no pure strategy Nash equilibrium, there exists a symmetric mixed
strategy Nash equilibrium. Greenwald and Kephart also show through simulations that
pricebots using a Myoptimal or a No-regret pricing strategy give rise to cyclic price-
wars. However, the Myoptimal and No regret pricing strategies studied in their work
are informationally intensive and require the details knowledge of the buyer demand
function, competitors' prices and payoffs. Here, we adopt the opposite scenario by assuming that the pricebots are relatively uninformed about the buyer's demand function
or their competitors' pricing strategies.

In our previous work on dynamic pricing strategies [4] we have viewed the price-setting problem for sellers as a Bertrand game where sellers choose prices and sell as much as they can. Simulations using our experimental e-market revealed that a predominantly bargain-hunting buyer population caused sellers to sell at the production cost of the good, while an increase in the number of randomly-selecting buyers resulted in cyclic price wars.

3   Dynamic pricing algorithms

In this section we detail the different dynamic posted pricing algorithms considered in this work, and highlight the motivation behind each approach.

3.1   Derivative Follower Pricing Strategy (DF)

This is the simplest possible dynamic pricing strategy and is the least computationally intensive. It simply experiments with incremental increases (decreases) in price, and as long as the observed level of profitability increases it continues to move its price in the same direction. If the profit level decreases, it changes the direction of the price movement. Thus

$$p_{t+1} = p_t + \delta_t \, \text{sign}(\pi_t - \pi_{t-1}) \, \text{sign}(p_t - p_{t-1})$$

where π_t is the profit made by the seller during time t and the step-size δ_t is distributed uniformly between $[a, b]$, where $a, b > 0$.

3.2   Adaptive Step-size Derivative Follower Strategy (ADF)

In our earlier work [4], we showed that the simple derivative following approach results in large oscillations in prices when the seller's price reaches a magnitude close its asymptotic value. The large fluctuations in the price dynamics occur because the step size is chosen from a uniform distribution whose range remains constant with respect to time. Also, due to the large oscillations, a seller can lose a significant amount of potential revenue.

We have refined the derivative follower algorithm to dynamically shrink or expand the step size at the end of each time step according to the following equation

$$\delta_t = \epsilon^{\text{sign}(\pi_t - \pi_{t-1})} \times \delta_{t-1}$$

where $\delta_{min} \leq \delta_t \leq p_{t-1}$ and $\epsilon > 1$. δ_{min} is the lower bound on the step-size for the adaptive derivative follower. The initial value of the step-size is given by δ_0 which is chosen uniformly between $[a, b]$, where $a, b > 0$. Dynamic step adjustment enables a seller to reduce the step size when the price is in the vicinity of the optimum and increase it otherwise.

3.3 Dynamic Pricing using the Model-Optimizer Strategy (MO)

A significant drawback of the derivative following algorithm is that the size of the history window of a seller spans only one time interval. One straightforward approach to extend the derivative following algorithm is to increase the time window beyond one time-step and fit a polynomial to the historical price-profit relationship. Once this relationship is modeled, a new price that provides the maximum profit in the model can be determined, and this new price can be posted to the market. As new price-profit information arrives, the model can be continuously updated to reset the posted price.

A major handicap of the above approach is that Internet markets consist of more than one independent seller, and thus, the dynamics of the entire system is non-stationary. In such a situation, it can be argued that a seller has less confidence in applicability of past price-profit relationships in determining its future pricing strategy. This suggests an approach which can assign weights to historical price-profit information in terms of some criterion such as relevance. For this purpose we have used a nonlinear regression approach using least squares. It should be emphasized that the underlying non-stationarity of the system would allow this approach to be applicable only for short-term decision making. Additional information such as consumer preferences and competitors' choices can then be used for more long-term pricing strategies.

Assuming that pricebots have exact information about prices (p) and the measured profits (π) contain all the error or noise, a regression of profit π on price p can be performed. Since π is expected to be non-linearly related to p, we use a high-degree polynomial to model the price-profit data. Let $\pi = c_0 + c_1 p + c_2 p^2 + \ldots + c_r p^r$, where c_i are the coefficients of the polynomial we want to determine. We assume there are m data points (p_t, π_t) each associated with weight w_t. The weights express our confidence in the accuracy or relevance of the points. (Note that m must be greater than r.) The deviation at each point is

$$e_t = c_0 + c_1 p_t + c_2 p_t^2 + \ldots + c_r p_t^r - \pi_t.$$

We now form the weighted sum of squares of the deviations for points (p_t, π_t) with $\tau \leq t \leq \tau + m$

$$F(c_0, c_1, \ldots, c_r) = \sum_{t=\tau}^{\tau+m} (c_0 + c_1 p_t + c_2 p_t^2 + \ldots + c_r p_t^r - \pi_t)^2 w(t)$$

By setting the partial derivatives of F with respect to the coefficients equal to zero we find the normal equations which can be expressed in the matrix form as

$$
\begin{bmatrix}
\sum w_t & \sum w_t p_t & \cdots & \sum w_t p_t^r \\
\sum w_t p_t & \sum w_t p_t^2 & \cdots & \sum w_t p_t^{r+1} \\
& & \vdots & \\
\sum w_t p_t^r & \sum w_t p_t^{r+1} & \cdots & \sum w_t p_t^{2r}
\end{bmatrix}
\begin{bmatrix}
c_0 \\ c_1 \\ \vdots \\ c_r
\end{bmatrix}
=
\begin{bmatrix}
\sum w_t \pi_t \\ \sum w_t p_t \pi_t \\ \vdots \\ \sum w_t p_t^r \pi_t
\end{bmatrix}
$$

By solving the matrix expression we can find the set of coefficients which best fits a given set of m data points (p_t, π_t) along with their corresponding weights w_t.

After obtaining the polynomial fit on the price-profit relationship, a non-linear optimization scheme must be used to locate the price that corresponds to the maximum profit. We have selected the Nelder-Mead algorithm [10, 11, 13] to identify the price corresponding to the maximum profit in the modeled price-profit relationship. The Nelder-Mead algorithm employs a simplex hill-climbing approach to solve unconstrained maximization problems. Our previous work has shown that this approach well suited for price-setting problems in information limited environments [2, 7]

4   Simulations

We have designed and implemented an electronic market in software to study the performance of the different price-setting algorithms. To simulate asynchronous buyer requests in our system we have implemented the buyers on independent threads using Java. Multi-threading also enables a seller to perform price setting calculations simultaneously while it is busy receiving quotes from buyers.

The parameters used for our simulations are the buyer's valuation $p_m = 1.0$, the seller's cut-off price $p_{co} = 0.1$, the lower bound on the step size for the adaptive step-size derivative follower $\delta_{min} = 0.01$, and $\epsilon = 2$ for the adaptive step-size derivative follower. The step size δ, for the the fixed step size derivative follower is drawn from the uniform distribution $[0.01, 0.02]$. The price adjustment interval for sellers is taken as $\tau_s = 20$ quote requests from buyers. We have selected number of quote-requests received from buyers as the unit for measuring time to equalize differences between sellers with different response times. For all the simulations, as a crude approximation to an e-commerce survey presented in [3], we used $B_{BH} = 750$ and $B_{RS} = 250$.

For our simulations we have successively compared the different dynamic pricing strategies. We begin with derivative following, identify its drawbacks and then verify the performance of the model optimizer. To contrast the performance of different pricing strategies, we have also used a seller agent employing the simplest pricing strategy; i.e., maintain a constant price $p = 0.5$.

4.1   Derivative Follower Strategy

Figure 1a illustrates the pricing pattern that results from competition between two fixed step-size derivative followers DF_1 (with $p_0 = 0.3$) and DF_2 (with $p_0 = 0.9$), and one adaptive step-size derivative follower ADF (with $p_0 = 0.4$). From the beginning of the simulation, DF_1 and DF_2 enter into a price war lowering their price until they reach $p_{co} = 0.1$ and continue to maintain their price in the vicinity of p_{co}. ADF however fails to discover that there is an ongoing price war to attract the bargain-hunting buyers. It raises its price close to p_m to extract maximum profit from the randomly-selecting buyers and then reduces its step size to keep the price near p_m. This illustrates that a derivative follower strategy can be incapable of discovering a better price that is not in the vicinity of the seller's price.

Derivative following also suffers from an inability to track prices over long time intervals. This is shown in Figure 1b where a fixed step-size derivative follower DF, an adaptive step-size derivative follower ADF, and a fixed-price seller FP compete against

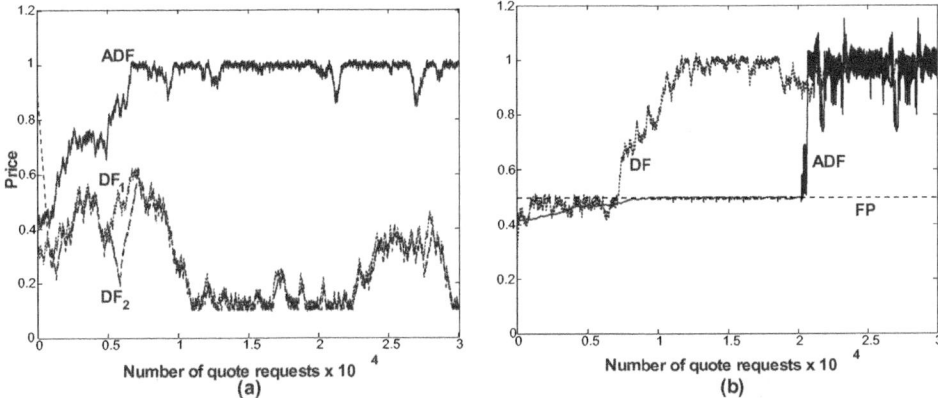

Fig. 1. (a) Price profile of two fixed step-size derivative followers (DF_1, DF_2) and one adaptive step-size derivative follower (ADF) competing against each other. (b) Price profile of an adaptive step size (ADF) and a fixed step-size derivative follower (DF) competing with a fixed-price seller (FP).

each other. Initially, DF succeeds in just under-cutting FP. However, around 7500 quote-requests, DF overshoots the price of FP by a small margin x. As a result, its profit decreases and in the next time interval it reverses the direction of the price change, and DF reduces its price by a step size of y. Note that the step size is drawn from a uniform distribution in $[0.01, 0.02]$, and since in this particular case the step size y was less than x, DF was unable to revert to under-cutting FP. Thus, DF's profit reduced further after reversing the direction of the price change. Since the history window of a derivative follower spans only one time step, DF became oblivious of its incorrect decision to increase its price beyond that of FP and continued to increase its price till it reached a value close to p_m. On the other hand, the adaptive step-size derivative follower ADF reduced its step-size to just under-cut the fixed price seller FP and it succeeded in avoiding the same mistake of crossing the price of the fixed price seller until 20000 quote-requests. However, once its price was more than that of FP it received less profit. In response, it increased its step size and rapidly reached p_m. Unlike in Figure 1a ADF exhibits large oscillations near p_m due to a price war with DF which also has a price close to p_m.

The fluctuations in the price around p_{co} in Figure 1a and around p_m in Figure 1b are due to the finite size of the buyer population and the stochastic nature of choosing sellers by the randomly-selecting buyers. This results in variation of the fraction of quote-requests from randomly-selecting buyers among the $\tau_s = 20$ quote-requests. Figure 2 illustrates this through a plot of the price-profit relationship when an adaptive step-size derivative follower that starts with $p_0 = 0.1$ competes against a fixed price seller with $p = 0.5$. Initially the derivative follower's profit increases as it increments its price towards the fixed price seller's price. In this interval the derivative follower attracts the entire bargain-hunting buyer population since it has the lowest price in the market. In this scenario, $p = 0.5$ corresponds to the optimum price in the system, since

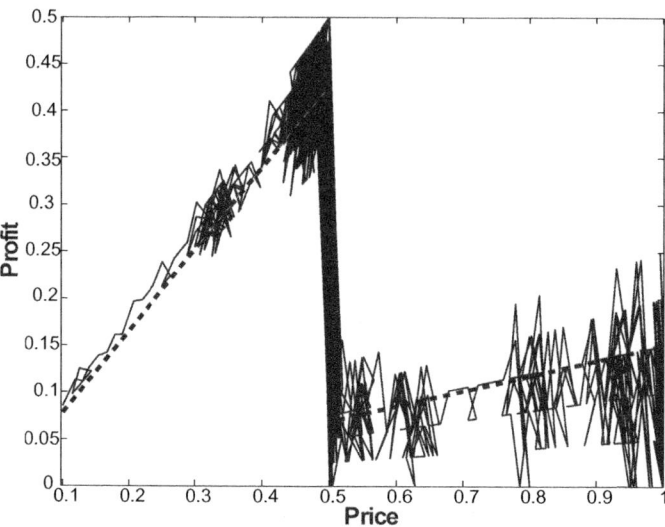

Fig. 2. Price-profit profile for an adaptive step-size seller competing against a fixed price seller with price set to $p = 0.5$. The size of the buyer population is 750 bargain-hunting buyers and 250 randomly-selecting buyers. The dotted line represents the theoretical price-profit relationship for an infinite size buyer population.

it guarantees the highest profit. The presence of large number of points around $p = 0.5$ indicates that the adaptive step-size derivative follower discovers and frequently sets its price at this optimum. However, due to the inability of derivative followers to track prices, the adaptive step-size derivative follower makes a wrong decision to increase its price beyond that of the fixed price seller and fails to revert its price back to the optimum. Thereafter, its profit is derived from solely from randomly-selecting buyers as it raises its price close to p_m. The broken line in Figure 2 shows the price vs. profit profile for the theoretical case when the size of the buyer population is infinite.

4.2 Model-Optimizer Strategy

The derivative follower algorithm performed poorly because its history window spans only one time interval. In the model optimizer algorithm we have addressed this problem by increasing the size of the history window to cover the last h time intervals. We ran our simulations for $h = 3$ and $h = 5$ and found, as expected, that with a larger window size the model optimizer estimates a better price to set during the next time interval. For all the simulation results of the model optimizer reported here, the history window was $h = 5$. In the beginning of the simulation, before the history window gets

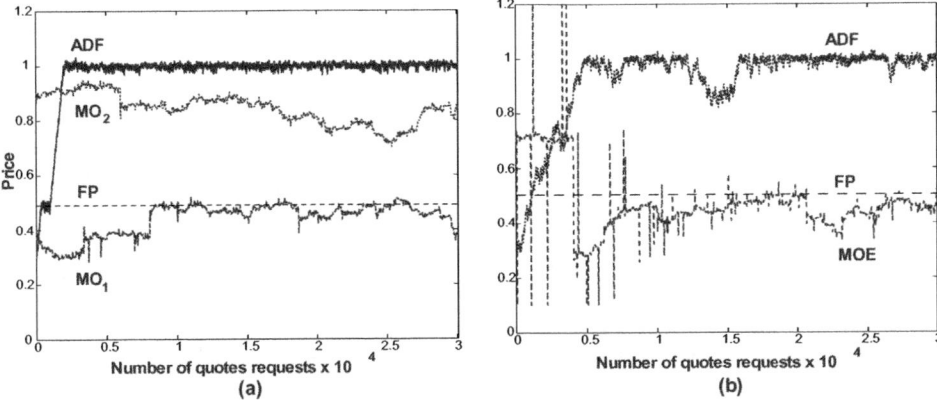

Fig. 3. (a)Price profile of a competition between a fixed-price seller (FP), an adaptive step-size derivative follower (ADF), and a model optimizer (MO). (b) Price profile of a fixed-price seller (FP), an adaptive step-size derivative follower (ADF), and a model optimizer with exploration (MOE) competing against each other.

initialized, the sellers move the price in a random direction with a step-size distributed uniformly in $[0.01 - 0.02]$. The weights w_t, denoting the relevance of the previously seen price-profit values, were assigned linearly decreasing values with $w_1 = 0.9$ and $w_5 = 0.5$. Also, for simplicity the historical price-profit relationship was modeled with a second degree polynomial.

Figure 3a compares the performance of two model optimizers MO_1 and MO_2 competing with an adaptive step-size derivative follower ADF and a fixed price seller FP. MO_2 (with $p_0 = 0.3$) is initially under-cut by the derivative follower ADF (with $p_0 = 0.4$). However, at almost 1000 quote-requests ADF makes a wrong decision and increases its price beyond that of FP, while MO_2 discovers FP at $p = 0.5$ and thereafter resorts to under-cutting it. MO_1, starting at $p_0 = 0.9$, however, fails to discover the sellers charging lower prices than itself and maintains almost the same price all along. This indicates that although model optimizers are more efficient than derivative followers, they are not capable enough to discover a price that is not in the vicinity of their current price. One solution to this problem is to allow the model optimizer to occasionally explore the price space and search for better prices.

4.3   Model-Optimizer Strategy with Exploration

We extended the model optimizer algorithm to explore the price space intermittently for better prices. The interval between two successive explorations, measured in number of price resets, is distributed uniformly between $[40 - 60]$ quote-requests [1]. In the beginning, the range of prices chosen during exploration is drawn from a uniform distribution in $[p_{co}, 5p_0]$. We assume that the maximum buyer valuation lies below the upper limit of

---

[1] Preliminary experiments showed this to be a suitable distribution that balances exploration against exploitation.

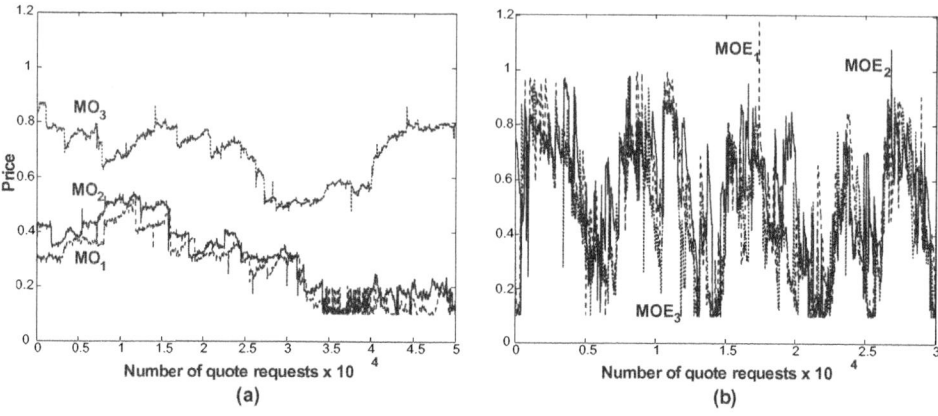

Fig. 4. (a) Price profile of three competing model optimizers without exploration (MO_1, MO_2, MO_3). (b) Price profile of three model optimizers with exploration (MOE_1, MOE_2, MOE_3) competing against each other.

this distribution. The upper limit of the distribution is adaptively adjusted at successive explorations to a price that returns positive profits.

The results of our simulation using the model optimizer strategy with exploration is shown in Figure 3b. All other parameter settings are retained from the simulation shown in Figure 3a. Although MOE starts with $p_0 = 0.9$, it explores the price space and discovers that profits increase when it reduces its price. It thus resets its price to $p = 0.3$ around 4000 quotes. Thereafter, it gradually increases its price and discovers the fixed price seller FP at $p = 0.5$, and resorts to under-cutting FP. Exploring the price space thus enabled the model optimizer to find new prices that were not in the vicinity of its current price.

Thus far we have considered competition among a heterogeneous population of sellers employing different price setting algorithms. Now we focus our attention on a homogeneous population of sellers. Figure 4a shows the price dynamics resulting from a competition between three model optimizers with three different starting prices: MO_1 starts with $p_0 = 0.3$, MO_2 begins with $p_0 = 0.4$, and MO_3 has $p_0 = 0.9$. Initially, sellers MO_1 and MO_2 engage in a price war with each other until they reach their cutoff price $p_{co} = 0.1$. Thereafter, their prices hover near p_{co}. However, as exploration was not enabled, seller MO_3, fails to discover the sellers charging a price lower than itself and keeps on maintaining a high price.

Figure 4a can be contrasted with Figure 4b which provides the results of similar experiment with three competing model optimizers with exploration. The sellers start at the same initial price as those from the last simulation. However, exploration of the price space enables them to discover each other's prices and they start a price war even before receiving 1000 quotes. The price war causes each seller to reduce its price till it reaches the cut-off price $p_{co} = 0.1$. However, unlike Figure 4a, the sellers' prices no longer fluctuate around p_{co}. Exploration of the price space now enables sellers to discover that they are better off by charging a price in the vicinity of p_m and attracting only the randomly-selecting buyers. This results in repeated cycles of price wars at intervals of approximately 5000 quotes as illustrated in Figure 4b. Our results also show that exploration of the price space can increase the income of the model optimizers since a successful exploration yields more profits. The income of model optimizers with exploration in Figure 4b were approximately 1.5 times the income obtained by model optimizers without exploration shown in Figure 4a.

The behavior observed in Figure 4b is similar to the cyclic price wars obtained for the shopbot economy [8, 9] where the sellers had detailed knowledge about buyer preferences and their competitors' prices. Our results suggest that similar cyclic price wars also occur in agent economies even when seller agents are ignorant of competitors' prices or profits.

5 Conclusion

This work addresses the problem of dynamic posted pricing for sellers in an environment where they have limited market information. We studied derivative following as a possible strategy in such an information limited situation and found it to be handicapped due to the limited size of its history window. We developed a model-optimizer algorithm which sets price more efficiently. by making use of historical price-profit relationship.

The objective of a seller agent in our system was to maximize its immediate profit by reseting a single attribute; viz., its price at regular intervals. In the real world, electronic goods and services can have multiple attributes, such as the quality of the good, its price per unit, or its bundle price. In such situations, a pricebot will need to set a number of attributes in response to sparse feedback from the market. Work is in progress to extend the dynamic pricing algorithms developed in this paper for electronic goods and services with multiple attributes.

In this work, we have used a relatively simple model for studying an information economy using pricebots that are selfish and myopic and aim to maximize their immediate profits. Competing pricebots engage in price wars under-cutting each other even when they are ignorant of the prices and profits of competitors, and perhaps, of each others existence. Therefore, we envisage that in the absence of cooperation there exists little friction in the economy and the market price will be repeatedly driven down to the production cost of the sellers giving rise to cyclic price wars. The work reported in this paper indicates that repeated cycles of price wars is a common phenomenon in agent-mediated electronic commerce even when the sellers possess limited information about the market.

References

1. C. H. Brooks, E. H. Durfee, and R. Das. Price wars and niche discovery in an information economy. In preparation, 2000.
2. C. H. Brooks, S. Fay, R. Das, J. K. Mackie-Mason, J. O. Kephart, and E. H. Durfee. Automated search strategies in an electronic goods market: Learning and complex price scheduling. In *Proceedings of the ACM Conference on Electronic Commerce*, 1999.

3. D. Clark. Shopbots become agents for business change. *IEEE Computer*, 33:18–21, February 2000.

4. P. Dasgupta and R. Das. Dynamic service pricing for brokers in a multi-agent economy. In *Proceedings of the Fourth International Conference on Multi-agent systems*. Springer-Verlag, July 2000.

5. A. R. Greenwald and J. O. Kephart. Shopbots and pricebots. In *Lecture Notes on Artificial Intelligence: Proceedings of the IJCAI Workshop on Agent-mediated Electronic Commerce*. Springer-Verlag, 2000.

6. A. R. Greenwald, J. O. Kephart, and G. J. Tesauro. Strategic pricebot dynamics. In *Proceedings of 1st ACM Conference on E-Commerce*, 1999.

7. J. O. Kephart, R. Das, and J. K. Mackie-Mason. Two-sided learning in an agent economy for information bundles. In *Lecture Notes on Artificial Intelligence: Proceedings of the IJCAI Workshop on Agent-mediated Electronic Commerce*. Springer-Verlag, 2000.

8. J. O. Kephart and A. R. Greenwald. Shopbot economics. In *Proceedings of Fifth European Conference on Symbolic and Quantitative Approaches to Reasoning with Uncertainty*, 1999.

9. J. O. Kephart, J. E. Hanson, and A. R. Greenwald. Dynamic pricing by software agents. To appear in Computer Networks, 2000.

10. J. A. Nelder and R. Mead. A simplex method for function minimization. *Computer Journal*, 7:308–313, 1965.

11. W. H. Press, B. P. Flannery, S. A. Teukolsky, and W. T. Vetterling. *Numerical Recipes in C: The Art of Scientific Computing*. Cambridge University Press, Cambridge, 1988.

12. G. J. Tesauro and J. O. Kephart. Pricing in agent economies using multi-agent q-learning. In *Proceedings of Fifth European Conference on Symbolic and Quantitative Approaches to Reasoning with Uncertainty*, 1999.

13. P. Tseng. Fortified-descent simplical search method: a general approach. Department of Mathematics, University of Washington, Seattle, 1998.

14. H. R. Varian. Market structure in the network age. In proceedings, Understanding the Digital Economy Conference, Department of Commerce, Washington, DC, USA, May 1999.

Multi-agent Cooperative Transactions for E-Commerce

Qiming Chen and Umesh Dayal

HP Labs, Hewlett-Packard, 1501 Page Mill Road, MS 1U4, Palo Alto, CA 94303, USA
{qchen,dayal}@hpl.hp.com

Abstract. E-Commerce is a distributed computing environment with dynamic relationships among a large number of autonomous service requesters, brokers and providers. With the increasing automation of e-commerce applications, we will see the use of software agents that cooperate to perform business transactions. Multi-agent cooperative transactions are different in their requirements both from conventional atomic transactions executed under centralized control and from nested transactions executed under hierarchical control. Cooperative transactions require peer-to-peer protocols based on inter-agent communication. In this paper, we develop a cooperative mulit-agent transaction model that includes peer-to-peer protocols for commit control and failure recovery. The significance and feasibility of this approach have been demonstrated in a prototype implemented at HP Labs, using our dynamic agent infrastructure.

1. Introduction: E-Commerce Automation

This work focuses on providing a framework for multi-agent cooperative transactions that occur in E-Commerce automation. E-Commerce applications operate in a *dynamic environment*, they typically rely on distributed and autonomous tasks for information search, fusion, extraction and processing, without centralized control. Today, these tasks are initiated and executed primarily by humans. In the future, with the increasing automation of e-commerce, we see them being conducted by software agents.

Software agents are personalized, continuously running and semi-autonomous computational entities that are driven by a set of beliefs, desires and intentions (BDI) [8,9]. They can be used to *mediate* between users (clients) and servers (service providers) to automate a number of the most time-consuming tasks in E-Commerce [2]. Moreover, agents can selectively preserve data and themselves become *dynamic information sources*, or *data containers*. E-Commerce automation can thus be accomplished through multi-agent cooperation, where agents perform various market activities and cooperate by exchanging data as well as programs.

One feature that distinguishes Internet-based e-commerce from traditional "brick and mortar" commerce is that agents can form *dynamic partnerships* that exist for only as long as they are needed. Further, multi-agent cooperation often requires that agents participate in distributed transactions. There exist several efforts for dealing

O. Etzion and P. Scheuermann (Eds.): CoopIS 2000, LNCS 1901, pp. 311 322, 2000.

with transactions carried by a single agent. However, we have not seen an adequate treatment of multi-agent cooperative transactions, which we believe are critical to e-commerce automation.

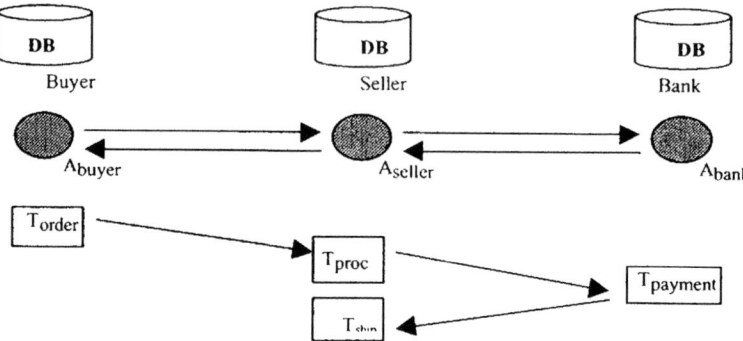

Figure 1. An example of a multi-agent cooperative transaction

In this paper, we shall discuss the cooperation of multiple agents for carrying out e-commerce transactions. Figure 1 shows an example of a cooperative transaction that involves three agents, representing a buyer, a seller, and a bank. The transaction consists of several steps: the buyer agent initiates the transaction by placing an order; the seller agent processes the order; the bank agent approves payment; and the seller agent ships the items ordered.

Multi-agent cooperative transactions have the following characteristics that distinguish them from conventional distributed "flat" or nested transactions [1,10,11].

❑   For conventional transactions, commit control is either centralized (e.g., a TP monitor coordinates two-phase commit among the sub-transactions comprising a distributed transaction), or strictly hierarchical (for nested transactions, each parent sub-transaction controls its children sub-transactions; commits pass up the transaction hierarchy from child to parent, until the entire transaction commits through the top level). In contrast, a multi-level cooperative transaction is not centrally controlled, but based on a *peer-to-peer protocol*, as the transaction may involve multiple agents with self-interests, acting on behalf of different parties. Each party typically has its own databases and possibly its own TP monitor. There is no single controller or top level transaction.

❑   Failure recovery also requires cooperation. For example, sub-transactions carried by multiple agents may fail individually; a peer belonging to another party may not cooperate; a transaction (e.g. purchase) may be cancelled by one party unilaterally (e.g., a buyer may switch to another vendor); and the effects of one agent may need to be compensated by another agent.

❑   In conventional nested transactions, the delegation of work from a parent sub-transaction to a child sub-transaction is "conceptual" -- the parent initiates the child and passes to it the locks that it holds; when the child completes, it commits its updates to the parent by releasing its locks to the parent. In multi-agent cooperative transactions, the delegation of work between sub-transactions is not conceptual, but 'physical" through inter-agent communication.

These features, however, imply that inter-transaction dependencies are set up as participating agents are bound by peer-to-peer protocols. We shall discuss the cooperative transaction commit control and failure recovery mechanisms underlying these protocols. In previous work, we had developed mechanisms for nested transactions, flexible commit control, and failure recovery across transaction hierarchies [4-6]. We adapt these mechanisms to work for multi-agent cooperative transactions.

Although our cooperative transaction mechanisms are independent of the underlying agent infrastructure, our experience has shown that implementing these mechanisms using a *dynamic agent infrastructure* we have developed at HP Labs, has several advantages [3]. The infrastructure allows us to create transaction services and launch transactions dynamically on demand. Thus, a business partnership can be created dynamically and maintained only for the required duration such as a single transaction. Agents can flexibly switch roles and modify their capabilities to participate in such dynamic business partnerships. Furthermore, agents may cooperate in different application domains. Thus, a purchasing agent may participate in one transaction to buy printers, and then switch to another transaction to buy office supplies or building maintenance services. Our dynamic agent infrastructure allows multi-agent cooperation to be based on *dynamic ontology*. By dynamic ontology, we mean that the vocabulary, concepts, rules and facts underlying agent interaction may be different from domain to domain, and may vary from transaction to transaction. To automate agent cooperation, it is necessary to provide a standard format for encoding messages with meaningful structure and semantics, as well as a domain ontology that agents can readily exchange and interpret. This format should be common for agent communication as well as for E-Commerce data exchange in general. Since the extensible markup language, XML, is becoming the standard for data interchange on the Web, we use it as the standard for inter-agent communication.

Our dynamic agent infrastructure for E-Commerce supports *dynamic behavior modification* of agents, a significant difference from other agent platforms [3,8,9]. A dynamic agent does not have a fixed set of predefined functions, but instead, it *carries application-specific actions*, which can be loaded and modified on the fly. This allows a dynamic agent to participate in different transactions and dynamically formed partnerships. Dynamic agents communicate using XML, and can *dynamically load and exchange different ontologies and XML interpreters* for tasks in different domains. Through messaging, dynamic agents can expose their knowledge, abilities and intentions, present requests and exchange objects. They can move to the appropriate locations for high-bandwidth conversation with other agents. They can also manage their own resources across actions. With these features, our dynamic agent infrastructure provides a suitable platform for deploying and managing multi-agent cooperative transactions for e-commerce automation applications. Resource, event and request brokering agents are introduced to handle the transaction dispatching, tracking and notification among multiple agents *belonging to the same party or agent group*. Agent communication across enterprises is supported by a global naming service such as HP E-speak.

In Section 2, we give an example of a multi-agent cooperative transaction and contrast such transactions with conventional distributed transactions, nested transactions, and workflow models. In Sections 3, we describe our multi-agent cooperative transaction model, and the mechanisms for commit control and failure recovery. Related work will be covered in Section 4 with conclusions.

2. Example of a multi-agent cooperative transaction

Let us consider a purchase process including individual transactions, T_{order}, T_{proc}, $T_{payment}$, and T_{ship}, which is carried out by agents belonging to a *buyer*, a *seller* and a *bank* that issued a credit card to the buyer. We compare the implementation of this process by transactional agent cooperation with other approaches, distributed tran sactions, nested transactions, and transactional workflow (Although each of the constituent transactions may be nested, for simplicity we do not discuss transaction nesting in this example.)

2.1 Purchase Process as a Distributed Transaction

In the typical approach to implementing a distributed transaction, a TP-monitor has to be employed for providing *centralized control*. The constituent (sub) transactions, T_{order}, T_{proc}, $T_{payment}$, and T_{ship} participate in a two-phase commit protocol coordinated by the TP-monitor, as shown in Figure 2. In our purchase process, however, the buyer, seller, and bank agents belong to different enterprises, and hence the use of a single TP-monitor is unrealistic.

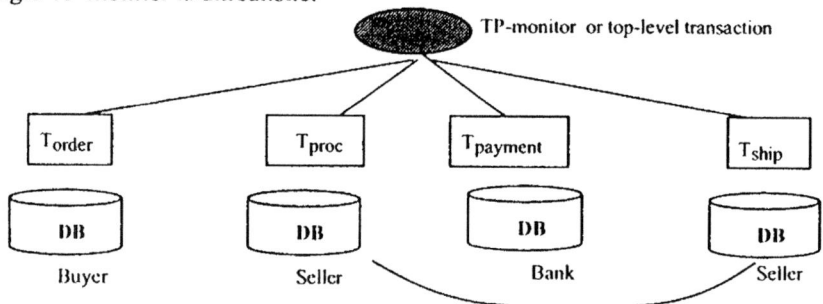

Figure 2. Centralized transaction control with TP monitor

2.2 Purchase Process as a Nested Transaction

In order to model the purchase process as a nested transaction, a *top-level* transaction, T_{top}, must be introduced (Figure 2). Then, T_{order}, T_{proc}, $T_{payment}$, and T_{ship} have to commit to T_{top}, i.e., their effects are made persistent through T_{top}. Again, the problem is that the buyer, the seller and the bank are independent enterprises, and hence transactions T_{order}, T_{proc}, $T_{payment}$, and T_{ship} commit to their own databases. It's not clear how to implement the conceptual transaction T_{top}.

2.3 Purchase Process as Transactional Workflow

The purchase process may be modeled as a transactional workflow (Figure 3). A workflow system provides flow control for business process automation. A business process often involves multiple steps, such as T_{order}, T_{proc}, $T_{payment}$, and T_{ship} . Each step represents a logical piece of work that contributes to the process. A workflow process represents the integration and synchronization of multiple actions. Although these actions and the agents executing the actions can be distributed, they are scheduled and coordinated by a centralized workflow engine. However, in our example, the purchase process involves tasks that are executed in different enterprises, which are not under the control of a single workflow engine.

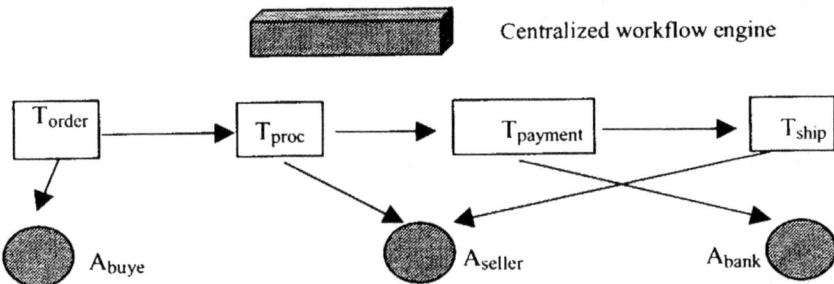

Figure 3. Centralized workflow control

2.4 Purchase Process as Transactional Agent Cooperation

Agent cooperation is *protocol based*, rather than centrally controlled by any coordinator. A multi-agent cooperative activity is the interaction of multiple autonomous activities, possibly bound by certain protocols. The success of a cooperative activity requires the common understanding of and agreement on the underlying protocols by all the participating agents.   Refer to Figure 1, our example purchase process, which includes individual transactions, T_{order}, T_{proc}, $T_{payment}$, and T_{ship}, is carried out through the cooperation of agents belonging to the *buyer*, the *seller* and the *bank*.that issued credit card to the buyer. These agents are denoted A_{buyer}, A_{seller} and A_{bank} respectively.

- ❑ Transaction T_{order} is executed by agent A_{buyer} and commits to the database on the buyer's side. The tasks of this transaction include filling a shopping basket, making an order with the credit line for payment.
- ❑ Transaction T_{proc} is executed by agent A_{seller} and commits to the database on the seller's side. The tasks of this transaction include processing the order, checking inventory, sending a payment request to the bank, etc.

❑   Transaction $T_{payment}$ is made by agent A_{bank} and commits to the database on the bank's side. The tasks of this transaction include verifying the payment request, checking credit, approving the payment, etc.

❑   Transaction T_{ship} is made by agent A_{seller} and commits to the database on the seller's side. The major tasks of this transaction are making the shipment and updating inventory.

The entire purchase process is not controlled by any common top-task, but accomplished through conversation among agents. An agent can request another agent to perform an action, or can delegate an action to another agent. For example, the buyer agent may delegate a price comparison task to another agent; the buyer agent requests the seller agent to process an order; the seller agent requests the bank agent to approve the buyer's credit. The results of these transactions are passed between agents via messaging. Agents are autonomous and act in their own self-interests. An agent may fail, or the transaction may be cancelled by any participating agent. If any exception condition occurs, such as the credit checking fails, or the shipment cannot be made, certain compensation transactions are executed. For instance, the buyer needs to update his database entry, indicating that the purchase and the payment were not made.

2.5 Difference between Multi-agent Cooperative Transactions and Conventional Transactions

In summary, multi-agent cooperative transactions differ from conventional transactions in the following aspects.

❑   The participating agents may represent different enterprises with self-interests.

❑   The component transactions forming a business process may be individual transactions running in different enterprises and committing to different databases.

❑   The component transactions are not controlled by a central TP monitor or workflow engine.

❑   In general, there is no top-level transaction to which the component transactions can commit.

❑   The synchronization of agents carrying out the component transactions is protocol-based and accomplished through peer-to-peer communication.

3. A Multi-agent Cooperative Transaction Model

Transactions are atomic operations. However, agents have typically been characterized as autonomous carriers of operations. How to support atomic transactions by autonomous agents is the key to dealing with cooperative transactions. We consider the following two situations: cooperation of multiple agents belonging to the same party (i.e., within a single enterprise), and belonging to different but contracting parties (i.e., between different enterprises).

3.1 Nested Transactions for Multi-agent Cooperation within a Single Enterprise

First, we focus on processes executed within a single enterprise. Modeling such a process as a single flat transaction is unnecessary in most cases. Such processes are often organized as nested transactions. A transaction may consist of hierarchically structured sub-transactions to be executed by the same or different agents. A sub-transaction represents a logical piece of work that contributes to the whole transaction, and may be delegated by an agent to another. Thus, a transaction tree may actually map to an agent organization tree, with each agent corresponding to one or more sub-transactions. The agent carrying a (sub) transaction, T, maintains the templates of sub-transactions beneath T. These sub-transactions may consist of all the descendant transactions of T, or only the child transactions of T, should the detailed steps of those child transactions be determined by their respective hosting agents.

We incorporate the ideas of *contingency* and *non-vital* transactions for providing failure protection. The failure of a non-vital transaction can be ignored by its parent, and a failed transaction T may be replaced by the contingency transaction T^* associated with it. A transaction at any level may be paired with a contingency transaction that may in turn have its own contingency transaction. A transaction T may also be paired with a *compensation* transaction T° that can logically undo its effects (e.g. a flight reservation may be compensated for by canceling that reservation). The contingency transaction or the compensation transaction associated with a transaction T may be executed by a different agent. The notion of vitalness underlies the failure recovery of multi-agent transactions, namely, when and via which path to eliminate or compensate for, certain previous effects.

3.2 Task Delegation between Agents

In a transaction hierarchy, a parent transaction may delegate tasks to a child transaction [10,11], and such delegation is typically implemented by passing locks [10]. When these transactions are carried by separate agents, task delegation is made by exchanging data containers through inter-agent communication. Thus, we adopt a container model rather than the lock model for dealing with the data flow between agents; that is, agents pass data, rather than locks, during transaction delegation. Delivering locks to agents running remotely has many more sensitive security and implementation problems than checking out data.

Each transaction carried by an agent is associated with a data container managed by the hosting agent. This container holds the data checked out from databases or passed from other agents. The data objects in the container are accessible only to the transaction carried by the hosting agent. When agent A delegates a transaction T to agent B, it is A's responsibility to deliver sufficient data to B for executing T, according to the transaction specification.

Agent-based task delegation offers certain flexibility in transaction control. For example, when the agent, say P, carrying a parent transaction determines that the agent carrying a child transaction is dead without performing the assigned task, P can re-assign the task to another agent.

However, when a parent transaction and a child transaction are carried by different agents, additional dependencies are introduced between these agents. For instance, suppose that after a child transaction has purchased a ticket, the carrying agent, C, became unreachable by the agent, P, carrying the parent transaction. Then, how does P know whether the ticket was purchased or not. In order to support reliable task delegation and commit control, the following protocols have to be followed.

❑   All communication between agents involved in a transaction is based on a handshake protocol with acknowledgement.

❑   A 2PC-like protocol should be used in the commitment of a child transaction to its parent transaction if the child transaction is an open transaction [10] that updates the database;

❑   An agent delegating a task to another agent must keep a copy of the delegated task and corresponding data container in order to re-delegate to another agent, if necessary.

❑   Every agent that carries a transaction in a transaction hierarchy must log the status of the whole family of transactions, including all its direct ancestors and all the descendents beneath it. In this way, the persistent effects made by open transactions are known to their ancestors, so if the internal results are lost due to the failure of the carrying agents, they can be re-generated. The agent coordinator keeps track of all the agents.

3.3 Contracting Transactions for Inter-enterprise Multi-agent Cooperation

A basic assumption is that an inter-enterprise cooperative transactional process, such as a purchase process or an auction process, is considered as an atomic transaction only conceptually, meaning that every participating party honors the results based on certain "contracts". The concept of contract is rather broad, such as making an agreement, exchanging information, making a purchase, and so on. A contract involves multiple parties, and usually is not controlled by a single party. For example, a purchase is made by two separate but contracting transactions, one on the buyer side and the other on the seller side. The contract, representing the interaction of multiple participating transactions belonging to different business processes, is not a single transaction physically carried by any agent. It is initiated by one agent sending a request to another, and completed along with the completion of a buying transaction and a selling transaction. The results of a contract are shared by the participating transactions, and thus visible to the interactive business processes. The agents participating in a contract communicate in terms of messaging.

In [6] we modeled a contract transaction as either the parent transaction or the child transaction of the participating transactions. However, since agent-carried transactions are physically handled by different "engines" (agents), such a model would be impractical. It cannot be assumed that when a buyer agent sends an order to a seller agent, a third agent should be necessarily introduced to hold a contract transaction "purchase". Nor is it reasonable to assume that the contract transaction is carried by the buyer agent or the seller agent. In fact, such a contract transaction is just a virtual entity, representing the combination of two actual transactions, buy and sell, with cross-transaction dependencies introduced between them.

Certain component transaction templates such as shopping, negotiation, auctions, are provided as common protocols for interaction among agents. These templates serve as the building blocks for transactional agent interaction.

3.4 Commit Control

In nested transactions, data objects held by a transaction are visible to its descendants, meaning that a sub-transaction can access without conflict any object currently accessed by one of its ancestors. Thus, a transaction T can acquire objects from databases or inherit objects from its parent or ancestors; these objects form the *access set* of T. A transaction T_i may *delegate* the commit/abort responsibility of its operations on certain objects to another transaction T_j, which form a *delegate set*.

Unlike conventional transactions, the access-set of a transaction T is physically carried by the hosting agent of T, A_T. When we say that set is visible by T's sub-transactions, we mean that those sub-transactions can send a query to A_T for checking out the data objects in the access set visible to them. A_T must validate the requesters before sending out the data.

The data about a contract are visible to all participating transactions and their hosting agents. Since a contract is simply conceptual, rather than a transaction carried by a hosting agent, contract related data is acquired through message exchange between the agents participating in the contract.

For applications requiring enhanced concurrency and transaction protection at selected levels of a transaction hierarchy, the atomicity property of closed nesting is too rigid and the data protection of open nesting is too weak. In order to balance concurrency and protection in a flexible way, we introduced the notion of *scoped transaction* [5] to intermediate the effects of closed and open transactions. This extension allows the results of a sub-transaction to be visible to the top-level transaction (and hence to all the sub-transactions) of a process, but they are still kept internally within the scope of that process.

3.5 Failure Recovery

Transactions are characterized by logical atomicity, but agents are characterized by autonomy. When multiple agents are involved in a logically atomic transaction, each agent may individually fail. A failure may be caused by the transaction itself, referred to as a *transaction failure*, or by the failure of a component, such as an agent, a communication channel, or a computer, referred to as a *component failure*. Using agents provides flexibility for transaction failure recovery. For example, a sub-transaction may be delegated to an alternative agent in case of failure. In general, failure recovery also requires cooperation among multiple agents.

For agent specific component failure handling, the mechanisms listed in Section 4.2 are necessary. Next we shall further discuss the following special issues in multi-agent cooperative transaction failure handling.

❑   Failure recovery along a single transaction hierarchy, where sub-transactions may be carried by multiple agents.

❑   Failure recovery across transaction hierarchies; this usually means across enterprises as well. For example, a purchase may be considered as an atomic activity logically, but actually involves two related but individual transactions, one for the buyer side and one for the seller side. A failure on one side may have impact on the other, and the failure recovery in this situation requires certain special mechanisms.

3.5.1 Hierarchical Failure Handling

Failure handling in a transaction hierarchy consists of two tasks: identifying the failure recovery scope, and top-down undoing of the sub-transactions in that scope. We described a detailed *two phase failure handling* algorithm in [4]. This mechanism is applicable to a distributed agent environment.

The failure recovery scope is represented by a Recovery Root (RR),T_{RR}, from there a logical undo is performed through aborting or compensating for the transactions underneath. Whether the effects of a transaction under T_{RR} should be aborted or *compensated for*, depends on the visibility scope of these effects. In general, if a transaction is in-progress or tentatively committed (to parent), then it should be aborted (with its committed sub-transactions compensated for). This is because its effects are still internal to the subtree rooted by T_{RR}. Otherwise, if it has committed over T_{RR} to the top-level transaction or database, then it should be compensated for in the corresponding scope (if its effects are not compensated for at a higher level) since its effects have been externalized beyond T_{RR} already. However, for a closed sub-transaction that has committed to its parent, compensation is never applicable; its effects may be eliminated either by aborting or by compensating an ancestor at a higher level. Compensating for the effects of a transaction may be done by the agent that originally carries that transaction, or by another agent.

3.5.2 Cross-Transaction Tree Failure Handling

Many e-commerce processes are transactional. Very often, such a process is conceptually atomic but actually made by separate transactions running by different parties. In case of failure, the participating transactions are recovered individually. However, due to the presence of contracts between those transactions, a failure occurring in one transaction tree (or sub-tree) may have to be transferred to the other sub-trees, which gives rise to the need for failure handling across transaction hierarchies. In [6], we introduced a "contract transaction" as the conceptual unit for linking the transaction trees. Here we treat contracts as conceptual, and implement them by pure peer-to-peer transaction interactions in the form of inter-agent communications.

In the transaction tree where a failure originally occurs, the parent and (direct) ancestors up to the RR of the originally failed transaction, are still *in-progress*, since they may not terminate until all its child transactions terminate. However, in a tran s-action tree where a failure is transferred in, the transaction to which the failure is transferred in, and its ancestors, may be committed and need to be compensated for, since their results have become invalidated as a result of such failure. To handle such a situation both RR and *scoped-rollback* algorithm should be extended.

Let us consider two cooperative transactions with sub-transactions T_a and T_b respectively, which are involved in a contract. Assume that the contract is vital to both sides. When T_a fails itself or in the undo scope as a result of other sub-transaction's failure, the failure is transferred to T_b, then each transaction tree has an individual recovery scope for undoing. When T_a fails, its parent and (direct) ancestors up to the RR of it, are still *in-progress*. However, when this failure is transferred to T_b, the situation may be different.

❑ T_b *has not started*: failure handling on T_b is not necessary at this time.
❑ T_b *is in-progress*: it can be treated as the original failure point in the transaction tree; the RR of T_b, should be determined as the root of recovery in the same way as described before.
❑ T_b *has completed*: it should be invalidated, that is, compensated for at the same or a higher level.

In the last case, the invalidation of T_b causes its parent to be aborted (if the parent is in-progress and T_b is vital to it), or invalidated (if the parent has committed). Such an invalidate/abort signal may propagate up to T_b's ancestors, but may or may not terminate at the RR of T_b, if the RR of T_b has committed. In general, if the RR of T_b is in-progress, then it can be treated as the root of recovery; if the RR of T_b has committed, but its own parent is in-progress, then the latter can be chosen as the root of recovery; otherwise, if the RR of T_b and its parent or even other ancestors have committed, first we need to find out such a transaction, say, T_h, that is the highest committed ancestor of the RR of T_b, and then consider the RR of T_h. If the RR of T_h is an in-progress transaction, then it is taken as the *extended rollback root* (eRR) of T_b for recovery; otherwise RR of T_h must be T_h itself, in this case the parent of T_h is taken as the eRR of T_b for recovery. We have described more details in [4].

4. Related Work and Conclusions

The development of agent-mediated e-commerce automation has given rise to the need for supporting cooperative transactions [12]. In this paper we discussed several issues of cooperative transactions involving multiple autonomous agents that are rarely addressed before.

E-commerce applications require the cooperation of multiple *in-progress* transactions. This is actually a missing link in the previous work. Because of the atomicity property, *in-progress* atomic transactions and closed nested transactions [7,11] cannot exchange partial results for cooperation. Open nested transactions [10] may exchange partial results only by making them persistent. Cooperating through e x-changing interleaved persistent partial results suffers the loss of data protection, since those partial results are accessible not only to the participating processes but also to others when these processes are still in progress.

Cooperating transactions carried by multiple agents are also different from handling transaction groups in the conventional sense. The cooperative transactions are individual transactions belonging to different parties. However, traditionally a transaction group represents a single piece of work hosted by a single party.

To support multi-agent cooperative transactions, it is necessary to handle failures across transactions. Common to all the existing approaches is that they lack the capabilities for allowing the interaction of multiple transaction hierarchies and for handling failure over and across transaction trees.

In summary, by merging the extended multilevel transaction commit and recovery mechanisms we proposed in [4-6], In this work we have developed a cooperative mulit-agent transaction model based on peer-to-peer protocols. Our experience also shows the flexibility of dynamic agents for supporting cooperative transactions. This infrastructure supports a new kind of dynamic computation paradigm, and we believe that such a paradigm is essential for implementing cooperative transactions occurring in e-commerce automation applications. The significance and feasibility of this approach have been demonstrated in a prototype implemented at HP Labs.

References

1   Yuri. Breitbart, Hector Garcia-Molina, Abraham Silberschatz: Overview of Multidatabase Transaction Management. VLDB Journal 1(2): 181-293(1992)
2   A. Chavez and P. Maes, Kasbah: An Agent Marketplace for Buying and Selling Goods, Proc. of PAAM96, 1996.
3   Q. Chen, P. Chundi, Umesh Dayal, M. Hsu, "Dynamic-Agents", International Journal on Cooperative Information Systems, 1999, USA.
4   Q. Chen and Umesh Dayal, "Failure Recovery across Transaction Hierarchies", Proc. of 13th International Conference on Data Engineering (ICDE-97), 1997, UK.
5   Q. Chen and Umesh Dayal, "Commit Scope Control in Nested Transactions", Proc. of EDBT'96, 1996, France.
6   Q. Chen, Umesh Dayal, "Contracting Transaction Hierarchies", Proc. of RIDE'96, 1996.
7   P.K. Chrysanthis and K.Ramamritham"Acta: The saga continues", A. Elmagarmid (ed) Transaction Models for Advanced Database Applications, Morgan-Kaufmann, 1992.
8   T. Finin, R. Fritzson, D. McKay, R. McEntire, "KQML as an Agent-Communication Language", Proc. CIKM'94, 1994.
9   Foundation for Intelligent Physical Agents(FIPA)- FIPA97 Agent Specification, http://www.fipa.org/.
10   J.Gray and A.Reuter"Transaction processing: Concepts and techniques"Morgan Kaufmann Publishers, 1993.
11   E.Moss"Nested transactions", MIT Press, 1985.
12   Evaggelia Pitoura, Transaction-Based Coordination of Software Agents. DEXA 1998.

Cross-Organizational Transaction Support for Virtual Enterprises *

Jochem Vonk[1], Wijnand Derks[2], Paul Grefen[1], Marjanca Koetsier[1]

[1] Center for Telematics and Information Technology (CTIT), University of Twente
{vonk, grefen, marjanca}@cs.utwente.nl
[2] KPN Research
w.l.a.derks@kpn.com

Abstract. In recent years, workflow management systems have become an accepted technology to support automation in process-centric environments. Lately, organizations concentrate more and more on their core business processes while outsourcing supporting processes to other organizations, thereby forming virtual enterprises. To apply workflow management technology in these virtual enterprises, support for cross-organizational processes is necessary. Transaction support, already considered an important issue in intra-organizational workflow management systems, must be extended to deal with the cross-organizational aspects as well. This paper presents a high-level transaction model and architecture for cross-organizational workflow processes. Characteristic of the model is the flexibility in rollback semantics by combining rollback modes and rollback scopes, supported by a dynamically generated architecture that is configured conforming to an electronic contract that has been established between the different organizations. The transaction model and architecture are independent of the underlying workflow management system platform, however, in the CrossFlow project the presented technology is being implemented on top of IBMís MQ Series Workflow.

1   Introduction

Nowadays, workflow management is an accepted technology to support process-centric environments. The focus of organizations with respect to workflow management is now turning from secondary processes towards primary business processes. For this reason, it is important that the workflow management system ensures that these business processes are executed in a reliable and consistent manner. This can be ensured by incorporating transaction semantics in the processes [6, 9, 12, 16].

Besides the focus-shift of organizations to apply workflow management for primary business processes, organizations are focussing more and more on their core business while leaving non-core businesses to other specialized organizations. This

---

* The work presented in this paper is supported by the European Commission in the CrossFlow Project (ESPRIT No. 28635). Partners in CrossFlow are IBM Zurich Research Labs in Switzerland, IBM France, SEMA Group sae. in Spain, Church and General in Ireland, GMD-IPSI and IBM Bˆblingen in Germany, KPN Research and University of Twente in the Netherlands.

O. Etzion and P. Scheuermann (Eds.): CoopIS 2000, LNCS 1901, pp. 323–334, 2000.
© Springer-Verlag Berlin Heidelberg 2000

introduces the concept of dynamic virtual enterprises. Multiple organizations with their own primary processes combine forces in a virtual enterprise for a period of time. Afterwards, the virtual enterprise is dismantled again.

The CrossFlow project [10] aims to develop support for cross-organizational workflow management in these dynamically formed virtual enterprises, resulting in fine-grained contract-based cooperation. Although a virtual enterprise can consist of more than two organizations, the scope within the CrossFlow project is limited to the commonly used consumer/provider paradigm. In the consumer/provider paradigm, one organization acts as a (service) consumer that outsources part of its business process to another organization, called the (service) provider. The thereby formed cooperation between the organizations is specified in an electronic contract. The transaction support presented here is developed within the CrossFlow project.

This paper discusses a three-level transaction model for cross-organizational workflow management that ensures reliable execution of the workflow processes within virtual enterprises, for which a standard transaction model is not sufficient. The developed transaction model offers different rollback modes and rollback scopes that allow for flexible rollbacks of executed processes. Rolling back processes is based on executing compensating activities that semantically undo the effects of already executed activities. The presented architecture that supports the transaction model consists of a static intra-organizational infrastructure layer and a dynamically generated cross-organizational infrastructure layer.

The structure of this paper is as follows. Section 2 discusses related work. In Section 3, the intra- and cross-organizational process models are explained and an example scenario is introduced. The architecture to support cross-organizational workflow processes is presented in Section 4. The X-transaction model that ensures reliable executions of workflow processes is presented in Section 5. The architecture and implementation issues to support the X-transaction model are discussed in Section 6, together with the CrossFlow project, which is the context of the work described in this paper. The paper ends with conclusions and a discussion of future work.

2   Related Work

Numerous advanced transaction models have been proposed in the past, see e.g. [6, 12, 15], that offer specific transaction properties required in advanced application areas, like workflow management (WfM). The cross-organizational transaction model presented in this paper is not created from scratch, but combines aspects of existing advanced transaction models, extended to deal with cross-organizational issues. The WIDE advanced transaction model [9] is taken as a basis, and specific cross-organizational transaction aspects have been added. In the WIDE model, compensating activities are used to undo already executed and committed activities. The safe-point concept offers the possibility to rollback only parts of a process besides rolling back the entire process. Using compensations to rollback long-running processes, like workflow processes, is first described in [7] and is called the saga transaction model. Also based on compensations is the transaction model developed in the Exotica project [2], however, it relies on statically computed compensation patterns, while our model dynamically computes a compensation process only when a rollback is necessary. The transaction model described in [16] presents atomicity spheres and isolation spheres. As in the previously mentioned models, both the atomicity and isolation properties of the standard ACID transaction model are relaxed using compensations. All transaction models mentioned above do not deal with cross-organizational aspects but are limited to intra-organizational workflow support.

Distributed execution of workflow process has also received a lot of attention in recent years. The workflow management coalition has created a standard [19] to facilitate the interoperability between heterogeneous workflow management systems, albeit without transactional properties. Aspects related to the specific cooperation between different organization are not mentioned either. Key problems related to cross-organizational WfM, a special kind of distributed WfM, is discussed in [17]. Modeling and analysis of cross-organizational WfM processes is presented in [1]. As transaction issues are not covered, the transaction model presented in this paper can be seen as complementary to it.

Transaction support in distributed WfM is dealt with in [4, 21, 18]. However, only intra-organizational processes are considered. The concept of INCAs (INformation CArriers) is introduced in [4]. INCAs contain all necessary information to execute a workflow process over multiple autonomous systems. Transaction support is determined by the transaction support offered by the autonomous systems. In the Mentor project [21], a transaction processing monitor is used to ensure reliable distributed workflow executions. Transactions are, however, restrictive as they comply to the strict ACID transaction properties. Compensation based transaction support in distributed WfM is described in [18], but only for intra-organizational processes.

The WISE project [3] covers cross-organizational WfM and an infrastructure for virtual enterprise business processes is presented. Execution guarantees for processes are given based on spheres of atomicity and isolation, the model of which is not elaborated upon.

3   Process Model and Example Scenario

The business processes of organizations are specified in workflow process models so that they can be executed by a workflow management system (WfMS). This section describes the intra-organizational and cross-organizational process model. Both models are illustrated by an example scenario.

3.1   Intra-Organizational Process Model

To apply workflow management, the business processes of an organization must be modeled in a workflow process model. A workflow process model consists of the activities that must be performed and the order in which they must be performed, called the control flow. Within the control flow it is possible to specify parallelism of activities, choices between activities and loops over activities [20] using different control connectors. Most business processes are complex in nature, consisting of numerous activities and a complex control flow. For this reason, it is possible to

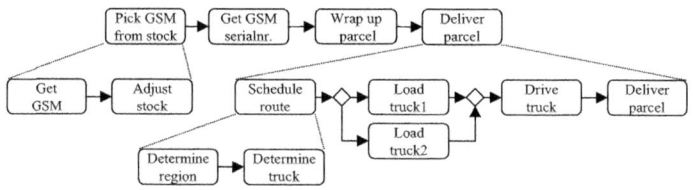

Fig. 1. Logistics process

model the business processes in a hierarchical manner, in which activities can be refined into smaller, more detailed, activities or grouped into coarser grained activities. This process of refinement or hierarchical decomposition results in a nested workflow process structure, consisting of basic activities, which are the activities that are actually executed, and subprocesses, which are activities that consist of other basic activities or subprocesses.

Fig. 1 shows an example of a nested workflow process, representing the business process of a logistics organization that delivers GSM phones from a warehouse to a customer. In the remainder of this paper, this process will be further elaborated. The rounded rectangles represent activities and the arrows represent the control flow. The diamond is a control connector representing an OR-split, meaning that one of the following activities can be executed, and an OR-Join, meaning that the following activity is executed whenever one of the preceding activities has been completed. The dotted lines represent hierarchical decomposition. The control flow in this example is relatively simple. However, the full set of control connectors as specified in [20] is offered in the intra- and cross-organizational process models described in this section.

3.2   Cross-Organizational Process Model

In a virtual enterprise based on the consumer/provider paradigm, two organizations are involved in the execution of a cross-organizational process. The provider organization executes a process on behalf of a consumer organization. However, the provider organization does not want to disclose all details of the process it executes. In addition, most consumer organizations would rather have an abstract view of the provider process. This abstract view is specified and agreed upon in the contract signed between the two organizations and is called the contract level. It encapsulates the details and presents a common view of the process. For example, in the logistics process of Fig. 1, the logistics company can act as a provider organization, but is willing to show only the top four activities, constituting the contract level. The other activities are encapsulated by the contract level and are thus not visible to a consumer organization. The encapsulated part of the process is called the internal level.

To incorporate the outsourced process in the consumer process, the placeholder concept is introduced. The placeholder is a special activity that represents the outsourced process, i.e. a process executed under the control of another organization.

Fig. 2 shows an example of a cross-organizational workflow process of a virtual enterprise established by a telecom company and a logistics company, acting as the consumer and provider organization, resp. An electronic contract, in which the cooperation including the outsourced process on the contract level, has been agreed upon by the two organizations. This example is based on one of the real-world scenarios

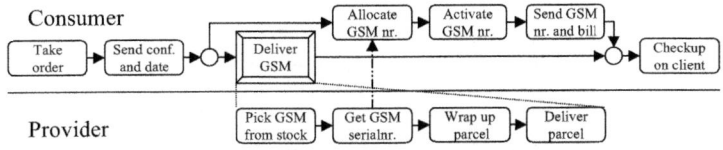

Fig. 2. Cross-organizational process with outsourced logistics process

used within the CrossFlow project [5]. In the example, the telecom organization sells GSM phones. After an order is received, a confirmation is sent to the client together with an estimate of the delivery date. Then, in parallel to the continued execution of the consumer process, the outsourced process is started (shown as a double lined rectangle, i.e. the placeholder). In the provider organization, the GSM phone is taken from stock and the serial number of the GSM phone is sent to the consumer (the dashed arrow). The consumer can then allocate a telephone number to the serial number, activate it and send the telephone number together with the bill to its client. At the same time in the provider process, the GSM phone is delivered, ending the outsourced process. Finally, the telecom company checks up on the client for marketing and customer satisfaction purposes.

4   Basic Architecture for Cross-Organizational WfM

Support for cross-organizational WfM requires more than just connecting the WfMSs of the involved organizations, for which a standard has been specified by the workflow management coalition [19]. In a cross-organizational setting, autonomous organizations are involved that each have their own business rules and culture. Besides this, both organizations have a common view on the contract level and do not want to show the details of their core business processes. The contract contains all specific information necessary to perform the cross-organizational process including the rights and obligations of both organizations, which must be enforced by the cross-organizational workflow management architecture. This requires a mechanism that maps the contract to an infrastructure that controls all cross-organizational aspects of the process. From this, it follows that the architecture is multi-layered. One layer deals with the internal processes of the consumer and provider organizations and consists of the individual WfMSs of the involved organizations. This architecture layer is static because it is also used to execute the intra-organizational processes of the organizations. A second layer deals with the processes on the contract level, which is only required for the time that the contract is valid and hence is a dynamic layer. A third layer is an isolation layer that shields the other two layers from each other.

The basic architecture is shown in Fig. 3. The upper half of the architecture is the dynamic cross-organizational infrastructure, which is configured according to the contract and is dismantled when the contract expires. The cross-organizational infrastructure consists of the necessary modules to provide dedicated support for different aspects of the cross-organizational workflow process execution, called cooperative support services (CSSs) and a proxy-gateway (PG) that provides a communication mechanism to handle all communication between the involved organizations. As the rights and obligations of both organizations are different, its CSSs and PG are config-

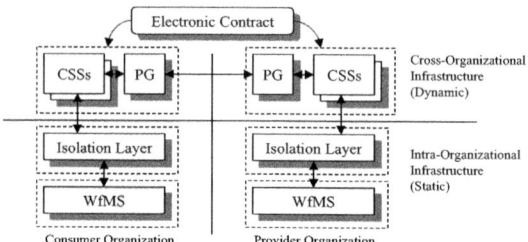

Fig. 3. Basic Cross-Organizational WfM Architecture

ured differently. The bottom half of the figure is the static intra-organizational infra-structure, consisting of the local WfMS and the isolation layer. The isolation layer maps the WfMS independent contract level processes to the WfMS dependent internal level processes. This way the cross-organizational infrastructure is independent of the underlying WfMS, which can be different for each organization.

5   The Cross-Organizational Transaction Model

Integrating transaction management support into workflow management systems provides for reliable and consistent process executions. The traditional flat transaction model originating in the database community that ensures the ACID transaction properties, is however too strict for the inherently long-running workflow processes. Cross-organizational workflow processes involving autonomous organizations require transaction support to deal with specific cross-organizational aspects as well.

5.1   Intra-Organizational Transaction Model

Various advanced transaction models [6] have been proposed to overcome the problems related to the long-livety of intra-organizational workflow processes by relaxing the atomicity and isolation constraints. Instead of inventing yet a new transaction model from scratch, we have taken the existing WIDE transaction model [9] as a basis and extended it to handle the specific requirements imposed by cross-organizational workflow processes. The WIDE transaction model is based on the saga transaction model [7], extended with the safe-point concept that allows flexible process rollbacks.

Long-running workflow processes are divided into smaller, relatively short running, process steps that commit the results after the step completes. As these steps are related to the intra-organizational workflow process, they are called I-steps. A compensating counterpart is specified for each I-step that semantically undoes the effect of the original I-step. If no compensating counterpart has been specified, it means that the original I-step cannot or should not be undone. In case of failures, the process is rolled back by executing the compensating steps in the reverse order in which their original counterpart I-steps have been executed. Marking I-steps as safe-points indicates that a rollback could be stopped at those steps, because a consistent state in the process has been reached. Whether the rollback actually stops at those safe-points is determined by the compensation algorithm, which is described formally in [8]. If a rollback request is issued, its rollback mode indicates whether the rollback should be partial, i.e. compensate the process until a suitable (set of) safe-points is encountered or complete, i.e., the entire process execution will be compensated.

5.2   Cross-Organizational Transaction Requirements

Transaction support for cross-organizational workflow management must satisfy additional requirements imposed by the autonomy of the involved organizations. When autonomous organizations participate in a tight cooperation within a virtual enterprise, they want to preserve their autonomy as much as possible. This rules out the use of one global transaction system that governs the transactional behavior over the involved organizations using for example a two-phase commit protocol as is common in multi-database environments. In such a protocol, the organization that wants to commit its results must wait until the other organization is ready to commit its results as well and the global transaction support system signals that the commit can be executed. Obviously, such a protocol seriously reduces the autonomy of the involved organizations, which is even more severe if the consumer/provider paradigm is extended to include more than two organizations. Thus, to preserve the autonomy of the involved organizations, cross-organizational workflow processes require transaction support that offers loose transaction properties.

Similar to dividing the intra-organizational processes, the contract level process is divided into smaller steps, called X-steps, that each commit their results when the step finishes and are compensated in case they need to be undone. As the X-steps form the abstract view of the provider process, it is the provider organization that specifies the compensating counterparts, which are also contained in the contract so that the consumer knows how its outsourced process might be compensated by the provider.

From the issues described for the intra-organizational transaction model, the cross-organizational transaction requirements and the cross-organizational process model described in Section 3, it follows that a cross-organizational workflow process consists of three levels that have transactional semantics. These three levels are:
1. The *outsourcing level*. The entire workflow process of the consumer organization on the level of I-steps. The placeholder in the consumer process is a regular I-step and must therefore have a compensating activity specified for it.
2. The *contract level*. The X-steps as they are specified in the contract.
3. The *internal level*. The entire workflow process steps of the provider organization on the level of I-steps.

5.3   Cross-Organizational Transaction Model

The cross-organizational transaction model, called X-transaction model, combines the three transactional levels described in the previous subsection into one transaction model, i.e. a three-level transactional workflow process model. It offers the required loose transaction properties for the intra- as well as cross-organizational workflow processes. An X-transaction consists of all X-steps and I-steps of the cross-organizational workflow process, together with the corresponding compensating steps. Similar to specifying I-steps as safe-points, it is also possible to specify X-steps as safe-points, providing the flexibility of partial rollbacks at the contract level as well. The X-transaction model offers a flexible rollback mechanism that allows rollbacks to take place at any of the three different transactional levels:

1. At the outsourcing level. A rollback on the outsourcing level is performed entirely by the consumer organization. If the outsourced process needs to be compensated, the compensating activity of the placeholder is executed, which does not necessarily involve the provider organization that executed the outsourced process.
2. At the contract level. A rollback on the contract level will involve only the X-steps by executing the compensating activities that correspond to those X-steps.
3. At the internal level. A rollback will involve the I-steps of the provider process.

Similar to the rollback mode, it is possible to indicate a rollback scope, i.e. intra- or cross-organizational, when a rollback is requested. Intra-organizational means that the rollback will involve only the organization that issues the rollback. Cross-organizational means that the rollback will involve the other organization as well. When the rollback scope is cross-organizational, the rollback can occur on any combination of the three transactional levels, e.g. if the consumer starts a cross-organizational rollback, the rollback will involve the outsourcing level and the contract level. The combination of different rollback modes and scopes determines the operational semantics of the rollback execution, presented in the table below.

Rollback starts at:	Consumer Organization	Provider Organization
Rollback Scope / mode:		
Intra-Organizational / Complete	Entire consumer process is rolled back (placeholder)	Entire provider process is rolled back.
Intra-Organizational / Partial	Consumer process is rolled back until a safe-point is found. (placeholder)	Provider process is rolled back until a safe-point is found.
Cross-Organizational / Complete	Consumer process is rolled back in its entirety. Outsourced process is rolled back by the provider.	Entire provider process is rolled back, then the consumer process is rolled back partially.
Cross-Organizational / Partial	Consumer process is partially rolled back. Outsourced process is rolled back by the provider.	Not possible.

5.4   Rollback Example

To illustrate the effects of different rollback modes and rollback scopes in a rollback request, the example scenario introduced in Section 3 is used. Fig. 4 shows the execution history of the X-transaction. The process is being executed and has progressed to the activities ëSend GSM nr. and billí and ëDeliver GSMí in the consumer organization, and to ëWrap up parcelí in the provider organization. This means that those three activities are still running and all preceding activities have finished. The thick-lined rectangles in the figure represent the safe-points that are specified in the process.

Suppose that the running activity at the provider fails, as indicated by the shaded rectangle in the figure, because during packaging it is discovered that the GSM phone is not the correct model. In this case, the provider will start a rollback to bring its process into a consistent state. For this, the entire process needs to be rolled back, thus the rollback mode is complete. Both processes are closely linked, because the GSM number is linked to the GSM serial number. Therefore, it is stated in the contract that

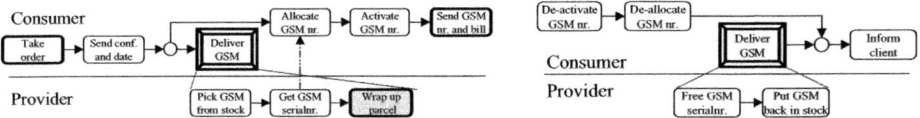

Fig. 4. Cross-organizational Rollback example   Fig. 5. Example compensation process

the provider can only issue a rollback with complete rollback mode if the rollback scope is cross-organizational, which implies that the consumer process will also be rolled back (in partial mode, see table). The resulting compensation process, consisting of the compensating counterpart activities, is shown in Fig. 5.

Parallel to the rollback at the provider, which frees the GSM serial number and puts the GSM phone back in stock, the consumer de-activates and de-allocates the GSM number. After that, the consumer informs its client that there is a delay in the delivery of the GSM phone (the compensating activity of ëSend conf. and dateí) and the original process is restarted again with activity ëSend conf. and dateí.

6   Transaction Architecture for Cross-Organizational WfM

In this section, the basic cross-organizational workflow management architecture presented in Section 4 is extended to offer support for the X-transaction.

6.1   Cross-Organizational Transaction Architecture

The cross-organizational transactional architecture is shown in Fig. 6. The basic architecture of Fig. 3 has been expanded and the CSS modules have been replaced with cross-organizational transaction managers (XTM) and workflow state modules (WFS), which are the CSS modules providing cross-organizational transaction support. In addition to this, the intra-organizational infrastructure is extended with the ITM that provides the intra-organizational transaction support.

The WFS is a module that registers activity and process state changes at the internal level and maps these to the contract level.

The XTM provides the cross-organizational transaction support. It has the necessary algorithms to calculate compensating workflow processes that undo executed X-steps. To determine which X-steps have been executed, it uses the information provided by the WFS. Although the cross-organizational architecture includes a XTM module for both organizations, only the provider side XTM requires the algorithms to calculate compensating processes, because the contract level activities are executed by the provider and must also be compensated at the provider. The consumer side XTM determines whether the contract level process must be compensated whenever a rollback is started within the consumer process itself.

The proxy-gateways (PG) interact with each other using Java RMI and handle the communication between the different organizations, thereby providing security mechanisms to protect the organizations.

The intra-organizational transaction manager (ITM) provides transaction support for intra-organizational workflow processes. Because transaction support is currently

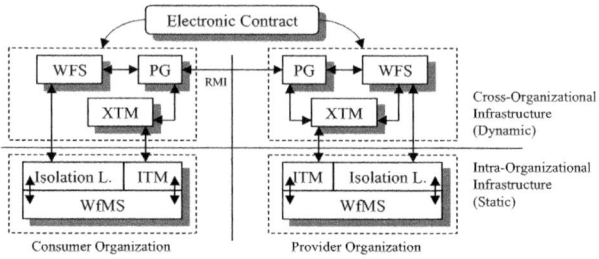

Fig. 6. Cross-Organizational Transaction Architecture

not offered by any commercial WfMS, the ITM is a separate module on top of the WfMS. The workflow execution history necessary for the ITM to calculate the compensating workflow process is retrieved from the WfMS. When the compensating workflow process is created by the ITM, the WfMS can execute it.

Note that, when a rollback occurs that involves a combination of the three transactional levels as described in Section 5, the compensation process will be computed by a combination of XTMs and ITMs. The entire compensation process will consist of multiple separate compensation processes, one for each involved transactional level, which are however, tightly related to each other.

6.2   The CrossFlow Context

As stated before, the work presented in this paper is part of the CrossFlow project [10]. Within the project, not only the support for the actual execution of cross-organizational workflow process is covered, but also the dynamic creation of a virtual enterprise based on the consumer/provider paradigm. Organizations find each other in an electronic marketplace where organizations offer their services or search for services on offer (business-2-business e-commerce). Using a matchmaking facility [11], compatible organizations form a virtual enterprise, the cooperation in which is described and established in an electronic contract [14]. The electronic contract not only contains the specification of the service, but also the rights and obligations that the service entails. To facilitate a smooth cooperation between the organizations in a virtual enterprise, the business processes that are to be performed in the involved organizations must be interconnected. The architecture presented in Section 4 is developed to handle the specific issues that arise as a consequence of the cooperation between the different organizations. Dedicated CSSs are developed that each deal with a different aspect of the cross-organizational WfM requirements. The CSSs covered in CrossFlow are transaction management as presented in this paper, Level of Control, Quality of Service and Flexible Change Control [13].

6.3   Implementation Issues

In the CrossFlow project, a prototype is built to test and demonstrate the described X-transaction model. The underlying workflow management system (WfMS) in the prototype is IBMís MQ Series Workflow, and the intra-organizational transaction support is based on the transaction manager built in the WIDE project. An additional module is implemented that resets activity states so that compensated activities reflect the correct state, which is currently not offered by MQ Series Workflow. The XTM module is a dynamic event-based software module that contains the algorithms to compute compensation processes on the contract level. It passes contract level compensation processes to the ITM, which has the functionality to make them persistent. The entire prototype will be built in Java. Although the prototype is built on top of a specific commercial WfMS, the the isolation layer ensures that only a small effort is required to exchange the WfMS used in CrossFlow with another WfMS.

7   Conclusions and Future Work

This paper describes an advanced transaction model and architecture to support cross-organizational workflow process executions within virtual enterprises. Although the cross-organizational process model consists of an arbitrary number of nesting levels, only three levels have transactional semantics. The advanced transaction model is called the X-transaction model and relies on compensations to undo already executed workflow activities. The combination of rollback scope (three transactional levels) and rollback mode (safe-points) in the X-transaction model offers a highly flexible rollback mechanism for cross-organizational workflow management.

The cross-organizational transactional architecture facilitates the implementation of the X-transaction model and consists of three layers. The dynamically created cross-organizational infrastructure layer handles the transactional aspects related to the outsourcing of workflow processes. The static intra-organizational infrastructure consists of a layer that incorporates the local WfMSs and a layer that includes an isolation layer and a transaction manager that provides intra-organizational transaction support. The architecture is highly flexible in the sense that other cooperative support services, e.g. Quality of Service, can be plugged into it, i.e. the architecture consists of a software bus to which cooperative support services can be connected.

The prototype built in the CrossFlow project will be tested using two real-world scenarios. One scenario is an extended version of the scenario presented in Section 3. The other scenario is a motor damage claim process of an insurance company, in which the damage assessment subprocess is outsourced to another organization.

Further development with respect to cross-organizational transaction management will include an extension of the consumer/provider paradigm so that more than two organizations can be involved in the outsourcing of processes. This offers the possibility of nested outsourcing, in which provider organizations can again outsource part of their processes, thereby acting as a consumer organization as well. It also offers the opportunity for a consumer organization to outsource multiple parts of its process to multiple provider organizations, which implies that multiple contracts have to be established. Both situations require an extension of the X-transaction model to refine the rollback scope so that it can be indicated which organizations are involved in the rollback. Because multiple organizations are involved that can all issue a rollback request simultaneously, the X-transaction model must be further extended to deal with concurrent rollback requests, similar to the work described in [18].

Acknowledgements

All members of the CrossFlow project are acknowledged for their role in the realization of the X-transaction model, architecture and implementation described in this paper. Pascal van Eck is acknowledged for his feedback on this paper.

References

[1] W. M. P. van der Aalst; Interorganizational Workflows ñ *An approach based on Message Sequence Charts and Petri Nets*; Systems Analysis ñ Modelling ñ Simulation, 34(3), 1999.

[2] G. Alonso, D. Agrawal et al.; *Advanced Transaction Models in Workflow Contexts*; Procs. Int. Conference on Data Engineering; USA, 1996.

[3] G. Alonso et al.*; WISE: Business to Business E-Commerce*; Procs. Int. Workshop on Research Issues in Data Engineering; Australia, 1999.

[4] D. Barbar· , S. Mehrotra, M. Rusinkiewicz; *INCAs: Managing Dynamic Workflows in Distributed Environments*; Journal of Database Management 7(1), 1996.

[5] Z. Damen, W. Nijenhuis, M. Verwijmeren; *Transport Scenario Description*; Public CrossFlow Deliverable, 2000. (available via: http://www.crossflow.org)

[6] A. K. Elmagarmid (Ed.); *Database Transaction Models for Advanced Applications*, Morgan Kaufmann; USA, 1992.

[7] H. Garcia-Molina, K. Salem; *Sagas*; Procs. 1987 ACM SIGMOD Int. Conf. on Management of Data,; USA, 1987.

[8] P. Grefen, J. Vonk, E. Boertjes, P. Apers; *Semantics and Architecture of Global Transaction Support in Workflow Environments*; Procs. Int. Conf on Cooperative Information Systems (CooPIS), United Kingdom; 1999.

[9] P. Grefen, B. Pernici, G. S·nchez (Eds.); *Database Support for Workflow Management ñ The WIDE Project*; Kluwer Academic Publishers, 1999.

[10] P. Grefen, K. Aberer, Y. Hoffner, H. Ludwig; *CrossFlow: Cross-Organizational Workflow Management in Dynamic Virtual Enterprises*; To appear in Int. Journal of Computer Systems Science & Engineering, 2000.

[11] Y. Hoffner; *Supporting Contract Match-Making*; Procs. IEEE 9th Int. Workshop on Research Issues in Data Engineering; Australia, 1999.

[12] S. Jajodia, L. Kerschberg (Eds.); *Advanced Transaction Models and Architectures*; Kluwer Academic Publishers, 1997.

[13] J. Klingemann*; Controlled Flexibility in Workflow Management*; Procs12[th] Conf. on Advanced Information Systems Engineering, Sweden, 2000.

[14] M. Koetsier, P. Grefen, J. Vonk; *Contracts for Cross-Organizational Workflow Management*; Procs. EC-Web, UK, 2000.

[15] V. Kumar, M. Hsu; *Recovery Mechanisms in Database Systems*; Prentice Hall, 1998.

[16] F. Leyman; *Supporting Business Transactions Via Partial Backward Recovery In Workflow Management Systems*; Procs. BTW í95.

[17] H. Ludwig, C. Bussler, M. Shan, P. Grefen; *Cross-Organizational Workflow Management and Co-ordination ñ WACC í99 Workshop Report*; ACM SIGGROUP Bulletin 20(1), 1999.

[18] J. Vonk, P. Grefen, E. Boertjes, P. Apers; *Distributed Transaction Support for Workflow Management Applications*; Procs. 10th Int. Conf. on Database and Expert System Applications (DEXA); Florence, Italy, 1999.

[19] WfMC; *Interface 4: Interoperability Abstract Specification v1.0*; 1996.

[20] WfMC; *Terminology & Glossary v3.0*; 1999.

[21] D. Wodtke, J. Weissenfels, G. Weikum, A. Dittrich; *The MENTOR Project: Steps Towards Enterprise-wide Workflow Management*; Procs. Int. Conf. on Data Engineering, USA, 1996.

Author Index

Lecture Notes in Computer Science

For information about Vols. 1–1825
please contact your bookseller or Springer-Verlag

GPSR Compliance

*The European Union's (EU) General Product Safety Regulation (GPSR)
is a set of rules that requires consumer products to be safe and our
obligations to ensure this.*

*If you have any concerns about our products, you can contact us on
ProductSafety@springernature.com*

In case Publisher is established outside the EU, the EU authorized
representative is:

Springer Nature Customer Service Center GmbH
Europaplatz 3
69115 Heidelberg, Germany

Batch number: 09624486

Printed by Printforce, the Netherlands